제8판

교원임용고시
일반영어 필독서

임용영어 수험생 대다수가 선택하는
전공영어의 보통명사

- 교원임용고시 전공영어 독보적 전국 1위
  (2025년 예스24 전공영어 부문 박문각 누적 판매량 1위)
- 미국 버클리대학 유희태 박사의 일반영어 필독서
- 일반영어의 기본이론 완성

유희태 일반영어

2S2R ❶ 기본

LSI 영어연구소 유희태 박사 저

박문각 임용 동영상강의 www.pmg.co.kr

박문각

PREFACE

2026년 《2S2R 기본》 8판을 내며

《2S2R 기본》은 지금은 사라진 비욘드 출판사에서 2009년 첫 출간되어 세상에 나온 지 벌써 17년이 되었다. 처음 출간됐을 때의 제목은 《2S2R 최고의 독해 비결》이었는데, 당시 많은 수험생들이 '최독비'란 애칭으로 불렀었다. 아직도 마감 일정을 맞추느라 당시 LSI 영어연구소의 연구원들과 출판사 직원들이 몇 날 밤을 새웠던 기억이 또렷하다. 그만큼 애정도 많았고 연구에 시간도 많이 들였던 책이었다. 비록 완벽하진 않지만, 한국의 Reading Comprehension 분야에 일조한다는 마음으로 준비한 책이었다. 처음 이 교재를 출간했을 때 가졌던 생각과 다짐 그리고 방법은 여전히 유효하리라 생각하여 여기에 다시 옮겨본다.

노량진에 있는 국공립학교 영어교사 양성시험을 대비하는 교원임용고시학원에서 일반영어를 강의하며 많은 수험생들로부터 받아왔던 공통적인 질문이 하나 있다. "어떻게 하면 글을 정확히, 그리고 빨리 읽을 수 있나요?" 아마 한국에서 시행되는 대부분의 영어시험을 준비하는 다른 수험생들도 마찬가지의 고민을 지니고 있을 줄로 안다. 이것은 우리나라 수험생들뿐만 아니라 미국의 수험생 또는 대학생들(매주 상당한 양의 논문과 책을 읽고 과제보고서를 제출하는)에게도 유사하게 해당하는 질문이기도 하다. 미국의 한 대학에서 학부생들에게 읽기 지도를 하면서 그 학생들도 마찬가지의 고민을 하고 있음을 보며, '영어'를 '이해'하는 문제가 얼마나 보편적인 것인지를 깨닫게 된다. 영어 독해를 할 때, 지문이 말하고자 하는 내용도 다 알겠고, 독해도 다 된 것 같은데, 문제를 풀면 항상 한두 문제는 틀리는 일이 발생하는 것은 왜일까? '나의 이해'와 '정답' 사이의 거리는 왜 항상 발생하는 것일까? 도대체 뭐가 문제일까? 저자는 그것이 근본적으로 영어를 넘어선 '언어'에 대한 논리적 이해의 결핍에서 오는 것이라 본다. 그렇다면 어떻게 하면 영어, 더 넓게는 '언어'를 잘 이해할 수 있을까? 저자는 그 하나의 가설적 대안으로 **"대화적 읽기"**를 제시하고자 한다. 대화적 읽기는 처음엔 시간이 오래 걸리겠지만 결국 실전 문제 풀이에서 **분석적(구조적)**으로 지문을 읽을 때 큰 도움이 될 것이다.

'대화적 읽기'란

우리는 매일 일상에서 수많은 읽을거리를 접하게 된다. 잡지의 기사, 신문의 사설 또는 한 조각의 광고 문구를 읽으며 스스로 "이것의 메시지는 뭐지?", "이것이 함축하는 것은 또 뭘까?" 등의 질문을 던지게 된다. 액면 그대로(at face value) 받아들이기보다 그것의 표면 아래(beneath the surface)를 보려는 노력이 필요함은 물론이다. 우리는 어렴풋이 다음과 같은 질문을 글쓴이에게 하게 된다.

❶ 이 글은 도대체 무엇에 관한 것인가요?
❷ 그것을 통해 당신이 말하고자 하는 바는 무엇인가요?
❸ 당신의 그 진술을 뒷받침할 수 있는 것인가요?
❹ 근거가 너무 주관적인 것 아닌가요?
❺ 사실관계가 명확한 것인가요?
❻ 그 용어를 어떻게 정의하는 것인가요?
❼ 어떻게 그런 결론을 내렸나요?
❽ 그래서 어떻다는 거죠? 왜 그것이 중요한 것인가요?
❾ 당신 도대체 어떤 태도로 대상을 바라보는 것이죠? 비꼬는 것인가요?
❿ 왜 이런 패턴으로 글을 쓴 것이죠? 너무 나열식 아닌가요?
⓫ 당신 글엔 모순이 있군요.
⓬ 당신 주장은 알겠는데, 동의할 순 없군요.
⓭ 좋은 주장이군요. 결코 생각하지 못했는데.

의식적이든 무의식적이든 위와 같은 반응은 이미 여러분이 읽은 것에 대해 '대화적으로(dialogically)' 사고한다는 것을 나타낸다. 개념에 대해 질문을 하고, 정보를 평가하고, 증거를 찾고, 가설을 하며, 그리고 판단한다. 한마디로 여러분은 다른 사람의 말(주장)을 그대로 흡수하는(take in) 수동적 관찰자로서가 아니라 그 주장을 가공(process)하고 있는 능동적 대화자의 자질이 있는 것이다. 글을 읽을 때, 읽는 '나'와 읽히는 '너'가 만나 새로운 하나의 '나와 너'가 만들어져 '지문(텍스트)에 나타나 있는 의미'를 넘어서는 새로운(창조적) 의미를 발견하는 것이 대화적 읽기이다.

왜 대화적 읽기인가?

하나, 대화적 읽기는 발견의 역동적 과정이기 때문이다. 여러분은 어느 한 주제에 관한 글쓴이의 관점을 발견하게 된다. 그런 다음, 그가 말하는 내용 또는 주장의 강함과 약함을 발견한다. 그리고 그 주장을 동의할지 동의하지 않을지를 결정하게 된다. 저자에게 질문을 하고, 그 저자가 서 있는 지점과 여러분이 서 있는 지점이 대비 또는 충돌이 됨으로써 평면적이 아닌 입체적인 이해를 하도록 해준다. 마지막 귀결점으로 글을 쓴 저자와 그 이슈에 대해 더 잘 이해하게 된다.

둘, 대화적 읽기는 다른 이의 글을 목수가 집을 바라보듯이 읽도록 해준다. 그는 세부 사항을 꼼꼼히 보며, 그런 다음 어떻게 그 세부 사항이 전체와 연결되고 동시에 전체를 만들어 내는지를 본다. 또한 대화적 읽기는 자신이 읽은 글에 대해 스스로 평가를 하도록 해준다. 남의 글에 대해 충실히 분석하고 반응할수록 그 글에 대한 이해에 대해서도 더욱 그렇게 하게 된다.

PREFACE

셋, 대화적 읽기는 교원임용고시, 수능, 공무원, 편입, 토익, 토플, 심지어 GRE 등 한국에서 시행되는 대부분의 시험에서 단골로 출제되는 유형인 빈칸추론, 요지찾기, 제목(주제)찾기, 순서맞추기, 글의 흐름 파악하기, 요약하기 등 '논리'를 물어보는 문제에 적극적으로 대처할 수 있도록 만들어 준다.

어떻게 대화적으로 읽을 것인가? 독해전략 4단계 2S2R
글을 '대화적'으로 읽기 위해 **구체적 방법론**으로 저자는 **2S2R 독해전략**을 제시하고자 한다. 2S2R 독해전략은 '빠르고 정확한 읽기'를 위한 훈련의 과정이다.

1단계) Survey 개관하기
2S2R 독해전략의 1단계로 텍스트(읽을거리)를 미리 훑어보는 것을 말한다. 개관하기는 각 문단의 첫 문장과 끝 문장을 유심히 읽은 다음 나머지를 훑어본다. 이것은 주어진 지문의 주요 화제(topic), 구조, 부분 그리고 특색 등에 대한 전체적인 생각을 갖도록 해준다. 이 1단계에서 여러분이 구체적으로 해야 할 것은 1) key words 찾기 2) signal words 찾기이다. 이 단계를 마치면, 여러분은 각각의 구체적인 문단들과 부분들이 얼마나 잘 짜여 있는지 이해하게 만들어 주는 '지적 얼개(a mental framework)'를 형성하게 된다.

2단계) Reading 읽기
2S2R 독해전략의 2단계는 읽기 단계로 여러분이 해야 할 것은 다음과 같다.
하나, 글의 목적(purpose) 파악하기
둘, 글의 어조(tone) 파악하기
셋, 글의 구조(pattern) 파악하기: 2S2R 독해전략에서 가장 강조하는 부분이다.
넷, 글의 요지(main idea) 파악하기

3단계) Summary 요약하기
2S2R 독해전략의 3단계는 2단계 Reading에서 했던 내용을 요약하는 것이다.
요약하기는 글의 중요한 부분을 훨씬 짧은 길이로 다시 서술하는 것으로, 요약을 잘 하기 위해서는 다음의 조건을 지켜야 한다.
하나, 좋은 요약은 요지와 주된 논거(major supporting points)를 포함한다. 요지는 가능하면 첫 문장에 제시한다.
둘, 좋은 요약은 단서가 되는 단어들(signal words)을 포함한 각 단락의 핵심어를 포함한다.
셋, 좋은 요약은 작은 세부 사항, 반복되는 세부 사항, 읽는 이의 의견을 포함하지 않는다.

넷, 좋은 요약은 본문에 있는 단어나 어구를 그대로 사용하지 않고 가능하면 다른 말로 바꿔 쓰기(paraphrase)한다.

다섯, 일반적으로 원 본문의 길이를 25%로 줄이는 것을 원칙으로 한다.

4단계 Recite 요약한 것 소리 내어 말하기

2S2R 독해전략의 4단계는 3단계에서 했던 것을 입으로 정리하는 것을 말한다. 3단계가 철저히 훈련되었다면 자연스럽게 진행될 수 있는 단계이다. 지문을 읽은 후 멈춰 서서 읽은 것에 대해 정리를 한다. 이때 반드시 입 밖으로 정리한 것을 소리를 내야 한다는 점에 유념하자. 머릿속에만 가지고 있는 것, 즉 **언어로 표현되지 않은 것은 내 것이 아니다.**

우리는 '유전자'가 모든 것을 결정한다는 이야기를 요즘 들어 더욱 자주 듣게 된다. 타고난, 즉, 부모로부터 물려받은 좋은 머리(높은 IQ로 상징되는)야말로 우리의 성공의 근원이라는 것이다. 그러나, 과연 그럴까? 최근의 연구들에 따르면, 유전자가 우리의 성공을 결정지을 확률은 '집적된 시간'이 끼치는 영향보다 훨씬 적다는 것이다. 우리가 꾸준히 노력을 해서 1만 시간에 가까운 시간을 자신의 전공 분야에 기울인다면, 누구나 성공에 이를 수 있다는 것이다. 비틀즈(The Beatles)의 성공에는 바로 1만 시간에 가까운 그들의 반복된 노력에 있었지, 그들의 유전자에 있었던 것이 아니었다고 한다. 애플 컴퓨터의 창립자인 스티브 잡스(Steve Jobs)가 성공한 것도 그의 유전자가 좋아서라기보다는 오히려 자신이 살던 곳인 마운틴뷰—지금은 너무나 유명해진 실리콘밸리 지역—가 그에게 많은 기회를 주었기 때문이라고 전문가들은 지적한다. 그의 이웃에는 휴렛패커드의 엔지니어들로 가득해서 그는 그들로부터 어린 시절 컴퓨터에 관한 수많은 이야기를 들을 수 있었고, 심지어 휴렛패커드의 창립자인 빌 휴렛(Bill Hewlett)과 개인적으로 접촉하여 직접 영향을 받을 수 있었다. 그것을 통해 그는 어린 시절부터 자신이 좋아하는 것을 정확히 알 수 있었고, 그 좋아하는 것을 꾸준히 노력 및 반복함으로써 성공을 할 수 있었다. 이때 그가 들인 시간이 약 1만 시간 정도라고 한다.

필자는 이 1만 시간이란 말을 은유로 받아들인다. 곧이곧대로 1만 시간이 중요하다는 것이 아니라, 그만큼 자신이 하고자 하는 것을 성취하기 위해서는 그에 요구되는 꾸준한 노력과 반복 학습이 필요하다는 것이다. 이것보다 더 확실한 것은 없다. 단, 그 노력과 반복 학습을 좀 더 나은 방식으로 한다면 더할 나위 없이 좋을 것이다. A라는 사람이 하루에 단어를 10개 외우고, B라는 사람이 20개를 외운다고 하자. 그렇다면, 이 둘의 집적된 시간은 어떻게 될까? A에게 하루가 24시간이라면 B에게는 하루가 48시간이 된다. 시간은 절대적이지만 동시에 상대적이기도 하다. 그렇다면, A가 아니라 B가 되도록 하는 것이다. 이 교재가 여러분을 A가 아닌 B가 되도록 하는 데 조금이라도 도움이 된다면 더 바랄 나위가 없겠다. 이제 '난 머리가 나빠서 안 되나 봐!'라는 좌절감에 빠질 필요는 전혀 없다. 스스로 부족하다 싶은 것은 더 많은 시간과 그 시간을 좀 더 효율적으로 만들 수 있는 좋은 방법론으로 만회하면 된다. 그 하나의 방법으로 2S2R 독해전략을 권하고 싶다.

PREFACE

임용고시 영어를 준비하는 대다수의 수험생이 일반영어의 시작을 《2S2R 기본》으로 공부한다고 한다. 저자로서는 기쁘면서도 무거운 책임감을 동시에 느낀다. 그래서 현재에 안주하지 않고 최선을 다해 좀 더 나은 지문과 분석력으로 한 걸음 더 진보된 교재를 만들어야겠다는 다짐을 항상 하곤 한다.

『유희태 2S2R 시리즈』를 효과적으로 활용하는 방법은, 대학 1학년 때 《2S2R 기본》을 최소 3회독, 평균 5회 독하여 일반영어 기본이론을 확실하게 다진 뒤, 2학년 때 《2S2R 유형》을 최소 3회독하여 임용 유형에 기본이론을 확장 적용하는 훈련을 하고, 3학년 때 《2S2R 기출》을 2회독한 다음, 처음으로 임용시험을 치르는 4학년 때 《2S2R 문제은행》을 가지고 공부하는 것이다. 이 과정에서 《기출 VOCA 30 days》는 1학년 때부터 주 6회 매일 20분씩 꾸준히 공부하기를 추천한다. 그러면 4학년 11월 임용시험을 치를 때가 되면, 임용에 필요한 어휘의 80%는 머릿속에 차곡차곡 쌓여서, 독해를 하는 데 있어 어휘의 부족은 느끼지 않을 것이다.

이 8판 작업을 하면서 많은 분들의 도움을 받았다. 원고를 보기 좋은 최종 결과물로 만들어준 박문각의 변수경 편집자와 박용 회장님께 고마움을 전한다. 또한 영어지문의 함축의미, 문화적 맥락, 그리고 답안 등을 두고 토론하고 때로는 격렬한 논쟁을 했던 LSI 영어연구소의 Sean Maylone 수석연구원에게도 인사를 전한다. 아무쪼록 이 《2S2R 기본》 8판 교재가 수험생 여러분의 합격에 일조하기를 깊은 마음으로 바란다.

2026년 새해를 앞두고 LSI 영어연구소에서
유희태

CONTENTS

PART 01　2S2R 원리　　　10

Chapter 01　General & Specific　　10
Chapter 02　Fact & Opinion　　21
Chapter 03　Signal Words & Transitions　　26
Chapter 04　Topic　　42
Chapter 05　Patterns of Organization　　52
Chapter 06　Main Idea & Supporting Details　　71
Chapter 07　The Writer's Technique-Purpose and Tone　　92
Chapter 08　Summarizing　　103

PART 02　2S2R 적용　　　116

PART 03　2S2R 심화　　　412

2S2R

유희태 일반영어
① 기본

PART 01

2S2R 원리

CHAPTER 01 General & Specific

모든 영어 논리의 기본은 바로 일반적인 것과 세부적인 것을 구분하는 것에서부터 시작한다는 점을 명심하자. General(일반적)이란 말은 'broad'하면서 'not limited'란 뜻이다. 누군가가 어떤 단어나 생각을 'general하다'라고 말하면, 그것은 **하나의 큰 것 속에 많은 다양한 작은 것들(세부사항들)**이 들어있음을 의미한다.

예를 들어, sports라는 하나의 범주 안에는 football, baseball, and basketball 등의 다양한 종류의 세부사항들이 들어있다. 여기서 sports는 general이고 football, baseball, and basketball은 specific한 것이 된다. 이렇듯 specific은 하나의 큰 그룹 안에 속해 있는 세부적인 것을 말한다.

> 영어의 거의 대다수의 글은 'general한 것에서 specific한 것'으로 진행된다!

모든 영어 독해의 가장 기본이 되는 것이 general과 specific을 정확하게 구별하는 능력이라 할 수 있다. 따라서 이 책에 실린 연습문제들을 푸는 과정에서 영어 논리력의 기본이 쌓일 것이라 생각한다.

General과 specific의 관계를 정확히 아는 것이 중요한 이유는 여러 가지가 있겠지만, 특히 순서 맞추기나 글의 흐름상 어색한 것 고르기 문제 등에선 이것을 모르고는 좋은 점수를 얻을 수 없다. 아래에 제시되어 있는 예제를 풀다 보면, 여러분은 general과 specific의 개념이 무엇인지 자연스럽게 체득할 것이라 본다.

예제

[1-2] 다음을 general에서 specific한 순서로 배열하시오.

01 a. physician   b. man   c. Dr. Anthony

_____ → _____ → _____

02 a. company   b. Success Publishing company   c. organization

_____ → _____ → _____

[3-9] Read each pair of sentences. Then label the general sentence G and the specific one S.

03   a. In Japan, readily revealing one's emotions to others is not encouraged, but in America the opposite is true. _____
   b. Culture affects behavior in a number of ways, particularly within the context of personal relations. _____

04   a. The temperature of Antarctica is changing; it is not as cold as it used to be. _____
   b. Current Antarctic temperatures are nine degrees higher than they were fifty years ago. _____

05   a. When some young computer executives became rich in the 1990s, they decided to donate money to groups that help children. _____
   b. In 1997, thirty young computer programmers who made their fortunes at the Microsoft company gave $50 million to schools and youth centers. _____

06   a. In wintertime, the body temperature of a woodchuck undergoes a steep drop of many degrees. _____
   b. In wintertime, the body temperature of a woodchuck drops from 90°F to around 40°F. _____

07   a. The fats found in fish, nuts, and vegetables may actually help protect you from heart disease. _____
   b. Not all fats are bad; in fact, some may be good for you. _____

정답   01 b-a-c
       02 c-a-b
       03 a-S, b-G
       04 a-G, b-S
       05 a-G, b-S
       06 a-G, b-S
       07 a-S, b-G

08　a. Heart disease is the leading cause of death in the United States. _____
　　b. Heart disease is a killer. _____

09　a. Many records claim that baseball was first played in 1846, but there is evidence suggesting that the game is older than that. _____
　　b. In her 1818 novel *Northanger Abbey*, author Jane Austen refers to a game called baseball, suggesting that the game was played before 1846. _____

[10-11] 다음의 문장을 가장 general한 것으로부터 가장 specific한 것으로 재배열하시오.

10　a. Dessert is my favorite part of a meal.
　　b. I especially love to eat pie.
　　c. The after-dinner treat I like most to eat is a slice of warm cherry pie.

　　_____ → _____ → _____

11　a. Many great artists are famous for being temperamental.
　　b. It's not unusual for great opera singers to be temperamental.
　　c. The great opera singer Maria Callas was known for her explosive temperament.
　　d. On one occasion, Callas refused to continue a performance because she considered the audience unappreciative.

　　_____ → _____ → _____ → _____

[12-18] 주어진 3개의 specific sentences에 대한 가장 알맞은 general sentence 하나를 고르시오.

12

> a. During World War II, German invaders destroyed Russia's richest agricultural regions.
> b. According to official reports, more than seven million Russians were killed while defending their country against German attacks.
> c. Many Russians lost their lives in concentration camps.

① The Russians suffered heavy losses in World War II.
② Russia suffered more losses than any of the other great powers.
③ Russia has never recovered from the tragedy of World War II.

13

> a. Between 1933 and 1939, about 150,000 square miles of U.S. farmland lost its topsoil.
> b. Huge dust storms turned day into night all over the Great Plains.
> c. During the same period, more than 500 million tons of rich earth dried out and turned to powder.

① American land has been overplowed and overplanted for decades.
② In the 1930s, a large part of the United States turned into what came to be called the "Great Dust Bowl."
③ Poor farming techniques cause hardships for many countries.

정답
08 a-S, b-G
09 a-G, b-S
10 a-b-c
11 a-b-c-d
12 ①
13 ②

14

> a. During World War II, the War Department finally approved the training of African American pilots.
> b. In 1941 Benjamin O. Davis Jr. became the first African American to lead a squadron of pilots.
> c. President Franklin D. Roosevelt's Executive Order 8802 required employers in defense industries to make jobs available "without discrimination because of race, creed, or color."

① For many African Americans, World War II offered a chance to break down racial barriers.
② During World War II, racial violence broke out on several military bases.
③ World War II brought out the best in Americans.

15

> a. The tradition of using candles at funerals began with the Romans, who used them to frighten away evil spirits.
> b. Tombstones originated as a way of keeping the dead in the underworld.
> c. The original purpose of coffins was to keep the dead safely underground.

① Anthropologists have found evidence that funeral traditions existed during the Neanderthal age (100,000-40,000 BC).
② Different cultures have different ways of mourning their dead.
③ Many of the modern customs associated with mourning came from a fear of the dead and what they might do to the living.

16

> a. The citizens of Sparta, a city-state of ancient Greece, were not allowed to become farmers; they were made to train as warriors instead.
> b. Family life in Sparta was severely limited because both boys and girls spent long hours in physical training.
> c. From age seven to age thirty, the boys received instruction in the art of waging war.

① The Spartans were obedient to the laws of their land.
② The Spartan life was hard and devoted to war.
③ Spartan men and women were known for their heroism in war.

17

> a. In sign language, we use hands and other body parts to make gestures that stand for letters, words, and concepts.
> b. Morse code requires a wire telegraph machine to produce sounds—dots and dashes—that are translated into letters, numbers, and punctuation.
> c. Often seen at airports, the semaphore, or flag signaling system, works this way: A person stands holding a flag in each hand, then moves his or her arms to positions that indicate letters and numbers.

① Mass communication means that messages are sent to large audiences.
② Some communication methods do not rely on written language.
③ Simple writing systems date back to the Sumerians of 3000 BC.

정답 14 ①
　　 15 ③
　　 16 ②
　　 17 ②

18

> a. Using the milk from 6,000 cows, a 13,440-pound cheese was produced for an exhibit at the 1937 New York State Fair.
> b. In 1801, a Massachusetts preacher, John Leland, presented President Andrew Jackson with a 1,200-pound Cheshire cheese made in Leland's hometown.
> c. The Wisconsin Cheese Foundation collected 183 tons of milk for its display in the 1964 World's Fair: a cheese wedge that weighed more than 34,500 pounds and stood six feet high.

① Over the years, cheese-loving Americans have produced some pretty big cheeses.
② Canadians proudly show their skill at cheese making during the annual Toronto Fair.
③ Ancient Romans who created huge cheeses were considered quite eccentric.

[19-20] 먼저 general sentence를 읽고, 그런 다음 그 general sentence를 뒷받침 또는 설명해주는 specific sentences의 기호를 모두 써넣으시오.

19 Several famous cities in ancient Greece were reserved for specific purposes.

a. The city of Delphi held an important temple where priestesses were said to receive messages from the gods.
b. History records that many naval battles took place near Greek islands.
c. Enthusiastic crowds flocked to Olympia, which was set aside for athletic games and physical contests.
d. Rulers organized Greece into city-states, large areas that were dominated and run by towns at their centers.
e. The teachings of the philosophers Socrates, Plato, and Aristotle influenced Greek citizens no matter where they lived.
f. The ancient city of Corinth earned fame as a busy trading center that linked Greece with the eastern and western worlds.

20 Because many Americans are fascinated by the idea of life on other planets, Roswell, New Mexico, has become a popular tourist town.

- a. Visitors spend $5 million in Roswell each year, hoping to find proof that a flying saucer landed in the desert in 1947 and was hidden by the U.S. Air Force.
- b. From 1991 to 1996, more than 100,000 people traveled to Roswell for a glimpse of its UFO Museum & Research Center.
- c. Roswell's annual UFO Festival now draws about 150,000 people; the six-day event includes lectures, concerts, bus tours, banquets, a "spaceship derby," and a costume ball.
- d. A book by Kal Korff, *The Roswell UFO Crash*, contends that the damaged spacecraft was actually a classified military balloon intended to track Soviet nuclear tests.
- e. When Walker Air Force Base closed in 1967, many of Roswell's 48,000 residents lost their jobs and the town was deprived of its main source of income.
- f. Most people who claim to have seen beings from outer space describe the creatures as small, with large heads, gray-green skin, and almond-shaped eyes.

정답 18 ①
19 a, c, f
20 a, b, c

한글번역

예제 03
a. 일본에서는 한 개인의 감정을 다른 사람에게 손쉽게 드러내는 것은 권장되지 않지만, 미국에서는 그 반대의 경우가 적용된다.
b. 문화는 행동에, 특히 인간관계의 맥락 안에서 여러 가지 방식으로 영향을 미친다.

04
a. 남극의 온도는 변화하고 있는데 기온이 예전만큼 낮지 않다.
b. 현재 남극의 온도는 50년 전에 비해서 9도가 높다.

05
a. 몇몇 젊은 컴퓨터 회사의 경영인들이 1990년대 부를 얻었을 때, 그들은 아이들을 도와주는 재단에 돈을 기부하기로 결정했다.
b. 1997년에 마이크로소프트 회사에서 많은 돈을 번 30명의 젊은 컴퓨터 프로그래머들은 학교와 청소년센터에 5000만 달러를 기부했다.

06
a. 겨울 동안, 마멋(woodchuck)의 체온은 급격하게 떨어진다.
b. 겨울 동안, 마멋(woodchuck)의 체온은 90°F에서 40°F 정도로 떨어진다.

07
a. 생선, 견과류, 그리고 야채에서 찾아볼 수 있는 지방은 실제로 당신을 심장 질환으로부터 보호해 줄 수 있다.
b. 모든 지방이 나쁜 것은 아니다. 사실, 몇몇 지방은 당신에게 이로울 수 있다.

08
a. 심장 질환은 미국에서 사망의 주요 원인이다.
b. 심장 질환은 살인자이다.

09
a. 많은 기록들은 야구가 1846년에 처음으로 개최됐다고 주장하고 있지만, 야구 경기가 더 이전에 시작됐다고 주장하는 근거가 있다.
b. 제인 오스틴이 1818년에 쓴 소설인 〈노생거 사원〉에 따르면, 그녀는 그 경기를 야구라고 불렀는데, 이는 야구 경기가 1846년 이전에 시작됐다는 것을 의미한다.

10
a. 디저트는 식사 시간 중에서 내가 가장 좋아하는 부분이다.
b. 나는 특히 파이를 먹는 것을 좋아한다.
c. 저녁 식사 후 나는 따뜻한 체리 파이 한 조각 먹는 것을 가장 좋아한다.

11
a. 많은 위대한 예술가들은 그들의 괴팍한 성미로 유명하다.
b. 오페라 가수들에게 있어서 괴팍한 성질은 찾아보기 쉽다.
c. 위대한 오페라 가수인 마리아 칼라스는 그녀의 욱하는 기질로 유명하다.
d. 어느 날 한 번은 칼리스가 공연을 계속하기를 거절했는데 그 이유는 그녀가 관객들이 감상력이 없다고 생각했기 때문이다.

12
a. 제2차 세계대전 동안, 독일군들은 러시아의 가장 비옥한 농경지들을 파괴했다.
b. 공식적인 기록에 따르면, 700만 명의 러시아인들이 독일군으로부터 자신들의 나라를 지키다가 죽었다.
c. 많은 러시아인들은 강제 수용소에서 목숨을 잃었다.

① 러시아인들은 제2차 세계대전에서 비롯되는 많은 손실로부터 고통받았다.
② 러시아는 그 어떤 다른 거대한 힘을 가진 국가보다도 많은 것을 잃었다.
③ 러시아는 제2차 세계대전의 비극으로부터 결코 회복되지 못했다.

13
a. 1933년에서 1939년 사이에, 미국 농지의 150,000평방 마일의 표토가 유실됐다.
b. 거대한 먼지 폭풍이 대평원을 시꺼멓게 뒤덮었다.
c. 같은 기간 동안, 500톤에 해당하는 비옥한 땅이 마르고 가루가 됐다.

① 미국 땅은 수십 년 동안 과잉으로 경작되고 재배됐다.
② 1930년대에 미국 땅의 많은 부분들이 "Great Dust Bowl"이라고 불리는 것으로 변했다.
③ 부실한 작농기법은 많은 나라들의 어려움을 초래했다.

14 a. 제2차 세계대전 동안, 미 육군성은 미국 흑인 비행사들을 훈련시키는 것을 승인했다.
   b. 1941년 벤자민 O. 데이비스 주니어는 비행중대를 이끈 최초의 미국 흑인이 됐다.
   c. 프랭클린 D. 루스벨트 대통령의 행정명령 8802는 방위산업에서 일하고 있는 노동자들이 "인종, 교의, 피부색 등에 의해 차별을 받지 않고" 일할 수 있도록 했다.

   ① 많은 미국 흑인들에게, 제2차 세계대전은 인종 간의 장벽을 무너뜨릴 수 있는 기회를 제공했다.
   ② 제2차 세계대전 동안, 인종 간의 폭동이 몇몇 군사 부대에서 발생했다.
   ③ 제2차 세계대전은 미국인들의 능력을 최대한 이끌어냈다.

15 a. 장례식에서 촛불을 사용하는 전통은 로마 사람들로부터 시작됐는데, 그들은 악령이 두려워해 떠나가도록 만들기 위해서 촛불을 사용했었다.
   b. 묘비석은 지하 세계에 있는 죽은 자들을 지키기 위한 방안에서 유래됐다.
   c. 관의 본래 목적은 지하에 죽은 자를 안전하게 지키기 위함이었다.

   ① 인류학자들은 장례식 전통이 구석기 시대(100,000-40,000 BC)에 존재했다는 증거를 발견했다.
   ② 다른 문화들은 죽은 자를 기리는 다른 방법들을 가지고 있다.
   ③ 애도와 관련된 현대의 많은 문화들은 죽은 자와 그리고 그들이 산 사람들에게 무엇인가를 할지도 모른다는 두려움과 관련이 있다.

16 a. 고대 그리스 도시 국가였던 스파르타의 시민들은 농부가 되는 것이 허락되지 않았다. 대신에 그들은 전사로서 훈련받도록 만들어졌다.
   b. 스파르타에서의 가정생활은 심하게 제약을 받았는데 왜냐하면 소년과 소녀들 모두 신체적인 단련을 하는 데 있어서 오랜 시간을 보내야 했기 때문이다.
   c. 7세에서부터 30세에 이르기까지, 소년들은 전쟁을 수행하는 방법을 배웠다.

   ① 스파르타 사람들은 그들의 토지와 관련된 법에 매우 순종적이었다.
   ② 스파르타 사람들의 삶은 힘겨웠으며 그들의 삶은 전쟁을 위해 바쳐지는 삶이었다.
   ③ 스파르타의 남자와 여자들은 전쟁에서의 그들의 영웅적 행위로 유명했다.

17 a. 수화에서, 우리는 글자, 단어, 그리고 생각들을 나타내는 몸짓을 하기 위해 손과 몸의 다른 부분들을 사용한다.
   b. 모스 부호는 유선 전신기를 필요로 하는데 이는 점과 대쉬를 통해 글자, 숫자, 그리고 구두점으로 번역되는 소리들을 만들기 위함이다.
   c. 공항에서 자주 볼 수 있는 수기 신호 즉 깃발신호 시스템은 다음과 같은 방법으로 작동하는데, 한 사람이 양손에 깃발을 쥐고 선 다음에 글자와 숫자들을 가리키는 위치로 자신의 팔을 움직인다.

   ① 대중 전달(매스컴)은 다수의 청중들에게로 전달되는 메시지를 의미한다.
   ② 몇몇 의사소통 방식은 문자 언어에 의존하지 않는다.
   ③ 단순한 표기 체제는 BC 3000년 수메르까지 거슬러 올라간다.

18 a. 6,000마리의 암소로부터 나오는 우유를 사용해서 만든 13,440 파운드의 치즈가 뉴욕주 박람회에 전시되기 위해 생산됐다.
   b. 1801년 매사추세츠주의 설교가였던 존 릴런드는 대통령이었던 앤드류 잭슨에게 자신의 고향에서 만들어진 1,200 파운드의 체셔 치즈를 선물했다.
   c. 위스콘신 치즈 재단은 1964년에 있을 세계박람회에 치즈를 전시하기 위해서 183톤의 우유를 모았는데 이는 34,500 파운드 이상의 무게가 나가고 세로로 6피트 정도나 되는 치즈 조각이었다.

   ① 수년간, 치즈를 너무나 좋아하는 미국인들은 꽤나 큰 치즈들을 생산했다.
   ② 캐나다인들은 토론토 박람회 기간 동안 자신들의 치즈 만드는 기술을 자랑스럽게 선보였다.
   ③ 거대한 치즈를 만들어낸 고대 로마인들은 꽤나 이상한 사람들로 여겨졌다.

19 고대 그리스의 몇몇 유명한 도시들은 특정한 목적으로 보존됐다.

  a. 델포이시에는 여자 사제들이 신으로부터 신탁을 받는 중요한 사원이 위치해 있었다.
  b. 역사는 많은 해전들이 그리스 섬 근처에서 일어났다고 기록하고 있다.
  c. 열광적인 관중들은 운동 경기와 신체적인 경쟁을 위해 따로 마련돼 있던 Olympia로 몰려들었다.
  d. 통치자들은 그리스를 도시국가로 조직했는데 이는 중앙에 있는 마을들에 의해서 지배되고 운영되는 큰 규모의 지역이었다.
  e. 소크라테스, 플라톤, 그리고 아리스토텔레스와 같은 철학자들의 가르침은 그리스 시민들이 어디에 사는지 관계없이 그들에게 영향을 끼쳤다.
  f. 코린트의 고대 도시는 그리스를 다른 동방 및 서방 세계와 연결해주는 분주한 무역의 중심지로서 명성을 얻었다.

20 많은 미국인들이 다른 행성에서의 삶에 관한 생각들에 매료돼 있기 때문에 뉴 멕시코의 로스웰은 인기 있는 관광 마을이 됐다.

  a. 방문객들은 비행접시가 1947년 사막에 착륙했고 미국 공군에 의해 숨겨졌다는 증거를 찾기 위해 로스웰에서 매년 500만 달러를 지출한다.
  b. 1991년부터 1996년까지, 100,000명이 넘는 사람들이 UFO 박물관과 연구센터를 보기 위해서 로스웰로 여행을 왔다.
  c. 로스웰에서 매년 개최되는 UFO 축제는 이제 150,000명의 사람들을 불러모은다; 6일간에 걸쳐 진행되는 이 행사에는 강의, 콘서트, 버스여행, 연회, "우주선 경주", 그리고 가장무도회 등이 포함된다.
  d. 칼 코르프의 저서인 The Roswell UFO Crash에 따르면, 파괴된 우주선은 사실 소련의 핵실험을 추적하기 위한 기밀 군사용 열기구였다고 주장한다.
  e. 워커 공군기지가 1967년에 문을 닫았을 때, 48,000명에 이르는 로스웰의 인구 중 많은 수가 직장을 잃었고 마을은 중요 수입원을 잃어버렸다.
  f. 우주 공간에서 생명체들을 봤다고 주장하는 대부분의 사람들은 그것들이 큰 머리와 회녹색의 피부, 그리고 아몬드 모양의 눈을 가진 작은 생명체들이라고 묘사한다.

CHAPTER 02 Fact & Opinion

    2S2R 독해전략을 이해하기 위해 우리가 가장 먼저 해야 할 것은 general과 specific을 구별하는 것이었다. 이제 그 다음으로 중요한 것은 사실과 의견을 구별하는 일이다. 우리는 영어 독해를 배우면서도 실제 이것의 중요성은 많이 간과하는 오류를 범하기 쉽다. 하지만, 글에서 저자의 주장이 설득력이 있는지 아니면 억측에 기반한 비논리적인 것인지를 판단할 때 가장 기본이 되는 것은 사실과 의견을 구별하는 능력에 있다.

    Fact사실란 조사나 증명이 가능한 정보나 진술a piece of information or a statement that can be checked or proven을 말한다. 가장 알기 쉬운 fact는 통계, 사건, 날짜 등과 같은 데이터를 포함한다. 예를 들어, '60살 넘는 사람들은 20대보다 투표율이 2배가 높다'는 fact이다. 여러분이 이 진술을 읽는다면, 여러분은 그것이 옳은 것이라 가정한다. 왜냐하면, 이 진술의 사실성은 투표 조사를 통해 사실인지 아닌지 조사와 검증이 가능하기 때문이다.

    Opinion의견이란 사실에 대한 해석an interpretation of facts으로, 믿음, 감정, 판단, 태도, 선호를 나타낸다. 이것들은 세계에 대한 자기 자신의 인식에 기반하고 있기에 확증하기가 쉽지 않다. 따라서 끊임없이 논쟁이 되고 다른 의견이 제기될 수 있다.

    하나의 예를 들어 보자. '60살 넘는 사람들은 20대보다 투표율이 2배가 높은 이유는 투표하는 방식이 젊은 사람들에겐 공정하지 못하기 때문이다.' 여기선 '60살 넘는 사람들은 20대보다 투표율이 2배가 높다'는 fact에 대해 글쓴이가 자신의 해석, 즉 '투표하는 방식이 젊은 사람들에겐 공정하지 못하기 때문이다'라는 해석을 가미하고 있다. 따라서 이 문장은 opinion이다. 이렇게, opinion엔 facts를 포함시킬 수도 있다. 하지만, 그렇지 않고 자신의 의견만을 진술하는 경우가 일반적으로 더욱 많다.

    위에서 말했듯이, 2S2R 독해전략에선 이 둘을 구별하는 능력이 영어 논리를 이해하는 데 있어서 중요함을 강조한다. 사실에 기반한 근거를 대는가, 아니면 자신의 의견만을 강요하는 글인가를 정확하게 이해함으로써 글을 비판적, 논리적으로 읽는 데 도움이 되기 때문이다. 아래에 제시된 예제를 풀다 보면, 여러분은 영어 논리력의 기본 중 하나인 사실과 의견을 구별하는 안목이 자연스럽게 쌓일 것이라 생각한다.

다음의 어구들이 나오면 fact보다는 opinion일 확률이 높다.

1. I think; I believe
2. good; bad; awful; ridiculous; (un)fair; wonderful; interesting; boring; disgusting; beautiful; difficult; terrific; fantastic; discouraging
3. bigger; most important; strangest; silliest
4. some; several; many; quite a few; most; large numbers; often; usually
5. sometimes; frequently; seldom; rarely
6. all; every; never; each; always; none; no
7. may be; could be; seems; appears; probably; apparently; seemingly

다음의 것들이 의견을 표현하는 대표적인 예들이다.

BELIEF 믿음: If you want to live an ethical life, you must follow the Ten Commandments.
FEELING 감정: We should be ashamed of our failure to get homeless people the help they need.
JUDGMENT 판단: People who don't keep their lawns neatly trimmed are lazy and inconsiderate toward their neighbors.
ATTITUDE 태도: A mother with a preschooler should not work outside the home full time.
PREFERENCE 선호: Singers should not try to improve upon "The Star-Spangled Banner" because the melody is fine the way it was written.

번역 BELIEF: 윤리적인 삶을 살고 싶으면 십계명을 따라야 한다.
FEELING: 우리는 노숙자들이 필요한 도움을 받지 못하게 된 것을 부끄럽게 느껴야 한다.
JUDGMENT: 자기 집 잔디밭을 깨끗이 깎지 않는 사람들은 게으르고 이웃에 대한 배려를 하지 않는 것이다.
ATTITUDE: 유아원 다니는 아이가 있는 엄마는 집 밖에서 풀타임으로 직장을 가져서는 안 된다.
PREFERENCE: 멜로디가 쓰여진 그대로 좋기 때문에, 가수들은 미국 국가인 "The Star-Spangled Banner"에 뭔가를 가미해 더 잘하려고 해서는 안 된다.

> 예제

[1-14] 다음 문장을 읽고 사실에 대한 진술이면 F, 의견에 대한 진술이면 O를 쓰시오.

01 In 1860 American Civil War broke out. _____

02 In 1860 there were probably 300,000 Indians in the United States, most of them living west of the Mississippi. _____

03 In an age without heroes, the Indian leaders are perhaps the most heroic of all Americans. _____

04 Public schools are better than private schools. _____

05 You never see a diverse student population in a private school class, yet public school classes often have students from all over the globe. _____

06 The buildings in my town are clean, fairly new, and updated often. _____

07 America cannot solve its energy problems by finding more oil in our own lands. _____

08 The Arctic yielded 1.5 million barrels a day at peak production in 2020. _____

정답 01 F 02 F 03 O 04 O 05 O 06 O 07 O 08 F

09 Their claim that the Arctic could yield 1.5 million barrels a day at peak production in 2020 is not believable. _____

10 Protecting kids may be as simple as turning off the tube, hoofing it around the block, or stocking the fridge with fruits and veggies instead of cakes and cookies. _____

11 One out of every four children in this country is dangerously overweight. _____

12 With increasing obesity rates, there has been an explosion in Type 2 diabetes, a disease once so rarely seen in children it was called "adult-onset diabetes." _____

13 Ten years ago, Type 2 diabetes accounted for just 4 percent of diabetes cases in children. But today, that figure has jumped to as high as 45 percent in some parts of the country. _____

14 According to the U.S. Department of Energy, this country accounts for about 25 percent of global oil consumption but only has about 3 percent of proven global oil reserves. _____

정답 09 O   10 O   11 F   12 F   13 F   14 F

한글번역

예제

01 1860년에 미국 남북전쟁이 발발했다.

02 1860년 당시 미국에는 약 30만 명의 인디언이 있었으며, 대부분은 미시시피 강 서쪽에 거주하고 있었다.

03 영웅이 없던 시대에, 인디언 지도자들은 아마도 모든 미국인 가운데 가장 영웅적인 존재였다.

04 공립학교들이 사립학교들보다 더 낫다.

05 사립학교 교실에서는 다양한 학생군을 거의 볼 수 없지만 공립학교 교실에는 세계 여러 곳에서 온 학생들이 있다.

06 우리 마을에 있는 건물들은 깨끗하고 상당히 새것이며 자주 보수된다.

07 미국은 우리 자신의 땅에서 더 많은 석유를 찾으려 해서는 에너지 문제를 해결할 수 없을 것이다.

08 2020년에 북극에서 하루 최고 150만 배럴의 석유를 생산했다.

09 그들은 가령 2020년에 북극에서 하루 최고 150만 배럴의 석유를 생산할 수 있다고 주장하는데 그것은 믿을 만하지 못하다.

10 텔레비전을 끄고, 집 주변을 돌며 냉장고를 케익과 쿠키 대신 야채와 과일로 채우는 것 같은 간단한 방법으로 당신의 아이들을 보호할 수도 있다.

11 우리나라의 4명 중 한 아이가 심각한 비만이다.

12 그리고 비만율의 증가에 따라 2군 당뇨병, 즉 한때는 어린이에게서는 거의 보이지 않았기 때문에 "성인 당뇨병"으로 불렸던 질병이 폭발적으로 증가하고 있다.

13 10년 전에는 4% 정도의 당뇨병이 어린이에게서 나타났다. 그러나 오늘날 우리나라의 어느 지역에서는 이 숫자가 45%로 급증했다.

14 미 에너지국에 의하면 우리나라는 전 세계의 25%의 석유를 사용하지만 단지 3%의 입증된 석유를 보유하고 있다.

CHAPTER 03 Signal Words & Transitions

　　2S2R 독해전략의 1단계인 Survey에서 연결어와 패턴을 나타내주는 단어나 구와 같은 signal words를 찾는 것은 매우 중요하다. 그것을 미리 파악함으로써 2S2R 독해전략의 2단계인 Reading에서 할 것을 미리 예측하여 전체 독해의 큰 그림을 그릴 수 있기 때문이다.

　　예를 들어 글의 중간에 '그러나'라는 연결사가 나오고 그 다음에 어떠한 signal word(s)가 나온 것이 없다면, 그 글은 '그러나' 다음에 나오는 내용이 저자가 말하고자 하는 주장이 될 확률이 높다. 따라서 시험시간이 부족할 경우 여러분은 '그러나' 이하의 문장만 꼼꼼히 읽어도 전체 내용을 파악할 수가 있고, 저자의 요지도 파악할 수 있다. 1단계에서 signal word(s)를 빨리 체크함으로써 글 전체에 대한 지도를 그릴 수 있는 것이다.

01　연결어의 특징들(Characteristics of Transitions)

　　Transition의 세 가지 성격에 주의해야 한다.
1. 일부는 동의어이다. 즉, 같은 의미이다. 예를 들어, also와 in addition, too는 모두 의미가 같으므로 보통 상호 간에 바꿔 쓸 수 있다.
2. 어떤 transition은 세부사항 간의 한 종류 이상의 관계를 보이는 데 사용될 수 있다. 예를 들어, 단어 next는 항목의 나열에서도 보이고, 과정에서의 단계를 설명하는 문단에서도 보인다.

> The next component of love is commitment.
> Next, prepare an agenda for the meeting.

3. 별개의 transition은 문장들의 의미에서 미묘하면서도 중요한 변화를 만들 수 있다. 예를 들어, 대조 접속사가 들어간 예문을 읽어보자.

> She was afraid of guns. But she bought a gun and learned to use it to protect herself.
> * but은 그녀가 무서운데도 불구하고 총을 샀다는 것을 암시한다.
>
> She was afraid of guns. So she bought a gun and learned to use it to protect herself.
> * 인과관계의 접속사 so로 바꿈으로써 무서움을 극복하려고 총을 샀다는 것을 암시한다. Transition 하나를 고치면 두 문장의 의미가 확연히 바뀐다.

02 다양한 패턴의 Signal Words

1. Series(열거)를 나타내는 Signal Words

✓ Series의 Signal Words

also	in addition	too	another	moreover
furthermore	first, second, third	first of all	and	for one thing
finally	lastly	most importantly	examples	next
several	many	one, two, three, etc.	a number of	numerous
advantages	reasons	points	classes	types
categories	groups	goals	kinds	characteristics
methods	ways	tips	forms	problems

예제

다음 글을 읽고 series pattern의 signal words에 밑줄을 치시오. 그런 다음 topic을 쓰시오.

> Computer language can be funny at times. For example, we say computers have a "memory." We know they do not really remember or think. But we still say "memory." Also, computer programs have "menus." Of course, we are not talking about restaurants or food. This is a different kind of menu, one for choosing a program or section of the memory. Another example is the "mouse" we use to "talk to" the computer. It is hard not to think about a real mouse when you hear the word. But there are no little gray animals in the machine.

Topic : _____

정답 Computer language can be funny at times. **For example**, we say computers have a "memory." We know they do not really remember or think. But we still say "memory." **Also**, computer programs have "menus." Of course, we are not talking about restaurants or food. This is a different kind of menu, one for choosing a program or section of the memory. **Another** example is the "mouse" we use to "talk to" the computer. It is hard not to think about a real mouse when you hear the word. But there are no little gray animals in the machine.
Topic : computer language

2. Comparison and Contrast(비교와 대조)를 나타내는 Signal Words

⊘ Comparison의 Signal Words

alike	similar	same	(and) also	both

⊘ Contrast의 Signal Words

but	however		
different	unlike	비교급(more... than / less... than 등)	in spite of
although	instead (of)	in opposition	as opposed to
just the opposite	though	nevertheless	rather
on the on hand / on the other hand		unlike	while
on the contrary	actually	despite	even though
unfortunately	in contrast	conversely	in reality
still	nonetheless	whereas	

예제

다음 글을 읽고 comparison and contrast의 signal words에 밑줄을 치시오. 그런 다음 topic을 쓰시오.

> The way people pay for health care is very different in Canada and in the U.S. In Canada, everyone has a chance to have health care. People pay a tax to the government, and the government pays most of the doctor, dentist, and hospital bills. In the U.S., on the other hand, some people pay insurance companies, and the insurance companies pay doctor, dentist, and hospital bills. But in the U.S., unlike Canada, many poor people cannot pay insurance companies. So they have very little health care.

Topic : _____

정답 The way people pay for health care is very **different** in Canada and in the U.S. In Canada, everyone has a chance to have health care. People pay a tax to the government, and the government pays most of the doctor, dentist, and hospital bills. In the U.S., **on the other hand,** some people pay insurance companies, and the insurance companies pay doctor, dentist, and hospital bills. **But** in the U.S., **unlike** Canada, many poor people cannot pay insurance companies. So they have very little health care.

Topic: medical care (or health care system) in Canada and in the U.S.

3. Time Order(시간순서)를 나타내는 Signal Words

✓ Time Order의 Signal Words

first, second, third	before	now	then
after	while	next	soon
in the beginning	once	today	previously
often	as	when	until
later	eventually	last	meanwhile
finally	over time	in the end	history
during, in, on, or by *(followed by a date)*		over time	originally
increasingly	in just one year	from~ to~	events
steps	stages	developments	procedure
process			

예제

[1-2] 다음 글을 읽고 time order의 signal words에 밑줄을 치시오. 그런 다음 topic을 쓰시오.

01

　　Albert Einstein was born near the end of the nineteenth century in Ulm, Germany. He graduated from the University of Zurich in Switzerland at the age of 26. That was also when he did his famous work in physics. Sixteen years later he won the Nobel Prize for physics. For the next ten years he lived in Germany. He also traveled a lot to talk with other scientists. Then in the early 1930s he had to leave Germany because of Hitler and the Nazi Party. He moved to the United States. From that time until his death he lived in Princeton, New Jersey. He died at the age of 76.

Topic : _____

02

In the United States, some people did not want the war. In the early 1960s only a few people felt this way. But by the late 1960s many people believed Americans should not be fighting in Vietnam. Finally, the U.S. government had to listen to these people. In May 1968, the Americans began to talk to North Vietnam about stopping the war. For the next few months, fewer bombs were used against the North. By the end of the year, the bombing stopped. It still took a long time to end the war. American soldiers started to go home in 1970. The last Americans left three years later.

Topic : _____

정답 01 Albert Einstein was born **near the end of the nineteenth century** in Ulm, Germany. He graduated from the University of Zurich in Switzerland **at the age of 26. That was also when** he did his famous work in physics. **Sixteen years later** he won the Nobel Prize for Physics. **For the next ten years** he lived in Germany. He also traveled a lot to talk with other scientists. **Then in the early 1930s** he had to leave Germany because of Hitler and the Nazi Party. He moved to the United States. **From that time until his death** he lived in Princeton, New Jersey. He died **at the age of 76**.
Topic : the life of Albert Einstein

02 In the United States, some people did not want the war. **In the early 1960s** only a few people felt this way. But **by the late 1960s** many people believed Americans should not be fighting in Vietnam. **Finally**, the U.S. government had to listen to these people. **In May 1968**, the Americans began to talk to North Vietnam about stopping the war. **For the next few months**, fewer bombs were used against the North. **By the end of the year**, the bombing stopped. It still took a long time to end the war. American soldiers started to go home in **1970**. The last Americans left **three years later**.
Topic : the process of ending the Vietnam War in the US
또는 how the Americans stopped fighting in Vietnam

4. Cause and Effect(인과관계)를 나타내는 Signal Words

✓ Cause and Effect의 Signal Words

If the arrow goes C(cause) ────────────► E(effect), use these signal words:

so	can make	is a cause of	produces
leads to	stops	results in	creates
causes	can help	had an effect (or influence) on	contribute
is responsible for	aggravate	effects	is the reason for
increase			

If the arrow goes E(effect) ◄──────────── C(cause), use these signal words:

(is) the effect of	is(are) caused by	is due to	results from
because (of)			

기타 signal words:

consequences	outcomes	factors	impact
chain reaction			

예제

다음 글을 읽고 cause and effect의 signal words에 밑줄을 치시오. 그런 다음 topic과 main idea를 쓰시오.

> In the United States, many of the poor city children have health problems. Some of the children are ill because of their diet. They do not get enough food, or they do not get healthy food. Their poor health is also caused by bad housing. Many children live in poor apartments which have no heat in the winter and little fresh air in the summer. Some of the children have poor health because they do not receive good medical care. Many poor children do not see a doctor for checkups or for shots to keep them healthy.

Topic : _____

Main idea : _____

정답 In the United States, many of the poor city children have health problems. Some of the children are ill **because of** their diet. They do not get enough food, or they do not get healthy food. Their poor health **is also caused by** bad housing. Many children live in poor apartments which have no heat in the winter and little fresh air in the summer. Some of the children have poor health **because** they do not receive good medical care. Many poor children do not see a doctor for checkups or for shots to keep them healthy.
Topic : the poor city children's health problems in the United States
Main idea : The poor city children's health problems in the United States are caused by several factors.

5. Definition(정의)을 나타내는 Signal Words

정의 패턴은 종종 하나 또는 그 이상의 보기examples를 포함하는데, 따라서 다음과 같은 signal words들이 주로 나타난다.

✓ **Definition의 Signal Words**

means	−(dash)	definition	define	meaning
is/are	is/are called	for example	for instance	to illustrate
as an illustration	in one instance	such as	in one case	describe
more precisely	specifically	what one calls		

[예제]

다음 글을 읽고 definition의 signal word를 제시하고, 글의 패턴은 무엇인지 밝히시오.

> The World Health Organization defines obesity as a condition in which a person's body-mass index, or MBI, is greater than 30.

Signal words의 중요성은, 일반적인 영어시험에서는 빈칸 채우기 형식으로 출제되는 문제에서 두드러진다. 이런 유형에선 signal words를 아는 것이 문제를 푸는 핵심이며, 답을 정확하면서도 빨리 풀 수 있도록 해준다. 다음의 문제를 보자.

[정답] 이 글의 signal word는 "defines"이다. 따라서, 글의 패턴은 'definition'이 된다.

01 Read the passage and follow the directions.

Language consumes a large proportion of time within a day while activating regions across the entire brain. Ellen Bialystok and her team tested the theory that bilingualism can increase cognitive reserve and thus delay the age of onset of Alzheimer's disease symptoms in elderly patients. Their study investigates conversion times from mild cognitive impairment to Alzheimer's disease in monolingual and bilingual patients. Although bilingualism delays the onset of symptoms, Bialystok says, once diagnosed, the decline to full-blown Alzheimer's disease is much faster in bilingual people than in monolingual people because the disease is more severe.

Imagine sandbags holding back the floodgates of a river. At some point the river is going to win. The sturdiness of the sandbag barrier is holding back the flood and at the point when they are diagnosed with mild cognitive impairment they already have severe pathology but there has been no evidence of it because they have been able to function thanks to their high cognitive reserve. Even the most resilient people have their limits. When they can no longer resist, the floodgates get completely washed out. As a result, they crash faster.

In the five-year study, researchers followed 158 patients who had been diagnosed with mild cognitive impairment. For the study, they classified bilingual people as having high cognitive reserve and monolingual people as having low cognitive reserve. Patients were matched on age, education, and cognitive level at the time of their diagnosis of mild cognitive impairment. The researchers followed their six-month interval appointments at a hospital memory clinic to see the point at which diagnoses changed from mild cognitive impairment to Alzheimer's disease. The conversion time for bilinguals, 1.8 years after initial diagnosis, was significantly faster than it was for monolinguals, who took 2.6 years to convert to Alzheimer's disease. This difference suggests that bilingual patients had more severe neuropathology at the time they were diagnosed with mild cognitive impairment than the monolinguals, even though they showed the same level of cognitive function.

> These results contribute to the growing body of evidence demonstrating that bilinguals are more _____ in dealing with neurodegeneration than monolinguals. They operate at a higher level of cognition because of their cognitive reserves, which means that many of these individuals will withstand the neuropathology longer. This study adds new evidence by showing that the decline is steeper once a clinical threshold has been crossed, presumably because there is more disease already in the brain.

Fill in the blank with the ONE most appropriate word from the passage.

친절한 해설

자 우리 기억합시다. "좋은 빈칸 문제는 항상 논리성을 띄고 있다"는 것을. (물론 때대로 출제위원이 개념 없이 출제하는 경우도 있긴 하지만, 우리 그냥 그렇지 않을 거라 믿어버리자구요.) 빈칸 채우기 문제가 나오면, ① 글 전체의 Topic sentence를 찾을 수 있으면 찾아보고(일반적으로 첫째나 둘째 문장에 있지만 항상 그런 것은 아님), ② 빈칸의 앞뒤 문장을 꼼꼼히, 특히 signal words에 주목해서 두 번 이상 읽기 바랍니다.

우선 비교급 표현과 대조를 나타내는 signal words에 주목해야 합니다.

1. 핵심 Signal Words 분석

비교급 표현:
"much faster in bilingual people than in monolingual people" (1단락)
"significantly faster than it was for monolinguals" (3단락)
"more severe neuropathology... than the monolinguals" (3단락)
"bilinguals are more (빈칸) in dealing with neurodegeneration than monolinguals" (4단락)
여기서 "than"은 두 집단(이중언어 사용자와 단일언어 사용자)을 지속적으로 비교하고 있음을 보여주는 중요한 signal word입니다.

대조 표현:
"Although bilingualism delays the onset of symptoms... once diagnosed, the decline... is much faster" (1단락)
여기서 "Although"와 "once"는 초기 단계와 진단 후 단계의 대조를 보여주는 signal words입니다.

인과 관계:
"because they have been able to function thanks to their high cognitive reserve" (2단락)
"because there is more disease already in the brain" (4단락)
여기서 "because"는 현상의 원인을 설명하는 signal word입니다.

2. 글의 논리적 흐름 분석

첫 번째 단락: 이중언어 사용자들은 알츠하이머 증상 발현이 지연되지만, 일단 진단되면 더 빠르게 악화됨을 설명합니다.

두 번째 단락: 모래주머니 비유를 통해 "Even the most resilient people have their limits"라고 명시합니다. 여기서 "resilient"(회복력 있는, 저항력 있는)이라는 단어가 직접 사용되었습니다.

세 번째 단락: 실제 연구 결과를 제시하며, 이중언어 사용자들이 단일언어 사용자들보다 알츠하이머로의 전환이 더 빠름을 보여줍니다.

네 번째 단락(빈칸 포함): "bilinguals are more _____ in dealing with neurodegeneration than monolinguals"은 앞선 내용들의 결론으로, 이중언어 사용자들이 신경퇴행에 대처하는 데 있어 어떤 특성이 더 강하다는 의미입니다. 특히 "more... than"이라는 비교급 표현이 사용된 것에 주목해야 합니다.

3. 빈칸에 적합한 단어 도출

위의 분석을 종합하면, 빈칸에 적합한 단어는 "resilient"입니다. 그 이유는:

두 번째 단락에서 직접 "esilient"라는 단어가 사용되었습니다.

글 전체가 이중언어 사용자들의 '저항력'과 '회복력'에 대해 설명하고 있습니다.

빈칸 이후 문장 "They operate at a higher level of cognition because of their cognitive reserves, which means that many of these individuals will withstand the neuropathology longer"에서 "withstand"(견디다, 저항하다)라는 단어가 "resilient"의 의미를 뒷받침합니다.

비교급 표현 "more... than"은 이중언어 사용자들이 단일언어 사용자들보다 이 특성이 더 강하다는 것을 나타내며, 이는 "resilient"(회복력 있는)이 가장 적합합니다.

따라서 빈칸에 들어갈 가장 적절한 단어는 "resilient"입니다. 이 단어는 글의 논리적 흐름, signal words, 비교급 표현, 그리고 글 전체의 주제와 완벽하게 일치합니다.

02 Read the passage and follow the directions.

> Fashion criticism should be rigorous, clearly stated, and historically informed. It should neither oversimplify (as current fashion criticism often does) nor be unnecessarily obscure (as current art criticism often is). It should look for vitality and boldness, and distinguish the original from the derivative. It should track a designer's development—or point out standstill or regression—and attempt to figure out what led the designer to make these specific aesthetic choices, elaborate on the techniques and materials that have been used—and finally pass judgment. As already mentioned, a proper judgment is something more than *mere* opinion—it is a *reasoned* or *justified* opinion which aims for broader validity. Criticism can never be completely objective. It must necessarily to a great extent be subjective, saying as much about the critic as about the object under scrutiny. Which is why writing criticism necessarily means exposing yourself. Writing criticism is about struggling to come to terms with what you do not yet know exactly how to deal with, to pass judgment, to expose yourself, knowing that you expose yourself, putting your prestige and your very identity at risk. As Pierre Bourdieu formulated it: "Taste classifies, and it classifies the classifier." This is a truth that holds for all of us, but it is especially acute in the case of the critic, whose judgment is at the greatest public scrutiny. Writing real criticism is about putting yourself on the line every single time.
>
> What about disagreements between critics? They should be welcomed. It is never a good sign when too many people are in agreement about too much. It almost always means that we are thinking too little. There *should* be disagreements between critics. Two critics can certainly disagree about the relative merits of two designers, such as for instance Alexandre Herchcovitch and Phoebe Philo. However, one should also note that there will usually be a high degree of convergence between critics in their judgments. One might prefer Herchcovitch and the other Philo, and even find a certain collection plain tasteless, but it would be highly surprising if one of them argued that Herchcovitch or Philo is a designer with virtually no aesthetic merit. Would a serious critic pass such a judgment? There will be disagreements, but disagreements are possible only against a much larger background of _____.

Fill in the blank with the ONE most appropriate word from the passage.

친절한 해설

이 빈칸 채우기 문제를 해결하기 위해서는 글의 논리적 흐름과 핵심 단서들을 면밀히 분석해야 합니다. 좋은 빈칸 문제는 항상 논리성을 띄고 있기 때문에, 글의 구조와 signal words에 주목하여 답을 찾아내야 합니다.

1. 빈칸 주변의 논리 구조 분석

   빈칸이 포함된 문장을 살펴봅시다.

   "There will be disagreements, but disagreements are possible only against a much larger background of _____."

   이 문장에서 주목해야 할 signal word는 "but"입니다. 이는 역접의 접속사로, 앞뒤 내용이 대조된다는 것을 알려줍니다. 즉, "의견 불일치가 있을 것이지만, 그 의견 불일치는 오직 더 큰 배경 위에서만 가능하다"는 논리 구조입니다. 여기서 "의견 불일치(disagreements)"와 대비되는 개념이 빈칸에 들어가야 합니다.

2. 글 전체의 맥락 분석

   두 번째 단락의 첫 문장부터 중요한 단서가 있습니다.

   "What about disagreements between critics? They should be welcomed. It is never a good sign when too many people are in agreement about too much."

   여기서 "agreement"라는 단어가 직접 등장하며, "disagreements"와 대비되는 개념으로 사용되었습니다.

   더 결정적인 단서는 다음 문장에 있습니다.

   "there will usually be a high degree of convergence between critics in their judgments."

   여기서 "convergence"(수렴, 일치)는 "agreement"의 유의어로, 비평가들 사이에 기본적인 합의가 있다는 것을 강조합니다. 그 다음 예시에서도 이를 뒷받침합니다.

   "One might prefer Herchcovitch and the other Philo... but it would be highly surprising if one of them argued that Herchcovitch or Philo is a designer with virtually no aesthetic merit."

   이 예시는 비평가들이 개인적 선호도는 다를 수 있어도, 기본적인 미적 가치 판단에는 공통된 합의가 있다는 것을 보여줍니다.

3. 논리적 추론 과정

   이러한 단서들을 종합해보면 :

   빈칸에는 "disagreements"와 대비되는 개념이 필요합니다. 글에서 직접 "agreement"라는 단어를 사용하여 이러한 대비를 보여주고 있습니다. "convergence"라는 유사 개념으로 이를 강화합니다. 예시를 통해 비평가들 사이의 기본적인 합의가 존재함을 증명합니다.

   따라서 빈칸에 들어갈 가장 논리적이고 타당한 단어는 "agreement"입니다. 이는 "의견 불일치는 오직 더 큰 합의의 배경 위에서만 가능하다"라는 글의 핵심 주장을 완성시킵니다.

   이 답은 단순히 문맥상 적절한 것이 아니라, 글의 논리 구조와 핵심 단서들을 통해 명확하게 도출된 것입니다. 비평에 관한 이 글의 전체 주장—비평가들이 세부적인 판단에서는 다를 수 있지만 기본적인 가치 체계에서는 공통된 합의가 있다는 것—을 "agreement"라는 단어가 가장 잘 표현하고 있습니다.

＊ 왜 "convergence"가 아닌 "agreement"인지에 대한 설명

1. 원문에서의 단어 사용 패턴

본문에서 두 단어가 모두 사용되었지만, 사용 방식과 맥락이 다릅니다.

"agreement"는 직접적으로 "disagreements"와 대비되는 개념으로 사용되었습니다: "It is never a good sign when too many people are in agreement about too much."

"convergence"는 비평가들의 판단이 자연스럽게 모이는 현상을 설명하는 데 사용되었습니다: "there will usually be a high degree of convergence between critics in their judgments."

2. 문장 구조와의 관계

빈칸이 포함된 문장은 "disagreements are possible only against a much larger background of _____"입니다. 이 문장에서는 "disagreements"(불일치)의 직접적인 반대 개념이 필요합니다. 언어적으로 "agreement"(일치)가 "disagreement"(불일치)의 정확한 반대어입니다. 반면 "convergence"(수렴)는 과정이나 결과를 더 강조하는 개념입니다.

3. 글의 핵심 논지와의 연결성

글의 핵심 주장은 비평가들 사이의 의견 차이(disagreements)는 더 큰 공통 기반 위에서 가능하다는 것입니다. 이 공통 기반은 정적인 상태의 "합의"(agreement)를 의미합니다. 반면에 "convergence"는 서로 다른 견해가 점차 가까워지는 동적인 과정에 가깝습니다. 하지만 빈칸에서는 이미 존재하는 배경(background)을 언급하고 있으므로, 정적인 상태를 나타내는 "agreement"가 더 적합합니다.

4. 출제자의 의도 추론

빈칸 채우기 문제는 종종 지문에서 직접 사용된 단어를 그대로 활용하도록 구성됩니다. "agreement"는 텍스트에서 직접적으로 "disagreements"와 대비되어 사용되었기 때문에, 출제자가 의도한 정답일 가능성이 높습니다. 또한 이 지문은 빈칸 직전에 "disagreements"를 언급했으므로, 그 반대어인 "agreement"를 사용하는 것이 가장 자연스러운 언어적 흐름을 만듭니다. 이러한 종류의 문제에서는 단순히 의미상 적합한 단어를 찾는 것이 아니라, 글의 논리 구조와 언어적 패턴을 정확히 분석하여 출제자가 의도한 정확한 단어를 찾는 것이 중요합니다.

한글번역

예제

1. Series(열거)를 나타내는 Signal Words

   가끔 컴퓨터 언어는 웃길 때가 있다. 예를 들면 우리는 컴퓨터가 "기억"이 있다고 말한다. 우리는 그것들이 실제로 기억하거나 생각하지 못한다는 것을 알고 있다. 그러나 우리는 여전히 "메모리"라고 말한다. 또한 컴퓨터 프로그램은 "메뉴"가 있다. 물론 우리가 식당이나 음식을 말하고 있는 것은 아니다. 이것은 다른 종류의 메뉴로 프로그램이나 메모리의 섹션을 선택할 때 쓰는 것이다. 또 다른 예는 우리가 컴퓨터에게 말을 걸기 위해 사용하는 "마우스"이다. 이 말을 들을 때 실제 쥐를 생각하지 않기란 쉽지 않다. 하지만 이 기계에 작은 회색 동물은 없다.

2. Comparison and Contrast(비교와 대조)를 나타내는 Signal Words

   미국과 캐나다에서 사람들이 의료혜택에 돈을 지불하는 방식은 아주 다르다. 캐나다에서는 모든 사람들이 의료혜택을 받을 수 있다. 사람들은 정부에 세금을 내고 정부는 대부분의 의사와, 치과의사 그리고 병원비를 지불한다. 반면 미국에서는 일부 사람들이 보험회사에 돈을 지불하고 보험회사가 의사, 치과의사, 병원비를 지불한다. 그러나 미국에서는 캐나다와는 다르게 많은 가난한 사람들이 의료보험 회사들에 돈을 지불할 능력이 없다. 그래서 그들은 의료혜택을 거의 받지 못한다.

3. Time Order(시간순서)를 나타내는 Signal Words

   01 알버트 아인슈타인은 19세기 말엽 독일 울름에서 태어났다. 그는 26세의 나이에 취리히 대학을 졸업했다. 이때는 또한 그가 물리학에서 유명한 업적을 이룬 때이기도 했다. 16년이 지난 이후 그는 노벨 물리학상을 받았다. 이후 10년 동안 그는 독일에 살았다. 또 그는 다른 과학자들과 교류하기 위해 많은 여행을 했다. 그리고 1930년대 초 그는 히틀러와 나치당 때문에 독일을 떠날 수밖에 없었다. 그는 미국으로 갔다. 그때부터 죽을 때까지 그는 뉴저지주 프린스턴에 살았다. 그는 76세의 나이로 사망했다.

   02 미국에서 일부 사람들은 전쟁을 원치 않았다. 1960년대 초반에는 이렇게 생각하는 사람이 많지 않았다. 그러나 1960년대 후반에는 많은 사람들이 미국이 베트남에서 싸워서는 안 된다고 믿었다. 마침내 미국 정부는 이들의 말을 들어야 했다. 1968년 5월 미국인들은 월맹(북 베트남)과 정전을 논하기 시작했다. 이후 몇 달 동안 전보다 적은 양의 폭탄이 월맹에 사용됐다. 그 해 말, 폭격은 멈췄다. 그러나 여전히 전쟁이 끝나는 데는 오랜 시간이 걸렸다. 1970년 미국 군인들은 귀환하기 시작했다. 3년 후 마지막 미국인들이 떠났다.

4. Cause and Effect(인과관계)를 나타내는 Signal Words

   미국에서 가난한 도시의 많은 아이들이 건강에 문제가 있다. 일부 어린이들은 식생활 때문에 몸이 아프다. 그들은 충분한 음식을 얻지 못하거나 건강한 음식을 얻지 못한다. 그들의 열악한 건강의 원인은 주거에 있기도 하다. 많은 아이들이 겨울에는 난방이 잘 안 되고 여름에는 환기가 잘 안 되는 열악한 아파트에 산다. 또 일부 아이들은 양질의 의료혜택을 받지 못해 건강이 나쁘다. 많은 아이들이 건강을 지키기 위한 정기검진이나 예방접종을 받기 위해 의사를 찾지 못한다.

5. Definition(정의)을 나타내는 Signal Words

   세계보건기구는 비만을 체질량지수 혹은 MBI가 30보다 높은 상태로 정의한다.

실전 문제

01 언어는 뇌 전체의 영역을 활성화하면서 하루 종일 많은 시간을 소비한다. 엘렌 비알리스톡과 연구팀은 이중언어 사용이 인지적 예비력을 증가시킴으로써 노인 환자들의 알츠하이머병 증상의 시작 연령을 지연시킬 수 있다는 이론을 실험했다. 그들의 연구는 단일언어와 이중언어 환자의 가벼운 인지장애에서 알츠하이머병으로의 전환 시간을 조사한다. 비알리스톡 박사는 이중언어 사용이 증상들의 시작은 지연시키지만, 일단 진단을 받고 나면, 병이 더 심한 상태에 있기 때문에 알츠하이머병이 정점으로 악화되는 것이 이중언어 사용자가 단일언어 사용자보다 훨씬 빠르다고 말한다.

모래주머니가 강의 수문을 막고 있다고 상상해보자. 언젠가는 강이 이길 것이다. 모래주머니 둑방의 견고함이 홍수를 지연시키고 있고, 경도인지장애 진단을 받는 그 시점에는 이미 심각한 병리 현상이 있지만, 높은 인지적 예비력 덕분에 기능을 발휘할 수 있었기 때문에 병의 증거가 없었던 것이다. 결국 아무리 (회복탄력이) 강한 사람도 한계가 있다. 그들이 더 이상 저항할 수 없을 때, 수문은 완전히 씻겨나간다. 결과적으로, 그들은 더 빨리 침몰한다.

5년간의 연구에서, 연구원들은 가벼운 인지장애로 진단받은 158명의 환자들을 추적했다. 이 연구를 위해, 그들은 이중언어 사용자들을 높은 인지능력을 가진 사람으로, 단일언어 사용자들을 낮은 인지능력을 가진 사람으로 분류했다. 환자들의 경도인지장애 진단 당시 연령, 교육, 인지 수준을 일치시켰다. 연구원들은 병원의 기억 클리닉에서의 6개월 간격의 진찰을 통해 진단이 가벼운 인지장애에서 알츠하이머병으로 바뀌는 시점을 알아봤다. 초기 진단 후 1.8년이 지난 이중언어 사용자의 전환 시간은 알츠하이머병으로 전환하는 데 2.6년이 걸린 단일언어 사용자의 전환 시간보다 상당히 빨랐다. 이 같은 차이는 이중언어 환자들이 동일한 수준의 인지기능을 보여줬음에도 불구하고 경도인지장애 진단 받았을 당시 신경병리증이 단일언어 환자들보다 더 심각했음을 시사한다. 이러한 결과는 이중언어 사용자가 단일언어 사용자보다 신경 퇴화를 처리하는 데 더 탄력적이라는 것을 보여주는 증거가 늘어나는 데 기여한다. 그들은 인지적 예비력 때문에 더 높은 수준의 인지 능력을 가동시킬 수 있고, 이는 이들 중 많은 사람들이 신경병증을 더 오래 견딜 것이라는 것을 의미한다. 이 연구는 임상적 한계를 넘어서면 감소가 더 가파르다는 것을 보여줌으로써 새로운 증거를 보태고 있으며, 아마도 이는 뇌에 이미 더 많은 질병이 있기 때문인 것이다.

02 패션비평은 엄격하고, 명확하게 진술돼야 하며, 역사적으로 풍부한 지식을 지니고 있어야 한다. 패션비평은 지나치게 단순화하거나(현재의 패션비평이 흔히 그렇듯이), 불필요하게 모호해선 안 된다(현재의 패션비평이 흔히 그렇듯이). 패션비평은 활력과 대담성을 찾아야 하고, 독창적인 것과 파생적인 것을 분별할 줄 알아야 한다. 패션비평은 디자이너가 어떻게 발전해 왔는지를 — 또는 정지 상태에 있는지, 아니면 (심지어) 퇴행을 하고 있는지 — 추적하고, 그런 다음 이 디자이너가 이러한 특정한 미적 선택을 하게 된 원인을 파악해 사용된 기술과 재료에 대해 자세히 설명한 뒤에, 최종적으로 비평적 판단을 내려야 한다. 이미 언급했듯이 적절한 판단은 단순한 의견을 넘어선 어떤 것이다. 즉, 그것은 더 넓은 타당성을 목표로 하는 일리 있고 정당한 의견이다. 비평은 결코 완전히 객관적일 수 없다. 비평이 크게 주관적일 수밖에 없는 것은 필연적이다. (왜냐하면) 비평이란 비평가가 검토하고 있는 대상에 대한 것만큼이나 비평가 자신에 대해서 말하는 것이기 때문이다. 비평문을 쓴다는 것은 필연적으로 결국 비평가 자신을 드러내는 것임을 의미하는 이유도 바로 여기에 있다. 비평문을 쓴다는 것은, (첫째) (비평문을 쓰는) 당신이 현재 정확히 어떻게 처리해야 될지를 알지 못한다는 것을 받아들이려 애쓰고, (둘째) 판단을 내리기 위해 애쓰고, (셋째) 비평 본인의 위신과 바로 그 정체성을 위험에 빠뜨린다는 것을 알면서도, 비평가 본인을 드러내기 위해 애쓰는 것에 관한 것이다. (프랑스 철학자) 피에르 부르디외가 말했듯이, "취향은 분류하며, 취향은 분류하는 사람을 분류한다." 이것은 우리 모두에게 적용될 수 있는 사실이지만, 이 사실은 특히 비평가 — 이들의 판단은 대중들에 의해 가장 꼼꼼히 검토되기에 — 의 경우에 더욱 예리하게 적용된다. 진정한 비평문을 쓴다는 것은 스스로를 매번 위험에 처하게 만드는 것이다.

비평가들 간의 불일치는 어떠한가? 그 불일치는 환영받아야 한다. 너무 많은 사람들이 너무 많은 것들에 동의하는 것은 결코 좋은 신호가 아니다. 그것이 의미하는 바는 거의 항상, 우리가 너무 얕게 사고하고 있다는 것이기 때문이다. 비평가 사이의 불일치는 반드시 존재해야만 한다. 예를 들면, 두 명의 비평가는 분명히 알렉산드르 헤르치코비치(브라질 태생의 세계적 디자이너)와 피비 파일로(영국의 세계적 디자이너) 같은 두 디자이너들의 상대적인 장점에 대해 동의하지 않을 수 있다. 하지만 이 비평가들의 판단에는 상당한 정도의 수렴되는 지점이 있다는 것은 주목할 만하다. 한 비평가는 헤르치코비치를 선호하고 다른 비평가는 파일로를 선호해서, 심지어는 어떤 컬렉션은 정말 아무런 취향이 없는 밋밋한 것이라 말할 수도 있다. 하지만, 만약 그 비평가들 중 한명이, 헤르치코비치나 파일로는 미학적 가치가 없는 디자이너라고 주장한다면 아마도 엄청나게 놀랄 것이다. 그 어떠한 진지한 비평가가 이러한 판단을 내릴까?(이런 판단을 하지 않을 것이란 의미). 불일치는 존재한다, 하지만 불일치는 더 큰 일치(동의)를 배경으로 할 때만 가능하다.

CHAPTER 04 Topic

　일반적인 글 읽기의 과정을 포함해서 대화적 읽기에서 가장 기본이 되고 가장 먼저 확인해야 할 것은 이 글이 **'무엇'에 관한** 글인지를 파악하는 것이다. 해당 글이 '무엇에 관한 글인가about what?'라는 질문을 던지고 그에 대한 답을 찾았다면 글의 주제topic를 파악했다고 할 수 있다. 단락 혹은 전체 글이 말하고자 하는 바가 요지main idea인데 그 요지의 근본이 되는 것이 주제이므로, **2S2R 독해전략**의 모든 과정에서 일관되게 고려되어야 할 것도 '주제'라고 할 수 있다.

　2S2R 독해전략의 1단계 개관하기Survey에서 지문의 주요 화제를 찾는 것이 곧 주제를 파악하는 것이다. 그리고 각각의 구체적인 문단들이 얼마나 잘 짜여 있는지를 평가하는 것도 주제를 중심으로 평가되어야 한다. 2단계 읽기Reading에서 주석을 달거나 주장과 근거들을 도식화하는 과정에서도 주제를 중심으로 작업이 진행되어야 한다. 3단계 요약하기Summarizing에서 좋은 요약이 각 단락의 주제어를 포함해야 함은 당연한 것이다.

01　주제와 요지의 구별

　주제와 요지는 구별되어야 한다. 다음의 예문을 보자.

> ① 서울은 외국 관광객에게 인기가 없다.
> ② 서울은 500년 동안 조선의 수도였다.
> ③ 서울은 자동차가 아주 많아 대기가 깨끗하지 않다.

　위의 세 문장은 모두 서울을 주어로 하여 주장이나 설명을 하고 있다. 이때 서울이 topic이며 세 문장은 모두 요지에 해당한다. 즉 요지는 topic을 통해서 글쓴이가 독자에게 말하고자 하는 요점이다. 따라서 topic을 이해한다는 것은 그 주제에 대해서 글쓴이가 어떤 주장 혹은 설명을 하고자 하는지를 이해하기 위한 관문에 해당한다. 요지가 드러나는 문장을 주제문이라고 할 때, 주제와 주제문의 관계는 아래와 같은 구조로 나타낼 수 있다. 따라서 '무엇'에 대한 글인지를 잘못 이해한다면 글의 핵심 주장을 파악할 수 없음은 자명한 이치이다.

> 주제문(topic sentence) = 주제(topic) + 서술어(controlling idea)

예 서울은 외국 관광객에게 인기가 없다(topic sentence) = 서울(topic) + 외국 관광객에게 인기가 없다(controlling idea)

02 주제 찾기 방법

일반적으로 주제를 파악하는 방법은 2가지로 제시할 수 있다. **먼저 단락에서 가장 많이 언급되는 대상을 찾는 방법이다.** 일반적으로 주제는 ① **반복되어 나오는** ② **개념어**가 될 가능성이 가장 높다. 따라서 지문에서 언급되는 대상 혹은 개념들의 빈도를 파악하는 것은 주제를 찾는 한 방법이 된다.

✓ Key Point

Topic은 다음의 3가지 원칙을 지켜야 한다.
1. Topic은 too general해서는 안 된다.
2. Topic은 too specific해서는 안 된다.
3. Topic엔 읽는 사람 개인의 생각이 들어가선 안 된다.

다음의 예를 들어 보자.

예 다음 중 어느 것이 topic이 될 수 있나?
① Korea ② Japan ③ Thailand ④ Nations ⑤ Asian nations

여기서, ①, ②, ③번은 너무 세부적(too specific)이다. 왜? 만약 ①이 답이 된다면 ②, ③도 답이 되어야 하니까 말이 안 된다. 서로 등가의 것이니까. 그러면, ④번에 있는 Nations는? 이것은 또 너무 포괄적(too general)이다. 아시아에 있는 나라를 다루는 데 국가라는 큰 개념을 쓸 필요는 없기 때문이다. 그래서 답은 ⑤ Asian nations가 된다. 만일 ⑤가 선택지에 없다면? 물론 ④가 답이 된다.

우리는 1장에서 general과 specific에 대해서 공부를 하였다. 그것을 기반으로 하여 지금부터 topic을 알아보도록 하자.

예제

[1-3] What is the topic? Write it.

01 nose / ears / eyes / head / mouth

Topic : _____

02 doctor / X-rays / medicine / hospital / patients

Topic : _____

03 Colorado / California / Florida / Arizona / Texas

Topic : _____

[4-5] One word does not belong with the others. Cross out the word. Then write the topic.

04 ice cream / candy / cake / carrots / pie / cookies

Topic : _____

05 pen / fountain pen / paper / ink / test

Topic : _____

06 What is the topic of the passage? Write it.

> Many American scientists are worried about the drinking water in the United States. They think that soon there may be no more clean drinking water. Dirt, salt, and chemicals from factories can get into the water, making it unsafe to drink. This is already true in some places. One example is a small town in Massachusetts. Many children in this town became sick because of chemicals in the water. Another place with water problems is California. The water near old Air Force airports is not safe to drink. Many other cities and towns have water problems, too.

Topic : _____

해설 원리를 적용하여 한번 풀어보자. 우선 가장 많이 반복되는 단어나 구를 찾아보자. drinking water란 어구가 첫째, 둘째 그리고 셋째 문장에 모두 반복되어 나온다. 그렇다면 이것은 틀림없이 중요한 key words에 해당한다. 그런 다음 그것에 대해 어떠한 말들이 언급되는지 보자.

첫 번째 문장 : Many American scientists are **worried about** the drinking water in the United States.
두 번째 문장 : They think that soon there may be **no more clean** drinking water.
세 번째 문장 : **Dirt, salt, and chemicals from factories** can get into the water, making it **unsafe** to drink.

위에서 밑줄 친 것들을 다시 한번 읽어보자. '걱정하다', '더 이상 깨끗하지 않은', '공장에서 나오는 쓰레기, 염류, 화학약품들', '안전하지 않은' 따위의 부정적인(negative) 의미를 지닌 것들뿐이다. 이제 이것들을 한마디로 요약하는 것이 필요하다. 무엇이라고 할까? 답을 내기 전에 다시 원리로 돌아가보자. 앞에서 우리는 다음과 같은 것을 배웠다.

physics / chemistry / astronomy / geology / biology ⇨ 이 5개를 한 단어로 정리하면, 답은 sciences이다.

그렇다면, 이 원리를 여기에 적용해보자. 'worried about', 'no more clean', 'Dirt, salt, and chemicals from factories', 'unsafe' 이것들의 의미의 공통 속성을 끄집어내어보자. 그렇다면, problems이란 단어가 가장 적합할 것이다. 여기까지 정리해보면, problems with drinking water가 topic이 된다. 하지만, 이것은 topic이 되기엔 too general하다. 왜냐하면, 위의 글은 한국의 문제도 중국의 문제도 우간다의 문제도 아닌, 바로 미국의 문제이기 때문이다. 따라서 다시 정리를 해보면, American problems with drinking water 또는 problems with drinking water in the United States가 topic이 된다.

정답 01 head
02 hospital
03 states in the United States
04 뺄 것 : carrots / Topic : sweets or desserts
05 뺄 것 : test / Topic : writing utensils (필기도구)
06 Topic : American problems with drinking water 또는 problems with drinking water in the United States

[7-10] Which of the following is not relevant to the rest of the passage in terms of coherence?

07
① The Los Angeles Lakers is a championship basketball team.
② Their home court is the Forum, a modern stadium near Hollywood, California.
③ Among their fans are many big names in the entertainment industry, including Jack Nicholson and Johnny Carson.
④ Most basketball teams are based in large cities.
⑤ Whenever the Lakers play home games, they can be sure of a few movie stars to cheer for them.
⑥ Lakers fans have a lot to cheer about : their team has won four championships in recent years.

08
① The Boston Celtics is another championship basketball team.
② They have won first place among American basketball teams sixteen times.
③ Their home court for many years was the Boston Garden, an old stadium near the waterfront, but they have recently moved to a brand-new arena.
④ Although few famous movie stars attend their games, the Celtics have many fans in Boston.
⑤ Boston fans also support a baseball team, an ice hockey team, and a football team.
⑥ On evenings when the Celtics are playing an important game, the theaters and clubs are half empty.
⑦ All the fans are either at the game or at home watching it on television.

09 ① Everybody knows that cigarette smoking is harmful to one's health.
② However, many parents who are smokers may not be aware that it is also bad for their children.
③ Cigarette smoke can have harmful effects not just on the smoker, but also on people who live with the smoker.
④ Children, naturally, are more easily affected than adults.
⑤ In fact, studies have shown that children of smokers get sick more often than children of non-smokers.
⑥ Many people smoke in order to feel more relaxed in social situations.
⑦ One experiment, for example, studied a very common problem among small children: earaches.
⑧ The statistics clearly proved that children of smokers got earaches more often than children of non-smokers.
⑨ Their earaches were also more difficult to cure and tended to last longer.

10 ① In some poorer countries, over twenty percent of the children die in their first year of life.
② One reason for this is the lack of medical care and medicines.
③ Many children die from diseases that could easily be prevented with the right medicines or the right care.
④ Another cause of death among children is the food.
⑤ It often is not clean or fresh and can make children very sick.
⑥ Milk is a very important source of vitamins and minerals.
⑦ Getting enough food is another problem.
⑧ When children are weak from lack of food, they die more easily from diseases.
⑨ And finally, dirty water also kills many children every year.
⑩ Because of water shortages, people often are forced to drink water from dirty rivers or lakes.
⑪ This water may carry serious diseases, or it may contain harmful chemicals from pollution.

정답 07 ④
       08 ⑤
       09 ⑥
       10 ⑥

What is the best title and main idea of the passage?

> First is the concern that only the rich will have access to such life-saving technologies as genetic screening and cloned organs. Such fears are justified, considering that companies have been patenting human life. The obesity gene, the premature aging gene, and the breast cancer gene, for example, have already been patented. These patents result in gene monopolies, which could lead to astronomical patient costs for genetic screening and treatment. A biotechnology industry argues that such patents are the only way to recoup research costs that, in turn, lead to further innovations. The commercialization of technology causes several other concerns, including issues of quality control and the tendency for discoveries to remain closely guarded secrets rather than collaborative efforts. In addition, industry involvement has made government control more difficult because researchers depend less and less on federal funding. Finally, although there is little doubt that profit acts as a catalyst for some scientific discoveries, other less commercially profitable but equally important projects may be ignored.

Title : _____

Main idea : _____

정답 Title : Commercialization of biotechnology
Main idea : Commercialization of biotechnology causes several problems.

친절한 해설

우선 중요한 key words나 signal words에 밑줄을 그어보세요. 그런 다음 topic도 찾아보지요. 그런 다음 글의 pattern of organization과 main idea도 찾아보고요. 그리고 맨 마지막에 summary도 해보지요. 자 준비됐나요?!

First is the concern that only the rich will have access to such life-saving technologies as genetic screening and cloned organs. Such fears are justified, considering that companies have been patenting human life. The obesity gene, the premature aging gene, and the breast cancer gene, for example, have already been patented. These patents result in gene monopolies, which could lead to astronomical patient costs for genetic screening and treatment. A biotechnology industry argues that such patents are the only way to recoup research costs that, in turn, lead to further innovations. The commercialization of technology causes several other concerns, including issues of quality control and the tendency for discoveries to remain closely guarded secrets rather than collaborative efforts. In addition, industry involvement has made government control more difficult because researchers depend less and less on federal funding. Finally, although there is little doubt that profit acts as a catalyst for some scientific discoveries, other less commercially profitable but equally important projects may be ignored.

우선 signal words나 key words에 밑줄을 치니 위와 같이 되네요. 이미 앞에서 설명했듯이, topic은 너무 구체적(too specific)이거나 너무 일반적(too general)이지 않은 "반복되는 단어나 어구"(특히 개념어)라고 말했던 것 기억나시죠? 그러면, topic이 될 만한 것을 찾아보죠. 우선 ① concern(s)-그것의 유사어인 fear(s) ② patent 등이 나오다가 조금 있으니, ③ commercialization of technology라는 단어가 반복해서 나오는군요. 여기서 저자는 paraphrase를 계속 사용하고 있는데, industry, companies 등을 commercialization과 같은 개념으로 서로 번갈아 가면서 쓰고 있네요. ① concern은 too general하고 ② patent는 too specific하네요. 따라서 가장 타당한 것은 ③ commercialization of technology이네요. 그런데 좀 더 정확히는 단순한 technology가 아니라 life-saving technologies라는 구체적인 것을 언급하므로 biotechnology가 돼야 해요. 따라서 이 글의 topic은 commercialization of biotechnology가 되네요.

그러면 다음으로 요지를 찾아보죠. 다음 5장에서 배우겠지만, 이 글은 series의 패턴으로 쓰여졌어요. 이 패턴의 signal words가 First; other; In addition; Finally이고요. 이 유형에서 가장 중요한 것은 일반화(generalization)의 기술이에요. 즉, 다른 말로 하면, 각각의 supporting details의 공통 속성을 찾아내는 것이 중요하다는 말이죠. (이 방법에 대해 우리는 본문 3장과 5장 Signal words와 Patterns of Organization에 대한 이론에서 좀 더 자세히 살펴볼 것이기에 여기선 간략히 다루겠음). 이 지문에서 First; other; In addition; Finally 사이엔 사소하고 지엽적인 내용상 차이가 있을 뿐, 그 어떠한 외적·범주적인 큰 차이도 없어요. 다시 말하면, First 다음에 나오는 것도 concern에 관한 것이고 other; In addition; Finally 다음에 나오는 것도 모두 concern에 관한 것일 따름이지요. 좀 더 부연하면, 첫 번째 우려처럼 오직 부자들만이 생명을 살리는 기술에 접근하고 가난한 사람들은 접근 못할 것이란 점이든; 두 번째 우려처럼 품질 관리를 어떻게 할 것인가와 협동 노력보다는 자기들끼리 몰래 함으로써 남게 되는 문제점 등을 지적하든; 세 번째 우려처럼 정부의 통제를 더욱 어렵게 만드는 등 총 4가지의 이유를 제시하고 있지만, 이것들 각각에서 하나의 공통 속성을 뽑아내면, 그것은 바로 concern(fear)이라는 점이네요.

그러면, 도대체 뭐 때문에 concern이 쭉 열거가 될까요? 이 질문을 품고 글의 구조를 좀 더 꼼꼼히 보니 또 하나의 pattern이 사용됐네요. 바로 인과관계(cause and effect) 패턴이네요. 나중에 본문에서 꼼꼼히 다루겠지만, 인과관계 패턴에 많이 사용되는 signal words는 다음과 같지요.

so	can make	is a cause of	leads to	stops
results in	causes	makes	had an effect on	can help
creates	effects	is the reason for	is the effect of	the effect of
are caused by	because of	is caused by	is the reason for	is due to
results from	because			

이런 경우 대다수의 글의 요지는 "A가 B에게 (이러저러)한 영향을 주었다"라든가 "A는 B라는 결과를 야기시켰다" 따위와 유사한 것이 되지요. 이 지문엔 result in; lead to; causes; has made; because 등의 signal words들이 있어요. 따라서 이 글의 main idea를 써보면, commercialization of biotechnology causes several concerns가 되지요. 다음의 공식을 명심하세요.

주제문(topic sentence or main idea) = 주제(topic) + 서술어(controlling idea)

예 commercialization of biotechnology causes several concerns = commercialization of biotechnology(topic) + causes several concerns(controlling idea)

자 그럼 이 지문을 summary한다면, 어떻게 해야 할까요? 마지막 장에서 나오겠지만, 미리 한 번 보죠. 다음에 나오는 summary의 원리를 적용하면 쉽게 풀 수가 있어요.

✓ Summary의 원리

1. 좋은 요약은 요지와 주된 논거(major supporting points)를 포함한다. 요지는 가능하면 첫 문장에 제시한다.
2. 좋은 요약은 단서가 되는 언어들(signal words)을 포함한 각 문단의 핵심어를 포함한다.
3. 좋은 요약은 작은 세부사항, 반복되는 세부사항, 읽는 이의 의견을 포함하지 않는다.
4. 좋은 요약은 본문에 있는 단어나 어구를 그대로 사용하지 않고 다른 말로 바꿔쓰기(paraphrase)한다.
5. 일반적으로 원 본문의 길이를 25%(4분의 1)로 줄이는 것을 원칙으로 한다.

→ 이 원칙을 따르면, 본문을 다음과 같이 요약할 수가 있겠네요.
Biotechnology for profit has several problems. These include the rising cost of genetic treatment and the possibility of companies withholding discoveries. Since governments no longer provide the major research funding, their control has slackened. Research becomes guided by profit than by true benefit.

한글번역

 06 많은 미국 과학자들은 미국의 식수에 대해 우려를 한다. 그들은 곧 깨끗한 식수가 없어질 거라고 생각한다. 공장에서 나오는 오염물, 염분, 화학물질이 물로 들어갈 수 있고 먹기에 안전하지 않게 만들 것이다. 일부 지역에서는 이것이 이미 사실이다. 하나의 예는 메사추세츠의 작은 마을이다. 이 마을의 많은 아이들은 물에 든 화학물질 때문에 병이 났다. 물 문제가 있는 또 다른 지역은 캘리포니아다. 오래된 공군 비행장 주변의 물은 먹기에 안전하지 않다. 다른 많은 도시들과 마을들 역시 물 문제가 있다.

07 ① 로스앤젤레스의 레이커스는 우승 농구팀이다.
② 그들의 홈 경기장은 캘리포니아 할리우드 근처의 현대적인 운동장인 포럼이다.
③ 그들의 팬 중에는 잭 니콜슨과 자니 카슨과 같은 연예계의 많은 유명인이 있다.
④ 대부분 야구팀들은 대도시에 본거지를 두고 있다.
⑤ 레이커스의 홈경기가 있을 때마다, 그들은 많은 영화배우들이 응원을 하러 오리라 확신할 것이다.
⑥ 레이커스 팬들은 그들의 팀이 최근에 4번이나 우승했다는 것에 아주 신이 나있다.

08 ① 보스턴 셀틱스는 또 다른 우승 농구팀이다.
② 그들은 미국 농구팀 경기에서 16번이나 우승을 거머쥐었다.
③ 그들의 홈 경기장은 수년간 해안 가까이에 위치한 오래된 경기장인 보스턴 가든이었으나, 최근에 새로운 경기장으로 옮겼다.
④ 그들의 경기에는 소수의 영화배우들이 참석하지만, 셀틱스는 보스턴에 많은 팬을 거느리고 있다.
⑤ 보스턴 팬들은 또 야구팀과 아이스하키팀, 그리고 축구팀도 응원한다.
⑥ 셀틱스의 중요한 경기가 펼쳐지고 있던 저녁, 극장과 클럽들은 절반 가까이 비었다.
⑦ 모든 팬들은 경기장이나 집에서 텔레비전을 통해 관람하고 있었다.

09 ① 흡연이 건강에 해롭다는 것은 모든 사람들이 알고 있다.
② 그러나 흡연을 하는 많은 부모들은 자녀들에게도 나쁠 수 있다는 것에 조심을 하지 않는다.
③ 흡연은 흡연자뿐만 아니라, 그들과 함께 사는 사람들에게도 악영향을 끼칠 수 있다.
④ 자연적으로 아이들은 어른보다 더 쉽게 영향을 받는다.
⑤ 연구들은 실제로 흡연자들의 자녀가 비흡연자의 자녀보다 더 병에 걸리기 쉽다는 것을 보여준다.
⑥ 많은 사람들이 사회 정세 속에서 긴장감을 더 풀기 위해 흡연을 한다.
⑦ 예를 들면, 한 실험에서 어린 아이들이 공통적으로 귀앓이를 한다는 문제점이 발견됐다.
⑧ 흡연자의 자녀들이 비흡연자의 자녀들보다 더 많이 귀앓이를 한다는 통계가 명확히 증명됐다.
⑨ 그들의 귀앓이는 치료도 어려우며 오래 지속되는 경향이 있었다.

10 ① 몇몇 저소득 국가에서는 20%가 넘는 아이들이 1살 때 사망한다.
② 이러한 것의 한 가지 이유는 의학적인 치료와 약의 결핍이다.
③ 많은 아이들이 올바른 약과 치료로 쉽게 예방이 가능한 병임에도 사망한다.
④ 사망의 또 다른 이유는 아이들의 음식이다.
⑤ 대개 위생적이거나 신선하지도 않아서 아이들로 하여금 병에 걸리게 할 수 있다.
⑥ 우유는 비타민과 미네랄의 매우 중요한 성분이다.
⑦ 충분한 음식 섭취도 다른 문제점이다.
⑧ 식량의 부족으로 아이들이 야위게 되면, 병에 걸려 더 쉽게 사망한다.
⑨ 그리고 마지막으로, 비위생적인 식수 또한 매년 많은 아이들을 사망케 한다.
⑩ 식수 부족으로 인해, 사람들은 대개 더러운 강이나 호수로부터 물을 마시도록 강요당한다.
⑪ 이러한 물은 심각한 병을 옮기거나, 오염으로 인해 해로운 화학물질을 포함할 수 있다.

실전문제 첫 번째 우려는 오직 부자들만이 (개인의 유전적 질병의 발견과 예방을 위한 조사인) 유전자 검사나 복제된 기관들과 같은 생명을 살리는 기술에 접근할 것이란 점이다. 그와 같은 걱정은, 기업체들이 인간 생명을 특허를 내는 것을 고려할 때, 정당한 근거가 있다. 예를 들어, 비만 유전자, 정상보다 빨리 노화되는 유전자, 그리고 유방암 유전자 등은 벌써 특허를 내고 있다. 이런 특허는 유전자 독점이란 결과를 낳게 되는데, 이 독점은 유전자 검사와 (그런 다음) 치료를 해야 하는 부모들에게 천문학적인 비용을 들게 할 수 있다. 생명공학 산업계는 그와 같은 특허는 연구비용을 벌충하는 유일한 방법인데, 이걸 통해 앞으로 더 나은 혁신을 가져올 수 있다는 주장을 한다. 기술을 상업화하는 것은 여러 우려를 낳게 하는데, 품질 관리의 문제와 협동노력보다는 연구 성과나 발견이 다른 사람들 모르게 보호되는 경향성 등이 거기에 포함된다. 게다가, 산업의 개입은 정부의 통제를 더욱 어렵게 만드는데, 왜냐하면 연구자들이 연방정부의 기금에 덜 의존하게 되기 때문이다. 끝으로, 이윤이란 것이 어떤 과학적 발견을 촉진시키는 촉매제라는 것은 거의 의심의 여지가 없음에도, 상업적으론 덜 이익이 나는 것이긴 하지만 마찬가지로 앞의 것 만큼이나 중요한 다른 계획들이 무시될 수도 있다는 점이다.

CHAPTER 05 Patterns of Organization

01 글의 패턴의 파악과 2S2R

주어진 글의 구성 유형patterns of organization을 파악하는 것이 '빠르고 정확한' 읽기에 어떤 도움이 되는지는 아래와 같은 간단한 실험을 통해 쉽게 이해할 수 있다.

> 다음의 숫자들을 한 번 읽고서 암기해보자.
>
> a. 1, 5, 9, 13, 17, 21, 25
> b. 1, 2, 6, 10, 16, 17, 22
> c. 1, 3, 5, 7, 9, 11, 13
> d. a, b, c, d, e, f, g, h

먼저 a의 경우는 맨 처음의 숫자 1에서부터 차례로 4씩 더해지고 있음을 알 수 있다. c의 경우는 홀수로 구성되어 있다. 그리고 d는 알파벳의 순서로 되어 있다. 따라서 a와 c, 그리고 d는 굳이 암기하지 않고도 정보를 이해하고 기억하는 것이 더 용이하다. 즉 유형pattern화된 정보는 '빠르고 정확한' 이해와 암기에 큰 도움을 준다. 결국 글의 **구성 유형**을 파악하는 것은 글 전체의 정보를 구조화시켜서 정확하게 이해할 뿐만 아니라, 읽은 정보를 빠르게 기억해내는 데 기여함을 알 수 있다.

2S2R 독해전략에서 주어진 글의 유형 파악이 이루어져야 할 부분은 **Reading** 단계이다. 각 단락의 주제topic를 잠정적으로 이해한 뒤에 그 topic sentence를 뒷받침하는 세부사항(논거)들인 supporting details들을 통해서 전체적인 글의 구성 유형을 떠올려본다. 이때 글이 어떻게 조직화(패턴화)되어 있는지를 알면 다음 단계에 나올, 저자가 글에서 말하려는 요점, 즉 요지를 정확하게 이해하는 데 큰 도움을 준다. 특히, **2S2R 독해전략**에서는 글의 구성 유형을 철저하게 이해하는 것을 매우 중시한다. 왜냐하면, 다시 강조하지만 글의 요지를 파악하는 데 있어서 supporting details가 어떻게 구성되어 있는지를 파악하는 것이 가장 급선무이기 때문이다. 다음의 글을 한 번 보자.

> The name *Arkansas* comes from the Sioux word *quapaw*, which means "downstream people." The word *Illinois* comes from the Algonquin word *illini*, "warrior men." *Kentucky* comes from the Iroquois word *kentake*, which means "meadow" or "plains." The name *Michigan* comes from the Chippewa *mica gama*, meaning "grand waters." *Oklahoma* is named after the Choctaw term for "red people," *okla humma*.

번역 알칸사스라는 이름은 '하류쪽의 사람들'을 뜻하는 수족의 단어 *quapaw*에서 온 것이다. 일리노이는 '전사'를 뜻하는 알곤퀸 족의 단어 *illini*에서 온 말이다. 켄터키는 '초원'이나 '평야'를 뜻하는 이로쿼이 족의 말 *kentake*에서 온 것이다. 미시간은 '거대한 물'을 뜻하는 취페와족의 용어 *mica gama*에서 온 것이다. 오클라호마는 '붉은 사람들'을 뜻하는 촉타우족의 *okla humma*에서 유래 했다.

이 글의 topic과 main idea는 무엇인가? 그냥 무작정 추측할 수는 없는 노릇이다. 그렇다면, 위에서 말했지만 글의 패턴을 파악하는 것이 급선무이다. 그런 다음 각각 문장 하나하나를 꼼꼼히 읽고 각 문장의 주제subject를 찾아 리스트화하는 것이다. 자, 우선 이 글의 패턴은 series (examples)이다. 미국의 5개 주의 이름이 나열되어 있다. 구체적으로 각 문장의 주제를 써보면 다음과 같다.

- Sentence 1 subject : the name Arkansas
- Sentence 2 subject : the word Illinois
- Sentence 3 subject : Kentucky
- Sentence 4 subject : the name Michigan
- Sentence 5 subject : Oklahoma

그러면, 이 다섯 문장에서 언급된 것의 공통 속성을 끄집어내보자. Arkansas, Illinois, Kentucky, Michigan, Oklahoma 등의 공통 속성은 미국의 '주'라는 것이다. (예를 들어 대전, 부산, 인천, 광주 등 4개가 있다고 할 때 이것들의 공통 속성은 한국의 광역시라는 것이듯이.) 그런데 각 문장에서 또 하나의 공통적 요소가 있는데, 그것은 그 주의 이름들의 기원에 대한 것이다. 그런데 그 이름들의 기원이 모두 인디언에게서 왔음을 알 수 있다. 따라서 이 예시examples로 나열되어 있는 다섯 문장을 종합해 보면, '(미국의) 주의 이름+이름의 기원+인디언 언어'라 할 수 있다. 그러므로 이 글의 topic은 'origins of names of several states of the United States'이 되며, main idea는 "Names of several states of the United States originated from Indian languages"가 될 수 있다.

만일 이 글의 구성이 contrast나 definition, 또는 cause/effect 등으로 되어 있었다면, 이 글은 전혀 다른 글이 되었을 것이며, 요지를 찾는 방법도 달랐을 것이다. 하지만, 이 글은 예시로 되어 있기 때문에 그것들의 공통 속성을 찾아내서 일반화하면 요지를 찾을 수가 있는 것이다.

02 문단의 패턴 유형

1. Series 열거에 따른 패턴

이 유형에서 저자의 요지main Idea는 일반화generalization의 형태로 제시된다. 따라서 바로 앞의 예문에서 봤듯이, 각각의 supporting details의 공통 속성을 찾아내는 것이 중요하다. 보통 문단의 맨 앞에 일반화되어 제시된 단어를 'key words'라고 한다. key words가 앞에 제시된 열거 방식의 글의 경우 key words와 관련된 항목을 순차적으로 나열하는 것이 일반적이다. 이렇게 제시된 항목들은 대등하게 제시된 경우도 있고 점층적으로 제시된 경우도 있다. 따라서 항목들 간의 관계가 어떠한지 살피는 것이 필요하다. 보통 열거의 구성은 ① 예시examples ② 이유reasons ③ 유형types ④ 분류classification ⑤ 다양한 항목들의 특질 설명하기kind of point 등이 대표적이다.

> The Spanish kings and queens sent many people to find out about America. Christopher Columbus was **one** of these people. Ponce de Leon was **another**. Vasco da Gama was **a third**.

위의 예문은 열거의 패턴으로 되어 있다. 첫째 문장이 topic sentence이고 나머지 세 문장은 그것을 뒷받침하는 supporting details에 해당하며, one, another, a third는 signal words에 해당한다. 만일 위의 문장이 다음과 같다면?

> Christopher Columbus was **one** of many people who went to find out America. Ponce de Leon was **another**. Vasco da Gama was **a third**.

이 예문은 주어진 topic sentence가 없다. 그러면 어떻게 글의 요지를 파악할 것인가? 이런 경우 어쩔 수 없이 여러분은 이 글의 요지를 추론해야만 한다. 이럴 때 유용한 방법은 다음과 같다. (나중에 Main Idea를 다루는 장에서 더 구체적으로 언급이 될 것이다.)

Step 1. topic과 관련이 있는 supporting details를 목록화하고,
Step 2. 글이 어떤 패턴으로 되어 있는지를 파악한 다음,
Step 3. 그 supporting details의 공통 속성을 찾아내서 그것을 일반화하는 것이 필요하다.

이 예문은 크게 3개의 문장으로 되어 있는데, 각각의 문장에서 세 사람이 등장한다. 이들을 나열해보면, Christopher Columbus와 Ponce de Leon과 Vasco da Gama다. 그런 다음 이 글엔 중요한 signal words가 있다. 그것을 나열해보자. one, another, a third가 그것이다. 이것은 전형적인 열거의 패턴으로 되어 있는 글이다. 즉, key words와 관련된 항목을 순차적으로 대등하게 나열하고 있다.

그렇다면, 각각의 내용은 유사한 것들을 담고 있을 것이다. 즉, Christopher Columbus가 미국을 발견하기 위해 갔던 것처럼, 다른 두 사람도 마찬가지인 것이다. 따라서 이 세 사람의 공통 속성을 찾아낼 수가 있다. 그것은 그들이 스페인 사람이란 점도, 그들이 축구를 좋아한 다는 점도, 그들이 왕의 총애를 받았다는 점도 아닌, 바로 미국을 발견하기 위해 갔던 사람들 이란 점이다. 그것을 찾을 수 있는 중요한 힌트가 one; another; a third 등의 signal words가 있는 열거의 패턴으로 되어 있다는 것이다.

따라서, 지금까지 언급한 것을 정리해보면, 이 글의 요지는 "There were many people who went to find out America_{미국을 발견하기 위해 많은 사람들이 갔다.}"가 되며, "Christopher Columbus was one of many people who went to find out America. Ponce de Leon was another. Vasco da Gama was a third."는 논거(supporting details)가 된다.

다음의 예도 보자.

> People have many different ideas about what makes a great vacation. **Some people** like to go for long walks in the forest, where they won't see anyone for days. **Others** prefer to spend their holiday in an exciting city. There they can visit museums, theaters, and good restaurants. **Still others** enjoy the fresh air at the seashore. They can spend their days at the beach and listen to the ocean waves at night. **A few people** decide to stay at home and do some major household projects.

번역 사람들은 어떻게 휴가를 보내야 잘 보내는 것인지에 대해 여러 다른 생각들을 가지고 있다. 어떤 이들은 며칠 동안 아무도 보이지 않는 숲에서 긴 산책을 하고 싶어 한다. 다른 이들은 흥미로운 도시에서 휴가를 보내고 싶어한다. 그들은 그 도시에 있는 박물관이나 영화관, 훌륭한 레스토랑을 방문할 수 있다. 그리고 또 다른 이들은 바닷가에서 시원한 공기를 즐긴다. 낮에는 해변에서 시간을 보내며 밤에는 파도 소리를 듣는다. 또한 몇몇 사람들은 집에 머물며 중요한 집안일을 하려고 한다.

해설 이 글의 main idea는 "People have many different ideas about what makes a great vacation"이다. 진하게 표시한 부분들은 여러분에게 main idea를 보충설명해주는 역할을 한다. 이런 것들을 'signal words'라고 한다. 그것들은 교통신호(traffic signals)와 같은 기능을 한다. 각각의 signal은 여러분의 시선을 집중시키도록 만든다.

다음의 글도 Series 패턴으로 구성되어 있다. 진하게 표시한 부분들이 signal words에 해당한다.

> This book has **a lot of information** about Poland. **First** it tells about the history. It **also** explains how to travel around the country. **Finally**, it lists some interesting places to visit.

번역 이 책에는 폴란드에 관한 많은 정보가 담겨 있다. 먼저 역사에 대해 이야기하고, 이어서 그 나라를 여행하는 방법을 설명한다. 마지막으로 방문할 만한 흥미로운 장소들을 소개한다.

해설 이 글의 main idea는 "This book has a lot of information about Poland"이다. 밑줄 친 부분들은 main idea를 보충 설명해주는 역할을 한다. 'First', 'Also', 'Finally'와 같은 단어들이 바로 signal words이다. 이런 signal words는 글의 전개 순서를 알려주면서, 독자가 어떤 내용에 주목해야 하는지 알려주는 역할을 한다. 따라서 이 글에서는 책에 담긴 정보가 역사, 여행 방법, 관광지라는 순서로 제시되고 있음을 알 수 있다.

2. Comparison and Contrast 비교와 대조에 따른 패턴

Comparison은 similarity에 기반하고 있고, Contrast는 difference에 기반하고 있음을 명심하자.

> The twins are as different as two people can be. Sally, who is always hoping someone will have a party, has black hair, brown eyes, and an outgoing personality. She wants to be an actress or a popular singer. Susan, more serious and studious, has blonde hair, blue eyes, and a somewhat shy manner. Since she has done well in all her classes in graphic arts and math, she plans to become an architect or an engineer.

번역 쌍둥이는 서로 다른 두 사람만큼 다르다. 누군가가 파티를 열기를 항상 바라는 샐리는 검은 머리에 갈색 눈, 그리고 외향적인 성품을 갖고 있다. 그녀는 배우나 유명한 가수가 되기를 바란다. 좀 더 심각하고 공부벌레인 수잔은 금발에 푸른 눈 그리고 좀 수줍은 편이다. 미술과 수학 수업에서 잘하기 때문에 수잔은 건축가나 엔지니어가 되기를 바란다.

해설 이 글은 contrast 패턴으로 구성되어 있다. 따라서 차이성(difference)에 기반하고 있다.

> Most Americans would say it is not really possible to establish an ideal society. But time after time, a small dedicated group of people will drop out of the mainstream of American society to try, once more, to live according to the group's concept of an ideal society. Most of these groups have believed in holding their property in common. Most have used the word *family* to refer to all members of the group. Many of these groups, however, have differed widely in their attitudes toward sex and marriage.

번역 대부분의 미국인들은 이상적인 사회를 만드는 것은 진정 불가능하다고 말할 것이다. 하지만 계속해서 소수의 헌신적인 사람들은 미국 주류 사회에서 벗어나 한 번 더 단체의 이상 사회의 개념에 의거해 살아보려고 노력할 것이다. 대부분의 이들 단체들은 재산을 공유하는 신념을 갖고 있다. 대부분은 가족이라는 단어를 단체 전체의 구성원들을 부를 때 쓴다. 그러나 많은 단체들이 성과 결혼의 문제에 있어서 대단히 다른 입장을 취한다.

해설 이 글은 Mixed Comparison and Contrast 패턴으로 구성되어 있다. 따라서 유사성(similarity)과 차이성(difference) 둘 모두에 기반하고 있다.

> Leif Ericson probably had a more difficult trip across the Atlantic Ocean than Christopher Columbus did. Ericson sailed across the cold northern part of the Atlantic, but Columbus sailed across the southern part, where it was warmer.

번역 리프 에릭슨은 대서양을 건널 때 콜럼버스보다 더욱 어려운 여행을 했을 것이다. 에릭슨은 추운 북대서양을 가로질러 항해했지만, 콜럼버스는 좀 더 따뜻한 남대서양을 가로질러 항해했다.

해설 이 글은 contrast 패턴으로 구성되어 있다. 따라서 차이성(difference)에 기반하고 있다.

3. Time Order 시간 순서에 따른 패턴

(1) **Narrative** 서사적 패턴

Narrative란 **이야기를 함축하고 있는** 글의 구성을 말한다. 서사를 위해서는 수행자인 '인물'과 수행되는 '사건', 그리고 이 둘을 매개하는 시간의 흐름이 필요하다. 이러한 구성의 글은 글 전체를 하나의 이야기화(누가 무엇을 수행하는가)하여 맥락을 파악하는 것이 필요하며, 이를 통해 주제를 도출할 수 있어야 한다.

> Gold was first found in California in **about 1840**. **The next ten years** in American history are called the California Gold Rush. Many people moved to the West **during those years** to look for gold. **By 1850**, there were many new Gold Rush towns in California.

번역 금은 캘리포니아에서 1840년 처음 채취됐다. 미국 역사의 다음 10년 동안은 캘리포니아 골드러시의 시대라고 일컬어진다. 많은 사람들이 금을 찾으려고 이 시기에 서부로 이주했다. 1850년이 돼서는 캘리포니아에 여러 새로운 골드러시 마을이 생겼다.

해설 이 글은 Time order 중에서도 narrative로 구성되어 있다. 진하게 표시한 것들이 signal word(s)에 해당한다. 이렇게 시간 순서로 진행되어 있는 것에서 다음과 같은 요지를 도출할 수 있다. "1840년에서 1850년까지 캘리포니아엔 많은 골드러시 마을이 생겼다 (Between 1840 and 1850, many Gold Rush towns appeared in California)."

> A small, hand-propelled German submarine, the Brandtaucher, sank **in 1851** in sixty feet of water, with her captain, Wilhelm Bauer, and two crew members aboard. Her hull **immediately** began to collapse under the pressure of the sea. Captain Bauer, who had built the tiny craft, knew that if he could keep his two companions from panicking while allowing the water to rise steadily inside her, the interior and exterior pressure would equalize and they would be able to open the hatch and get out. They did. As Bauer wrote **later**, "We came to the surface like bubbles in a glass of champagne." The world made little note of this first escape from a sunken submarine.

번역 소형 독일 수동 추진 잠수함 브란트타우허는 1851년 수심 약 60피트에서 침몰했는데, 당시 함장 빌헬름 바우어와 두 명의 승무원이 탑승해 있었다. 선체는 곧바로 바닷물의 압력에 의해 무너지기 시작했다. 이 작은 잠수정을 직접 제작한 바우어 함장은, 내부에 물이 서서히 차오르게 해서 내외부의 압력이 같아지면 해치를 열고 탈출할 수 있다는 사실을 알고 있었다. 그는 두 동료가 공포에 휩싸이지 않도록 진정시키며 이 과정을 실행했고, 결국 세 사람은 탈출에 성공했다. 나중에 바우어는 "우리는 마치 샴페인 잔 속의 거품처럼 수면 위로 떠올랐다"라고 기록했다. 그러나 세상은 이 최초의 잠수함 침몰 탈출 사건을 거의 주목하지 않았다.

해설 이 글은 Time order 중에서도 narrative로 구성되어 있다. 진하게 표시한 것들이 signal word(s)에 해당한다. 이렇게 시간 순서로 진행되어 있는 것에서 다음과 같은 요지를 도출할 수 있다. "The sailors successfully made the first escape from a sinking submarine, the Brandtaucher, by letting the water flow in and equalize the pressure."

> Franklin D. Roosevelt, the thirty-second president of the United States, served his county for most of his life. He was the only president to be elected four times. He was born in Hyde Park, New York, **on January 30, 1882**, and he began his studies at Harvard **in 1903**. **In 1905**, he married Eleanor Roosevelt, a distant cousin, and they had six children. **After** serving in the New York State Senate, Roosevelt worked in Washington as Secretary of the Navy **until 1921**. **At that time**, he became very ill with polio and lost the use of his legs. **In 1928**, Roosevelt ran for governor of New York. **After** serving two terms as governor, he was elected to the presidency **in 1933**. Roosevelt died in office **on April 12, 1945**.

번역 미국의 32대 대통령인 프랭클린 D. 루스벨트는 평생 대부분을 자신의 지역에서 봉사했다. 그는 유일하게 4번이나 선출된 대통령이었다. 그는 1882년 1월 30일, 뉴욕의 하이드파크에서 태어났으며, 1903년 하버드에서 공부를 시작했다. 1905년, 그는 먼 사촌인 엘리너 루스벨트와 결혼해서 6명의 자녀를 뒀다. 뉴욕주 상원의원으로 일한 뒤, 루스벨트는 1921년까지 워싱턴에서 해군 차관으로 일했다. 당시 그는 소아마비로 매우 아팠으며 그로 인해 걸을 수가 없었다. 1928년, 루스벨트는 뉴욕의 주지사로 출마했다. 그는 주지사로 두 번 재임한 뒤, 1933년 대통령으로 선출됐다. 루스벨트는 1945년 4월 12일 직무실에서 사망했다.

해설 이 글은 Time order 중에서도 narrative로 구성되어 있다. 진하게 표시한 것들이 signal word(s)에 해당한다. 이렇게 시간 순서로 진행되어 있는 것에서 다음과 같은 요지를 도출할 수 있다. "Franklin D. Roosevelt served his county for most of his life".

(2) **Process** 단계적 패턴

Process란 각 단계별로 어떤 것이 행해지는 방식을 설명하는 구성이다. 따라서 세부사항 details들은 단계들 steps or stages로 조직화되어 있다.

> Making orange juice concentrate from fresh oranges is done entirely by machines. **First**, oranges are dumped onto a moving belt. They travel into a machine which washes them with detergent. **Next** they are rolled into juicing machines, where seven hundred oranges per minute are split and squeezed. **Then** the rinds (the skin of the oranges) are thrown out the end of a long tube. **At the same time**, the juice goes through small holes in the bottom of the tube. **Next**, the juice goes into another machines called the finisher. There, the seeds and other tiny objects are removed. **Last**, the juice goes into large tanks, where most of the water is removed.

번역 신선한 오렌지를 응축해 오렌지 주스를 만드는 것은 전부 기계를 통해 이루어진다. 첫 번째로 오렌지는 움직이는 벨트 위해 올려진다. 그것들은 세척기 안으로 이동한다. 그 다음, 분당 700개의 오렌지를 쪼개서 즙을 내는 기계 안으로 들어가게 된다. 그리고 나서 오렌지의 껍질은 기다란 용기의 끝부분에 던져진다. 동시에 즙은 용기의 바닥에 있는 작은 구멍을 통과한다. 다음, 즙은 마무리 기계 안으로 들어간다. 그 기계에서 씨와 다른 작은 물질들이 제거된다. 마지막으로, 즙은 수분의 대부분을 제거하는 커다란 탱크로 들어가게 된다.

해설 이 글은 Time order 중에서도 process로 구성되어 있다. 진하게 표시한 것들이 signal word(s)에 해당한다. 이것을 도식화해보면 다음과 같다.

Step 1: Oranges are dumped onto a moving belt. They travel into a machine which washes them with detergent.
Step 2: They are rolled into juicing machines, where seven hundred oranges per minute are split and squeezed.
Step 3: The rinds (the skin of the oranges) are thrown out the end of a long tube. The juice goes through small holes in the bottom of the tube.
Step 4: The juice goes into another machines called the finisher.
Step 5: The juice goes into large tanks, where most of the water is removed.

이렇게 시간 순서로 진행되어 있는 것에서 다음과 같은 요지를 도출할 수 있다. "Making orange juice concentrate from fresh oranges is done entirely by machines."

Photocopying machines use a **process** known as xerography. In transfer xerography, a photoconductive plate, cylinder, or belt is electrostatically charged. A photoconductor, such as selenium, allows charge to leak away when exposed to light. **Then** the material to be copied is placed face down on the photocopying machine, and a projected image of the page falls on the charged plate. **Next**, the illuminated portions become conducting and discharge, leaving a charged electrostatic image of the dark regions or print of the page. The photoconductor copy **then** comes into contact with toner. **Finally** the toner is attracted to the paper, and heating causes it to be permanently fused to the paper. All this takes place very quickly—and outcomes your copy.

번역 복사기는 제로그래피라고 알려진 과정을 이용한다. 전사 제로그래피 과정에서 광전도의 판금, 실린더 또는 벨트가 정전기적으로 충전된다. 셀레늄과 같은 광전도체가 빛에 노출될 때 방전이 새 나가도록 한다. 그리고는 복사될 물체는 뒤집어서 복사기에 놓이고 투사된 이미지는 충전된 판에 떨어진다. 다음으로 빛을 받은 부분은 광전도되고 발사되어 검은 부분 또는 페이지의 프린트 부분의 정전기적 이미지를 남긴다. 그러면 광전도체 사본은 토너와 접촉하게 된다. 마지막으로 토너는 종이에 붙게 되고 열이 종이 위에 이것이 영구적으로 남게 한다. 이 모든 것이 아주 빨리 진행되고 당신의 복사본이 나오게 된다.

해설 이 글은 Time order 중에서도 process로 구성되어 있다. 진하게 표시한 것들이 signal word(s)에 해당한다. 이것을 도식화해보면 다음과 같다.

Step 1: Photoconductive plate, cylinder, or belt is electrostatically charged.
Step 2: Image of original document is projected onto charged plate.
Step 3: Illuminated portions leave a charged image of the dark print on the page.
Step 4: Photoconductor copy comes into contact with toner.
Step 5: Heat fuses toner to paper.

이렇게 시간 순서로 진행되어 있는 것에서 다음과 같은 요지를 도출할 수 있다. "There are several steps in transfer xerography."

4. Cause and Effect 인과관계에 따른 패턴

Cause and Effect는 원인과 결과에 따라 글을 구성하는 것이다. 일반적으로 원인은 결과보다 먼저 존재하므로 인과관계의 글에서는 시간적인 순서에 따라 글을 이해하는 것이 한 요령이 된다. 또한 인과관계에서 원인은 구체적이고 결과는 일반적인 경우가 많은데, 이러한 글의 경우 귀납적인 논리 전개법을 따르고 있을 가능성이 크므로 글의 요지를 파악하는 데 참고할 필요가 있다. 먼저 이해를 쉽게 하기 위해 우리말로 된 글들을 읽어보자.

아래의 글을 인과관계에 따라 요약해 보자.

> 1997년 외환 금융 위기 이후, 자본 시장 개방으로 대규모 외국 자본이 유입되면서 주주의 이익을 극대화하는 경영에 부합하는 가치관과 제도들이 확산되었다. 주주 대표 소송 등 소액 주주의 권한 행사 요건과 절차가 개선되었으며, 사외 이사가 확대되고 사외 이사 중심의 독립적인 감사 위원회가 설치됨으로써 내부 감시 기능도 강화되었다. 소유 구조 및 회계의 투명성도 높아졌다. 이 '주주 가치 경영'은 시장 질서의 확산과 함께 우리나라 기업들의 기업 지배 구조를 개선하고, 기업 경영을 감시하여 기업 가치를 높이는 긍정적인 효과를 낳은 것으로 평가된다.

먼저 지문에서 언급하고 있는 사건이나 변화된 상황을 정리해보자.

> 1997년 외환 금융 위기 ⇨ 자본 시장 개방 ⇨ 외국 자본의 유입 ⇨ 주주의 이익을 극대화하는 경영 가치관과 제도들의 확산(주주대표 소송, 사외 이사의 확대, 독립적인 감사 위원회의 설치, 소유 구조 및 회계의 투명성 개선) ⇨ 기업 지배 구조 개선 ⇨ 기업 가치의 상승

가만히 살펴보면 끝부분의 기업 가치의 상승은 주주대표 소송, 사외 이사의 확대, 독립적인 감사 위원회의 설치 등과 같은 주주 이익 극대화 경영의 가치관과 제도의 확산에 따른 결과물이다. 마찬가지로 그러한 가치관과 제도의 도입은 외국 자본의 유입에 따른 결과물인 것이며, 외국 자본의 유입은 자본 시장 개장을 통해서 가능했던 것이다. 자본 시장 개방은 외환 금융 위기에 대처하기 위해 이루어졌다. 따라서 위의 글은 원인과 결과의 관계를 시간적인 순서에 따라 진술하고 있음을 알 수 있다. 이제 영어로 된 예문을 살펴보자.

Fewer fans are attending football and baseball games **because** they are turned off by the commercialism of these teams.

번역 극소수의 팬들만이 축구와 야구 경기에 참석했는데, 그 이유는 사람들이 이 스포츠들의 상업주의에 흥미를 잃었기 때문이다.

해설 이 글의 signal word는 "because"이다. 따라서, 글의 패턴은 'cause and effect'가 된다.

Ethical behavior in business **results in** a variety of benefits for an organization.

번역 비즈니스에서의 윤리적인 행동은 한 조직에 다양한 이득을 안겨주게 된다.

해설 이 글의 signal word는 "results in"이다. 따라서, 글의 패턴은 'cause and effect'가 된다.

Parents who cater to their kids' every whim and demand too little of them in return will negatively **affect** their children's character development.

번역 아이들의 모든 변덕을 충족시키지만 그 대가로 거의 어떤 것도 요구하지 않는 부모들은 아이들의 성격 형성에 있어 부정적인 영향을 끼치게 된다.

해설 이 글의 signal word는 "affect"이다. 따라서, 글의 패턴은 'cause and effect'가 된다.

유희태 일반영어 ❶

> To save money in the early 1980s, Illinois released 21,000 prisoners an average of three months early. The early releases **produced** 23 homicides, 32 rapes, 262 arsons, 681 robberies, 2,472 burglaries, 2,571 assaults and more than 8,000 other crimes. According to Harvard researchers, the $60 million the state saved cost Illinois crime victims $304 million, directly or indirectly.

번역 1980년대 초반 비용을 절감하기 위해, 일리노이주는 2만 천 명의 죄수들을 평균 석 달 일찍 출감시켰다. 이 감형은 23건의 살인, 32건의 강간, 262건의 방화, 681건의 강도, 2472건의 도둑질, 2571건의 폭력, 그리고 8000건 이상의 다른 범죄들을 유발시켰다. 하버드 연구진에 의하면, 주 정부가 절감한 6천만 달러는 일리노이의 범죄 피해자들에게 직간접적으로 3억 4백만 달러의 비용을 들게 한 것이다.

해설 원인: the early release of prisoners
결과: an increase in crimes
Main idea: the early release of prisoners caused an increase in crimes in Illinois.

다음 글을 읽고 빈칸을 채워보자.

> Smoking is responsible for more preventable illnesses and deaths than any other single health-compromising behavior. Smoking is associated with cancer of the lung, larynx, oral cavity, and esophagus; it is also a major risk factor for other cancers throughout the body. Smoking is also related to cardiovascular illness and mortality. Smoking increases the risk of emphysema, chronic bronchitis, peptic ulcers, cirrhosis of the liver, and respiratory disorders and aggravates the symptoms of allergies, diabetes, and hypertension. In women, smoking increases the risk of osteoporosis and lowers the age of menopause.

Words that indicate cause/effect pattern: _____

번역 흡연은 어떤 특정한 건강에 해를 끼치는 행동보다 더 예방할 수 있는 질병들과 죽음들에 책임이 있다. 흡연은 폐암, 후두암, 구강암, 그리고 식도암과도 관련되어 있다. 이것은 또한 몸 전반에 걸친 다른 암들의 주요 위험 요인이다. 흡연은 또 심혈관계 질환과 죽음에도 관련되어 있다. 흡연은 기종, 만성 기관지염, 위궤양, 간경변, 그리고 호흡기 장애와 알러지의 악화, 당뇨병, 고혈압의 위험도 증가시킨다. 여성들에게는, 흡연이 골다공증과 폐경기의 단축을 증가시킨다.

해설 is responsible for, factor, increases, aggravates, increases

5. Definition 정의에 따른 패턴

   Definition은 어떤 특정한 단어나 용어 또는 개념의 의미를 진술한 다음 그것을 설명해주기 위해 하나 또는 그 이상의 예를 드는 것이 일반적이다. 앞 3장에서 봤듯이, 주로 "means; definition; define; meaning; is/are; is/are called, is described as" 같은 signal words들이 사용된다. 다음과 같은 것이 그 예들이다.

   Harmful substances that invade the womb and result in birth defects **are called** teratogens.

번역 자궁에 침입해 선천적 기형을 유발하는 유해 물질을 기형유발인자(teratogens)라고 한다.

   A term that has become a buzz word among media executives **is** synergy. Synergy **describes** a situation in which the whole is greater than the sum of its parts. When Time Warner's DC Comics provides the characters for Time Warner's Warner Brothers movies that provide the inspiration for Batman clothing sold at the Warner Brothers Stores—and when all of these elements get publicity through Time Warner's TNT and TNS cable networks—that **is** synergy.

번역 미디어 경영진 사이에서의 유행어가 된 용어는 시너지이다. 시너지는 전체가 그것의 합보다 큰 상황을 묘사한다. Time Warner's DC Comics가 Warner Brothers Stores에서 판매된 배트맨 의상의 영감을 제공한 Time Warner's warner Brothers의 영화의 특징을 제공할 때-그리고 이 모든 요소들이 Time Warner's TNT와 TNS 케이블 네트워크를 통해서 매스컴의 관심을 받았을 때 이것을 시너지라고 한다.

6. Description 묘사에 의한 패턴

Description이란 어떤 특정한 사람이나, 장소에 대한 기호, 또는 어느 특정한 대상의 외양 등을 마치 '그림을 보는 듯이 생생하게' 묘사해 강한 인상을 남기는 것을 말한다. 소위 우리가 중·고등학교 시절 배웠던 '붓 가는 대로' 써지는 글에 해당하는 것들이 주로 이 패턴에 속한다고 보면 된다. 수필이라든가 문학작품이 여기에 많이 속한다. narrative와 유사한 면이 있긴 하지만, narrative가 주로 시간 속에서 일어나는 일을 서술한다면, description은 구체적인 대상에 대한 세부적인detail 묘사가 중심이 되며 살아 뛰는 언어를 많이 쓴다. 다음의 예를 보자.

> The chair was the one piece of furniture I wanted to take with me when I closed up my parents' house for the final time. To look at it, sitting in the same kitchen corner where it had been for fifty years, you'd wonder how it could be my favorite chair. It was nothing but a straight-backed wooden chair, its seat scratched here and there from the soles of a small boy's shoes. The only thing unusual about it was the intricate design carved into its back. But the carving was what made the chair meaningful to me. I had sat in that chair many times as punishment for errors in my ways. I suppose my mother thought it was defiance that led me to sit cross-legged on the seat with my back to her in the kitchen. But it was not defiance. Rather, in that position my eyes and then my fingers could trace the intertwining leaves and flowers of the design carved in the back of the chair. Each time I sat there I seemed to see lines and shapes I hadn't seen before: a heart-shaped leaf, a budding rose, a blade of grass. Perhaps that chair had something to do with my lasting interest in well-made antique furniture. Who knows? I do know that when I drove away on that last day, the chair, carefully wrapped in several old quilts, lay tenderly cradled on the back seat of my car.

번역 그 의자는 내가 부모님 집을 마지막으로 정리할 때 가지고 오고 싶었던 가구였다. 지난 50년간 부엌 가장자리에 한결같이 있던 그 의자의 겉모습만 보면 왜 내가 그 의자를 가장 좋아하는지 의아할 것이다. 이것은 등받이가 반듯하고, 어린 시절 내 신발 밑창 때문에 여기저기 긁힌 나무 의자일 뿐이었다. 유일하게 특이한 점은 등받이에 새겨진 복잡한 디자인이었다. 하지만 그 새긴 무늬가 그 의자를 내게 의미 있는 것으로 만들었다. (어린 시절) 내가 한 잘못에 대한 처벌로 그 의자에 여러 번 앉았었다. 지금 생각해보면 어머니는 내가 의자에 책상다리를 한 채, 부엌에 있는 엄마에게 등을 돌리고 앉아 있던 것이 어머니에 대한 나의 반항이라고 생각하셨던 것 같다. 하지만 그것은 반항이 아니었다. 바로 그 자세에서 나의 눈과 손가락은 의자 뒤쪽에 새겨져 있던 나뭇잎과 꽃이 서로 뒤엉켜 있는 디자인을 따라갈 수 있었다. 매번 거기 앉을 때마다 예전에는 보지 못했던 선이나 모양들, 예를 들어 하트 모양의 나뭇잎, 싹트기 시작한 장미, 풀잎 따위를 볼 수 있었던 것 같았다. 아마도 그 의자는 훌륭한 고가구에 대해 내가 계속 관심을 갖는 것과 연관이 있을 것이다. 누가 알겠는가? 그 마지막 날 차를 타고 떠날 때 여러 가지 옛날 이불로 잘 싸여진 그 의자가 뒷좌석에 부드럽게 안겨져 놓여 있었다는 것을 난 알고 있다.

해설 이 글에서 의자는 단지 등받이가 반듯한 나무 의자이며, 앉는 자리가 어린 소년의 구두창으로 여기저기 긁힌 의자라고 묘사되어 있다. 하지만 글쓴이는 이 단순한 것을 살아 뛰는 언어로 생생하게 묘사하고 있다.

7. Combination of Patterns

종종, 지문들은 하나가 아니라 두 개 이상의 패턴으로 되어 있는 경우가 있다. 주로 major supporting details가 어느 한 패턴으로, 하지만 minor supporting details는 다른 패턴으로 되어 있는 경우가 많다.

> Quitting smoking is difficult **because of** the **effects** of nicotine in cigarettes. Nicotine **produces** pleasurable feelings and acts as a depressant. As the nervous system adapts to nicotine, smokers tend to **increase** the number of cigarettes they smoke and, **thus**, the amount of nicotine in their blood. **Therefore**, when a smoker tries to quit, the absence of nicotine **leads to two types** of withdrawal. The **first type** of withdrawal is physical, which may include headaches, increased appetite, sleeping problems, and fatigue. The **second type** of withdrawal is psychological. Giving up a habit can **result in** depression, irritability, or feelings of restlessness.

번역 금연이 어려운 이유는 담배 속 니코틴의 영향 때문이다. 니코틴은 유쾌한 감정을 만들어내고 진정제로서 역할을 한다. 신경계가 니코틴에 적응하게 되면서, 흡연자들이 피우는 담배의 수가 증가하고, 따라서, 그들 혈액 속 니코틴의 양이 증가하게 된다. 따라서, 흡연자가 담배를 끊으려고 하면, 니코틴 결핍은 두 가지의 금단현상을 야기시킨다. 첫 번째는 두통, 식욕 증가, 수면 장애 그리고 피로감을 포함하는 육체적 금단현상이다. 두 번째는 심리적인 금단현상이다. 습관을 버리는 것은 우울, 짜증, 불안감 등을 유발할 수 있다.

해설 이 지문은 cause/effect가 major supporting details, series가 minor supporting details이다.

> **In 1994**, the Women's Bureaus of the Department of Labor conducted a landmark survey of how working women in America feel about their jobs. More than a quarter of a million women told of their concerns and experiences. **After** the results of the survey were studied, the workplace was identified as the greatest single source of stress. The **causes** of such stress can range from the anxieties **produced** by corporate downsizing to factors that **result in** physical disorders such as carpal tunnel syndrome. Stress **also** can **result from** simply a feeling on the part of the individual worker that he or she is not appreciated on the job or is being overwhelmed by family obligations.

번역 1994년 여성 노동부는 미국의 직장 여성들이 그들의 직업에 대해 어떻게 생각하는지에 관한 획기적인 설문조사를 시행했다. 25만 명 이상의 여성들이 그들의 걱정과 경험을 털어놨다. 설문조사 결과가 연구된 후, 직장은 가장 큰 스트레스를 주는 요인으로 드러났다. 이러한 스트레스의 원인은 기업 축소에서 오는 불안함부터 손목 터널 증후군처럼 신체적 장애를 유발하는 요소들까지 이른다. 스트레스는 또한 단순히 직장에서 인정받지 못하거나 가족의 의무로 억압된 근무자 개인의 감정으로부터 유발될 수 있다.

해설 이 지문은 cause/effect가 major supporting details, series와 time order가 minor supporting details이다.

An overwhelming **amount of evidence** shows that social support has therapeutic **effects** on both our psychological and physical health. **David Spiegel**, of Stanford University's School of Medicine, came to appreciate the value of social connections many years ago when he organized support groups for women with advanced breast cancer. Spiegel had fully expected the women to benefit, emotionally, from the experience. **But** he found something else he did not expect: These women lived an average of eighteen months longer than did similar others who did not attend the groups. In **another study**, Lisa Berkman and Leonard Syme surveyed seven thousand residents of Alameda County, California; conducted a nine-year follow-up of mortality rates; and found that the more social contacts people had, the longer they lived. This was true of men and women, young and old, rich and poor, and people from all racial and ethnic backgrounds. **James House and others** studied 2,754 adults interviewed during visits to their doctors. He found that the most socially active men were two to three times less likely to die within nine to twelve years than others of similar age who were more isolated.

번역 압도적인 양의 증거들은 사회적 지지가 심리적이고 신체적인 건강 모두에 치료 효과가 있다는 것을 보여준다. 스탠포드 의과대학 소속 데이비드 슈피겔은 유방암 말기의 여성들을 위한 지지 그룹들을 결성했던 수 년 전, 사회적 유대감이 가지는 가치를 인정하게 됐다. 슈피겔은 이 여성들이 이러한 경험을 통해 정서적으로 득을 보리라 크게 기대했었다. 하지만 슈피겔은 그가 예상했던 것과는 다른 무언가를 발견했다. 이 여성들은 모임에 참석하지 않았던 다른 유사한 여성에 비해 평균 18개월을 더 살았다. 또 다른 연구에서 리사 버크만과 레너드 시메가 7,000명의 캘리포니아주 알라미다 카운티 주민들을 조사했다. 이후 9년 동안 사망률 추적 연구를 했으며, 사람들은 사회적 접촉이 더 많을수록 더 오래 산다는 것을 알아냈다. 이는 남녀노소, 빈부, 그리고 모든 인종과 민족적 배경 출신에 관계없이 해당됐다. 제임스 하우스와 다른 이들은 2,754명의 성인들이 병원에 왔을 때 인터뷰를 했다. 그는 사회적으로 가장 활발한 사람들이 비슷한 연령대의 고립된 다른 이들보다 9년에서 12년 내에 죽을 가능성이 두세 배 낮다는 것을 알아냈다.

해설 이 지문은 series와 cause/effect의 패턴이 혼합되어 사용되고 있다.

예제

[1-12] What is the main pattern of organization for each writing?

01 When you study for an exam, you should follow three steps. First, you should make sure you have all the information you need. Next, you should put that information in order. Finally, you should make a list of the most important things.

① Series ② Time order ③ Cause/effect
④ Comparison ⑤ Definition

02 A parakeet is a small bird that lives in tropical forests. The parrot is similar to a parakeet, but it is larger. Both birds sometimes can learn how to say words.

① Series ② Time order ③ Cause/effect
④ Comparison ⑤ Definition

03 Some kinds of birds cannot fly. The penguin is one of these birds. It lives mostly in the very cold Antarctic climate. Another kind of bird that cannot fly is the ostrich. It lives in Africa.

① Series ② Time order ③ Cause/effect
④ Comparison ⑤ Definition

04 Some people do not like to use computers for writing. They prefer to use typewriters. They know computers are faster and more accurate, but they feel more comfortable with typewriters.

① Series ② Time order ③ Cause/effect
④ Contrast ⑤ Definition

05 Leif Ericson was probably the first European to see America. He visited some of the northern areas in about 1000. The next European visitor to America was Christopher Columbus in 1492.

① Series ② Time order ③ Cause/effect
④ Comparison ⑤ Definition

정답 01 ② 02 ④ 03 ① 04 ④ 05 ②

06 Cola and ginger ale are both kinds of soft drinks. Both these drinks have a lot of sugar in them, but cola has caffeine in it and ginger ale does not.

① Series   ② Time order   ③ Cause/effect
④ Comparison/contrast   ⑤ Definition

07 Some of the early Americans did not want to come to this country. For example, many Africans had to come as slaves. Some Europeans had to come for religious freedom.

① Series   ② Time order   ③ Cause/effect
④ Comparison/contrast   ⑤ Definition

08 Lisa plans to travel in Europe this summer. In June, she will visit Sicily. In July, she will bicycle in northern Italy. In August, she will travel through France. By September, she hopes to be in Paris.

① Series   ② Time order   ③ Cause/effect
④ Comparison/contrast   ⑤ Definition

09 The clambake is a popular New England dinner. It usually includes many different kinds of seafood. Clams are the most common kind of seafood at a clambake. There may also be lobster and mussels.

① Series   ② Time order   ③ Cause/effect
④ Comparison/contrast   ⑤ Definition

10 Many American Indians died soon after the Europeans arrived. There was one important reason for this. The Europeans brought new kinds of diseases with them. These diseases caused thousands of deaths in a short time.

① Series   ② Time order   ③ Cause/effect
④ Comparison/contrast   ⑤ Definition

11 During the war in the Vietnam in 1970s, many villages were destroyed. People were left homeless, so they moved to the city. The cities were often overcrowded, with little hope for a good life. This led many people to leave their homeland and move to the United States. Now, many schools and colleges in the United States are expanding their English language programs.

① Series   ② Time order   ③ Cause/effect
④ Comparison/contrast   ⑤ Definition

12
> Maya Angelou, an African-American author, had many difficult experiences while she was growing up. Born in 1929 in Long Beach, California, her original name was Marguerite Johnson. Her parents separated when she was three. Then she and her brother went to live with their grandmother in Stamps, Arkansas. Later on, she lived for a while with her mother and grandmother in St. Louis, Missouri. When she was only eight years old, Maya experienced abuse from her mother's boyfriend. Wherever she lived, she was often badly treated because of racial prejudice. But her life was also shaped by the strong influence of love. In her childhood, she learned of love from her grandmother and her brother. As she grew older, she also began to love literature. After junior high school, Maya went to live with her mother in San Francisco. There, in 1945, she graduated from high school. A few months later, she had a baby son, who became the center of her life. In later years, Maya included all of these experiences in her novels, plays, and poems. She has received many honors as a writer and spokes-woman for Afro-Americans. But perhaps her greatest honor came in 1993. President Bill Clinton asked her to write the official poem for his inauguration. Then she read the poem aloud at the ceremony in front of the American public.

① Series   ② Time order   ③ Cause/effect
④ Comparison   ⑤ Definition

정답 06 ④ 07 ① 08 ② 09 ① 10 ③ 11 ③ 12 ②

한글번역

예제 01 당신이 시험 공부를 할 때, 3가지 순서를 따라야 한다. 우선, 필요한 정보가 모두 갖춰져 있는지 확인해야 한다. 다음으로 그 정보를 차례대로 정리해야 한다. 마지막으로 가장 중요한 것들의 목록을 만들어야 한다.

02 잉꼬는 열대우림에 사는 작은 새이다. 앵무새는 잉꼬와 비슷하지만 더 크다. 두 새 모두 때때로 말을 할 수 있다.

03 어떤 종류의 새들은 날지 못한다. 펭귄은 이러한 새들 중 하나이다. 펭귄은 대부분 아주 추운 남극 지방에서 산다. 또 다른 날지 못하는 새는 타조이다. 타조는 아프리카에 산다.

04 몇몇 사람들은 글을 쓸 때 컴퓨터를 사용하는 것을 좋아하지 않는다. 그들은 타자기를 사용하는 것을 선호한다. 그들은 컴퓨터가 더 빠르고 정확하다는 것을 알지만 타자기를 사용할 때 더 편안함을 느낀다.

05 리프 에릭슨은 아마도 미국을 본 최초의 유럽인이다. 그는 대략 1000년에 일부 북쪽 지방을 방문했다. 그 다음 미국을 본 유럽인은 1492년 크리스토퍼 콜럼버스이다.

06 콜라와 진저에일은 둘 다 청량음료의 한 종류이다. 두 음료는 모두 많은 당분을 포함하고 있지만, 콜라는 카페인이 있는 반면, 진저에일은 카페인이 없다.

07 초기 몇몇 미국인들은 이 나라에 오기를 원하지 않았다. 예를 들어, 많은 아프리카인들이 노예로서 미국에 와야만 했다. 몇몇 유럽인들은 종교적 자유를 위해 와야만 했다.

08 리사는 이번 여름에 유럽을 여행하기로 계획했다. 6월에 그녀는 시실리를 방문할 것이다. 7월에는 이태리 북부를 자전거를 타고 갈 것이다. 8월에는 프랑스를 여행할 것이다. 그녀는 9월까지는 파리에 있기를 희망한다.

09 해산물 파티는 뉴잉글랜드의 유명한 만찬이다. 이 만찬은 많고 다양한 종류의 해산물을 포함하고 있다. 조개는 해산물 파티에서 가장 흔한 종류의 해산물이다. 또한 랍스터와 홍합도 있다.

10 많은 아메리칸 인디언들은 유럽인들이 온 뒤 곧 죽었다. 여기에는 가장 중요한 원인이 있다. 유럽인들은 신종 질병들을 함께 가지고 왔다. 이 질병들은 짧은 시간 안에 무수한 사람들을 죽게 만들었다.

11 1970년대에 베트남 전쟁 기간 동안, 많은 마을이 파괴됐다. 사람들은 집을 잃은 채 남겨져, 도시로 이동했다. 도시들은 풍요로운 삶에 대한 희망 없이 포화상태가 됐다. 이것은 사람들로 하여금 고국을 버리고 미국으로 이주하게 만들었다. 현재 미국에 있는 많은 학교와 대학은 그들의 영어 프로그램을 확대하고 있다.

12 아프리카계 미국인 작가 마야 안젤로우는 그녀가 성장하는 동안 많은 어려운 일을 겪었다. 1929년, 캘리포니아 주의 롱비치에서 태어난 그녀의 본명은 마가렛 존슨이었다. 그녀가 3살 때 그녀의 부모님은 별거했다. 그리고 그녀와 오빠는 아칸소주의 스탬스에서 할머니와 함께 살았다. 나중에 그녀는 잠시 동안 미주리 주의 세인트루이스에서 그녀의 어머니와 할머니와 함께 살았다. 그녀가 8살이 됐을 때, 마야는 어머니의 남자친구로부터 학대를 받았다. 그녀가 어디에서 살든 간에, 인종 차별로 인해 종종 모진 대우를 받았다. 그러나 그녀의 인생은 또한 강력한 사랑의 영향을 받으며 만들어졌다. 어린 시절 그녀는 할머니와 오빠로부터 사랑을 배웠다. 성장하면서, 그녀는 또한 문학을 사랑하기 시작했다. 중학교를 졸업한 뒤, 마야는 샌프란시스코에서 어머니와 함께 살았다. 1945년 그곳에서, 그녀는 고등학교를 졸업했다. 몇 달 후, 그녀는 인생의 중심이 된 아들을 가졌다. 후에, 마야는 이런 모든 경험을 그녀의 소설과 연극, 시에 포함했다. 그녀는 작가이자 아프리카계 미국인을 위한 연설가로서 많은 존경을 받아왔다. 그러나 아마도 그녀에게 가장 명예로운 순간은 1993년이었을 것이다. 빌 클린턴 대통령은 그녀에게 그의 취임사를 써줄 것을 요청했고 그녀는 취임식에서 미국 대중 앞에서 큰소리로 시를 낭송했다.

CHAPTER 06 Main Idea & Supporting Details

Main idea요지란 무엇인가? 저자가 **topic**을 통해서 독자에게 말하려고 하는 것으로, 보통 완전한 문장으로 이루어져 있다. 이미 우리는 topic을 다루는 장에서 설명을 했다. 하지만, 다시 한번 살펴보자.

> **예** Topic : 의사
> Possible main ideas :
> ① 의사라는 직업은 힘들다.
> ② 의사는 환자와 가까이 지내야 한다.
> ③ 의사는 부자가 되는 지름길이다.
>
> **예** Topic : 술
> Possible main ideas :
> ① 술은 몸에 해롭다.
> ② 술은 위암의 주범이다.
> ③ 술은 한국으로 많이 수입된다.

이상에서 보듯이 하나의 topic에는 무수히 많은 main ideas가 나올 수 있다. 이 세 가지 말고도 여러분은 더욱 많은 main ideas를 쓸 수가 있다. 하지만 한 단락paragraph에서는 단 하나의 요지main idea만 가능하다는 점을 명심하자.

다음 글을 읽어보자.

> Many bosses share two weaknesses. First, they are often poor communicators. They tell people what to do and how and when to do it, without explaining the reasons for their rules, and they do not welcome feedback or questions. In addition, many bosses are not well-rounded people. Their jobs tend to be their lives, and they expect everybody who works for them to think and act the way they do. These bosses frown upon hearing that a family matter will keep an employee from working late, and they come out of their office looking irritated if there is too much talk or laughter during a coffee break.

번역 많은 사장들이 두 가지 약점을 공유하고 있다. 첫째로 그들은 대개 대화 상대가 부족하다. 그들은 자신의 방식에 대한 이유를 설명하지 않은 채 무엇을, 언제, 어떻게 할 것인지에 대해 사람들에게 말하며, 상대방의 반응이나 질문에는 인색하다. 게다가 많은 사장들은 균형 잡힌 사람이 아니다. 그들의 직업은 삶이 되기 쉬우며, 모든 직원들이 본인이 하는 것처럼 생각하고 행동하기를 기대한다. 이러한 사장들은 집에 일이 있어서 늦게까지 일을 못한다고 하면 인상을 찌푸리고, 휴식 시간에 잡담을 오래 하거나 크게 웃기라도 하면 짜증을 내며 사무실에서 나온다.

그 어떠한 글을 읽더라도 여러분이 항상 마음속에 두고 질문해야 하는 것이 있다. 그것은 "What is the main point the writer is trying to make?"이다. 이것에 답하는 데 도움을 주는 것이 'topic'이다. 이 예제에서 topic은 'many bosses'이고, 그 topic을 가지고 저자가 말하려고 하는 바는 'share two weaknesses'이다. 그리고 글의 나머지는 그것에 대한 근거를 보여주는 'supporting details'이다.

단락의 topic을 찾으면 저자가 topic을 통해 표현하고자 했던 일반적인 관점인 main idea를 정할 수 있다. Main idea는 저자가 증명하거나 설명하고자 하는 것이다. 즉, 단락을 끝까지 읽었을 때, 저자가 당신으로 하여금 알거나 믿도록 요구하는 것이 요점이므로 main idea를 찾는 것은 완벽한 독해를 위한 필수적인 능력이다.

Main idea를 찾기 위해서, 저자가 topic에 대하여 말하고 있는 것이 무엇인지를 스스로에게 물어보라. 다음에 나오는 글을 읽고 생각해보자.

The Eagle's Greatest Hits album is the most successful album in history. It has sold 26 million copies, more than any other album. It was the first album ever to gain platinum status for sales of one million copies. Greatest Hits was the number one album on the Billboard Charts of five weeks, and it spent a total of 133 weeks on the chart altogether.

번역 이글스의 앨범「Greatest Hits」는 역사상 가장 성공한 앨범이다. 이 앨범은 2,600만 장이 팔려 그 어떤 앨범보다 많은 판매량을 기록했다. 또한 100만 장 판매를 달성해 최초로 플래티넘 인증을 받은 앨범이기도 하다. 「Greatest Hits」는 빌보드 차트에서 5주 동안 1위를 차지했으며, 총 133주 동안 차트에 머물렀다.

이 단락의 topic은 'Eagle's Greatest album'이다. 이것은 단락의 모든 문장에서 언급된 것이다. 그러면 이 topic에 대한 저자의 요지는 무엇인가? 첫 번째 문장에서 저자는 이 음반이 다른 어떤 것보다 성공적이었다고 언급하고 있으며, 그 다음에 나오는 모든 문장들은 그러한 생각을 보충하는 세부적인 내용을 제공하고 있다.

다음 글을 읽고 topic과 main idea를 찾아보자.

> Single mothers face many challenges. Their greatest difficulties are usually financial. They are the primary family breadwinners, so their greatest struggles, especially for those who are younger and less educated, often involve making ends meet. To make matters worse, single moms often do not receive regular child support from their children's fathers. They also must curtail their work hours due to childcare limitations, so many can't earn full-time wages.

번역 싱글맘들은 많은 어려움에 직면한다. 그중 가장 큰 어려움은 보통 경제적인 문제다. 이들은 가정의 주된 생계부양자이기 때문에, 특히 더 젊거나 교육 수준이 낮은 경우에는 생계를 유지하는 것이 가장 큰 고충이 된다. 상황을 더 악화시키는 것은, 많은 싱글맘들이 아이 아버지로부터 정기적인 양육비를 받지 못한다는 점이다. 또한 자녀 돌봄의 제약으로 인해 근로 시간을 줄여야 하므로, 상당수가 정규직 임금을 벌지 못한다.

'Single mother's financial challenges'가 topic이라고 생각하였는가? 그렇다면 정답이다. 이 단락의 모든 문장에서는 미혼모(single mother)나, 그를 지칭하는 대명사를 사용하고 있다. 또한, 각 문장들은 경제적인 어려움을 언급하고 있다. 두 번째 문장에서는 경제적 어려움이 그들의 가장 큰 고난이라 말하고 있다. 그리고 나서 단락의 나머지 부분은 읽는 이가 이 견해(주장)를 사실로 받아들여야만 하는 이유에 관해 설명하고 있다.

01 요지 혹은 주제문의 의미와 의의

다시 정리하면, 주제topic 혹은 화제話題가 필자가 진술하고자 하는 대상이라면 요지main idea 혹은 주제문topic sentence은 주제를 통해서 필자가 독자에게 말하고자 하는 핵심 주장 혹은 요점이라고 할 수 있다. 따라서 주제가 한 단어 혹은 간단한 어구로 표현된다면, 요지는 보통 완전한 문장으로 이루어진다. 요지를 찾는 것은 필자의 핵심 주장을 파악하는 것이므로 글을 읽는 궁극적인 목적이 될 뿐만 아니라, 세부적인 정보의 이해와 같은 여타의 글을 읽는 목적을 올바로 달성하기 위한 기본적인 전제가 된다. 또한 주제문의 파악이 정확해야 나머지 내용들에 대한 이해도 정교해진다. 올바른 주제문을 중심으로 해서 글을 구조화했을 때만 여타의 내용들이 주장을 뒷받침하는 논거인지, 부연설명인지, 세부 정보를 제공하는지를 정확하게 가릴 수 있다.

02 2S2R과 요지 찾기

실제 글 읽기 과정에서 주제문의 파악은 '주제의 파악 → 주제문의 파악 → 글 전체의 구조화 및 논거와 세부 정보의 확인'과 같은 단선적인 방식으로 진행되지 않는다. 잠정적 주제와 주제문을 통해 글을 구조화하고 글의 나머지 정보를 이해하는 과정에서 주제와 주제문은 끊임없이 정교하게 수정될 수밖에 없다. 이는 2S2R의 독해전략을 활용할 때도 마찬가지이다.

2S2R의 2단계인 Reading읽기 단계에서 주장과 근거들을 도표나 도식으로 정리하면서 핵심 주장을 도출하게 되지만, 최종적으로 읽은 것을 요약하는 단계로 접어들면서, 잠정적으로 이해된 주제문은 더욱 명료한 형태로 수정된다. 즉 잠정적으로 설정된 주제문을 중심으로 어떤 주제문일 때 글 전체가 가장 짜임새 있게 구조화되는지, 글 전체의 내용을 포괄하면서 요점을 가장 경제적으로 전달할 수 있는지의 여부를 확인한다. 이 과정을 거쳐서 글 읽기가 종료되는 시점에 주제문이 확정된다고 할 수 있다. 따라서 잠정적 주제문의 채택과 그 주제문을 통해 글을 구조적으로 이해하고 평가하는 과정은 순환적으로 반복되는 과정이다. 이를 2S2R의 과정으로 설명하자면, 글의 핵심 주장에 대한 정확한 이해를 위해서는 주장과 근거, 그리고 세부 정보들을 배치하는 윤곽잡기outline의 과정과 마지막 요약의 과정이 요구된다.

결국 주제문을 정확하게 파악하는 것은 잠정적 주제 및 주제문과 전체 글의 구조와 논거supporting details를 끊임없이 일치시켜가는 과정이라고 할 수 있는데, 특히 이러한 노력은 긴 지문을 독해할 때 반드시 요구된다. 문장이 길고 내용이 난해할수록 주제문을 명료화하기 위한 반복적 읽기가 더 요구되는 것은 분명하다. 반복적 읽기의 횟수를 줄이고 주제문을 정확하게 찾기 위한 가장 단순한 방법은 글을 많이 읽는 것이다. 그러나 글 읽기 훈련을 위한 충분한 시간이 주어지지 않는다는 것을 논외로 하더라도, 글을 단순히 많이 읽는다고 해서 글을 구조적으로 독해하고 행간의 의미를 파악하는 대화적 독해의 능력이 향상된다는 보장은 주어지지 않는다는 것에 문제가 있다.

때로 저자들은 자신이 언급하고자 하는 것을 직접적으로 말하지 않는다. 왜냐하면 독자 스스로 논리적 추론을 거쳐 핵심 주장에 이르게 될 경우, 주장의 설득력과 독자의 공감이 더 커지게 되기 때문이다. 즉 핵심 주장을 명시적으로 되풀이하는 것보다 제시된 논거와 세부 정보들을 통해서 자연스럽게 어떤 주장에 도달하게 될 때 독자의 공감이 커질 수 있다는 것이다. 따라서 고급 독해를 할수록 주제문을 찾기 위한 추론이 요구되며, 독자가 파악한 주제문이 필자의 의도와 쉽게 일치되지 않을 수도 있음을 명심해야 한다.

　우리에게 주어진 시간과 달성해야 할 독해의 수준을 고려할 때, 읽기 훈련의 과정에서부터 스스로 주제문을 찾고 검증하는 방법을 사용하는 것이 필요하다. 앞서 제시한 2S2R의 읽기 훈련과 그 훈련의 일부라고 할 수 있는 주제문을 찾고 검증하는 노력들은 비록 귀찮고 더디게 가는 방법처럼 보이지만 탄탄한 읽기 내공을 쌓는 정도이자 지름길이다.

03　주제문을 찾고 검증하는 방법

　주제문을 찾고 검증하는 방법은 앞서 이야기한 주제 topic를 확인하는 방법과 밀접하게 연관되어 있다. 다음을 잊지 말자.

> 주제문(topic sentence) = 주제(topic) + 서술어(controlling idea)

　글의 요지나 주제문을 파악하는 데 있어서 그 기초가 되는 훈련은 key ideas를 찾는 방법을 익히는 것이다.

⊘ Key Ideas를 찾는 방법

1. 이 글이 '누구 who'에 관한 것인지 또는 '무엇 what'에 관한 것인지를 묻는다.
2. 그 사람이나 대상 object이 무엇을 하고 있는지 또는 그 사람이나 대상에게 무슨 일이 일어나고 있는지를 질문한다.
3. when, what kind, where, why, how에 관련된 것은 details에 해당된다는 점을 염두에 두자. 즉 이것들은 key ideas가 아니다.

예제

[1-4] 다음 문장에서 key ideas를 찾아보시오.

01 Because of the new rules, most foreign automobiles in Korea now offer safety features at no extra charge.

Key idea(s) : _____

02 Inventions like the microwave oven dramatically reduce the amount of time necessary for cooking.

Key idea(s) : _____

03 Fast-food chains, which exist all over the country, provide a familiar place for Americans to eat, no matter where they go.

Key idea(s) : _____

04 Americans can even find fast-food chains in cities like Paris, Moscow, and Beijing.

Key idea(s) : _____

정답 **01** Automobiles offer safety features.
automobiles, offer safety features를 제외한 나머지 것들은 세부사항(details)일 따름이다. Because of the new rules('why'에 해당); most foreign('what kind'); in Korea('where'); now('when'); at no extra charge('how')
02 Inventions reduce time cooking.
03 Fast-food chains provide a familiar place to eat.
04 Americans find fast-food chains.

> **한글번역**
>
> 01 새로운 규칙 때문에, 한국 대부분의 외국 자동차들은 현재 추가비용 없이 안전장치를 제공하고 있다.
> 02 전자레인지와 같은 것들의 발명은 조리에 필요한 시간을 현저하게 줄여줬다.
> 03 전국에 있는 패스트푸드 체인점들은 미국인들이 어딜 가든 친숙하게 먹을 수 있는 장소를 제공해준다.
> 04 미국인들은 심지어 파리나 모스크바, 베이징 같은 도시에 가도 패스트푸드 체인점을 찾을 수가 있다.

04 Stated Main Ideas

글 안에 요지가 언급되어 있는 경우 그 요지가 있는 문장을 주제문topic sentence이라 하는데, 크게 다음과 같이 나눌 수 있다.

참고로, 글 안에서 topic sentence를 찾아내는 방법은 다음과 같다.

> 1단계: 주제 개념을 찾기 위해 전체 단락을 읽는다.
> 2단계: 전체 단락의 전반적인 그림을 보여주는지 보기 위해 첫 문장을 읽는다. 그렇지 않다면 첫 문장이 개론적인 배경이나 대조적인 정보를 주기 위한 것일 수 있다. 또는 첫 문장이 그 뒤 두세 문장의 답이 되는 질문을 던지는 것일 수도 있다.
> 3단계: 만약 첫 문장이 요지를 말하고 있지 않으면 전체 단락의 전반적인 그림을 제시하는지를 보기 위해 마지막 문장을 보라.
> 4단계: 첫 문장이나 마지막 문장이 단락의 전체적인 개요, 즉 요지를 제시한다면 당신은 주제문을 찾은 것이다.
> 5단계: 첫 문장이나 마지막 문장 둘 다 주제문이 아니라면 단락 중간의 문장들 중 하나가 개요나 요지를 말하고 있는지를 알기 위해 모든 문장을 평가해야 한다. 각 문장을 의문문으로 바꾸고 단락의 다른 문장들이 이 질문에 답변하는 것인지를 결정함으로써 각 가능성을 확인하라.

1. At(In) the Beginning

> **All of this suburban development occurred under the dominion of Euclidian zoning—zoning that requires the rigid segregation of housing, commerce, and industry.** That approach to zoning is a residue of the Industrial Revolution, which made it seem desirable to move people's homes away from the dark satanic mills. Such distancing is no longer necessary, of course, since most contemporary office parks and electronics plants make extraordinarily benign neighbors. Nevertheless, every generation of planners attempts to relive that last great victory of the planning profession by separating more and more elements, more and more functions: Even doctors' offices today are kept strictly isolated from the people who use them.

번역 이런 모든 교외 지역 개발은 주택과 상업 지구 그리고 산업 지구를 엄격하게 구분하는 유클리드적 용도지역제라는 정책의 지배 아래에서 발생했다. 이러한 용도지역제에 대한 관점은 산업혁명의 잔여물인데, 사람들의 거주지를 더럽고 악마 같은 공장(영국이 산업혁명을 거쳐 근대화를 이루는 과정에서 노동자들의 가난하고 비참한 빈곤 상태를 묘사할 때 사용한 용어)으로부터 멀리 떨어진 곳으로 옮기는 것이 바람직한 것으로 느껴졌기 때문이다. 이러한 거리두기는, 대다수의 현대 복합 상업 지구와 전자 공장들이 아주 친근한 이웃이 됐기 때문에, 더 이상 필요하지 않다. 그럼에도 불구하고, 모든 세대의 도시계획설계자들은 점점 더 많은 요소들과 기능들을 분리함으로써 도시계획이라는 직역의 최후의 위대한 승리를 되새기려고 한다. 요즘에는 심지어 병원조차도 그곳을 사용하는 사람들과 매우 떨어져 있다.

2. In the Second or Third Sentence

> It used to be that emergency rooms got swamped just during winter flu outbreaks, or just in inner-city neighborhoods on Saturday nights. **But now emergency departments are overwhelmed year-round.** They're maxed out in world-class institutions that consistently land on *U.S. News and World Report's* honor roll of Best Hospitals including Johns Hopkins Hospital, the University of California-San Francisco Medical Center, and the Cleveland Clinic, which last year turned away ambulance patients almost half the time. And they're struggling in wealthy suburbs like Fairfax County, a high-technology mecca with a median household income of more than $90,000 and home to Colin Powell and ABC newscaster Sam Donaldson. "When there's not enough room," says Thom Mayer, chairman of the Inova Fairfax emergency department, "there's not enough room."

번역 응급실은 겨울철 감기가 발병했던 동안이나, 토요일의 도심지역의 주민들 사이에 있을 때 아주 눈코 뜰 새 없이 바쁘곤 했다. 하지만 지금의 응급 병동들은 연중 내내 감당할 수 없는 지경에 이르렀다. 이런 응급실들은 U.S. News & World Report에서 미국 최고의 병원으로 평가한 존스 홉킨스 병원, 캘리포니아 대학교 샌프란시스코 메디컬 센터, 그리고 작년에 자주 응급 환자를 외면했던 클리블랜드 클리닉 등에서도 한계치에 다다르고 있다. 그리고 그것들은 페어팩스 카운티와 같은, 평균 가계 소득 90,000달러 이상인 첨단 기술의 메카이면서 콜린 파월과 ABC의 뉴스캐스터 샘 도날드슨의 고향인 부유한 교외의 마을들에서도 어려움을 겪고 있다. "충분한 병실이 없을 때는", 인오바 페어팩스 응급 부서장 톰 메이어가 말하기를, "충분한 병실이 없는 것이다."

3. In the Middle

> Maria Luisa Martinez uses the same routine for her face every day. First, she washes it, then she uses a nonirritating toner, and finally she gently rubs in a light moisturizer. Most important, she recognizes some truths about the skin care industry: **Spending more money does not guarantee getting a better product for your skin.** So, instead of going out and buying an expensive brand, Maria Luisa follows the advice of Paula Begoun, a well-recognized skin care expert and author of the book *Don't Go to the Cosmetics Counter Without Me*. Maria Luisa's use of skin care products proves the point well. She knows that expensive soap by Erno Laszlo is not better for her skin than an inexpensive bar of Dove. And a toner by Neutrogena that doesn't have irritants in it is as good or perhaps better than an expensive toner by Orlane or La Prairie.

번역 마리아 루이자 말티네즈는 얼굴을 위해 매일 같은 일을 반복한다. 첫째, 그녀는 얼굴을 씻고, 무자극의 스킨을 바르고, 마지막으로 가벼운 로션을 바른다. 가장 중요한 것은 그녀가 화장품 산업의 진실을 알고 있다는 점이다. 돈을 더 많이 들인다고 해서 당신 피부에 더 좋은 제품을 반드시 구하는 것은 아니라는 점이다. 그래서 그녀는 나가서 비싼 브랜드를 찾는 대신에 마리아는 유명한 스킨케어 전문가이며 '나 없이 화장품 판매대에 가지 마세요'라는 유명한 책의 저자인 파울라 베건의 충고를 따른다. 마리아 루이자의 화장품 사용은 중요한 점을 잘 파악한 것이다. 그녀는 에르노 라즐로의 비싼 비누가 값싼 도브 비누보다 자기 피부에 더 좋지 않음을 알고 있다. 또 무극성 뉴트로지나 스킨은 비싼 올랑이나 라 프레리 스킨보다 충분히, 어쩌면 더 좋을 수도 있음을 알고 있는 것이다.

먼저 이 글의 topic을 찾아보자. 즉 이 글은 무엇(또는 누구)에 관한 것인가?

① Maria Luisa Martinez
② the same routine for her face
③ skin care products
④ Paula Begoun, a well-recognized skin care expert
⑤ the skin care industry

이 다섯 가지 중에서 여러분은 어떤 것을 골랐는가?

우선, ① Maria Luisa Martinez가 topic이 되려면, Maria Luisa Martinez란 사람에 대한 이야기가 그 뒤에 supporting details로 언급되어야 한다. 예를 들어 Maria가 어떤 사람이고 어디에 살고 어떤 음식을 좋아하며 어떤 사람들과 어울리는지 등 그 개인에 대한 언급이 나와야 하는데, 그런 것이 없다. 따라서 topic이 될 수 없다.

② the same routine for her face가 topic이 되려면, 얼굴을 위해 매일 같은 일을 하는 것에 대한 구체적인 예가 글 전체에 나와야 한다. 얼핏 보면, 바로 다음 문장 "첫째, 그녀는 얼굴을 씻고, 무자극의 스킨을 바르고, 마지막으로 가벼운 로션을 바른다." 등의 supporting details가 나와 있어 topic이 될 만한 소지는 있는 것처럼 보인다. 하지만, 거기서 끝이다. 그 다음에 이어지는 문장들이 더 이상 '얼굴을 위해 매일 같은 일을 하는 것'을 뒷받침support하는 세부사항들details이 아니기 때문이다. 이것은 다음에 나올 요지를 언급하기 위한 도입introduction의 역할만을 할 따름이다.

③ skin care products가 topic이다. 왜냐하면, 그 다음 문장들에서 덜 비싼 화장품들이 더 비싼 것들만큼이나 좋다는 예시들이 계속 언급되고 있기 때문이다.

④ Paula Begoun, a well-recognized skin care expert는 근거를 들기 위해 사용된 예일 따름이고, ⑤ the skin care industry은 너무 포괄적too broad이어서 topic이 될 수 없다.

자, 이제 요지를 알아내보자. 우리는 다음과 같은 질문, 즉 '저자가 topic을 가지고 독자에게 말하려 하는 것이 무엇인가'라는 질문을 던져야 한다. skin care products가 topic이므로, 이것을 가지고 저자가 말하려는 요점은, "더 비싼 화장품을 쓰는 것이 더 나은 효과를 보장하는 것은 아니다Spending more money does not guarantee getting a better product for your skin"가 되는 것이다.

4. At the End

때때로 글쓴이는 자신의 주장을 먼저 제기하기 전에 여러 사실들을 먼저 나열하여 자신의 주장의 설득력을 높이는 전략을 구사하기도 한다. 이럴 때 글의 요지는 맨 마지막에 올 경우가 많다. 하지만 영어 구조에선 그렇게 흔한 것은 아니다.

> Everybody uses words to persuade people of something without actually making a clear argument for it. This is called using loaded language. For example, a newspaper writer who likes a politician call him "Senator Smith"; if he doesn't like the politician, he refers to him as "right-wing or left-wing senator as Smith." If a writer likes an idea proposed by a person, he calls that person "respected"; if he doesn't like the idea, he calls the person "controversial." If a writer favors abortion, she calls somebody who agrees with her "prochoice" (choice is valued by most people); if she opposes abortion, she calls those who agree with her pro-life ("life," like "choice," is a good thing). **Recognizing loaded language in a newspaper article can give you important clues about the writer's point of view**.

번역 모든 사람들은 실제로 명확한 논거 없이 사람들을 설득하는 말을 한다. 이것을 유도적인 언어라고 부른다. 예를 들어, 어떠한 정치가를 좋아하는 신문기자는 그를 '스미스 상원의원'이라 부르고, 만약 그 정치가를 좋아하지 않는다면, '스미스와 같은 우파 또는 좌파 의원'이라고 부른다. 만약 글쓴이가 어떤 사람에 의해 제안된 아이디어를 좋아하면, 그 사람은 '존경받는'이라 불리지만, 그가 그 아이디어를 좋아하지 않으면 그 사람은 '논란이 많은 사람'이라 지칭한다. 만약 글쓴이가 임신중절을 찬성한다면 그녀에게 동조하는 사람들은 '선택을 지지하는 사람'(선택은 대부분의 사람에 의해 가치 있게 여겨진다)이라고 부르지만, 임신중절에 반대한다면 '생명을 지지하는 사람'(선택과 마찬가지로 생명은 좋은 것이다)으로 부른다. 신문기사의 유도적인 언어는 기자의 견해에 관한 중요한 단서를 제공해준다.

5. In the First and Last

> **Hunting and gathering in the ocean does more than kill fish; it changes ecosystems.** Each species in an ecosystem is linked to many others, as a predator, a scavenger, or a source of food or shelter. Remove some peripheral species from the web and the system as a whole may continue to function just fine, so long as all the roles are still filled. But knock out a keystone 3 species and the system must find a new equilibrium, or balance. Other human impacts such as agricultural runoff and seafloor dredging may provide the final knockout blow to ecosystems, but in every case scholars analyzed, excessive fishing set the process in motion. According to author Jeremy Jackson, **we're causing fundamental shifts in ecosystems, and some of those shifts may be irreversible.**

번역 바닷속에서의 사냥과 채집은 물고기를 죽이는 것 그 이상이다. 즉, 그것은 생태계를 변화시킨다. 생태계 안의 종들은 다른 종들과 연결돼 있는데 서로 포식자, 청소부, 혹은 먹이나 피난처로서이다. 몇몇의 지엽적인 종들을 관계망에서 제거하더라도 모든 역할이 다 채워져있는 한 전체로서의 체계는 적절히 기능할 것이다. 하지만 핵심 3개 종을 없애버리면 시스템은 새로운 평형, 즉 균형을 찾아야만 한다. 농지유출수나 해저준설 같은 인간의 영향들은 생태계에 최후의 일격을 가하게 될 것이지만 많은 사례에서 학자들이 분석한 결과 지나친 어업이 그런 과정에 시동을 걸고 있다. 작가 제레미 잭슨에 따르면 우리는 생태계에 근본적인 변화를 일으키고 있고 변화들 중 일부는 돌이킬 수 없을 것이다.

6. Two-Step Topic Sentence

때때로 저자는 요지를 하나의 문장에 두는 대신, 요지의 각 부분들을 두 개의 서로 다른 문장에 넣기도 한다. 이때 독자는 이 둘을 하나로 통합하여 하나의 완전한 주제문으로 구성해야 한다.

> At one time, the right brain was regarded as the "minor" hemisphere. However, we now know that it has its own special talents. The right hemisphere is superior at recognizing patterns, faces, and melodies. It is also involved in detecting and expressing emotion. The right brain is also better than the left at visualization skills, such as arranging blocks to match a pattern, putting together a puzzle, or drawing a picture.

번역 한때, 우뇌는 '덜 중요한' 반구로 간주됐다. 하지만 지금 우리는 우뇌가 자기 자신만의 특별한 재질을 가지고 있음을 안다. 우뇌는 패턴이나 면, 멜로디 등을 인식하는 데 뛰어나다. 그것은 또한 감정을 인지하고 표현하는 데 연루돼 있다. 또한 우뇌는 모양을 맞추기 위해 블록을 정렬하거나, 퍼즐을 맞추거나, 그림을 그리는 등의 시각적 기술에 있어 좌뇌보다 뛰어나다.

첫 번째 문장은 글의 topic인 'the right brain'을 소개하고 있지만, topic sentence는 아니다. 이 글 전체가 우뇌가 '덜 중요한' 반구라는 점에 초점을 맞추고 있지 않기 때문이다. 첫 번째 문장은 도입 문장introductory sentence으로, 이 글의 요지인 '우뇌가 자기 자신만의 특별한 재질을 가지고 있음'을 말하는 두 번째 문장이 나오도록 단순히 길잡이 역할을 하고 있을 따름이다. 하지만, 두 번째 문장 'we now know that it has its own special talents'에서 it와 its가 무엇인지 명확하지 않기 때문에 완전한 주제문이 될 수 없다. 이 대명사를 명확히 언급을 해주어야만 완전한 주제문이 되기 때문이다. 따라서 첫 번째 문장과 두 번째 문장을 통합할 때만이 "The right brain has its own special talents."라는 완전한 주제문이 나오게 된다.

05 Unstated(Implied) Main Ideas

글 안에 요지가 있는 경우보다, 당연하게도 글 안에 없는 요지를 찾아내는 것이 더 어렵다.

따라서, 글 안에 없는 요지를 찾아내기 위해서 여러분은 체계적이면서도 꼼꼼하게 한 단계 한 단계씩 접근methodical and step-by-step approach하는 것이 필요하다. 이 과정은 기본적으로 ① supporting details에 있는 힌트clues를 찾고 ② 그것들을 함께 모아 ③ 그 근거에 기반하여 논리적 결론을 도출하는 것이다. 글 안에 없는 요지를 찾아내는 데 다음과 같은 방법이 도움 될 것이다.

Step 1. 글의 주제(Subject)를 찾아낸다. (그러기 위해선 우선 각각의 문장 하나하나를 꼼꼼히 읽고, 반복되는 단어나 어구를 본다.)
Step 2. topic과 관련이 있는 supporting details를 목록화한다.
Step 3. 그 supporting details이 어떤 패턴으로 되어 있는지 알아낸다.
Step 4. 그 supporting details의 공통 속성에 기반해서 an implied main idea를 결정한다.

다음 글의 요지를 써보자.

40 percent of Finns aged 24 to 65 have a college degree compared with twelve percent in the United States. Understandably, Finns are, per capita, the greatest consumers of literature in the world. School attendance is compulsory up to age 16, an earlier age than in Belgium, but schooling is rigorous. High school students attend classes 38 hours a week, compared with about 25 hours in the United States. Finnish students are also required to take more courses, including two foreign languages. All higher education is free, with most financial support coming from the state and the rest from private industries.

2S2R 기본

> **번역** 24세에서 65세 사이의 핀란드인 40%가 대학 학위를 갖고 있으며 이는 미국의 12%와 비교된다. 알려진 대로 핀란드인들은 개인당 세계에서 문학작품을 가장 많이 읽는 사람들이다. 16세까지 학교 교육은 의무이며 이는 벨기에보다 이른 나이기긴 하지만 학교생활은 대단히 엄격하다. 고등학생들은 미국의 25시간에 비해 일주일에 38시간의 수업을 받는다. 핀란드 학생들은 두 개의 외국어 과정을 포함해 더 많은 과목을 필수적으로 이수해야 한다. 모든 고등교육은 무료이며 대부분의 재정 지원은 국가에서 하고 나머지는 사기업들에서 한다.

자, 우선 첫 번째 질문을 던지자. 이 글은 무엇에 관한 것인가? 우선 반복되어 나오는 단어들을 확인해보자. 핀란드, 학교, 교육, 학비 등이다. 따라서 이것들을 정리해보면, Education in Finland 라는 걸 알 수 있다. 이 글은 미국과 핀란드를 비교하는 글이 아니다. 그렇다면, 중간에 벨기에가 나올 이유가 없다. 이것은 벨기에와 미국을 언급해서 핀란드의 교육에 대해 말하고자 하는 것일 뿐이다.

그러면, 두 번째 단계로 가보자. 이 글에 나오는 supporting details을 목록화해보자.

① <u>40 percent of Finns have college degrees</u> versus 12 percent in the United States.
② Finns consume <u>the most literature</u> (read the most) in the world.
③ <u>School attendance is compulsory</u> up to age 16.
④ <u>High school students</u> are in class <u>38 hours a week</u> versus 25 in the United States. Finns take <u>more courses</u>.
⑤ <u>All higher education is free</u>.

이 글의 supporting details는 Series열거의 패턴을 취하고 있다. 따라서 그것을 정리해보면 우선 맨 처음 ① 핀란드 국민의 대학 졸업률을 언급하며 ② 세계에서 가장 많이 읽는 사람들이란 것을 강조한다. 그런 다음 좀 더 구체적으로 열거하는데, 첫 번째로는 ③ 16살까지(즉, 고등학교 전까지) 학교가 요구하는 것이 많음을 말하고, 그다음에 ④ 고등학교 수업의 엄격함을, 그런 뒤엔 ⑤ 대학이 무상으로 제공된다는 점(즉, 누구나 대학에 갈 수 있음으로써 돈을 내고 다니는 나라의 학생들보다 훨씬 교육의 기회가 많음을 암시한다.)을 설명한다.

따라서 이 5가지의 supporting details를 일반화시킨 다음, 앞에서 파악했던 topic(Education in Finland)과 연결하면, 이 글의 요지가 추출될 수 있다. 이 글은 열거의 패턴으로 되어 있으므로 나열된 것의 공통 속성을 찾는 것이 요지를 찾는 핵심 방법이 된다. 앞의 5가지 details의 공통 속성을 먼저 파악해보면 모두 핀란드 교육제도의 장점들만을 언급하고 있다. 따라서 이 글의 요지는 "Finland has an outstanding educational system핀란드는 우수한 교육제도를 가지고 있다."가 된다.

06　Supporting Details

Topic은 글쓴이가 읽는 이로 하여금 글을 다 읽었을 때, 알게끔 하거나 믿도록 하는 일반적인 특징이다. 그러나 이러한 특징은 읽는 이가 종종 더 많은 정보를 얻지 못하는 한 이해하거나 받아들일 수 없게 만드는 경우가 있다. 글의 뒷받침 내용은 이러한 정보를 제공해준다.

Supporting details는 구체적인 사실과 통계, 예시, 단계, 일화, 이유, 묘사, 정의 등으로 주제문에 서술된 공통적인 main idea를 설명하고 증명하는 것이다. Supporting details는 이 main idea를 보충하거나 탄탄한 토대를 제공한다. Supporting details는 주제문에서 제시된 모든 문제에 답이 되어야 한다. 예를 들어, 다음 문장을 읽어보라.

> Female surgeons are treated differently from male surgeons by their colleagues, nurses, and patients.

이 문장은 즉각적으로 당신의 생각에 '어떻게, 왜'라는 질문들을 제기한다. 그 질문들에 답하기 위해서는 문단이 계속 이어져서 이 요점을 증명할 만한 이유와 기타 설명이 제시되어야 한다. 다음의 단락을 읽으면서, 뒷받침 내용이 굵은 글씨체로 쓰인 main idea를 어떻게 명료화시키는지 주시하고, 왜 참인지 설명하라.

> **If you want to become rich, you must follow four important rules.** The first rule is to establish a reasonable income base. To reach and maintain that stable, middle-income base, you should earn a college degree, marry someone with an equal or higher education and stay married, and work as long as you are able to. The second rule for becoming rich is to avoid frivolous temptations. For example, don't drive expensive luxury cars; instead, buy medium-priced cars. Following rule #2 will allow you to save more money, which is rule #3. Average people who become rich often do so because they save more of their money, even if they must make sacrifices to do so. Finally, the fourth rule to become rich is take advantage of compound interest. If you invested $2,000 every year from age 22 to age 65 and that money earned 10 percent interest per year, you'd have over a million dollars when you retired.

번역 부자가 되고 싶다면, 다음의 중요한 4가지 법칙을 따르라. 첫 번째 법칙은 적당한 수입의 토대를 마련하는 것이다. 안정적인 중산층이 되고 이를 유지하기 위해서는 학사 학위를 취득하고, 동등하거나 또는 더 높은 수준의 교육을 받은 사람과 결혼해 결혼 상태를 유지하고, 할 수 있는 한 계속 일을 해야 한다. 부자가 되기 위한 두 번째 법칙은 사소한 유혹을 피하는 것이다. 예를 들면, 사치스러운 차를 몰지 마라; 대신, 중간 가격대의 차를 구입하라. 두 번째 규칙을 따르는 것은 당신이 더 많은 돈을 절약하게 해줄 것이고, 그것이 바로 세 번째 규칙이다. 부자가 된 사람들의 대부분은 희생이 따르더라도 돈을 더 절약하기 위해 대개 그렇게 한다. 마지막으로, 부자가 되기 위해 필요한 네 번째 법칙은 복리를 이용하는 것이다. 만약 당신이 22세부터 65세까지 매년 2,000달러를 투자했다면 해마다 10%의 이자가 붙어서 은퇴 시에는 백만 달러 이상을 소유하게 될 것이다.

이 단락의 주제 문장에서는 '부자가 되는 이러한 법칙들은 무엇인가'라는 질문을 제기한다. 이어서 재산을 불리기 위해 해야 할 네 가지를 설명하면서 그 질문에 답한다. 단락의 뒷부분에 나오는 세부사항을 읽지 않고는 주제 문장을 이해할 수 없을 것이다.

07 Major and Minor Details

Supporting details는 큰 세부사항major details과 작은 세부사항minor details의 두 가지이다. 큰 세부사항은 글의 주요 내용으로 주제문에 있는 idea를 설명하고 보충한다. 큰 세부사항은 main idea를 이해하기 위해 있어야 하는 필수적 이유와 기타 정보를 제공한다. 작은 세부사항은 큰 세부사항을 부연 설명해준다. 작은 세부사항은 main idea를 이해하는 데 항상 큰 영향을 끼치는 것은 아니어도, 더 구체적 정보를 제공해서 단락 내에서 요점을 한결 명료하게 해준다. 이 두 가지의 차이를 알아보기 위해, 다음의 단락을 읽어보라.

> **Many Americans believe in the supernatural**. For one thing, they believe in supernatural beings. A recent Gallup poll revealed that 69 percent of people believe in angels, half of them believe they have their own guardian angels, and 48 percent believe that there are aliens in outer space. Americans also believe in the existence of supernatural powers. For example, over 10 million people have called the Psychic Friends Network to get advice about their present and future.

번역 많은 미국인들이 초자연주의를 믿는다. 하나의 예로, 그들은 초자연적인 존재를 믿는다. 최근 갤럽 투표에 따르면 69%의 사람들이 수호신을 믿고, 그들 중 절반이 자신을 지켜주는 수호신이 있다고 믿으며, 48%는 외부 세계에 외계인이 존재한다고 믿는 것으로 나타났다. 미국인들은 또한 초자연적인 힘의 존재를 믿는다. 예를 들면, 천만 명이 넘는 사람들이 그들의 현재와 미래에 대한 조언을 얻기 위해 Psychic Friends 통신망에 전화를 걸고 있다.

굵은 글씨체의 문장이 이 단락의 주제 문장이다. '어떤 종류의 초자연적인 일을 믿는가?'라고 질문을 제기한다. 단락의 둘째, 넷째 문장에서는 미국인들이 초자연적 존재와 초자연적 힘을 믿는다고 말한다. 단락 내 다른 문장들은 작은 세부사항을 제공한다. 이 경우에, 작은 세부사항은 사람들이 실재한다고 믿는 존재나 힘의 종류를 예로 든다. 그러므로 작은 세부사항은 main idea를 좀 더 설명해주는 비필수적인 정보를 제공한다. 이런 기타 문장들supporting details은 또한 총체적으로나 구체적으로 서로 연관되어 있다.

	MAIN IDEA	
MAJOR DETAIL	MAJOR DETAIL	MAJOR DETAIL
Minor Detail	Minor Detail	Minor Detail

글을 읽을 때 이해를 돕기 위해, 문장들을 도표로 시각화하려 할 것이다. 이러한 관계를 구분해 보는 것은 단락을 이해하는 데 중요할 뿐만 아니라, 당신이 작가의 생각에 동의할 수 있는지의 여부를 결정하는 데에도 중요하다.

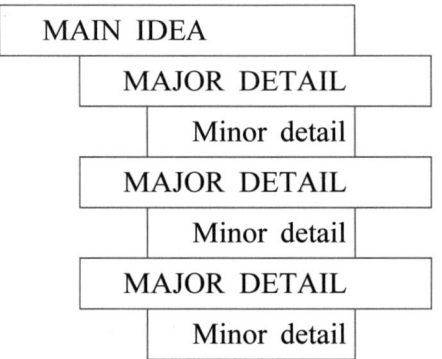

예제

[1-3] 각 문장의 주제(subject)를 쓰시오.

01

(1) Teachers, according to 79 percent of public high school students, are too easy on students when it comes to enforcing rules and assigning homework. (2) In addition, half of teens in public schools say their teachers and schools do not challenge them. (3) Too many disruptive students in classrooms, according to 70 percent of teenagers, are interfering with learning. (4) Schools' standards for graduation, say 70 percent of students, are too low. (5) According to three-fourths of students, diplomas are given to students even if they don't learn the required materials.

Sentence 1 subject : _____
Sentence 2 subject : _____
Sentence 3 subject : _____
Sentence 4 subject : _____
Sentence 5 subject : _____

정답 01 Sentence 1 subject : teachers
Sentence 2 subject : teachers and schools
Sentence 3 subject : disruptive students
Sentence 4 subject : Schools' standards
Sentence 5 subject : diplomas

02

(1) *Ladies' Home Journal* is a magazine that focuses on women's issues and is generally considered appropriate for women in their thirties, forties, and fifties. (2) *Glamour* is a magazine that devotes many pages to issues facing women in their twenties and early thirties. (3) *Mode* is a new magazine devoted entirely to issues affecting "plus-size" women. (4) *Allure* magazine has the most information on beauty products and is for women who are interested in the latest information on makeup and hairstyles. (5) For the most information on home life, however, the best magazine to buy is *Better Homes and Gardens*.

Sentence 1 subject : _____

Sentence 2 subject : _____

Sentence 3 subject : _____

Sentence 4 subject : _____

Sentence 5 subject : _____

03

(1) Thomas Jefferson, who wrote the Declaration of Independence, was lean, elegant, remote, and a bit sneaky. (2) John Adams, who contributed to the Declaration as well, was stout, cheap, and perhaps too honest about himself and everyone else. (3) Considered somewhat eccentric, or odd, Benjamin Franklin was a noted inventor and diplomat who was somewhat chubby and messy, but neither of those things interfered with his ability to help write the most important document in American history. (4) George Washington was a genius at lifting morale and knowing when to retreat to fight another day, so keeping the Founding Fathers agreeable and on task was his major contribution.

Sentence 1 subject : _____
Sentence 2 subject : _____
Sentence 3 subject : _____
Sentence 4 subject : _____

정답 02 Sentence 1 subject : Ladies' Home Journal
　　　　　Sentence 2 subject : Glamour
　　　　　Sentence 3 subject : Mode
　　　　　Sentence 4 subject : Allure
　　　　　Sentence 5 subject : Better Homes and Gardens
　　　03 Sentence 1 subject : Thomas Jefferson
　　　　　Sentence 2 subject : John Adams
　　　　　Sentence 3 subject : Benjamin Franklin
　　　　　Sentence 4 subject : George Washington

04 문장의 주제(subject)와 글의 패턴을 파악해보고, 이 글의 topic을 찾아내시오.

> (1) Judge Larry Standley of Harris County, Texas, required a man who slapped his wife to sign up for a yoga class as part of his punishment. (2) Municipal Judge Frances Gallegos in Santa Fe often sentences people convicted of domestic violence or fighting to a twice-a week, New Age anger-management class, where offenders experience tai chi, meditation, acupuncture, and Eastern philosophy as means of controlling rage. (3) Municipal Judge David Hostetler of Coshocton, Ohio, ordered a man who had run away from police after a traffic accident to jog for an hour every other day around the block where the jail is located. (4) Hostetler also received worldwide attention in 2001 when he ordered two men to dress in women's clothing and walk down Main Street as a sentence for throwing beer bottles at a car and taunting a woman. (5) Judge Mike Erwin of Baton Rouge ordered a young man who hit an elderly man in an argument to listen to a John Prine song, "Hello in There," about lonely senior citizens and write an essay about it.

Sentence 1 subject : _____
Sentence 2 subject : _____
Sentence 3 subject : _____
Sentence 4 subject : _____
Sentence 5 subject : _____
Pattern of organization : _____
General topic of paragraph : _____

정답 04 Sentence 1 subject : Judge Larry Standley
Sentence 2 subject : Judge Frances Gallegos
Sentence 3 subject : Judge David Hostetler
Sentence 4 subject : Hostetler
Sentence 5 subject : Judge Mike Erwin
Pattern of organization : Series
General topic of paragraph : Judges in the USA who have imposed unusual sentences

한글번역

예제 01 (1) 79%의 공립 고등학교 학생들에 의하면 교사들이 규칙을 강행하거나 숙제를 부과하는 데 있어 너무 너그럽다고 한다. (2) 게다가 공립학교를 다니는 십대의 절반이 그들의 교사와 학교가 그들이 도전하도록 하지 않는다고 말했다. (3) 수업에 방해를 주는 매우 많은 학생들이, 십대의 70%에 의하면, 학습을 방해한다. (4) 70%의 학생들은 학교의 졸업 기준이 너무 낮다고 말한다. (5) 학생들의 3/4에 따르면, 학위가 필수과목을 공부하지 않은 학생들에게도 주어진다고 한다.

02 (1) *Ladies' Home Journal*은 여성들과 관련된 이슈에 초점을 둔 잡지로 보통 30대, 40대, 50대 여성들에게 적합하다고 여겨지고 있다. (2) *Glamour*는 20대 및 30대 초반의 여성들이 직면한 이슈와 관련해 많은 페이지를 할애하고 있는 잡지다. (3) *Mode*는 전적으로 플러스 사이즈인 여성들과 관련된 이슈들로 구성돼 있다. (4) *Allure*은 화장품과 관련된 최신 정보가 있어 메이크업과 헤어스타일에 관련된 최신 정보에 관심이 있는 여성들을 위한 잡지다. (5) 그러나 가정생활과 관련된 최고의 정보를 위해서는 *Better Homes and Gardens*를 구입하는 것이 가장 좋다.

03 (1) 독립 선언문을 쓴 토마스 제퍼슨은 야위었고 우아하며 쌀쌀맞고 조금은 엉큼한 사람이었다. (2) 또한 선언문에 기여한 존 애덤스는 통통하고 천박한 성격에 본인 스스로와 다른 모두에게 너무나 솔직한 사람이었다. (3) 별나고 기이한 것으로 따지면 저명한 발명가이자 외교관이었던 벤자민 프랭클린이 있는데, 그는 조금 통통하며 지저분한 성격이나 미국 역사상 가장 중요한 문서를 작성하는 능력에는 전혀 방해가 되지 않았다. (4) 조지 워싱턴은 사기를 높이고, 후일에 다시 싸우기 위해 언제 후퇴할지에 대해 잘 알고 있는 천재여서 (독립 선언문의) 창시자들의 동의를 얻어 과업을 넘기는 것이 그의 주요한 공헌이었다.

04 (1) 텍사스주의 판사 래리 스탠드리는 와이프를 때린 남자에게 처벌의 일부로써 요가 클래스를 수강하도록 했다. (2) 산타페의 지방 판사 프랜시스 갤리고스는 가정 폭력이나 싸움으로 기소된 이들에게 이주에 한 번 뉴 에이지 분노관리 수업을 듣도록 종종 판결하는데 이 수업에서 범법자는 태극권이나, 명상, 침술 그리고 동양 철학 등을 분노 조절의 수단으로 경험하게 된다. (3) 오하이오 코섁튼의 지방판사 데이비드 호스틀러는 교통사고 이후 교통경찰로부터 도망간 남자에게 이틀에 한 번 감옥이 소재된 블록을 조깅하라는 명령을 내렸다. (4) 호스틀러는 2001년에도 세계적인 관심을 받았는데 그때 그는 차에 맥주병을 던지고 여성을 희롱한 두 사람에게 여자 옷을 입고 대로를 걸으라는 명령을 내리기도 했다. (5) 배턴 루지의 마이크 어원 판사는 말다툼 끝에 노인을 때린 젊은 남성에게 외로운 노인에 대한 존 프라인의 노래 "Hello in There"을 듣고 거기에 대한 글을 써오라는 명령을 내리기도 했다.

CHAPTER 07 The Writer's Technique – Purpose and Tone

01 목적(Purpose)의 파악과 2S2R

글의 목적purpose을 파악하는 것은 글의 요지를 이해하고 그와 관련된 문제들을 추론하는 데 있어 의미 있는 정보를 제공한다. 따라서 저자가 왜 글을 쓰는지를 파악하는 것은 2S2R Reading 단계에서 주제문을 파악하고, 주장main point과 논거supporting details를 구분하는 데 있어서 중요한 역할을 한다. 저자가 글을 쓸 때는 수많은 서로 다른 목적이 있기 때문에 매우 복잡할 수 있다. 하지만, 그렇게 복잡한 것은 한국에서 출제되는 시험의 영역 바깥에 있는 것이므로, 여기서는 가장 일반적인 글의 목적 3가지를 제시하고자 한다. 보통 대다수의 글은 넓게 보아 다음의 3가지의 틀 안에 포함된다.

1. To Entertain

글을 읽는 독자 여러분을 즐겁게 하거나 미소 짓게 하기 위한 것. 주로 소설, 단편, 시, 드라마 등 문학작품들과 그냥 흥밋거리로 붓 가는 대로 글을 쓰는 수필 등이 여기에 해당한다. 흥미로운 이야기를 전함으로써 독자 여러분에게 즐거움을 가져다주는 것이 가장 큰 목적이다.

2. To Inform

글을 읽는 독자 여러분에게 글의 topic에 대해 더 많은 정보를 주기 위한 것. 학교 교재, 신문 기사, 백과사전과 같은 참고문헌 등이 여기에 해당하는데 주로 여러분에게 뭔가를 가르치는 것teach을 목적으로 한다.

① 주제, 사건, 이슈 등을 개인의 의견 없이 묘사한다.
② 객관적인 어조에 의존한다.
③ 사실을 진술하거나 다른 이의 의견을 자신의 관점을 드러냄 없이 진술한다.
④ 일인칭 단수나 복수(I, We 등)의 사용을 피하고 독자를 직접적으로 언급하지 않는다.
⑤ 어떤 이슈에 대해 양쪽 모두의 견해를 제공한다.

3. To Persuade

글을 읽는 독자 여러분이 가지고 있는 세상에 대한 태도, 신념, 혹은 행위를 변화시키기 위해 설득하기 위한 것 또는 저자 자신의 생각에 동의하도록 만들기 위한 것. 신문의 사설과 광고가 대표적인 예이다.

① 주제, 사건, 이슈 등을 개인의 의견을 가지고 표현한다.
② 감정이나 태도를 드러내는 어조를 사용한다.
③ 상대방의 의견을 언급하는데, 그 의견을 반박하기 위해서다.
④ 한쪽의 관점을 편애하는 사실을 포함시킨다.
⑤ 자신의 의견이 왜 다른 이들에 의해서 받아들여져야 하는지 그 이유를 제공한다.

예제

[1-5] What is the author's primary purpose?

01 If you don't serve your time as a juror, you can't expect our legal system to be fair.

    a. to entertain   b. to inform   c. to persuade

02 The high rate of corporate crime proves that Korea needs to have much stricter law enforcement than now.

    a. to entertain   b. to inform   c. to persuade

정답 01 c   02 c

03

    Frankly, it seems pretty easy to come up with a new exercise. You just take something people are already doing—like eating—and add "exercise." Or say it's cardio-friendly. So how's about:

    R.C. Colaerobics: Soda shopping? Don't just grab a Coke. Stretch waaaaay down to reach the Royal Crown! Your abs will be glad—and so will your wallet!

    Karaoke Swim: Tired of singing on that stupid bike? Start singing as you swim across the pool! Pounds peel away as you struggle to clear your lungs and stay afloat. You go, gurgle!

    Lego Lifts: Step 1: Invite a child to play with Legos on your rug. Step 2: Have child leave after "cleaning up." Step 3: Remove your socks and run around. Yeow! Ouch. There's another one he missed! You're hopping your way to health!

a. to entertain   b. to inform   c. to persuade

04

    At least 12 women from the United States contracted bacterial infections after undergoing breast enlargement surgery or other cosmetic procedures in the Dominican Republic, the government said yesterday. The Centers for Disease Control and Prevention said the women developed soft tissue infections known as *mycobacterium abscesses* after traveling to Santo Domingo for procedures between May 2003 and February 2004. All have since recovered after being given antibiotics. Nine had to be hospitalized. An increasing number of Americans are getting cosmetic surgery abroad because it is cheaper. The CDC said that it has yet to establish the source of the infection but that previous outbreaks in other places have been attributed to contaminated surgical equipment.

a. to entertain   b. to inform   c. to persuade

05

> I'm a pretty good housekeeper. Ask anybody. No, wait: Don't ask my wife. She and I disagree on certain housekeeping issues, such as whether it's OK for a house to contain dirt. Also smells. If NASA scientists really want to know about life on Mars, instead of sending up robots that keep finding rocks, they need to send my wife and have her take a whiff of the Martian atmosphere. If there's a single one-celled organism anywhere on the planet, she'll smell it. And if the other astronauts don't stop her, she'll kill it with Lysol. This is why her approach to leftovers baffles me. I am opposed to leftovers. I believe the only food that should be kept around is takeout Chinese, which contains a powerful preservative chemical called "kung pao" that enables it to remain edible for several football seasons. All other leftover foods should be thrown away immediately.

a. to entertain   b. to inform   c. to persuade   d. to praise

정답 03 a   04 b   05 a

한글번역

예제

01 배심원으로서 봉사하는 시간을 내지 않는다면, 우리의 법적 제도가 공정하기를 바랄 수 없다.

02 높은 기업 범죄율은 한국이 훨씬 더 엄격한 법의 적용이 필요한 나라임을 보여준다.

03 솔직히, 새로운 운동을 생각해내는 것은 아주 쉬운 것 같다. 사람들이 이미 하는 일들(먹는 일처럼)을 택해서 '운동'을 붙이기만 하면 된다. 아니면 그것이 심장에 좋다고 말하면 된다. 자 그러면 다음은 어떤가?
R.C. 콜라에어로빅: 탄산음료를 사러 나왔는가? 그냥 콜라를 잡을 게 아니다. 로얄 크라운을 잡을 수 있도록 아래로 쭈우욱 몸을 펴라! 당신의 복근이 좋아할 것이고 당신의 지갑도 좋아할 것이다!
노래방 수영: 멍청한 자전거 위에서 노래하기가 싫증나는가? 수영장을 헤엄치면서 노래하는 운동을 시작해보라! 폐를 비우면서도 물에 뜨는 것을 동시에 하려고 버둥거리면서 살들이 빠질 것이다. 자 가라, 꾸르륵!
레고 집어들기: 1단계: 어린이를 한 명 오게 해서 당신의 카펫 위에서 레고를 가지고 놀게 하라. 2단계: 아이가 다 '치우기'를 한 다음 가게 하라. 3단계: 양말을 벗고 뛰어다녀라. 아야! 아이가 못 찾은 게 또 있다! 당신은 건강으로 깡총깡총 뛰어가고 있는 것이다.

04 적어도 12명의 미국 여성들이 도미니카 공화국에서 가슴 확대 수술이나 다른 미용 시술을 받은 이후에 박테리아성 질병에 감염됐다고 당국이 어제 밝혔다. 질병 통제 예방센터는 산토 도밍고로 2003년 5월에서 2004년 2월까지 수술 여행을 다녀온 여성들에게서 mycobacterium abscesses이라 알려진 연조직 감염이 발병했다고 밝혔다. 그들은 모두 항생제 처방을 받은 이후에 회복됐지만, 아홉 명은 병원에 입원했어야만 했다. (수술) 비용이 저렴하기 때문에 점점 더 많은 수의 미국인들이 성형 수술을 받기 위해 외국에 나가고 있다. 질병 예방 통제센터는 아직 감염의 원천을 밝혀내지 못했지만, 이전의 다른 지역에서의 감염은 오염된 외과용 수술 도구 탓이었다.

05 나는 꽤 훌륭한 살림꾼이다. 누구에게든지 물어보라. 아니, 기다려보라: 내 아내에게는 묻지 말라. 그녀와 나는 집에 먼지가 있거나 냄새가 나도 괜찮은지 아닌지와 같은 가사 문제에 있어서 의견의 불일치가 있다. NASA의 과학자들이 화성에 정말로 생물체가 있는지 없는지에 대해 알기를 원한다면 바위나 계속 찾는 로봇을 보내는 대신에 내 아내를 보내서 화성의 대기를 한 모금 마시게 할 필요가 있다. 그 행성의 어디엔가 단 하나의 세포를 가진 유기체라도 있다면 그녀는 그 냄새를 맡을 것이다. 그리고 다른 비행사가 그녀를 제지하지 않는다면 리졸로 그것을 죽일 것이다. 이것이 남은 음식에 대한 그녀의 접근법이 나를 당황하게 만드는 이유이다. 나는 음식을 남기는 것을 반대한다. 나는 보존돼야 하는 유일한 음식은 여러 번의 축구 시즌 동안 남겨서 먹을 수 있도록 하는 '쿵파오'라고 불리는 강력한 방부제를 함유하고 있는 포장 중국 음식이라고 믿는다. 다른 모든 남겨진 음식물들은 즉시 폐기돼야 한다.

02   어조(Tone)의 파악과 2S2R

 글의 어조tone를 파악하는 것은 글의 요지를 이해하고 그와 관련된 문제들을 추론하는 데 있어서 의미 있는 정보를 제공한다. 따라서, 글의 어조를 파악하는 것은 글의 목적과 더불어 2S2R Reading 단계에서 주제문을 파악하고, 주장main point과 논거supporting details를 구분하는 데 중요한 역할을 한다.

 어조란 글쓴이가 서술 대상을 바라보는 태도와 느낌을 나타내는 언어적 표현 방식이다. 어조는 글쓴이의 개성적인 **목소리**로 나타나거나 글을 지배하는 **분위기**로 나타남으로써 글의 의미 및 주제를 형성하는 데 이바지한다. 따라서 어조를 평가하는 것은 글의 주제와 글쓴이의 태도 및 관점을 정확히 짚어내는 데 기여할 수 있다. 특히 **반어적인 어조**의 경우는 파악하기가 까다로울 뿐더러, 잘못 판단하면 글의 중심 내용까지도 잘못 독해할 수 있으므로 주의해야 한다. 저자가 글을 쓸 때는 수많은 서로 다른 어조를 사용할 수 있을 것이기 때문에 수많은 어조가 있을 수 있다. 대표적인 것만 나열하면 다음과 같다.

① **Objective** : neutral
② **Sympathetic** : understanding the feelings of others
③ **Critical** : expressing disapproval or strong disagreement
④ **Ironical** : saying the opposite of what you mean
⑤ **Admiring** : praising, favoring, or supportive
⑥ **Angry** : indignant; outraged; bitter
⑦ **Disgusted** : feeling sickened or irritated
⑧ **Amused** : humorous(funny or witty) or playful
⑨ **Sad** : feeling down, depressed
⑩ **Worried** : concerned or frightened about what will happen
⑪ **Distressed** : anxious and upset; disturbed
⑫ **Sarcastic** : mean and hurtful
⑬ **Lighthearted** : not serious; carefree
⑭ **Excited** : emotionally aroused and active
⑮ **Optimistic** : not pessimistic or hopeful about the future

다음의 세 개의 예문을 보자. 아래 예문들은 하나의 내용을 다른 어조로 표현한 것이다.

ⓐ The Immigration and Naturalization Service ranks among the worst managed federal agencies rated by Government Executive magazine. It charges immigrants for doing basic paperwork and even for some informational phone calls. Additionally, its facilities aren't equipped to handle the volume of people it serves.

ⓑ The bureaucratic nightmare we call the Immigration and Naturalization Service ranks among the worst managed federal agencies rated by Government Executive magazine. It robs poor immigrants of their hard-earned money by charging them for basic paperwork, and it even has the nerve to require these people to pay for informational phone calls. Additionally, its embarrassingly substandard facilities aren't equipped to handle the volumes of people it serves.

ⓒ The overworked and struggling Immigration and Naturalization Service ranks among the worst managed federal agencies rated by Government Executive magazine. Its meager resources force it to charge immigrants for doing basic paperwork, and its pitiful lack of funding leaves it no choice but to charge people for informational phone calls. The agency has been ignored for so long that its cramped and outdated facilities just aren't equipped to handle the volumes of people it serves.

번역 ⓐ 정부 관보에 실린 내용에 따르면, 이민귀화국은 최악으로 운영된 연방 기관 중 하나이다. 이민귀화국에서는 기본적인 문서 작업과 심지어 정보 제공용 전화에도 요금을 부과하고 있다. 게다가 이용자들이 충분히 이용할 만큼 넉넉한 시설을 갖추고 있지 않다.
ⓑ 최악으로 운영된 연방 기관 중의 하나로 정부 관보에 순위가 오른 이민귀화국을 평가하기에 가장 좋은 표현은 '관료제의 악몽'일 것이다. 그곳에서는 간단한 문서 작성에도 요금을 부과하고, 정보 제공 전화 요금을 지불하라고까지 요구해서 가난한 이민자들이 힘들게 번 돈을 착취한다. 게다가 민망하게도 설비는 기준 이하인데다가 이용자들이 충분히 이용할 정도로 시설을 넉넉히 갖추고 있지도 않다.
ⓒ 정보 관보에 의해 최악으로 운영된 연방 기관 중의 하나로 평가된 이민귀화국은 늘 열악한 환경에 시달리고 있다. 이민귀화국에서는 만성적인 예산 부족 때문에 간단한 문서 작업이나 정보 제공 전화에도 요금을 부과할 수밖에 없다. 오랫동안 주력 부서로 취급되지 않았던 기관이기 때문에 설비는 노후하고 이용자들이 충분히 이용할 만큼 넉넉한 시설을 갖추고 있지도 못하다.

글 ⓐ의 경우 '이민귀화국이 최악으로 운영된 연방 기관 중 하나'라는 것을 정부 관보를 인용해서 이야기하고 있다. 즉 필자 자신의 의견으로 제시하고 있지 않다. 과다한 요금 부과나 시설 부족에 대해서도 같은 시각으로 평가할 수 있다. 따라서 예문 중에서 글 ⓐ는 중립적인 어조를 가졌다고 할 수 있다. 그러나 글 ⓐ가 절대적 중립성을 가지고 있는지는 여전히 의문이다. 왜냐하면 정부 관보에 실린 내용이 이미 이민귀화국에 대해서 특정한 가치평가를 담고 있기 때문이다. 마치 자신의 의견이 아닌 것처럼 권위 있는 기관이나 학자의 의견을 이용해서 주장을 펴는 것은 자신의 주장에 설득력을 더하기 위한 고전적인 수법이라고 할 수 있다.

따라서 관련된 주제topic에 대해서 다양한 의견이 균형감 있게 제시되고 있는지를 살피는 것은 중립적 어조의 글을 평가할 때 반드시 필요한 일이다. 글 ⓑ의 경우 '관료제의 악몽', '착취', '민망하게도' 등의 단어를 사용함으로써 이민귀화국에 대한 비판적 시각을 직접적으로 드러내고 있다. 글 ⓒ의 경우 이민귀화국에 대한 동정 혹은 비판에 대해서 해명하는 어조를 보여주고 있다.

예제

[1-5] What is the primary tone of the passage?

01

I was brought up in Europe. I came to the United States at age 25 in 1963, and for the past 41 years, I have been disturbed by the eating habits of Americans. Americans have come to demand that an endless quantity of foods be available at all times. I have seen them pile food on their plates at buffet-style restaurants. However, seldom have I seen them eat all of the items they put on their plates. Some restaurants, in a smart move, have had to resort to posting signs such as, "You may take as much as you want, but please eat all that you take."

a. disgusted b. optimistic c. humorous
d. sad e. ironic

02

Like to go to the beach, do you? Swim? Surf? Fish? Snorkel? Scuba dive? Wait! What can you be thinking? Don't you read the papers? Watch TV? Don't you know sharks are massing along our coastlines, biting bathers, eating people? Should you risk an attack by these JAWS wanna-bes?

a. critical b. angry c. neutral
d. ironic e. alarmed

정답 01 a 02 e

03

> Killing animals for their fur is wrong. Consider the cute mink, the cuddly raccoon, the lovable harp seal. These animals haven't hurt us, so why should we savagely murder these adorable creatures? Think of a puppy. Picture its soulful, trusting eyes. Would you want to wear spot's hide on your back? The answer, from any thoughtful individual, must be a resounding "No!"

a. critical　　　　b. sympathetic　　　　c. angry
d. ironic　　　　　e. neutral

해설 critical도 어느 정도 답이 될 수 있지만, angry가 전체적인 어조엔 더 맞다. 글 전체의 어조는 모피를 사용하는 행위에 대한 분노가 스며들어 있다. "wrong", "why should"(도대체 왜), "savagely", "spot's hide" 등의 단어에서 저자의 분노가 묻어나고 있다.

04

> It's not easy being a mother these days. Most work outside the home in addition to their parenting duties. Because of the high divorce rate, many are rearing their children alone or with only part-time help from fathers. In 2001, an ABC news columnist did some research that suggested if you paid mothers for all the things they do, they would draw down about $500,000 a year. Moms face a daunting task, whether they have other jobs or not.

a. admiring　　　　b. ironic　　　　c. neutral
d. sympathetic　　　e. worried

05

> Seabiscuit was one of the most remarkable thoroughbred racehorses in history. From 1936 to 1940, Americans thronged to racetracks to watch the small, ungainly racehorse become a champion. He had an awkward gait but ran with dominating speed; he was mild-mannered yet fiercely competitive; and he was stubborn until he became compliant.

a. admiring   b. sympathetic   c. neutral
d. ironic   e. worried

정답 03 c   04 d   05 a

한글번역

예제 01 나는 유럽에서 자랐다. 나는 1963년, 미국에 25살의 나이로 왔고, 지난 41년 동안 미국인들의 식습관에 심적으로 불편을 느껴왔다. 미국인들은 무한한 양의 음식이 항상 있기를 요구하고 있다. 나는 사람들이 뷔페 스타일의 식당에서 접시에 음식을 수북이 쌓는 것을 봐왔다. 하지만, 그들이 접시에 담은 모든 음식을 먹는 사람을 지금까지 나는 본 적이 단 한 번도 없다. 영리한 움직임의 일환으로, 일부 식당들은 "마음대로 가져가시되 가져간 것은 모두 드십시오"라는 문구를 붙여놓는 것에 의존할 수밖에 없었다.

02 해변에 가는 것을 좋아하지, 그렇지? 수영? 파도타기? 낚시? 스노클링? 스쿠버 다이빙? 잠깐! 대체 무슨 생각을 하고 있는 거야? 신문도 안 보나? TV는 보나? 상어들이 해안가를 따라 떼 지어 다니고, 수영하는 사람들을 물고, 잡아먹기도 하는 거 몰라? 이 죠스가 되고 싶어하는 놈들에게 공격당할지 모르는 위험을 감수해야 하겠어?

03 모피를 얻기 위해 동물을 죽이는 것은 잘못된 일이다. 귀여운 밍크와 꼭 껴안고 싶은 너구리, 사랑스러운 하프 바다표범을 생각해보라. 이 동물들은 우리를 해치지 않는다. 그런데 왜 우리는 이러한 사랑스런 동물들을 잔인하게 죽이는가? 강아지를 떠올려보라. 강아지의 영혼이 담긴 진심어린 눈을 그려보라. 당신은 자신의 몸에 오명의 가죽을 입기를 원하는가? 지각 있는 사람이라면 누구든 그 대답은 확실히 '아니오'일 것이다.

04 요즘 엄마가 된다는 것은 쉬운 일이 아니다. 대다수의 엄마들은 부모로서의 의무뿐 아니라 집 바깥에서도 일을 한다. 높은 이혼률로 인해서, 많은 엄마들은 자녀들을 홀로 키우거나 아이들의 아빠들로부터 시간제로 도움을 받아서 키우고 있다. 2001년, (미국의) ABC 방송의 한 뉴스 컬럼니스트는 연구를 했는데, 그것이 시사하는 바는 다음과 같다. 만일 엄마들이 하는 일들에 대해 임금을 지불한다면, 일 년에 약 50만 달러(6억 원 정도)를 지불해야 한다. 엄마들은 (집에서 하는 일이 아닌) 다른 직업이 있든 없든 간에, 벅찬 일에 직면해 있다.

05 씨비스킷은 역사상 가장 놀라운 순종 경주마 가운데 하나다. 1936년부터 1940년까지, 미국인들은 그 조그맣고 (움직임이) 어색한 경주마가 우승자가 되는 것을 보기 위해 경기장으로 몰려들었다. 그 말은 이상한 걸음걸이를 했지만, 압도적인 속도로 질주했다; 온유한 성품이었지만 놀랍도록 경쟁심이 강했다; 말을 들을 때까진 자기 고집이 강했다.

CHAPTER 08 Summarizing

    2S2R 전략적 독해의 3단계에 해당하는 요약하기summarizing는 요지를 정확하게 파악하는 데 도움이 되는데, 보통 100여 자 정도의 짧은 글의 요약은 요지와 유사하다. 따라서 요지를 잘 파악하려면 요약하기의 기술을 활용해야 한다. 좋은 요약은 작거나 반복되는 세부사항을 포함하지 않는다. 주제문은 일반적인 요약보다 더 짧은 요약이므로 핵심 주장만을 드러낼 뿐 논거와 부연설명을 포함하지 않는다. 정리해서 보자.

    요약하기는 글의 중요한 부분을 훨씬 짧은 형식으로 다시 말하는 것으로, 좋은 요약을 하기 위한 방법은 다음과 같다.

① 요약할 글의 전 지문을 꼼꼼하게 읽는다.
② main idea와 major supporting points에 밑줄을 긋거나 리스트를 따로 체크한다.
③ 지문의 main idea를 요약의 첫 번째 문장에 놓는다.
④ 원 지문에 있던 사실들과 개념들을 그것들 사이의 논리적 일관성을 보여주는 문장으로 재구성하여 쓴다. 이때 상호간의 논리적 연관관계가 명확해야 한다.
⑤ 지문에 있는 불필요한 내용들(minor details, repeated details)을 반복하지 않고, 지문에 없던 독자 자신의 의견(the reader's opinion)을 요약에 포함하지 않는다.
⑥ 요점과 요점 사이에 비약이 있어선 안 된다.
⑦ 요약을 여러분 자신의 언어로 "바꾸어 쓴다면(rephrase; paraphrase)" 더욱 좋은 요약이 된다.
⑧ 원래의 지문을 약 4분의 1로 줄이는 것이 가장 좋다.

✓ summary할 때 자주 사용되는 연결사(Transitional Signal Words)

Transition Signal	Common Terms		
To indicate addition to the original train of thought (원래 있던 것에 더 첨가하고자 할 때)	also further moreover too	in addition furthermore second	first last secondly
To indicate a change, challenge, or contradiction (이미 있던 것에 대해 변화, 도전, 또는 반박 등을 나타낼 때)	although by (in) contrast nevertheless rather yet	after all despite that fact on the other hand regardless	but however on the contrary still
To point out similarities (유사성을 강조할 때)	likewise similarly	by the same token	in the same vein
To introduce examples and/or illustrations (예시나 사례 따위를 도입할 때)	for example specifically	for instance that is	in other words
To introduce the effect of some cause (결과를 나타낼 때)	as a result in response	consequently therefore	hence thus
To help readers follow a time sequence (시간의 흐름을 나타낼 때)	afterward finally next then	after a while in the meantime of late thereafter	before in time soon
To repeat a point made before (반복, 정리할 때)	in brief in short to reiterate	in conclusion in summary to sum up	in other words on the whole to repeat

예제

01 다음을 3단어로 요약하시오.

The small cowboy put the saddle on his horse, untied him from the fence, waved good bye and rode off the sunset.

Summary : _____

해설 앞서 학습한 요약의 방법을 이용하여 보자. ④번의 원리, 즉, "원 지문에 있던 사실들과 개념들을 그것들 사이의 논리적 일관성을 보여주는 문장으로 재구성하여 쓴다. 이때 상호간의 논리적 연관관계가 명확해야 한다."를 응용해보면,
① put the saddle on his horse
② untied him from the fence
③ waved good bye
④ rode off the sunset
위의 4가지 사실들을 논리적 일관성의 측면에서 재구성해보면, 결국 그 카우보이가 '떠났다'라는 것을 뒷받침하는 것일 따름이다. 따라서 요약하면, "The cowboy left."가 되는 것이다.

02 다음을 한 문장으로 요약하시오.

> Although several early societies experimented with paper currency—most notably the Chinese during the 1st millennium B.C.—coins of silver and gold predominated as the major form of exchange over early experiences with paper currency. The reasons were understandable enough: coins were far more durable than paper and less likely to be destroyed by fire, and coins contained the very precious metals that made money worth its salt. It required a leap of both imagination and of courage to establish a form of currency that was only backed by a precious metal but of itself was intrinsically worthless.

Summary : _____

해설 2단계로 나누어 요약을 해보자.
Step 1. 다음의 A와 B 둘 중 더 타당한 요약을 골라보자.
A. Although several early societies experimented with paper currency—most notably the Chinese during the 1st millennium B.C.—coins of silver and gold predominated as the major form of exchange over early experiences with paper currency.
B. Coins of silver and gold predominated as the major form of exchange over early experiences with paper currency.
당연히 문장 B가 더 적절하다. 하지만 이것만으로는 불충분하다. 다음의 2단계를 보자.

Step 2. 이 글의 핵심 정보는 '동전이 종이돈보다 주요 통화수단이었다.'는 것만이 아니라 '왜' 그렇게 됐는지에 대한 것도 포함하고 있다. 따라서 이 둘의 주요 핵심 내용이 들어가야 올바른 요약이 된다. 여기서 항상 유념할 것은 여러분 자신의 언어로 '바꾸어 써야(rephrase; paraphrase)' 한다는 것이다.
다시 요약해보면, "Because silver and gold were more durable, less flammable, and more intrinsically valuable, they predominated over early paper money."가 적절한 요약이 된다.

 정답 01 The cowboy left.
02 Because silver and gold were more durable, less flammable, and more intrinsically valuable, they predominated over early paper money.

[3-6] 다음의 문장들을 요약하시오.

03 Sammy put on his raincoat, picked up his umbrella from the table near the door, turned off the lights, put out the cat, and got ready for his twenty-minute walk to the bus stop.

Summary : _____

04 In Sammy's library you can find mysteries, novels, biographies, travel books, how-to manuals, science fiction thrillers, and reference books.

Summary : _____

05 During the summer along the Charles River in Boston, you can go rollerblading, running, biking, or sailing, or you can have a picnic, listen to a concert, or watch a movie.

Summary : _____

06 When he heard the weather forecast, Sammy closed the windows, put tape across the glass, moved all of his plants and chairs indoors, and stocked up on bottles of fresh water.

Summary : _____

[7-8] 다음의 글들을 요약하시오.

07

> Shopping malls have produced a revolution in the United States shopping and living habits in just 45 years. Before 1950, there were no malls, but now almost every city or region has at least one. In fact, shopping malls have become a part of daily life. Many people even think of them as social centers. In a way, malls have taken the place of Main Street. Shops and services which were once spread over several city blocks are now in one place at the mall. Busy householders can save time by doing their shopping at the mall. And people young and old, with time on their hands, often say, "Let's go to the mall!"

Summary : _____

08

> By 1984, NASA, the United States space program, had carried out many successful flights of the space shuttle. In fact, Americans were beginning to take the whole NASA program for granted. Then, the president announced that the next shuttle would carry a school teacher into space. Hundreds of teachers from all parts of the country applied for the job. They all wanted to be "the first teacher in space." During the next year, these adventurous educators were tested and examined and trained. At last, the choice was announced. A teacher from New Hampshire, Christa McAuliffe, would be the first teacher-astronaut.

Summary : _____

정답
03 Sammy left the house.
04 Sammy has a variety of books.
05 You can do many things along the Charles in the summertime.
06 Sammy prepared for the storm.
07 Shopping malls have changed United States culture.
08 NASA chose Christa McAuliffe, a school teacher, to be an astronaut.

[9-10] Summarize the passage in approximately 100 words.

09

In nineteenth-century America, most migrants went west because the region seemed to promise a better life. Railroad expansion made remote farming regions accessible, and the construction of grain elevators eased problems of shipping and storage. As a result of population growth, the demand for farm products grew rapidly, and the prospects for commercial agriculture—growing crops for profit—became more favorable than ever.

Life on the farm, however, was much harder than the advertisements and railroad agents suggested. Migrants often encountered shortages of essentials they had once taken for granted. The open prairies contained little lumber for housing and fuel. Pioneer families were forced to build houses of sod and to burn manure for heat. Water was sometimes as scarce as timber. Few families were lucky or wealthy enough to buy land near a stream that did not dry up in summer and freeze in winter. Machinery for drilling wells was scarce until the 1880s, and even then it was very expensive.

The weather was seldom predictable. In summer, weeks of torrid heat and parching winds often gave way to violent storms that washed away crops and property. In winter, the wind and cold from blizzards piled up mountainous snowdrifts that halted all outdoor movement. During the Great Blizzard that struck Nebraska and the Dakota Territory in January 1888, the temperature plunged to 36 degrees below zero, and the wind blew at 56 miles per hour. The storm stranded schoolchildren and killed several parents who ventured out to rescue them. In the spring, melting snow swelled streams, and floods threatened millions of acres. In the fall, a week without rain could turn dry grasslands into tinder, and the slightest spark could ignite a raging prairie fire.

Nature could be cruel even under good conditions. Weather that was favorable for crops was also good for breeding insects. Worms and flying pests ravaged corn and wheat. In the 1870s and 1880s swarms of grasshoppers virtually ate up entire farms. Heralded only by the din of buzzing wings, a mile-long cloud of insects would smother the land and devour everything: plants, tree bark, and clothes. As one farmer lamented, the "hoppers left behind nothing but the mortgage."

Summary : _____

_____

_____

10

Where do museums get the objects they put on display? Many of a museum's artifacts come from archaeological excavations sponsored by government or educational institutions. Sometimes, however, museums acquire ancient objects by buying them or accepting them as gifts from dealers or private collectors. In that case, museums don't always know the provenance, or origin, of the artifacts. They might have been stolen from archaeological sites or looted from other museums. It is not unusual during times of war or political upheaval, as recent wars in Afghanistan and Iraq have illustrated, for artifacts to be stolen and offered for sale to the highest bidder. During the Gulf War of 1991, for example, more than 2,000 objects were looted from Iraqi museums; only a handful have ever been recovered.

To avoid acquiring stolen artifacts, some museums—the British Museum and Chicago's Field Museum—have adopted strict policies that prevent them from accepting any object with questionable provenance. There are, however, curators who insist that adding questionable artifacts to museum collections is both necessary and right. Some museum curators defend decisions to accept objects with uncertain origins on the grounds that they often come from legitimate sources. While museums obviously prefer clear proof of an artifact's origin, such documentation is not always available. Many unprovenanced objects have been in private collections for generations. Thus their exact sources cannot be traced when the objects finally become available for purchase or are donated. In other words, the lack of a centuries-old paper trail does not necessarily mean that an object was stolen.

Museum curators also argue that displaying only documented items would prevent them from exhibiting artifacts related to certain cultures. The Metropolitan Museum of Art in New York, for example, had to use several artifacts of unknown origin for its exhibit on the ancient country of Bactria, which was once located in present-day Afghanistan. If the museum had limited itself to objects with clear documentation, its exhibition about this particular civilization would have been incomplete.

As a result, many curators reason that banning artifacts of questionable provenance would prevent museums from fulfilling their mission—the imparting of knowledge about humanity's past. By not acquiring objects with uncertain origins, museums ensure that these objects will remain in private hands, where they are unavailable to scholars or to the general public. Thus the artifacts could never be used to reveal the secrets of the past.

Summary : _____

_____

_____

_____

정답 09 During the nineteenth century, countless men and women went west in the belief that farming was a way to make money and improve their life but most found it harder and more rigorous than expected. First, essentials like lumber and water were hard to come by. Second, the weather was both harsh and unpredictable. In winter, the temperature might plunge as low as 36 degrees below zero while the wind could blow at 56 miles per hour. In summer, scorching heat and drought would suddenly be followed by slashing rainstorms. In addition, insects were an additional problem and plagues of them could devour entire farms.

10 Museums face an ethical dilemma between acquiring artifacts with uncertain origins and maintaining strict provenance standards. Museums acquire artifacts primarily through archaeological excavations sponsored by institutions, but also through purchases and donations from private collectors. This latter source creates an ethical challenge when the provenance is unclear, as items might have been stolen or looted, especially during conflicts like recent wars in Afghanistan and Iraq. While some institutions like the British Museum maintain strict policies against accepting questionable items, other curators defend acquiring objects with uncertain origins. They argue that many unprovenanced artifacts come from legitimate sources but lack documentation due to generations in private collections. Furthermore, they believe rejecting these items could leave gaps in cultural exhibitions and keep potentially valuable historical pieces hidden from scholars and the public.

한글번역

예제

01 그 키 작은 카우보이는 말에 안장을 얹고, 말뚝으로부터 말을 풀고, 작별 인사를 하고, 석양 속으로 말을 타고 갔다.

02 비록 여러 초기 사회들이 지폐를 시험해봤지만-이것의 가장 주목할 만한 예로는 기원전 1000년 동안 중국인들이 있다-은화나 금화가 종이 화폐를 쓴 조기 경험을 뛰어넘고 주요한 교환수단으로 우세하게 자리 잡았다. 이유는 충분히 이해할 만하다. 동전은 종이보다 훨씬 내구성이 좋았고, 불에 파손될 우려가 적었으며, 제구실을 할 만한 귀금속을 가지고 있었다. 귀금속이 뒷받침만 해 줄 뿐 그 자체로는 내재적 가치가 없는 하나의 통화 형태를 만들기 위해서는 상상력과 용기 양쪽에서 도약을 해야 하는 일이었다.

03 새미는 비옷을 입고, 문 근처 테이블에 놓인 우산을 집어 들고, 불을 끄고, 고양이를 내보내고, 버스 정류장까지 20분 걸어갈 준비를 마쳤다.

04 새미의 서가에서 당신은 추리물, 소설, 전기, 여행 서적, 방법 매뉴얼, SF 소설, 그리고 참고 서적들을 볼 수 있다.

05 보스턴의 찰스 강변에서 여름 동안 롤러블레이드를 탈 수도 있고, 달리기도 할 수 있고, 자전거 타기나 배 타기를 할 수도 있고, 아니면 소풍을 가거나 음악회를 듣거나 영화를 볼 수도 있다.

06 기상예보를 들었을 때 새미는 창문을 닫고 유리창에 테이프를 두르고 화분들과 의자들을 집안으로 들여놓고 생수병을 쌓아 비축해 놓았다.

07 지난 45년 동안 쇼핑몰은 미국인들의 쇼핑과 생활 습관에 혁명적 변화를 야기시켰다. 1950년 이전엔 단 한 개의 몰도 없었지만 지금은 거의 모든 도시나 지역에 적어도 한 개 이상의 쇼핑몰이 있다. 실제로 쇼핑몰은 우리 일상생활의 한 부분이 됐다. 심지어 많은 이들은 쇼핑몰들을 사교의 중심지로 간주하기도 한다. 어떤 의미에서 몰들은 메인 스트리트를 대체하고 있다. 예전에 몇 블록에 걸쳐 늘어서 있던 가게와 서비스들은 이제는 몰 안에 한데 모여 있다. 바쁜 사람들은 몰에서 쇼핑을 함으로써 시간을 절약할 수 있다. 그리고 젊은 나이가 많은 시간이 있는 사람들은 "자 몰에 가지"라고 자꾸 말한다.

08 1984년까지 미국 우주 프로그램은 많은 우주 비행선의 성공적인 항해를 이루어내고 있었다. 사실상, 미국인들은 모든 NASA의 프로그램들을 당연하게 여기기 시작했다. 그리고 나서, 대통령은 다음 비행선이 학교 교사들을 우주로 보낼 것이라고 발표했다. 전국의 수백 명의 교사들이 이 일에 지원했다. 그들은 모두 '우주로 가는 첫 번째 교사'가 되기를 원했다. 다음 해에, 이러한 모험적인 교육자들은 시험을 치르고 검사를 받고 훈련을 받았다. 결국, 선출자가 발표됐다. 뉴햄프셔의 교사인 크리스트 맥컬리프가 첫 번째 교사-우주 비행사가 될 것이다.

09 19세기 미국에서 대부분의 이민자들은 서부로 갔다. 그 이유는 그 지역이 더 나은 삶을 약속한 것처럼 보였기 때문이다. 철도의 확장은 거리가 먼 농장 지역을 접근하기 쉽게 만들었고, 양곡기의 건설은 수송과 저장의 문제를 완화시켰다. 인구 증가의 결과로서, 농작물 생산을 위한 수요는 빠르게 증가했고, 이윤을 위한 작물들 같은 상업적 농업의 전망은 그 어떤 때보다 더 유리해졌다.

그러나 농장에서의 삶은 광고나 철도청에서 제시한 것보다 훨씬 더 힘들었다. 이주민들은 이미 한 번 그들이 양도받았던 본질적 요소들의 결핍에 자주 직면했다. 개방된 대초원은 집과 연료를 위한 적은 양의 제재들을 포함했다. 개척자 가족들은 뗏장으로 집을 지을 수밖에 없었고, 난방을 위해 동물들의 배설물을 태워야 했다. 물은 때때로 목재만큼이나 희귀했다. 거의 어떤 가정도 여름에 메마르거나 겨울에 얼지 않는 개울 근처의 땅을 살 수 있을 정도로 운이 좋거나 부유하지 않았다. 우물을 파기 위한 기계가 1880년대까지는 희귀했고, 심지어 매우 비싸기까지 했다.

날씨는 좀처럼 예측하기 어려웠다. 여름엔 타는 듯한 열과 바싹 마르게 하는 바람은 종종 강렬한 폭풍으로 변했고, 그 폭풍은 농작물들과 소유물들을 깡그리 쓸어버렸다. 겨울엔 눈보라로부터 나온 바람과 추위가 바깥에서의 모든 활동을 멈추게 하는 거대한 눈 더미를 쌓아 올렸다. 1888년 1월, 네브래스카와 다코타주 경계 지역에 몰아친 거대한 눈보라가 불었던 기간 동안, 그 당시 온도는 영하 36도로 곤두박질쳤고, 바람은 시속 56마일로 불었다. 그 폭풍은 학생들을 오도 가도 못하게 만들었고, 그 아이들을 구하기 위해 위험을 무릅쓴 몇몇 학부모들을 죽이기도 했다. 봄에는 녹은 눈이 시냇물의 수위를 높여, 홍수가 100만 에이커를 위협했다. 가을엔 비가 없던 주간에는 건조한 초원을 불쏘시개로 변하게 만들어 아주 작은 불꽃도 격렬한 대초원을 불바다로 만들 수 있었다.

자연은 좋은 상황에서도 무자비할 수 있다. 작물에게 유리한 날씨는 곤충을 번식시키기에도 좋은 조건이다. 벌레들과 날아다니는 해충들은 옥수수와 밀을 황폐화시켰다. 1870년대와 1880년대에 메뚜기 떼들은 모든 농작물을 사실상 먹어치웠다. 날개의 윙윙거리는 조그만 소리에 의해 예고된, 1마일 정도 하늘을 자욱하게 뒤덮은 곤충 떼가 땅을 완전히 덮어버리고, 식물들, 나무껍질, 그리고 직물 등 모든 것을 게걸스레 먹었다. 한 농부는 "메뚜기들은 저당 증서 빼고 모든 것을 앗아갔다."며 한탄했다.

10 박물관들은 그들이 전시할 물품들을 어디서 얻는가? 많은 박물관들의 물품들은 정부 혹은 교육기관으로부터 후원받은 고고학적 발굴로부터 온다. 하지만 때때로 박물관들은 고대 물품들을 구입하거나 거래처 혹은 개별 수집가로부터 선물 받은 방식으로 획득한다. 그러한 경우 박물관들은 때때로 그 물품들의 기원이나 출처를 알지 못한다. 그것들은 유적지로부터 도굴됐거나 다른 박물관으로부터 약탈됐을 수 있다. 최근 아프가니스탄과 이라크 전쟁에서 보여주듯이, 전시 혹은 정치적 격변 동안 물품들이 도난당하고 가장 높은 값을 부르는 응찰자에게 판매되는 것은 특별한 일이 아니다. 예를 들어, 1991년 걸프 전쟁 동안 2000개 이상의 물품들이 이라크 박물관들로부터 약탈당했다; 오직 몇 안 되는 수의 물품들만 되돌아왔다.

장물을 습득하는 것을 피하기 위해, 몇몇 박물관들은—대영 박물관과 시카고의 필드 자연사 박물관—의심스러운 출처를 가진 물품을 받아들이는 것을 예방하는 엄격한 정책들을 채택했다. 그러나 의문스러운 물품을 박물관 수집품에 추가하는 것이 어쩔 수 없이 정당하다고 주장하는 큐레이터들도 있다. 어떤 박물관 큐레이터들은 그것들이 종종 합법적인 원천에서 나온다는 것을 근거로 출처가 불분명한 물품을 받아들이는 결정을 옹호한다. 박물관이 분명 물품의 근거가 분명한 것을 선호하지만, 그러한 증거자료가 항상 있지는 않다. 수 세대 동안, 출처가 없는 많은 물건들이 개인 소장품으로 존재해왔다. 따라서 그들이 마침내 구매 가능한 상태가 되거나 기증될 때, 그들의 정확한 출처는 추적될 수 없다. 다시 말해서, 수백 년 된 문서기록의 부재가 반드시 그 물건이 도난당했음을 의미하진 않는다.

또한 박물관 큐레이터들은 오직 기원이 분명한 물품들만 전시하는 것은 특정 문화와 관련된 물품들을 전시하지 못하게 한다고 주장한다. 예를 들어, 뉴욕의 메트로폴리탄 미술관은 한때 현재의 아프가니스탄에 위치했던 고대 박트리아에 관한 전시를 위해 몇몇 기원이 불분명한 물품들을 사용해야만 했다. 만약 박물관이 출처가 증명된 물품들로만 한정시켰다면 이 특정 문명에 관한 전시는 불완전했을 것이다.

그래서 대다수의 큐레이터들은 기원을 알지 못하는 물품들을 금지하는 것이 박물관들로 하여금 그들의 미션인 인류의 역사에 관한 지식을 전하는 것을 충족시키지 못하게 한다고 판단했다. 불분명한 기원을 가진 물품들을 획득하지 않음으로써, 박물관들은 이러한 물품들이 학자들 혹은 일반 대중은 접할 수 없는 개인 소유로 남게 만드는 것이다. 그로 인해 그 물품들은 과거의 비밀을 드러내도록 사용될 수가 없는 것이다.

MEMO

2S2R

유희태 일반영어
① 기본

PART 02

2S2R 적용

PART 02 2S2R 적용

01 Read the passage and follow the directions.

> On December 1, 1955, an attractive Negro seamstress, Mrs. Rosa Parks, boarded the Cleveland Avenue Bus in downtown Montgomery. She was returning home after her regular day's work in the Montgomery Fair—a leading department store. Tired from long hours on her feet, Mrs. Parks sat down in the first seat behind the section reserved for whites. Not long after she took her seat, the bus operator ordered her, along with three other Negro passengers, to move back in order to accommodate boarding white passengers. By this time every seat in the bus was taken. This meant that if Mrs. Parks followed the driver's command she would have to stand while a white male passenger, who had just boarded the bus, would sit. The other three Negro passengers immediately complied with the driver's request. But Mrs. Parks quietly refuse. The result was her arrest.

MEMO

What is it about Mrs. Park's action that seems so symbolic of the early civil rights movement?

_____

NOTE

Step 1	**S**urvey
Key Words	
Signal Words	
Step 2	**Reading**
Purpose	
Pattern of Organization	
Tone	
Main Idea	
Step 3	**Summary**
지문 요약하기 (Paraphrasing)	
Step 4	**Recite**
	요약문 말로 설명하기

Answer Key

On December 1, 1955, an attractive Negro seamstress, Mrs. Rosa Parks, boarded the Cleveland Avenue Bus in downtown Montgomery. She was returning home after her regular day's work in the Montgomery Fair—a leading department store. Tired from long hours on her feet, Mrs. Parks sat down in the first seat behind the section reserved for whites. Not long after she took her seat, the bus operator ordered her, along with three other Negro passengers, to move back in order to accommodate boarding white passengers. By this time every seat in the bus was taken. This meant that if Mrs. Parks followed the driver's command she would have to stand while a white male passenger, who had just boarded the bus, would sit. The other three Negro passengers immediately complied with the driver's request. But Mrs. Parks quietly refuse. The result was her arrest.

effect

모범답안
It was non-violent, but a strong stand for her rights.

한글번역

1955년 12월 1일, 매력적인 흑인 재봉사인 로사 파크스는 시내 몽고메리에서 클리브랜드 애비뉴 버스를 탔다. 그녀는 몽고메리 페어—잘 나가는 백화점—에서 정규적인 업무를 마치고 집으로 돌아가는 중이었다. 서서 오래 근무한 탓에 피곤한 그녀는 백인을 위한 자리 뒤의 첫 번째 자리에 앉았다. 그녀가 앉은 지 얼마 되지 않아, 버스 기사가 그녀와 다른 세 명의 흑인 승객에게 백인 승객을 태우기 위해 뒤로 이동하라고 명령했다. 이쯤 버스의 모든 좌석이 가득 찼었다. 이것은 그녀가 운전기사의 명령에 따른다면 버스에 방금 탄 백인 남성 승객이 앉는 동안 서 있어야만 한다는 뜻이었다. 다른 세 명의 흑인 승객들은 즉시 기사의 요청에 따랐다. 하지만 그녀는 조용히 거절했다. 결과적으로 그녀는 체포됐다.

NOTE

Step 1	Survey
Key Words	Mrs. Rosa Parks; downtown Montgomery; the bus operator; her arrest
Signal Words	Result
Step 2	**Reading**
Purpose	To describe the result of Mrs. Rosa Parks' resistance
Pattern of Organization	Cause/effect
Tone	Objective; neutral
Main Idea	Mrs. Rosa Parks' refusal to white driver's order to move back to accommodate boarding white passengers caused her arrest.
Step 3	**Summary**
지문 요약하기 (Paraphrasing)	Mrs. Rosa Parks' refusal to white driver's order to move back to accommodate boarding white passengers caused her arrest.
Step 4	**Recite**

요약문 말로 설명하기

02 Read the passage and follow the directions.

The digital revolution caused a lot of… confusion. A clock radio, for example, used to have a face and a slender hand that you'd set pointing to the time you wanted to get up. Nowadays, a clock radio is a formidable machine : programmable to the minute, it can wake you and your mate at different times, let one or both of you "snooze" [and] even activate the coffee maker. But just unplug the thing for a tenth of a second, and you'll be back studying the owner's manual as the display automatically blinks out 12:00—as though time were standing still.

What can you set a digital clock radio to do? Second, what happens in the digital clock radio when it is unplugged?

NOTE

Step 1	**S**urvey
Key Words	
Signal Words	
Step 2	**R**eading
Purpose	
Pattern of Organization	
Tone	
Main Idea	
Step 3	**S**ummary
지문 요약하기 (Paraphrasing)	
Step 4	**R**ecite
	요약문 말로 설명하기

Answer Key

The digital revolution caused a lot of… confusion. A clock radio, for example, used to have a face and a slender hand that you'd set pointing to the time you wanted to get up. Nowadays, a clock radio is a formidable machine : programmable to the minute, it can wake you and your mate at different times, let one or both of you "snooze" [and] even activate the coffee maker. But just unplug the thing for a tenth of a second, and you'll be back studying the owner's manual as the display automatically blinks out 12:00—as though time were standing still.

모범답안

You can set it to wake up you and your mate at different times, snooze (sleep a little longer) and make coffee. longer), set it to the minute, and make coffee. Second, it resets to 12:00 and flashes at that number until set again.

한글번역

　　디지털 혁명은 많은 혼란을 불러왔다. 예를 들어, 예전의 시계 라디오는 눈금판과 원하는 기상 시간을 가리키도록 맞출 수 있는 가느다란 바늘이 달려 있었다. 하지만 오늘날의 시계 라디오는 훨씬 복잡한 기계가 됐다. 분 단위로 설정할 수 있을 뿐 아니라, 부부가 서로 다른 시간에 알람을 맞출 수도 있고, 한쪽 혹은 양쪽 모두가 '스누즈' 기능을 사용할 수도 있으며, 심지어 커피 메이커까지 작동시킬 수 있다. 그러나 전원을 0.1초라도 뽑아버리면, 화면에 자동으로 12:00이 깜빡이며 마치 시간이 멈춘 듯한 상태가 되고, 다시 사용 설명서를 펼쳐야 하는 상황에 직면하게 된다. (기술적으로는 전원을 잠깐만 꺼도 메모리가 지워지고 기본값(12:00)으로 돌아가는 불편함을 풍자적으로 표현한 것이다.)

NOTE

Step 1	Survey
Key Words	The digital revolution; a clock radio; confusion
Signal Words	For example
Step 2	**Reading**
Purpose	To give an example of confusion caused by the digital revolution
Pattern of Organization	Series
Tone	Objective
Main Idea	The digital revolution has brought about problems along with conveniences.
Step 3	**Summary**
지문 요약하기 (Paraphrasing)	The digital revolution has brought about problems along with conveniences. For example, a clock radio was simple to use but the current machine has many options and functions but can be reset easily and require study to setup again.
Step 4	**Recite**
	요약문 말로 설명하기

03 Read the passage below and follow the directions.

They create jobs, not destroy them. Immigrants from up and down the wealth scale have proved to be incredibly entrepreneurial. Many technologically savvy immigrants from Western Europe and India helped create thousands of jobs in Silicon Valley. One in six of these companies were started by immigrants. Many of America's best scientists, economists and engineers are not originally from Kentucky or Florida or Maine. They are from Beijing, Moscow and Bangalore. This reality is because American kids can't do math and science, so Microsoft and Google have had to find these geniuses somewhere else. Poorer immigrants have created thousands of restaurants, retail shops and other service-based companies. One visit to San Francisco, New York or Chicago will show you how many native-born Americans are earning a paycheck because of the incredible efforts immigrants have put into our quasi-capitalistic market. Immigrants without money and business plans have filled jobs in meat packing, textiles, lawn care and restaurants that Americans simply won't take. Sadly, it is beneath the dignity of the average American to pick onions or cut fat off a pig 10 hours per day. Who is supposed to fill this gap? Immigrants have also helped keep our rate of inflation down by supplying valuable labor in areas where shortages would otherwise exist. Imagine what the price of housing or restaurant meals would be if not for immigrant roofers and dishwashers with tremendous work ethics. We can also thank immigrants for having lower crime rates, higher graduation rates and lower participation in the welfare state than native-born Americans. Routinely, immigrants from the Caribbean show up, look around and find opportunity where many native-born Americans look around and give up on the chance to advance over time. If I were president of the United States, I would fly to New York and read the plaque on the Statue of Liberty. Then, I would go on television and announce to my fellow Americans that every one of us is a descendant of someone who originally was not from here. I might also mention that <u>if we want to help India and China pass us up in the economic superpower game, the surest way of achieving that is to keep immigrants from those nations out.</u>

Explain what the underlined "if we want to help India and China pass us up in the economic superpower game, the surest way of achieving that is to keep immigrants from those nations out" means.

NOTE

Step 1	**S**urvey
Key Words	
Signal Words	
Step 2	**R**eading
Purpose	
Pattern of Organization	
Tone	
Main Idea	
Step 3	**S**ummary
지문 요약하기 (Paraphrasing)	
Step 4	**R**ecite
	요약문 말로 설명하기

Answer Key

They create jobs, not destroy them. Immigrants from up and down the wealth scale have proved to be incredibly entrepreneurial. Many technologically savvy **immigrants** from Western Europe and India helped create thousands of jobs in Silicon Valley. One in six of these companies were started by **immigrants**. Many of America's **best scientists, economists and engineers** are not originally from Kentucky or Florida or Maine. They are from Beijing, Moscow and Bangalore. This reality is because American kids can't do math and science, so Microsoft and Google have had to find **these geniuses** somewhere else. **Poorer immigrants** have created thousands of restaurants, retail shops and other service-based companies. One visit to San Francisco, New York or Chicago will show you how many native-born Americans are earning a paycheck because of the incredible efforts immigrants have put into our quasi-capitalistic market. **Immigrants without money and business plans** have filled jobs in meat packing, textiles, lawn care and restaurants that Americans simply won't take. Sadly, it is beneath the dignity of the average American to pick onions or cut fat off a pig 10 hours per day. Who is supposed to fill this gap? **Immigrants** have also helped keep our rate of inflation down by supplying valuable labor in areas where shortages would otherwise exist. Imagine what the price of housing or restaurant meals would be if not for immigrant roofers and dishwashers with tremendous work ethics. We can also thank immigrants for having lower crime rates, higher graduation rates and lower participation in the welfare state than native-born Americans. Routinely, **immigrant**s from the Caribbean show up, look around and find opportunity where many native-born Americans look around and give up on the chance to advance over time. If I were president of the United States, I would fly to New York and read the plaque on the Statue of Liberty. Then, I would go on television and announce to my fellow Americans that every one of us is a **descendant of someone who originally was not from here**. I might also mention that if we want to help India and China pass us up in the economic superpower game, the surest way of achieving that is to keep immigrants from those nations out.

key words

①

②

③

③-1

③-2

tone : critical / cynical

모범답안

The writer uses irony to argue that blocking immigrants from India and China would weaken America's economic competitiveness while strengthening these nations' positions as global economic powers. 또는 It means that preventing talented immigrants from India and China from entering the US would weaken America's economic power while strengthening these rival nations.

한글번역

　　그들은 일자리를 창출하지, 파괴하지는 않는다. 높은 규모의 부에서부터 낮은 규모의 부를 가진 이민자들은 믿을 수 없을 정도로 기업가적임을 증명해왔다. 서유럽과 인도로부터 온 기술적으로 요령 있는 많은 이민자들이 실리콘 밸리에서 수천 개의 일자리 창출을 도왔다. 이 회사들의 6곳 중 한 곳은 이민자들에 의해서 시작됐다. 많은 미국 최고의 과학자, 경제학자, 공학자들 중 많은 이들이 원래 켄터키나 플로리다 혹은 메인 출신이 아니다. 그들은 베이징, 모스크바, 그리고 방갈로르 출신이다. 이러한 현실은 미국 아이들이 수학과 과학을 잘하지 못한 데에서 비롯됐고, 그래서 마이크로소프트와 구글은 이러한 천재들을 그 밖의 다른 곳에서 찾아야만 했다. 더 가난한 이민자들은 수천개의 식당, 소매점, 그리고 다른 서비스 기반 회사들을 만들어냈다. 샌프란시스코, 뉴욕 혹은 시카고에 한 번 방문해보면 이민자들이 우리의 준-자본시장에 쏟고 있는 엄청난 노력 덕분에 얼마나 많은 미국 토박이들이 자금을 회수하고 있는지 보여줄 것이다. 돈과 사업 계획이 없는 이민자들은 육류 포장, 섬유업, 잔디 관리, 미국인들이 그냥 받아들이지 않을 식당에서 일자리를 채우고 있다. 슬프게도, 하루에 10시간 동안 양파를 깎거나 돼지의 지방을 잘라내는 것은 평균적인 미국인들의 존엄성 아래에 있는 일이다. 누가 이러한 공백을 채워야만 할까? 이민자들은 또한 그렇지 않으면 노동력이 부족했을 곳에 값비싼 노동력을 제공함으로써 인플레이션을 낮추는 데 기여했다. 만약 엄청난 노동관을 가진 이민자 지붕 수리공과 설거지 담당자가 없었다면 주택과 식당 음식의 값이 얼마나 될지 상상해보라. 우리는 또한 이민자들의 낮은 범죄율과 높은 졸업률, 미국 토박이보다 낮은 사회 복지 제도 참여율에 대해 고마워할 수 있다. 관례적으로 카리브해 지역 출신 이민자들은 미국 토박이들이 둘러보고 포기했던 곳에 나타나서 둘러보고 여러 기간에 걸쳐 발전할 기회를 탐색했다. 만약 내가 미국의 대통령이라면, 나는 뉴욕으로 가, 자유의 여신상의 명판을 읽을 것이다. 그 후 방송에 나가 미국인 동료들에게 우리 모두는 원래 이곳 출신이 아닌 누군가의 후손이라고 알릴 것이다. 나는 또한 만약 우리가 인도와 중국이 경제적 초강대국 시합에서 우리를 이기도록 돕고자 한다면, 이를 이룰 수 있는 가장 확실한 방법은 그 나라 출신의 이민자들을 들이지 않는 것이라고 말할 것이다.

NOTE

Step 1	Ⓢurvey
Key Words	Immigrants
Signal Words	Also
Step 2	**Ⓡeading**
Purpose	To inform general people of the advantages immigrants provide
Pattern of Organization	Series
Tone	Persuasive
Main Idea	Immigrants provide many benefits to Americans and should be valued.
Step 3	**Ⓢummary**
지문 요약하기 (Paraphrasing)	Immigrants provide many benefits to Americans and should be valued. Immigrants with talents in math and sciences that Americans don't have created companies, jobs, and provided much needed expertise while poor immigrants generated service-sector jobs. Likewise, immigrants take on hard labor that Americans otherwise wouldn't do, to the benefit of the economy. For these reasons, they should be valued for the continued success of America.
Step 4	**Ⓡecite**
	요약문 말로 설명하기

04 Read the passage and follow the directions.

In the natural regime, budworm epidemics besiege the Maine woods every thirty to fifty years. Left to run its course, an outbreak kills some 40 percent of the fir and the red and white spruce in its path. Then the moths subside. Spraying the woods with insecticides began in the 1950s and has continued intermittently. Chemicals have prevented a lot of damage, but in doing so they have also kept alive enough forage for the budworm population to remain at the verge of an outbreak more widespread and virulent than if there had been no spraying. In this way, spraying has made more spraying inevitable. Insecticides now represent the only barrier against truly catastrophic losses of Maine's spruce and fir, but spraying cannot prevent substantial losses. The budworm has already eaten its way through large sections of spruce and fir. In the worst areas, evergreen canopies now stand all gray and powdery. For a time, industries in the Maine woods will have at their disposal more dead and dying trees than they can use, and then, probably, a time will come when there will be less of the right kinds of wood in the forest that the various mills are designed to handle. For the Maine woods, there seems to be no way around the _____ that won't have unpleasant consequences, both economic and environmental.

*forage : food
*virulent : severely destructive

Fill in the blank with the ONE most appropriate word from the passage.

NOTE

Step 1	**S**urvey
Key Words	
Signal Words	
Step 2	**R**eading
Purpose	
Pattern of Organization	
Tone	
Main Idea	
Step 3	**S**ummary
지문 요약하기 (Paraphrasing)	
Step 4	**R**ecite
	요약문 말로 설명하기

Answer Key

In the natural regime, **budworm epidemics** besiege **the Maine woods** every thirty to fifty years. Left to run its course, an outbreak kills some 40 percent of the fir and the red and white spruce in its path. Then the moths subside. **Spraying** the woods with **insecticides** began in the 1950s and has continued intermittently. **Chemicals** have prevented a lot of damage, but **in doing so** they have also kept alive enough forage for the budworm population to remain at the verge of an outbreak more widespread and virulent than if there had been no spraying. In this way, **spraying** has made more spraying inevitable. **Insecticides** now represent the only barrier against truly catastrophic losses of Maine's spruce and fir, but spraying cannot prevent substantial losses. **The budworm** has already eaten its way through large sections of spruce and fir. In the worst areas, evergreen canopies now stand all gray and powdery. For a time, industries in the Maine woods will have at their disposal more dead and dying trees than they can use, and then, probably, a time will come when there will be less of the right kinds of wood in the forest that the various mills are designed to handle. **For the Maine woods, there seems to be no way around the budworm that won't have unpleasant consequences, both economic and environmental.**

→ key words

모범답안
budworm

한글번역

자연 지역에서, budworm(나방의 애벌레)의 급속한 확산은 매 30년에서 50년 마다 메인주의 산림을 황폐화시킨다. 그러는 동안, 그 발병은 40%의 전나무와 빨간색과 흰색의 가문비나무를 죽인다. 그리고 나방의 무리가 줄어든다. 1950년대에 나무들에 살충제를 뿌리기 시작했고 이는 간헐적으로 지속됐다. 화학물질은 많은 손상을 예방했지만, 그로 인해 간신히 존재했던 나방의 애벌레 개체군이 생존할 수 있을 만큼의 먹을 것이 남겨졌고, 이는 살충제를 뿌리지 않았을 때보다 나방의 애벌레 발병을 더 넓고 활발하게 만들었다. 이렇게 살충제를 뿌리는 것은 더 많은 살충제를 뿌리는 것을 불가피하게 만들었다. 살충제는 이제 재앙적인 메인주의 가문비나무와 전나무 손실을 막을 유일한 방패이지만, 살충제를 뿌리는 것은 상당한 손실을 예방할 수 없다. 나방의 애벌레는 이미 넓은 범위의 가문비나무와 전나무를 먹어 치웠다. 제일 심하게 당한 지역에서는, 상록수들이 모두 회색과 먼지투성이가 된 채로 남아 있다. 얼마 동안, 메인주의 산림에서 활동하는 사업체들에서는 그들이 사용할 수 있는 것보다 더 많은 죽은 나무들을 처리해야 할 것이고, 아마도—그 지역의 제재소들이 처리할 수 있는 나무의 종류가 숲에서 부족할 시기가 올 것이다. 메인주의 산림은, 경제와 환경적인 모든 측면에서 나방의 애벌레과 관련된 유쾌하지 않은 결과가 없을 방법은 없을 것으로 보인다.

NOTE

Step 1	Survey
Key Words	Budworm epidemic; outbreak; insecticide; spraying
Signal Words	Not clear
Step 2	**Reading**
Purpose	To explain why simply spraying insecticides to kill the budworms is ultimately ineffective 또는 To point out how "controlled" insects in the end do more damage than if they had been left alone
Pattern of Organization	Cause/effect
Tone	Objective; analytical
Main Idea	Insecticides, which have been used since the 1950s to prevent budworm epidemics in the woods of Maine, seem to be leading to negative economic and environmental results.
Step 3	**Summary**
지문 요약하기 (Paraphrasing)	Insecticides, which have been used since the 1950s to prevent budworm epidemics in the woods of Maine, seem to be leading to negative economic and environmental results. While natural cycles kill 40% of certain trees every 30-50 years, chemical intervention has created a dependency that may trigger worse outbreaks, leaving the forest's future increasingly uncertain.
Step 4	**Recite**
	요약문 말로 설명하기

05 Read the passage and follow the directions.

We did it. With less than two months to go until our second child is scheduled to arrive, my husband and I swallowed our pride, plundered our savings and joined the much ridiculed ranks of minivan owners. It had to be done. Neither of our old vehicles had what it takes to handle two car seats, two parents, the odd grandparent and the sheer tonnage of baby paraphernalia required for even quick trips to the grocery. Still, it took multiple visits to the dealership before I came to terms with the sociological enormity of what we were about to do. In America, you are what you drive. And as everyone knows, cruising around in a shiny new minivan definitively announces to your fellow road warriors, "I am an unabashed suburban breeder."

MEMO

What is it that the writer and her husband did? What was the cause that made the writer and her husband take the action they did? Why do you think the writer resisted doing what she and her husband eventually did? What does the writer mean by "The sociological enormity" of what they did?

_____
_____
_____
_____

NOTE

Step 1	**S**urvey
Key Words	
Signal Words	
Step 2	**R**eading
Purpose	
Pattern of Organization	
Tone	
Main Idea	
Step 3	**S**ummary
지문 요약하기 (Paraphrasing)	
Step 4	**R**ecite
	요약문 말로 설명하기

Answer Key

　　We did it. With less than two months to go until our second child is scheduled to arrive, my husband and I swallowed our pride, plundered our savings and joined the much ridiculed ranks of minivan owners. It had to be done. Neither of our old vehicles had what it takes to handle two car seats, two parents, the odd grandparent and the sheer tonnage of baby paraphernalia required for even quick trips to the grocery. Still, it took multiple visits to the dealership before I came to terms with the sociological enormity of what we were about to do. In America, you are what you drive. And as everyone knows, cruising around in a shiny **new minivan** definitively announces to your fellow road warriors, "I am an unabashed **suburban breeder**."

→ key words

모범답안

They purchased a minivan. The practical necessity of the vehicle is to handle two children and their paraphernalia. The minivan is a cultural signal of a "suburban breeder" which they did not want to be seen in. By buying one, they are branding themselves with a new kind of identity.

한글번역

　　우리는 해냈다. 둘째 아이가 태어날 때까지 두 달도 안 남은 상황에서 내 남편과 난 자존심을 굽히고, 저축한 것을 다 사용해 미니밴을 끄는 사람으로서 놀림 당하는 지위에 합류했다. 그래야만 했다. 우리의 예전 차 중 그 어떤 것도 두 개의 카시트와 두 명의 부모, 한 명의 조부모와, 잠깐 식료품을 사러 나갈 때조차 필요한 많은 양의 아기 용품들을 실을 수 없었다. 그러나, 우리가 하려는 일의 사회적인 심각성을 받아들이기까지 그 자동차 딜러샵을 여러 번 왔다 갔다 해야 했다. 미국에서, 당신이 운전하는 것이 당신을 의미한다. 그리고 모든 이들이 알고 있듯이, 빛나는 새 미니밴을 타고 일주를 하는 것은 당연히 너의 친구 도로용사들에게 "나는 부끄러움을 모르는 시골의 애 키우는 사람이다."라고 공표하는 것이다.

NOTE

Step 1	Ⓢurvey
Key Words	New minivan; suburban breeder
Signal Words	None
Step 2	**Ⓡeading**
Purpose	To explain why the narrator bought a new minivan
Pattern of Organization	Cause/effect
Tone	Subjective; humorous
Main Idea	The demands of a growing family led the narrator to buy a minivan. 또는 The practical necessity of the vehicle led the narrator to buy a minivan.
Step 3	**Ⓢummary**
지문 요약하기 (Paraphrasing)	The practical necessity of the vehicle to handle two children, their parents, the grandparent, and paraphernalia caused the narrator to buy a minivan, which she and her husband had refused.
Step 4	**Ⓡecite**
	요약문 말로 설명하기

06 Read the passage and follow the directions.

Being unemployed creates many problems for my family and me. First of all, there are financial problems. We have cut back on the quality of groceries we purchase. We now buy two pounds of hamburger in place of two pounds of sirloin. This hamburger is also divided into quantities sufficient for three meals: one may be creole beef, one chili, and the other spaghetti. There is also less money for clothing. Dresses must be altered and made into blouses; pants make nice skirts after some alteration. I have two more very sticky problems. I've fallen behind in the rental payments for our apartment, and now I am experiencing difficulties trying to pay the back rent. The other sticky problem is my son's tuition payments. There does not seem to be any way that I can send a complete payment to his college. These are not the only problems I face. I also have psychological problems as a result of unemployment. Often I wonder why this has happened to me. Then depression and confusion take over, and I feel drained of all my abilities. The one question that fills my mind most often is the following: Why can't I get employment? This question evokes in me a lack of self-confidence and self-worth. I am haunted by an overall feeling of uselessness. My other problems center on trying to cope with the bureaucracy of the Employment Bureau. Once I get to the Employment Bureau, I stand in line to sign up. I then wait in another line to which I must report. Once I go through all of this, I am sent out for job interviews, only to find that the employer wants someone with more experience. To top everything off, I had to wait almost six months to receive my first unemployment check. As you can see, there is often a frustratingly long delay in receiving benefits. My family and I have suffered through many problems because of my unemployment.

What makes the writer feel "drained" of her abilities? What is the main idea of the passage?

_____
_____
_____

NOTE

Step 1	**S**urvey
Key Words	
Signal Words	
Step 2	**R**eading
Purpose	
Pattern of Organization	
Tone	
Main Idea	
Step 3	**S**ummary
지문 요약하기 (Paraphrasing)	
Step 4	**R**ecite
	요약문 말로 설명하기

Answer Key

> **Being unemployed** creates many **problems** for my family and me. First of all, there are **financial** problems. We have cut back on the quality of groceries we purchase. We now buy two pounds of hamburger in place of two pounds of sirloin. This hamburger is also divided into quantities sufficient for three meals: one may be creole beef, one chili, and the other spaghetti. There is also less money for clothing. Dresses must be altered and made into blouses; pants make nice skirts after some alteration. I have two more very sticky problems. I've fallen behind in the rental payments for our apartment, and now I am experiencing difficulties trying to pay the back rent. The other sticky problem is my son's tuition payments. There does not seem to be any way that I can send a complete payment to his college. These are not the only problems I face. I also have psychological problems as a result of unemployment. Often I wonder why this has happened to me. Then depression and confusion take over, and I feel drained of all my abilities. The one question that fills my mind most often is the following: Why can't I get employment? This question evokes in me a lack of self-confidence and self-worth. I am haunted by an overall feeling of uselessness. My other problems center on trying to cope with the **bureaucracy** of the Employment Bureau. Once I get to the Employment Bureau, I stand in line to sign up. I then wait in another line to which I must report. Once I go through all of this, I am sent out for job interviews, only to find that the employer wants someone with more experience. To top everything off, I had to wait almost six months to receive my first unemployment check. As you can see, there is often a frustratingly long delay in receiving benefits. My family and I have suffered through many problems because of my unemployment.

→ key words

모범답안

Depression and confusion, which is caused by doubt as a result of not being able to get a job. The main idea is that the speaker and her family have had many problems because of her unemployment.

한글번역

실직 상태에 있는 것은 나와 내 가족에게 많은 문제점을 안겨준다. 우선, 경제적인 어려움이다. 우리 집은 구입하는 식료품의 질을 낮춰야 했다. 우리는 2파운드 분량의 소 등심 대신 이제 2파운드의 햄버거용 고기를 사고 있다. 이 햄버거용 고기는 다시 세 끼에 맞는 양으로 나눈다: 한 끼는 크리올 소고기, 다른 끼니는 칠리, 또 다른 끼니는 스파게티일지도 모른다. 옷에 쓰이는 돈도 더 줄었다. 드레스는 수선해 블라우스로 만들어 입는다; 바지는 조금만 수선하면 멋진 스커트가 된다. 나에겐 매우 곤란한 문제가 두 가지 더 있다. 우리 아파트 임대 비용이 밀린 상태이고, 이것을 갚는 데 어려움을 겪고 있다. 또 다른 힘든 문제는 아들의 학비 문제이다. 아들의 대학교 학비를 완납할 방법이 없어 보인다. 내가 겪는 것은 이 문제들뿐만이 아니다. 난 실직의 영향으로 정신적 문제도 겪고 있다. 종종 왜 이런 일이 내게 일어났는지 궁금하다. 그러면 우울과 혼란이 날 덮치고 내 모든 능력이 소진된 것처럼 느낀다. 가끔 내 마음을 사로잡고 있는 한 가지 의문은 다음과 같다: 왜 나는 직업을 구할 수 없을까? 이 질문은 내게 자신감과 자부심 결여를 불러일으킨다. 내 자신이 무능한 존재라는 전반적인 생각이 나를 괴롭혔다. 나의 또 다른 문제는 고용관리국의 관리들을 상대하는 데 있다. 일단 고용관리국에 가면, 나는 등록하기 위해 줄을 선다. 그 다음 신고하기 위해 다른 줄에 서야 한다. 이 모든 것을 끝마치고 나면, 나는 구직 인터뷰를 하러 보내지는데, 고용주는 나보다 경험이 더 많은 다른 이를 원한다는 사실을 발견하게 될 뿐이다. 다른 것들은 제쳐두고, 나는 첫 실직 수당을 받는 데 거의 6개월을 기다려야 했다. 여러분도 알다시피, 혜택을 받는 데는 종종 절망스러울 정도로 긴 기다림이 필요하다. 나와 나의 가족은 내 실직으로 인해 많은 고초를 겪었다.

NOTE

Step 1	**S**urvey
Key Words	Being unemployed; problems; financial; psychological; bureaucracy
Signal Words	Creates; First of all; also; as a result of; other problems; because of
Step 2	**R**eading
Purpose	To explain how unemployment creates many problems
Pattern of Organization	Cause/effect; series
Tone	Critical; angry
Main Idea	The narrator and her family have had many problems due to her unemployment.
Step 3	**S**ummary
지문 요약하기 (Paraphrasing)	The narrator's unemployment causes a lot of problems for the narrator and her family. First, it creates financial problems such as curtailment of the quality of groceries, less money for clothing, difficulties of rental payment and tuition. Second, the narrator suffers from psychological problems such as depression and confusion. Finally, the bureaucracy of government makes the narrator frustrated.
Step 4	**R**ecite
	요약문 말로 설명하기

07 Read the passage and follow the directions.

Over the years Halloween has shown an enduring malleability and a terrierlike tenacity to survive religious persecution, class prejudice, Victorian politesse, and consumerist inflation. Still, all the adaptability and advertising and marketing in the world couldn't keep Halloween alive if Americans weren't yearning for what it has to offer. Candy Day, energetically touted in the early part of the twentieth century, never sent the nation out to buy boxes of sweets for loved ones on the second Saturday in October. Why have Americans, so admirably skeptical and adamantly opposed to adopting other holidays, taken to their hearts this originally scary, often silly festival? Many say it reminds them of their childhood, which baby boomers are notoriously reluctant to relinquish. And maybe it reminds some others of the childhood they wish they'd had. Since people don't go home for Halloween as they do for Thanksgiving and Christmas, there is less likelihood of parental disappointment, sibling squabbles, free-floating depression, and the other symptoms of the disquiet we are told afflict America's families. Moreover, though recently cornered by adults, Halloween is still identified with children, and while our society may quarrel over the expensive realities of raising children, like health care and education, it cherishes the idea of childhood. But perhaps the greatest attraction of the holiday is that it no longer has any reason for being. It is not a night to worship the God of our choice, honor the dead, celebrate the nation's past, take stock for the future, or woo a loved one. It is simply an occasion for fun. Costumes camouflage identity, blur status, and change gender. Men can be women, children adults, milquetoasts heroes, good girls bad, devils saints, and vice versa.

What is the main purpose of the passage? Write your answer in 5 words or so.

To discuss _____

NOTE

Step 1	ⓢurvey
Key Words	
Signal Words	
Step 2	**ⓡeading**
Purpose	
Pattern of Organization	
Tone	
Main Idea	
Step 3	**ⓢummary**
지문 요약하기 (Paraphrasing)	
Step 4	**ⓡecite**
	요약문 말로 설명하기

Answer Key

Over the years **Halloween** has shown an enduring malleability and a terrierlike tenacity to survive religious persecution, class prejudice, Victorian politesse, and consumerist inflation. **Still**, all the adaptability and advertising and marketing in the world couldn't keep **Halloween alive if Americans weren't yearning for what it has to offer**. Candy Day, energetically touted in the early part of the twentieth century, never sent the nation out to buy boxes of sweets for loved ones on the second Saturday in October. **Why have Americans, so admirably skeptical and adamantly opposed to adopting other holidays, taken to their hearts this originally scary, often silly festival?** Many say it reminds them of their childhood, which baby boomers are notoriously reluctant to relinquish. And maybe it reminds some others of the childhood they wish they'd had. **Since** people don't go home for Halloween as they do for Thanksgiving and Christmas, there is less likelihood of parental disappointment, sibling squabbles, free-floating depression, and the other symptoms of the disquiet we are told afflicts America's families. **Moreover**, though recently cornered by adults, Halloween is still identified with children, and while our society may quarrel over the expensive realities of raising children, like health care and education, it cherishes the idea of childhood. **But** perhaps the greatest attraction of the holiday is that it no longer has any reason for being. It is not a night to worship the God of our choice, honor the dead, celebrate the nation's past, take stock for the future, or woo a loved one. **It is simply an occasion for fun**. Costumes camouflage identity, blur status, and change gender. Men can be women, children adults, milquetoasts heroes, good girls bad, devils saints, and vice versa.

→ key word

question

answers
①

②

③

④

모범답안

the enduring popularity of Halloween

어휘

corner (시장을) 장악하다; 몰아넣다
free-floating 걷잡을 수 없는
milquetoasts ≪미≫ 대가 약한 남자[사람], 변변치 못한 남자
over the years 수년간, 오랜 세월 동안
relinquish 포기 · 단념하다
take ~ to one's heart ~를 따뜻이 맞이하다
tenacity 끈질김; 강인함
woo 구애하다

disquiet 불안
malleability 유연성; 순응성
politesse (특히 형식적으로) 예의 바름, 품위 있음
squabble 옥신각신, 아웅다웅(하다)
take stock ~을 고려하다; 자세히 조사하다
terrierlike (사냥개) 테리어처럼

한글번역

오랜 세월 동안 할로윈은 지속적인 적응력과 테리어(사냥개) 같은 끈질김을 보여주며 종교적 박해, 계층 편견, 빅토리아 시대의 품위와 걷잡을 수 없는 소비자중심주의를 견뎌냈다. 하지만, 할로윈이 주는 것을 갈망하는 미국인들이 없었더라면, 그 모든 적응력, 세상의 광고와 마케팅만으로는 할로윈을 살아남게 하지는 못했을 것이다. 20세기 초반 열심히 홍보됐던 '사탕 주고 받는 날'(10월 둘째 주 토요일-할로윈 이전의 사탕에 관한 공휴일)에 사람들은 더 이상 사랑하는 사람들을 위해 사탕을 사러 나가지 않았다. 왜 미국인들은 다른 공휴일을 받아들일 때는 너무나 회의적이고 강하게 반대하면서, 원래는 무섭고 가끔은 바보 같은 이 축제를 따뜻하게 맞이해왔는가? 많은 이들은 할로윈이 베이비 붐 세대 사람들이 포기하기 꺼렸던 그들의 어린 시절을 떠올리게 한다고 말한다. 또한 어떤 이에게는 그들이 이랬으면 하고 소망했던 어린 시절을 떠올리게 할 수도 있다. 사람들은 추수감사절이나 크리스마스에 집에 가는 것처럼, 할로윈에는 집에 가지 않기 때문에, 부모의 실망, 형제자매 간의 말다툼, 걷잡을 수 없는 우울함과 미국 가정을 위협하는 다른 불안의 징후들이 덜할 가능성이 있다. 게다가, 비록 최근에는 성인들에 의해 시장이 장악됐지만, 할로윈은 여전히 아이들과 동일시된다. 우리 사회가 의료 서비스나 교육과 같이 아이들을 양육하는 값비싼 현실에 언쟁을 높이는 동안에도, 할로윈은 어린시절이라는 아이디어를 소중히 여긴다. 그러나 할로윈의 가장 큰 매력은 존재를 위한 어떤 이유도 가지고 있지 않다는 것이다. 할로윈은 우리가 선택한 신을 숭배하거나, 죽은 사람을 기리거나, 국가의 과거를 찬양하거나, 미래를 고려하거나, 사랑하는 사람에게 구애를 하는 밤이 아니다. 할로윈은 단지 재미를 위한 날이다. 할로윈 의상은 자신의 정체를 위장하고, 신분을 흐릿하게 하며, 성을 바꾼다. 남자는 여자가, 아이는 어른이, 겁쟁이는 영웅이, 착한 소녀가 나쁜 소녀로, 악마가 성인이 될 수 있으며 그 반대도 마찬가지다.

NOTE

Step 1	ⓢurvey
Key Words	Halloween; enduring
Signal Words	Why; since; moreover; reason
Step 2	**ⓡeading**
Purpose	To discuss the reasons for the enduring popularity of Halloween in America
Pattern of Organization	Cause/effect; question/answer
Tone	Neutral
Main Idea	There are several reasons why Americans have loved Halloween for a long time.
Step 3	**ⓢummary**
지문 요약하기 (Paraphrasing)	Halloween has retained its mass appeal through many years in America for the following reasons: it reminds people of childhood; it doesn't induce conflict between family members; it celebrate childhood; and it is fun.
Step 4	**ⓡecite**
	요약문 말로 설명하기

08 Read the passage and follow the directions.

If you want to get a sense of how pervasive corporate influence in U.S. education is, just take a tour of your neighborhood school. Enter the cafeteria and you'll probably find wrappers from Taco Bell, Arby's, and Subway, fast food chains that provide school lunches. The third grade class may be learning math by counting Tootsie Rolls. Science curricula might well come from Dow Chemical, Dupont, or Exxon. It doesn't end there. Education in the U.S. has become big business. The 'education industry', a term coined by EduVentures, an investment banking firm, is estimated to be worth between $630 and $680 billion in the U.S. The stock value of publicly traded educational companies is growing twice as fast as the Dow Jones Average. Brokerage firms like Lehman Brothers and Montgomery Securities have specialists seeking out venture capital for the _____.

Analysts at the conservative think tanks, like the Heritage Foundation, Hudson and Pioneer Institutes, tell us that the problems in education stem from inefficient, bloated school bureaucracies. Conservatives talk about 'school choice,' referring to vouchers and other public/private schemes. Free marketeers strike a chord with many parents when they point out that families do not have the choices they deserve, especially in urban school districts.

However, according to progressive school activists, the problems in education have their roots on decades of unequal school funding. They say that as long as school districts are financed through property taxes, kids in poor, urban districts will never receive an equal education with suburban school kids. Wide disparities in school resources open the door for corporations to fill the gap (and their pockets), especially in inner city schools.

2S2R 기본

Fill in the blank with the TWO most appropriate consecutive words from the passage. Second, explain the main reason that prevents inner city students from getting an equal education.

_____

_____

_____

NOTE

Step 1	**S**urvey
Key Words	
Signal Words	
Step 2	**R**eading
Purpose	
Pattern of Organization	
Tone	
Main Idea	
Step 3	**S**ummary
지문 요약하기 (Paraphrasing)	
Step 4	**R**ecite
	요약문 말로 설명하기

Part 02 2S2R 적용 147

Answer Key

If you want to get a sense of **how pervasive corporate influence in U.S. education is**, just take a tour of your neighborhood school. Enter the cafeteria and you'll probably find wrappers from Taco Bell, Arby's, and Subway, fast food chains that provide school lunches. The third grade class may be learning math by counting Tootsie Rolls. Science curricula might well come from Dow Chemical, Dupont, or Exxon. It doesn't end there. **Education in the U.S. has become big business.** The **'education industry'**, a term coined by EduVentures, an investment banking firm, is estimated to be worth between $630 and $680 billion in the U.S. The stock value of publicly traded educational companies is growing twice as fast as the Dow Jones Average. Brokerage firms like Lehman Brothers and Montgomery Securities have specialists seeking out venture capital for the education industry.

Analysts at the **conservative** think tanks, like the Heritage Foundation, Hudson and Pioneer Institutes, tell us that the **problems in education** stem from inefficient, bloated school bureaucracies. **Conservatives** talk about 'school choice,' referring to vouchers and other public/private schemes. **Free marketeers** strike a chord with many parents when they point out that families do not have the choices they deserve, especially in urban school districts.

However, according to **progressive school activists**, the **problems in education** have **their roots** on decades of **unequal** school funding. They say that as long as school districts are financed through property taxes, kids in poor, urban districts will never receive an equal education with suburban school kids. **Wide disparities in school resources open the door for corporations to fill the gap (and their pockets), especially in inner city schools.**

— key words

— key words

→ signal word

모범답안

The words are "education industry". Second, Inner city students cannot receive an equal education primarily because of the school funding system based on property taxes. (Since property values are lower in poor urban districts, these schools receive significantly less funding compared to suburban schools, creating wide disparities in educational resources.)

> **어휘**
>
> **brokerage firm** 종합 증권회사(투자 은행업, 주식 매매 중개, 투자 운용 등 증권 업무 전반을 취급한다.)
> **voucher** 쿠폰(바우처 제도란 정부가 수요자에게 쿠폰을 지급하여 원하는 공급자를 선택하도록 하고, 공급자가 수요자로부터 받은 쿠폰을 제시하면 정부가 재정을 지원하는 방식을 말하는데, 이때 지급되는 쿠폰을 바우처라고 한다. 일종의 상품이나 서비스를 구매할 수 있는 증서와 같다.)
> **wrapper** 포장지

> **한글번역**
>
> 만약 미국 교육계에 기업의 영향이 얼마나 널리 퍼져있는지 알고 싶다면, 동네에 있는 학교를 한번 둘러보면 된다. 학교 카페테리아에 들어서면 아마도 타코벨이나 아비스, 서브웨이와 같은 학교에 점심을 제공하는 패스트푸드 업체의 포장지를 발견할 것이다. 3학년 학급에서는 아마도 Tootsie Roll을 세며 수학을 배우고 있을 것이다. 과학 교과 과정들은 다우 케미컬이나 듀퐁 또는 엑손에서 제공받았을 것이다. 하지만 여기서 그치지 않는다. 미국에서의 교육은 거대한 사업이 돼가고 있다. '교육산업'이라는 용어는 EduVentures라는 투자은행에 의해 고민된 용어로, 이 교육산업은 미국에서 6300~6800억 달러의 가치가 있는 것으로 추정된다. 상장된 교육기업의 주가는 다우존스 평균보다 2배나 빠르게 성장하고 있다. 리먼 브라더스나 몽고메리 시큐리티스 같은 증권회사들은 교육산업을 위한 투기자본을 찾아내기 위한 전문가들까지 두고 있는 실정이다.
>
> 헤리티지 재단과 허드슨 인스티튜트, 그리고 파이오니아 인스티튜트 같은 보수파 두뇌집단의 애널리스트들은 교육계의 문제들이 비효율적이고 지나치게 비대한 학교 관료주의에서 비롯된다고 말한다. 보수주의자들은 '학교 선택권'에 대해 주장한다. 이는 바우처나 그 밖의 정부나 민간 프로그램을 지칭한다. 자유 시장 경제 옹호자들은 응당 있어야 할 학교 선택권이 특히 도심지역의 학군에 없다는 사실을 지적해 많은 부모들의 공감을 얻고 있다.
>
> 하지만 진보적인 학교 운동가들에 따르면, 교육계의 문제는 수십 년 동안 지속된 불공평한 학교의 운영자금 제공 방식에 뿌리를 두고 있다. 그들은 학군이 재산세를 통해 지원되는 한 도시 빈민가의 가난한 아이들이 교외지역의 아이들과 동등한 교육을 받을 수는 없을 것이라고 말한다. 학교 재정의 극심한 격차가 기업들에게 격차를 줄이기 위한 (그리고 기업들의 주머니를 채우기 위한) 문을 열어주도록 했으며, 특히 도심 빈민가의 학교에서 이런 상황이 심각한 실정이다.

NOTE

Step 1	Survey
Key Words	Corporate influence; education industry; unequal school funding
Signal Words	Stem from; their roots; However

Step 2	Reading
Purpose	To explain concerns about the presence of corporations in schools and the causes for their presence
Pattern of Organization	Cause/effect; contrast
Tone	Critical
Main Idea	The problems in education come from corporate influence as a result of unequal funding.

Step 3	Summary
지문 요약하기 (Paraphrasing)	The problems in education come from corporate influence as a result of unequal funding. Conservative criticism cites bad organization and points out options available for parents, which free marketeers believe aren't plentiful. On the other hand, progressive activists argue that the unfair history of funding creates a wealth gap that corporations are taking advantage of.

Step 4	Recite
	요약문 말로 설명하기

MEMO

09 Read the passage and follow the directions.

Why do people value gold and precious stones? Not simply because of their rarity: there are a number of elements called "rare earths" which are much rarer than gold, but no one will give a penny for them except a few men of science. There is a theory, for which there is much to be said, that gold and gems were valued originally on account of their supposed magical properties. The mistakes of governments in modern times seem to show that this belief still exists among the sort of men who are called "practical." At the end of the last war, it was agreed that Germany should pay vast sums to England and France, and they in turn should pay vast sums to the United States. Every one wanted to be paid in money rather than goods; the "practical" men failed to notice that there is not that amount of money in the world. They also failed to notice that money is no use unless it is used to buy goods. As they would not use it in this way, it did no good to anyone. There was supposed to be some superstitious virtue about gold that made it worth while to dig it up in the Transvaal and put it underground again in bank vaults in America. In the end, of course, the debtor countries had no more money, and, since they were not allowed to pay in _____, they went bankrupt. The Great Depression was the direct result of the surviving belief in the superstitious properties of gold.

Fill in the blank with the ONE most appropriate word from the passage.

NOTE

Step 1	**S**urvey
Key Words	
Signal Words	
Step 2	**R**eading
Purpose	
Pattern of Organization	
Tone	
Main Idea	
Step 3	**S**ummary
지문 요약하기 (Paraphrasing)	
Step 4	**R**ecite
	요약문 말로 설명하기

Answer Key

Why do people value gold and precious stones? Not simply because of their rarity: there are a number of elements called "rare earths" which are much rarer than gold, but no one will give a penny for them except a few men of science. There is a theory, for which there is much to be said, that gold and gems were valued originally on account of their supposed **magical properties**. The mistakes of governments in modern times seem to show that this belief still exists among the sort of men who are called "practical." At the end of the last war, it was agreed that Germany should pay vast sums to England and France, and they in turn should pay vast sums to the United States. Every one wanted to be paid in money rather than goods; the "practical" men failed to notice that there is not that amount of money in the world. They also failed to notice that money is no use unless it is used to buy goods. As they would not use it in this way, it did no good to anyone. There was supposed to be some superstitious virtue about gold that made it worth while to dig it up in the Transvaal and put it underground again in bank vaults in America. In the end, of course, the debtor countries had no more money, and, since they were not allowed to pay in goods, they went bankrupt. **The Great Depression was the direct result of the surviving belief in the superstitious properties of gold.**

question

→ key word

모범답안
goods

한글번역

사람들은 왜 금과 보석을 소중하게 여길까? 그저 드물기 때문만은 아니다: 세상에는 금보다 훨씬 더 드문 '희토류'라는 원소가 몇 가지 있는데 몇 안 되는 과학자들 말고는 아무도 여기에 관심을 갖지 않는다. 논의할 여지가 많은 다음과 같은 이론도 있다. 즉, 금과 보석은 원래 마술적 성질을 지니고 있기 때문에 소중하게 여겨진다는 것이다. 현대의 각국 정부가 저지르는 실수를 보면 이러한 믿음은 이른바 '실용주의자'들 사이에도 여전히 존재하는 듯하다. 제1차 세계대전이 끝날 무렵 독일은 영국과 프랑스에 막대한 배상금을 지불하기로 합의했고, 뒤이어 두 나라 또한 미국에 막대한 채무를 갚기로 합의했다. 그들 모두 물건이 아닌 돈으로 지급받기를 원했다: '실용주의자'들은 그토록 많은 돈이 이 세상에 없다는 사실을 알아차리지 못했던 것이다. 게다가 그들은 물건을 사는 데 쓰지 않는 한 돈은 아무것도 아니라는 사실도 알아차리지 못했다. 그들이 돈을 이런 식으로(물건을 사는 식으로) 사용하려 하지 않았기 때문에 그 돈은 누구에게도 도움이 되지 못했다. 남아프리카의 트란스발에서 캐낸 금을 다시 미국에 있는 은행의 지하 금고에 묻은 것을 보면 그들은 금에 틀림없이 어떤 신비한 가치가 있다고 생각했을 것이다. 물론 채무국들은 결국 돈이 남아나지 않았고, 물건으로 지불하도록 허락받지 못한 탓에 파산하고 말았다. 대공황은 금의 마술적 성질을 끝끝내 믿으려 한 데서 비롯된 직접적인 결과였던 것이다.

NOTE

Step 1	Survey
Key Words	Gold; money; magical; superstitious
Signal Words	Because of; on account of; result
Step 2	**Reading**
Purpose	To show the risks of attaching superstitious value to gold
Pattern of Organization	Cause/effect
Tone	Cautioning; critical
Main Idea	The superstitious value attached to gold and money is impractical and creates problems.
Step 3	**Summary**
지문 요약하기 (Paraphrasing)	The superstitious value that is attached to gold and money instead of real, practical goods has led to many mistakes, including creating bankruptcy after WWI and causing the Great Depression.
Step 4	**Recite**
	요약문 말로 설명하기

10 Read the passage and follow the directions.

Society is losing its odor integrity. Some enterprising souls are actually marketing aerosol cans filled with the aromas of pizza, new cars, anything that might enhance people to buy something they would otherwise not. From the inexhaustible engine of commerce have come Aroma Discs, which when warmed in a special container (only $22.60) emit such scents as Passion, Fireplace and After Dinner Mints. And, in what may be the odor crime of the century, a company in Ohio is selling a cherry-scented garden hose. I may seem like a weird curmudgeon looking for something new to complain about, but it's only the fake smells I don't like, the ones that are meant to fool you. This is a dangerous business because the human nose is emotional and not very bright. Inside the brain, smell seems snuggled right up to the centers for cooking, sex and memory. I recently discovered a substance whose odor stimulates my memory of childhood like nothing else: Crayola crayons. I don't expect you to experience the effect of this odor memory just by thinking about crayons, since most people can't recall smells the way they can recall pictures or sounds. But once you get a good whiff of waxy crayon odor, the bells of childhood will ring. Go out and buy a box. Get your nose right down on the crayons and inhale deeply. Pull that crayon smell right up into the old reptile brain. You'll be flooded with a new-crayon, untouched-coloring-book feeling—you're young, the world is new, the next thing you know your parents may bring home a puppy. The smell is part of our culture in the same class as the Howdy Doody* song. Long after my daughters have stopped drawing with crayons, they will

MEMO

have in their brains, as I do now, the subconscious knowledge that if you smell stearic acid*—the major component in the smell of Crayola crayons—you're able to have a good time. We're responsible for what posterity will smell, and like to smell. If we're not careful, we may end up with a country in which everyone thinks garden hoses are supposed to smell like cherries.

*Howdy Doody: a famous American children's television program
*stearic acid: a saturated fatty acid with an 18-carbon chain

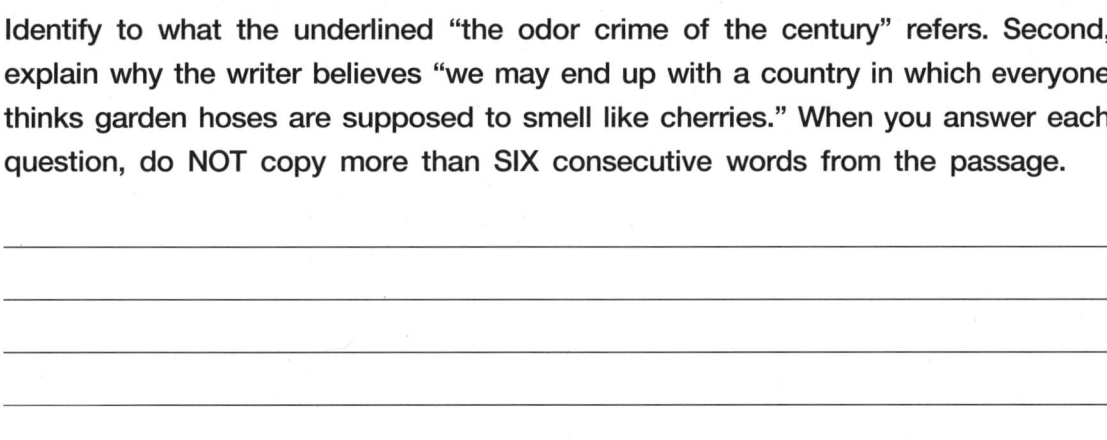

Identify to what the underlined "the odor crime of the century" refers. Second, explain why the writer believes "we may end up with a country in which everyone thinks garden hoses are supposed to smell like cherries." When you answer each question, do NOT copy more than SIX consecutive words from the passage.

NOTE

Step 1	**S**urvey
Key Words	
Signal Words	
Step 2	**R**eading
Purpose	
Pattern of Organization	
Tone	
Main Idea	
Step 3	**S**ummary
지문 요약하기 (Paraphrasing)	
Step 4	**R**ecite
	요약문 말로 설명하기

Answer Key

Society is losing its odor integrity. Some enterprising souls are actually marketing aerosol cans filled with the **aromas** of pizza, new cars, anything that might enhance people to buy something they would otherwise not. From the inexhaustible engine of commerce have come Aroma Discs, which when warmed in a special container (only $22.60) emit such scents as Passion, Fireplace and After Dinner Mints. And, [**in what may be the odor crime of the century**], a company in Ohio is selling a cherry-scented garden hose. I may seem like a weird curmudgeon looking for something new to complain about, but it's only **the fake smells** I don't like, the ones that are meant to fool you. **This is a dangerous business because the human nose is emotional and not very bright**. Inside the brain, smell seems snuggled right up to the centers for cooking, sex and memory. I recently discovered a substance whose **odor** stimulates my **memory** of childhood like nothing else: Crayola crayons. I don't expect you to experience the effect of this odor memory just by thinking about crayons, since most people can't recall smells the way they can recall pictures or sounds. But once you get a good whiff of waxy crayon odor, the bells of childhood will ring. Go out and buy a box. Get your nose right down on the crayons and inhale deeply. Pull that crayon smell right up into the old reptile brain. You'll be flooded with a new-crayon, untouched-coloring-book feeling—you're young, the world is new, the next thing you know your parents may bring home a puppy. **The smell is part of our culture in the same class as the Howdy Doody song**. Long after my daughters have stopped drawing with crayons, they will have in their brains, as I do now, the subconscious knowledge that if you smell stearic acid—the major component in the smell of Crayola crayons—you're able to have a good time. We're responsible for what posterity will **smell**, and like to smell. If we're not careful, we may end up with a country in which everyone thinks garden hoses are supposed to smell like cherries.

- main idea
- tone : critical
- key word
- key word
- opinion

모범답안

First, it refers to a company in Ohio selling a cherry-scented garden hose. Second, the writer believes that if businesses (or companies) are allowed to market fake odors, people will lose their ability to recognize real odors and, ultimately, society's odor memories will be distorted.

어휘

curmudgeon 괴팍한 사람
snuggle up to ~에 바짝 달라붙다
end up with 결국 ~하게 되다
stearic acid 스테아르산
posterity 후손
whiff (잠깐 동안) 훅 풍기는 냄새

한글번역

　　사회는 향기의 온전함을 잃어가고 있다. 몇몇 기업들은 사람들이 그렇게 하지 않으면 사지 않을 것들을 사게끔 강화할지도 모르는 피자, 새로운 차들과 같은 향으로 가득 찬 에어로졸 캔들을 판매하고 있다. 지칠 줄 모르는 상업의 엔진으로부터 애로마 디스크가 나왔는데 그것들은 특별한 용기 (22.60달러) 안에서 따뜻해질 때 열정, 벽난로, 그리고 애프터 디너 민트(식후 입가심용 민트향 사탕)와 같은 향들을 내뿜는다. 그리고, 세기의 향기 범죄인 오하이오주의 한 회사는 체리향의 정원 호스를 판매하고 있다. 나는 불평할 만한 새로운 것을 찾고 있는 괴팍한 사람처럼 보일지 모르지만, 내가 싫어하는 것은 단지 당신을 속이려고 의도된 가짜 냄새이다. 인간의 코는 감정적이지만 매우 똑똑하지는 않기 때문에 이것은 위험한 사업이다. 뇌 속에서, 향기는 요리, 성, 그리고 기억의 중심부에 바짝 달라붙어 있는 것처럼 보인다. 나는 최근에 한 물체를 발견했는데, 그것의 향기는 다른 것들과 같지 않게 나의 어린 시절 기억을 자극했다: 크래욜라 크레파스이다. 나는 당신이 크레파스들을 단지 생각함으로써 이러한 향기 기억 효과를 경험하기를 바라지 않는다, 왜냐하면 대부분의 사람은 사진이나 소리를 회상하는 것처럼 냄새를 회상할 수 없기 때문이다. 하지만 당신이 왁스 크레파스의 좋은 냄새를 한번 맡아본다면, 어린 시절의 벨이 울릴 것이다(추억이 회상될 것이다). 나가서 박스를 사라. 크레파스에 코를 갖다 대고 깊게 숨을 들여 마셔봐라. 크레파스 냄새를 파충류 뇌로 곧바로 집어넣어라. 당신은 새로운 크레파스로 감정이 벅찰 것인데, 당신은 어리고, 세상은 새롭고, 당신의 부모에 대해 당신이 알고 있는 다음의 것은 강아지를 집으로 데려오는 것이다. 그 냄새는 하우디 두디의 노래와 같은 분류의 우리 문화의 한 부분이다. 나의 딸들이 크레파스로 그림 그리기를 멈춘 한참 뒤로, 내가 지금 그렇듯, 나의 딸들도 그들의 크레파스 냄새에 대한 추억이 그들의 뇌에 있을 것인데, 이것은 만약 당신이 크래욜라 크레파스의 냄새의 주요한 요소인 스테아르산을 맡는다면, 당신도 좋은 시간을 보낼 것이라고 생각하는 잠재의식이다. 우리는 후손들이 냄새를 맡고, 냄새 맡길 좋아하는 것에 대한 책임이 있다. 만약 우리가 주의하지 않는다면, 우리는 결국 모두가 정원 호스가 체리향이라고 생각하는 나라에 살게 될 것이다.

NOTE

Step 1	Survey
Key Words	Society; odor integrity; fake smells
Signal Words	Not clear
Step 2	**Reading**
Purpose	To explain why society is losing its odor integrity
Pattern of Organization	Cause/effect
Tone	Critical; humorous
Main Idea	Artificial aromas, which are sold by businesses, cause a lack of odor integrity.
Step 3	**Summary**
지문 요약하기 (Paraphrasing)	Artificial aromas, which are sold by businesses, cause a lack of odor integrity. Recently it is common to be able to purchase products with fake smells like a cherry-smelling garden hose. Since our noses are prone to strong sense memories, like a Crayola crayon which will evoke childhood feelings vividly, these fake smells might cause us to hold inaccurate memories. In conclusion, our duty to preserve authentic scents for future generations is critical, as unchecked proliferation of artificial fragrances could normalize unnatural scents like cherry-scented garden hoses.
Step 4	**Recite**
	요약문 말로 설명하기

11 Read the passage and follow the directions.

> I learned, that if A is standing on a street corner and B wants his spot, B is within his rights if he does what he can to make A uncomfortable enough to move. In Beirut only the hardy sit in the last row in a movie theater, because there are usually standees who want seats and who push and shove and make such a nuisance that most people give up and leave. Another silent source of friction between Americans and Arabs is in an area that Americans treat very informally—the manners and rights of the road. In general, in the United States we tend to defer to the vehicle that is bigger, more powerful, faster, and heavily laden. While a pedestrian walking along a road may feel annoyed, he will not think it unusual to step aside for a fast-moving automobile. He knows that because he is moving, he does not have the right to the space around him that he has when he is standing still. It appears that the reverse is true with the Arabs who apparently take on rights to space as they move. For someone else to _____ into a space an Arab is also moving into is a violation of his rights. It is infuriating to an Arab to have someone else cut in front of him on the highway. <u>It is the American's cavalier treatment of moving space that makes the Arab call him aggressive and pushy.</u>

MEMO

Fill in the blank with the ONE most appropriate word from the passage. Second, what does the underlined "It is the American's cavalier treatment of moving space that makes the Arab call him aggressive and pushy" means?

_____
_____
_____

NOTE

Step 1	**S**urvey
Key Words	
Signal Words	
Step 2	**R**eading
Purpose	
Pattern of Organization	
Tone	
Main Idea	
Step 3	**S**ummary
지문 요약하기 (Paraphrasing)	
Step 4	**R**ecite
	요약문 말로 설명하기

Answer Key

> I learned, that if A is standing **on a street corner** and B wants his spot, B is within his rights if he does what he can to make A uncomfortable enough to move. **In Beirut** only the hardy sit in the last row in **a movie theater**, because there are usually standees who want seats and who push and shove and make such a nuisance that most people give up and leave. Another **silent source of friction between Americans and Arabs** is in **an area** that **Americans** treat very informally—the manners and rights of **the road**. In general, **in the United States** we tend to defer to the vehicle that is bigger, more powerful, faster, and heavily laden. While a pedestrian walking along a road may feel annoyed, he will not think it unusual to step aside for a fast-moving automobile. He knows that because he is **moving**, he does not have the right to the space around him that he has when he is standing still. It appears that the reverse is true with **the Arabs** who apparently take on rights to space as they **move**. For someone else to move into a space **an Arab** is also moving into is a violation of his rights. It is infuriating to **an Arab** to have someone else cut in front of him on the highway. It is **the American's** cavalier treatment of **moving space** that makes **the Arab** call him aggressive and pushy.

→ key word
→ key word
→ key word
→ key word

모범답안

The word is "move". Second, it means that Americans' casual disregard for others' right to space while in motion leads Arabs to perceive them as aggressive and pushy, due to differing cultural views about spatial rights while moving.

한글번역

만약 A가 길모퉁이에 서 있고 B가 그 자리를 원한다면, 나는 B가 A를 충분히 불편하게 만들어서 움직이게 할 수 있는 권리가 있다는 것을 배웠다. 베이루트에서는 강한 자만이 영화관 마지막 줄에 앉는데, 왜냐하면 거기엔 주로 앉고 싶어 하는 입석 관람객들이 있어서, 그들이 밀고 떠밀며 성가시게 만들어 대부분 관람객들이 포기하고 떠나게 만들기 때문이다. 미국인과 아랍인 사이의 또 다른 암묵적 마찰의 근원은, 미국인들의 공간에 대한 격식에 얽매이지 않는 태도이다—즉, 미국인들의 도로에 대한 매너와 권리에 관해서이다. 일반적으로 미국에서는 더 크고, 더 강력하고, 더 빠르고, 짐을 많이 실은 차량에 양보하는 경향이 있다. 도로를 걷는 보행자가 짜증이 날 수는 있지만, 그는 빠르게 움직이는 자동차를 위해 비켜서는 것을 이상하게 생각하지 않는다. 그는 자신이 움직이고 있을 때는 서 있을 때처럼 자신의 주변 공간에 대한 권리가 없다는 것을 안다. 아랍인들의 경우는 정반대인 것 같은데, 그들은 움직일 때 공간에 대한 권리를 가진다고 여기는 듯하다. 아랍인이 이동하고자 하는 공간으로 누군가가 이동하는 것은 그 아랍인의 권리에 대한 침해다. 아랍인에게 고속도로에서 누군가가 자신의 앞을 가로지르는 것은 매우 분노할 일이다. 움직이는 공간에 대한 미국인의 무신경한 태도가 아랍인들이 그들을 공격적이고 뻔뻔하다고 부르는 이유다.

NOTE

Step 1	Survey
Key Words	Arabs; Americans; space; moving; road
Signal Words	Friction between A and B; the reverse is true
Step 2	**Reading**
Purpose	To describe cultural differences between Arabs and Americans concerning the concept of space
Pattern of Organization	Contrast
Tone	Analytical; observational
Main Idea	There are cultural differences between Arabs and Americans in terms of the rights of space.
Step 3	**Summary**
지문 요약하기 (Paraphrasing)	There are cultural differences between Arabs and Americans in terms of the rights of space. An Arab believes he has the right to make another still person uncomfortable in order to take his place, while Americans believe someone in place has the right to be there. In terms of rights of the road, Arabs perceive that a person in motion has rights to the space as they move, while Americans do not.
Step 4	**Recite**
	요약문 말로 설명하기

12 Read the passage and follow the directions.

> She was my best friend, and hard as it may have been to figure by the looks of us, she was the good girl, I the bad. I suppose everyone has at least one friendship like this in their lives. We were dialectical, she the thesis, I the antithesis. She was direct, trustworthy, kind, and naive; I was manipulative, selfish, and clever. She laughed at all my jokes, took part in all my schemes, told everyone that I was the smartest and the funniest and the best. Like a B movie of boarding school life, we stole peanut butter from the refectory, short-sheeted beds, called drugstores and asked them if they had Prince Albert in a can. Whenever I hear a mother say, "If so-and-so told you to jump off the Brooklyn Bridge, would you do it?" I think of her. On my order, she would have jumped.

What words does the writer use to describe herself? Second, what simile does the author use to describe the friendship?

_____
_____
_____
_____
_____

NOTE

Step 1	**S**urvey
Key Words	
Signal Words	
Step 2	**R**eading
Purpose	
Pattern of Organization	
Tone	
Main Idea	
Step 3	**S**ummary
지문 요약하기 (Paraphrasing)	
Step 4	**R**ecite
	요약문 말로 설명하기

Answer Key

> She was **my best friend**, and hard as it may have been to figure by the looks of us, she was **the good girl**, I the **bad**. I suppose everyone has at least one friendship like this in their lives. We were dialectical, she the thesis, I the antithesis. She was direct, trustworthy, kind, and naïve; I was manipulative, selfish, and clever. She laughed at all my jokes, took part in all my schemes, told everyone that I was the smartest and the funniest and the best. Like a B movie of boarding school life, we stole peanut butter from the refectory, short-sheeted beds, called drugstores and asked them if they had Prince Albert in a can. Whenever I hear a mother say, "If so-and-so told you to jump off the Brooklyn Bridge, would you do it?" I think of her. On my order, she would have jumped.

→ key words

→ signal words

모범답안

She describes herself as bad, manipulative, selfish and clever. Her friend thinks she is the funniest and smartest person in school. Second, the simile is "Like a B movie of boarding school life."

한글번역

그녀는 나의 가장 친한 친구였고, 외모만으로 판단하기에는 힘들겠지만 그녀는 착한 소녀였고 나는 나쁜 소녀였다. 모든 사람들이 자신의 인생에서 이런 종류의 친구 관계를 하나쯤 갖고 있을 거라 생각한다. 우린 모두 변증법적인데, 즉 그녀가 정립이면 나는 반정립이다. 그녀는 단도직입적이고 신뢰할 만하고 상냥하고 순진한 반면 나는 교묘하고 이기적이며 똑똑했다. 그녀는 나의 모든 농담에 웃어줬고 내 계획에 참여했고 모든 사람들에게 내가 가장 똑똑하고 웃기며, 최고라고 얘기했다. 기숙학교 인생의 B급 영화처럼 우리는 식당에서 땅콩버터를 훔쳤고, 침대 시트로 장난을 쳤고, 약국에 전화해서 캔 속에 앨버트 왕자가 있는지를 물어봤다. 엄마가 "아무개가 너에게 브루클린 다리에서 뛰어내리라고 하면 할 거야?"라고 물어볼 때마다 나는 그녀를 떠올린다. 내 명령이라면 그녀는 뛰어내릴 것이다.

NOTE

Step 1	**S**urvey
Key Words	Best friend; good girl; bad girl
Signal Words	Dialectical; thesis; antithesis
Step 2	**R**eading
Purpose	To provide a candid assessment of an unbalanced friendship from the speaker's days at a boarding school for girls
Pattern of Organization	Comparison/contrast
Tone	Subjective; humorous
Main Idea	Though the speak is different from her friend in many ways, they can have a good friendship.
Step 3	**S**ummary
지문 요약하기 (Paraphrasing)	Though the speak is different from her friend in many ways, they can have a good friendship. As children, the speaker was selfish and bad while her friend was good, and the speaker led her friend to misbehave along with her.
Step 4	**R**ecite
	요약문 말로 설명하기

13 Read the passage and follow the directions.

Only two animals have entered the human household otherwise than as prisoners and become domesticated by other means than those of enforced servitude: the dog and the cat. Two things they have in common, namely, that both belong to the order of carnivores and both serve man in their capacity of hunters. In all other characteristics, above all in the manner of their association with man, they are as different as the night from the day. There is no domestic animal that has so radically altered its whole way of living, indeed its whole sphere of interests, that has become domestic in so true a sense as the dog; and there is no animal that, in the course of its centuries-old association with man, has altered so little as the cat. There is some truth in their assertion that the cat, with the exception of a few luxury breeds, such as Angoras, Persians and Siamese, is no domestic animal but a completely wild being. Maintaining its full independence it has taken up its abode in the houses and outhouses of man, for the simple reason that there are more mice there than elsewhere. The whole charm of the dog lies in the depth of the friendship and the strength of the spiritual ties with which he has bound himself to man, but the appeal of the cat lies in the very fact that she has formed no close bond with him, that she has the uncompromising independence of a tiger or a leopard <u>while she is hunting in his stables and barns</u>, that she still remains mysterious and remote when she is rubbing herself gently against the legs of her mistress or purring contentedly in front of the fire.

How do a dog and a cat differ in their association with their owners? Second, what does the underlined "while she is hunting in his stables and barns" means?

___

NOTE

Step 1	**S**urvey
Key Words	
Signal Words	
Step 2	**R**eading
Purpose	
Pattern of Organization	
Tone	
Main Idea	
Step 3	**S**ummary
지문 요약하기 (Paraphrasing)	
Step 4	**R**ecite
	요약문 말로 설명하기

Answer Key

Only two animals have entered the human household otherwise than as prisoners and become domesticated by other means than those of enforced servitude: **the dog** and **the cat**. Two things they **have in common**, namely, that both belong to the order of carnivores and both serve man in their capacity of hunters. In all other characteristics, above all in the manner of their association with man, **they are as different as the night from the day**. There is no domestic animal that has so radically altered its whole way of living, indeed its whole sphere of interests, that has become domestic in so true a sense as **the dog**; and there is no animal that, in the course of its centuries-old association with man, has altered so little as **the cat**. There is some truth in their assertion that **the cat**, with the exception of a few luxury breeds, such as Angoras, Persians and Siamese, is no domestic animal but a completely wild being. Maintaining its full independence it has taken up its abode in the houses and outhouses of man, for the simple reason that there are more mice there than elsewhere. The whole charm of **the dog** lies in the depth of the friendship and the strength of the spiritual ties with which he has bound himself to man, but the appeal of **the cat** lies in the very fact that she has formed no close bond with him, that she has the uncompromising independence of a tiger or a leopard while she is hunting in his stables and barns, that she still remains mysterious and remote when she is rubbing herself gently against the legs of her mistress or purring contentedly in front of the fire.

→ key words
→ key words

모범답안

First, cats remain independent while dogs form deep friendships and spiritual ties. Second, it means that even when a cat is actively hunting mice in human buildings (stables and barns owned by humans), it maintains its wild and independent nature like a tiger or leopard.

> **한글번역**
>
> 단 두 종류의 동물만이 포로로 잡혀 강제로 길러지는 방식이 아니라, 다른 방법으로 인간의 가정집으로 들어와 길들여지게 됐다. 바로 강아지와 고양이다. 다시 말해, 두 동물은 공통점이 있는데, 즉 이들은 모두 육식 동물 계열에 속하고 사냥꾼으로서의 능력을 통해 인간을 돕는다는 것이다. 다른 특징으로는 무엇보다도 인간과의 관계에서, 밤과 낮이 다르듯, 서로 차이가 있다. 개처럼 진정한 개로서 가정용이 되기 위해, 자신의 전체 생활 방식, 그의 전체적인 관심사 자체를, 그렇게 급진적으로 바꿔버린 애완동물은 없다. 그리고 고양이처럼 수 세기나 된 인간과의 관계에서 이렇게 변하지 않은 동물은 없다. 몇 개의 고급 종—앙고라, 페르시안, 샴—을 제외한 고양이는 애완동물이 아니라 완전히 야생 동물이라는 주장에는 어느 정도 진실성이 있다. 고양이는 자신의 완전한 독립심을 유지하면서 단지 다른 곳보다 쥐가 더 많다는 이유로 인간의 집안과 별채에 자신의 거주지를 차지한다. 개의 온전한 매력은 우정의 깊이와 자신이 직접 인간과 형성하는 정신적 교감의 힘에 있다. 하지만 고양이의 매력은 주인과 깊은 유대는 형성하지 않고 마구간과 헛간에서 사냥하면서 호랑이나 표범의 단호한 독립성을 가지고 있다는 데 있다. 또한 주인의 다리에 부드럽게 부빌 때와 만족스럽게 가르랑거릴 때에도 여전히 신비스러우며, 거리를 유지한다는 데 고양이의 매력이 있다.

NOTE

Step 1	**S**urvey
Key Words	Dogs; cats; domestication
Signal Words	Have in common; both; different
Step 2	**R**eading
Purpose	To describe what dogs and cats have in common and how they differ
Pattern of Organization	Comparison/contrast
Tone	Analytical; objective
Main Idea	Dogs and cats have some similarities and many differences.
Step 3	**S**ummary
지문 요약하기 (Paraphrasing)	Dogs and cats have some similarities and many differences. While both are carnivores and serve as hunters, they differ dramatically in their adaptation to domestication. Dogs have fundamentally changed their lifestyle to form deep emotional bonds with humans, while cats maintain their wild, independent nature despite living in human spaces, much like their wild relatives tigers and leopards.
Step 4	**R**ecite
	요약문 말로 설명하기

14 Read the passage and follow the directions.

In T'ai Chi class Dr. Young talked about yin and yang. In the beginning square form, each movement is followed by a pause; the movement is yin, the pause yang. To my Western ears this smacks of sexism; the masculine principle acting, the feminine doing nothing. But I eventually begin to learn the pause is not nothing. Given its proper weight, gravity, and time, the pause does its work, its stretch, its subtle modification of the quality of the move before and the one to come. Later in the round form, the movement is continuous. Yin and yang, though still opposite, are inscrutably simultaneous, engaged in an ancient abstract intercourse.

What is a yin and what is yang in the beginning square form of T'ai Chi? Second, why does the writer think the notion of yin and yang "smacks of sexism"?

___
___
___
___
___

NOTE

Step 1	**S**urvey
Key Words	
Signal Words	
Step 2	**R**eading
Purpose	
Pattern of Organization	
Tone	
Main Idea	
Step 3	**S**ummary
지문 요약하기 (Paraphrasing)	
Step 4	**R**ecite
	요약문 말로 설명하기

Answer Key

In T'ai Chi class Dr. Young talked about **yin** and **yang**. In the beginning **square form**, each movement is followed by a pause: the **movement** is yin, the **pause** yang. To my Western ears this smacks of sexism; the masculine principle acting, the feminine doing nothing. But I eventually begin to learn the pause is not nothing. Given its proper weight, gravity, and time, the pause does its work, its stretch, its subtle modification of the quality of the move before and the one to come. Later in the **round form**, the movement is continuous. Yin and yang, though still opposite, are inscrutably simultaneous, engaged in an ancient abstract intercourse.

→ key words

모범답안

The yin is pause, and the yang is movement in the beginning square form. Second, the concept analogizes the male as active and the female being passive.

한글번역

태극권 수업에서 Young 박사는 음과 양에 대해서 얘기했다. 처음에 네모 형태 자세에서, 각 움직임 이후에 정지가 뒤따른다. 움직임 뒤에는 음이 따라오고, 정지 뒤에는 양이 따라온다. 서양인인 나의 입장에서, 이것은 성차별주의의 기미가 보인다. 남성스러움의 원칙은 행동을 취하는 것이고, 여성스러움은 아무것도 하지 않는 것이다. 그러나 나는 결국 멈춰 있는 것이 아무것도 아닌 것은 아니라는 사실을 배우기 시작했다. 정지의 적절한 무게, 중력, 시간을 고려해봤을 때, 정지는 그것의 수행, 당기기, 이전 동작과 앞으로 올 동작의 질에 대한 미묘한 수정의 일을 하고 있다. 그리고 나서 원의 형태로 그 동작이 계속된다. 음과 양은 여전히 정반대이지만, 고대의 추상적인 소통에 참여하며, 불가사의하게도 동시에 일어난다.

Step 1	**S**urvey
Key Words	Yang; yin; pause; movement; square form; round form
Signal Words	But; opposite
Step 2	**R**eading
Purpose	To explain what yang is and what yin is
Pattern of Organization	Contrast; definition
Tone	Contemplative
Main Idea	In T'ai Chi, yin and yang, though opposite, are simultaneous and meaningful.
Step 3	**S**ummary
지문 요약하기 (Paraphrasing)	In T'ai Chi, yin and yang, though opposite, are simultaneous and meaningful.
Step 4	**R**ecite

요약문 말로 설명하기

15 Read the passage and follow the directions.

Physically and psychologically women are by far the superior to men. The old chestnut about women being more emotional than men has been forever destroyed by the facts of two great wars. Women under blockade, heavy bombardment, concentration camp confinement, and similar rigors withstand them vastly more successfully than men. The psychiatric casualties of civilian populations under such conditions are mostly masculine, and there are far more men in our mental hospitals than there are women. The steady hand at the helm is the hand that has had the practice at rocking the cradle. Because of their greater size and weight, men are physically more powerful than women—which is not the same thing as saying that they are stronger. A man of the same size and weight as a woman of comparable background and occupational status would probably not be any more powerful than a woman. As far as constitutional strength is concerned, women are stronger than men. Many diseases from which men suffer can be shown to be largely influenced by their relation to the male Y-chromosome. More males die than females. Deaths from almost all causes are more frequent in males of all ages. Though women are more frequently ill than men, they recover from illnesses more easily and more frequently. Women, in short, are fundamentally more resistant than men. With the exception of the organ systems subserving the functions of reproduction, women suffer much less frequently than men from the serious disorders which affect mankind. With the exception of India, women everywhere live longer than men.

MEMO

Describe the main idea of the passage in TEN words or less.

NOTE

Step 1	**S**urvey
Key Words	
Signal Words	
Step 2	**R**eading
Purpose	
Pattern of Organization	
Tone	
Main Idea	
Step 3	**S**ummary
지문 요약하기 (Paraphrasing)	
Step 4	**R**ecite
	요약문 말로 설명하기

Answer Key

Physically and psychologically women are by far the superior to men. The old chestnut about women being more emotional than men has been forever destroyed by the facts of two great wars. Women under blockade, heavy bombardment, concentration camp confinement, and similar rigors withstand them vastly **more successfully than men**. The psychiatric casualties of civilian populations under such conditions are mostly masculine, and there are far more men in our mental hospitals than there are women. The steady hand at the helm is the hand that has had the practice at rocking the cradle. // Because of their greater size and weight, men are physically more powerful than women—which is not the same thing as saying that they are stronger. **A man of the same size and weight as a woman of comparable background and occupational status would probably not be any more powerful than a woman.** As far as constitutional strength is concerned, **women are stronger than men**. Many diseases from which men suffer can be shown to be largely influenced by their relation to the male Y-chromosome. **More males die than females**. Deaths from almost all causes are more frequent in males of all ages. Though women are more frequently ill than men, they recover from illnesses more easily and more frequently. **Women, in short, are fundamentally more resistant than men.** With the exception of the organ systems subserving the functions of reproduction, women suffer much less frequently than men from the serious disorders which affect mankind. With the exception of India, women everywhere live longer than men.

- topic sentence
- psychologically
- physically

모범답안

Women are superior to men both physically and psychologically.

한글번역

　육체적으로 그리고 심리적으로 여성은 남성들보다 훨씬 우월하다. 여성이 남성들보다 더 감정적이라는 케케묵은 이야기는 두 건의 큰 전쟁에 대한 사실들로 인해 영원히 깨졌다. 봉쇄와 집중 포격, 강제 수용소 감금, 그리고 또 다른 비슷한 고초 하에 있는 여성들은 남성들보다 그런 고초들을 훨씬 더 성공적으로 이겨낸다. 그러한 상황하에 있는 시민들 중 정신질환을 가지고 있는 피해자들은 대부분 남성들이고, 정신병원에는 여자보다 남자가 훨씬 더 많이 있다. 안정적인 손은 요람을 흔든 경험을 가진 손이다. 그들의 큰 덩치와 무게 때문에 남자들은 여자들보다 힘이 넘친다. 이 말은 남자들이 강하다고 말하는 것과는 다르다. 비슷한 배경과 직업적 지위를 가진 여성과 같은 크기와 무게를 가진 남자는 아마도 여자보다 힘이 강하지 않을 것이다. 체질적인 힘이 고려되는 한, 여자들은 남자보다 더 강하다. 남자들이 고통스러워 하는 많은 질병들은 남성의 Y염색체의 영향을 크게 받은 것으로 보일 수 있다. 여성보다 많은 남성들이 죽는다. 온갖 원인에 의한 죽음은 모든 연령대의 남자들에게 더 빈번하다. 여자들은 남자들보다 더 자주 아픔에도 불구하고 더 쉽게, 더 자주 아픔을 회복한다. 즉 여자들은 남성들보다 근본적으로 내성이 더 강하다. 생식의 기능을 하는 장기 기관을 제외하고는 여자들은 인류에 영향을 미치는 심각한 장애로부터 남자들보다 덜 빈번하게 고통을 겪는다. 인도를 제외하면 여자들은 어디에서나 남자들보다 오래 산다.

NOTE

Step 1	**S**urvey
Key Words	Women; men; physical; psychiatric; strength
Signal Words	Superior to; more… than; because of; in short; with the exception of
Step 2	**R**eading
Purpose	To support the claim that women are superior to men both physically and psychologically
Pattern of Organization	Comparison/contrast
Tone	Argumentative; assertive
Main Idea	Women are superior to men both physically and psychologically.
Step 3	**S**ummary
지문 요약하기 (Paraphrasing)	Women are superior to men both physically and psychologically. They hold up better in stressful situations and recover more quickly from disease. Death from all causes, including disease, violence, and accidents, is more prevalent among men. Women live longer on the average.
Step 4	**R**ecite
	요약문 말로 설명하기

16 Read the passage and follow the directions.

Who talk more—men or women? Most people believe that women talk more. However, this is a stereotype. Women are more verbal—talk more—in private situations, where they use conversation as the "glue" to hold relationships together. But men talk more in public situations, where they use conversation to exchange information and gain status. We can see these differences even in children. Little girls often play with one best friend; their play includes a lot of conversation. Little boys often play games in groups; their play usually involves more doing than ⓐ_____. A recent study at Emory University helps to shed light on the roots of communication style differences. Researchers studied conversation between children age 3-6 and their parents. They found evidence that parents talk very ⓑ_____ to their sons than they do to their daughters. The startling conclusion was that parents use far more language with their girls. Specifically, when parents talk with their daughters, they use more descriptive language and more details. There is also far more talk about emotions, especially sadness, with daughters than with sons. Most parents would be surprised to learn this. They certainly don't plan to talk more with one child than with another. They don't even realize that this is happening. So why do they do it? Interestingly, it begins when the children are newborn babies.

Fill in each blank with the ONE most appropriate word from the passage. If necessary, change the word form.

NOTE

Step 1	**S**urvey
Key Words	
Signal Words	
Step 2	**R**eading
Purpose	
Pattern of Organization	
Tone	
Main Idea	
Step 3	**S**ummary
지문 요약하기 (Paraphrasing)	
Step 4	**R**ecite
	요약문 말로 설명하기

Answer Key

Who talk more—men or women? Most people believe that women talk more. However, **this is a stereotype**. Women are more verbal—talk more—in **private** situations, where they use conversation as the "glue" to hold relationships together. But men talk more in **public** situations, where they use conversation to exchange information and gain status. We can see **these** differences even in children. Little girls often play with one best friend; their play includes a lot of conversation. Little boys often play games in groups; their play usually involves more doing than talking. A recent study at Emory University helps to shed light on **the roots of communication style differences**. Researchers studied conversation between children age 3-6 and their parents. They found evidence that parents talk very differently to their sons than they do to their daughters. The startling conclusion was that parents use far more language with their girls. Specifically, when parents talk with their daughters, they use more descriptive language and more details. There is also far more talk about emotions, especially sadness, with daughters than with sons. Most parents would be surprised to learn this. They certainly don't plan to talk more with one child than with another. They don't even realize that this is happening. So why do they do it? Interestingly, it begins when the children are newborn babies.

question

key words

key words

모범답안

ⓐ talking ⓑ differently

어휘

gain status 지위를 얻다	glue 붙이다	hold together 단결하다; 뭉치게 하다
shed light on ~을 밝히다	specifically 특히, 분명하게	startling 아주 놀라운

> **한글번역**
>
> 누가 더 수다를 많이 떠는가? 남자인가 여자인가? 대부분의 사람들은 여자들이 수다를 더 많이 떤다고 생각한다. 그러나 그것은 고정관념이다. 여자들은 그들이 서로 관계를 유지하기 위해 '접착제'로 대화를 하는 사적인 상황에서 더 말이 많다. 그러나 남자들은 정보를 교환하거나 지위를 획득하기 위해 대화를 하는 공적인 상황에서 더 말이 많다. 우리는 심지어 이러한 차이점들을 아이들에게서도 발견할 수 있다. 어린 여자아이들은 종종 한 명의 가장 친한 친구와 어울리며, 그들의 놀이는 많은 대화를 포함한다. 어린 남자아이들은 종종 무리를 지어 게임을 하며 논다; 그들의 놀이는 말보다 행동을 더 많이 포함한다. 에모리 대학교의 최근 연구는 대화 방법의 차이점의 근원을 밝혀내는 데 일조를 했다. 연구자들은 3세부터 6세의 아이들과 그들의 부모 사이의 대화를 연구했다. 그들은 부모들이 딸들에게 하는 것에 비해 아들들에게는 다르게 이야기한다는 증거를 발견했다. 아주 놀라운 결과는 부모는 자신들의 딸에게 훨씬 더 많은 언어를 사용한다는 것이었다. 특히, 부모들이 그들의 딸과 대화했을 때, 더 서술적이고 자세한 언어를 사용한다는 것이었다. 또한 아들보다 딸에게 더 많은 감정들, 특히 슬픔을 이야기한다는 것이다. 대부분의 부모는 이 사실을 알고는 놀랄 것이다. 그들은 분명 다른 자녀보다 어느 한 자녀와 더 많이 이야기하려고 하지는 않기 때문이다. 그들은 심지어 이러한 사실이 일어나리라고는 생각지도 못한다. 그들은 왜 그러는가? 흥미롭게도 그것은 아이들이 갓난아이일 때부터 시작한다.

NOTE

Step 1	Survey
Key Words	Talk; men; women; private; public
Signal Words	However; differences; differently than; more; more… than
Step 2	**Reading**
Purpose	To outline the differences between the development of boys and girls, particularly in regard to their use of speech
Pattern of Organization	Comparison/contrast; cause/effect
Tone	Informative
Main Idea	Men and women have different styles of speaking which are influenced unconsciously from birth by their parents.
Step 3	**Summary**
지문 요약하기 (Paraphrasing)	Men and women have different styles of speaking which are influenced unconsciously from birth by their parents. Girls develop their language ability through differing influential factors such as socialization with other girls and language treatment by parents. Parents unknowingly use different, more verbal communication with girls than with boys from birth, nurturing this difference later in life.
Step 4	**Recite**
	요약문 말로 설명하기

17 Read the passage and follow the directions.

Researchers note three frequent attitudes among mothers of _____ⓐ_____ children. The first attitude is reflected by those mothers who reject their child or are unable to accept the child as a handicapped person. Complex love-hate and acceptance-rejection relationships are found within this group. Rejected children not only have problems in adjusting to themselves and their disabilities, but they also have to contend with disturbed family relationships and emotional insecurity. Unfortunately, such children receive even less encouragement than the normal child and have to absorb more criticism of their behavior. A second relationship involves mothers who overcompensate in their reactions to their child and the disorder. They tend to be unrealistic, rigid, and overprotective. Often, such parents try to compensate by being overzealous and giving continuous instruction and training in the hope of establishing superior ability. The third group consists of mothers who accept their children along with their defects. These mothers have gained the ability to provide for the special needs of their handicapped children while continuing to live a normal life and tending to family and home as well as civic and social obligations. The child's chances are best with parents who have accepted both their child and the _____ⓑ_____.

Fill in each blank with the ONE most appropriate word from the passage.

NOTE

Step 1	**S**urvey
Key Words	
Signal Words	
Step 2	**R**eading
Purpose	
Pattern of Organization	
Tone	
Main Idea	
Step 3	**S**ummary
지문 요약하기 (Paraphrasing)	
Step 4	**R**ecite
	요약문 말로 설명하기

Answer Key

Researchers note three frequent attitudes among mothers of handicapped children. **The first attitude** is reflected by those mothers who reject their child or are unable to accept the child as a handicapped person. Complex love-hate and acceptance-rejection relationships are found within this group. Rejected children not only have problems in adjusting to themselves and their disabilities, but they also have to contend with disturbed family relationships and emotional insecurity. Unfortunately, such children receive even less encouragement than the normal child and have to absorb more criticism of their behavior. // A **second** relationship involves mothers who overcompensate in their reactions to their child and the disorder. They tend to be unrealistic, rigid, and overprotective. Often, such parents try to compensate by being overzealous and giving continuous instruction and training in the hope of establishing superior ability. // The **third** group consists of mothers who accept their children along with their defects. These mothers have gained the ability to provide for the special needs of their handicapped children while continuing to live a normal life and tending to family and home as well as civic and social obligations. The child's chances are best with parents who have accepted both their child and the defects.

- topic sentence
- category 1 : rejection
- category 2 : overcompensation
- category 3 : acceptance

모범답안

ⓐ handicapped ⓑ defects

한글번역

연구자들은 장애 아동을 둔 어머니들의 세 가지의 흔한 태도에 대해 주목한다. 첫 번째는 그들의 자녀가 장애인이라는 것 자체를 거절하거나 용납할 수 없는 태도를 보이는 어머니들이다. 복잡한 (자식들에 대한) 사랑-증오와 인정-거부의 관계는 이러한 그룹 내에서 발견된다. 이렇게 거부당한 아이들은 그들 스스로 그들의 장애에 대해 적응하는 것에 있어서 문제가 있을 뿐만 아니라, 잘못된 가족 관계와 감정적인 불안정과도 맞서 싸워야만 한다. 불행하게도, 그러한 아이들은 비장애인 아동들보다 적은 격려를 받으며, 그들의 행동에 대해 더 많은 비난을 받아내야만 한다. 두 번째 관계는 그들의 아이와 장애에 대해 과잉보호를 하는 엄마들을 포함한다. 그들은 비현실적이고, 완고하며, 과잉보호하는 경향이 있다. 종종, 그러한 부모들은 과다하게 열정적이거나 지속적인 지시를 주고, 우수한 능력을 가질 수 있다는 희망을 가지고 훈련시킴으로써 보상하려고 한다. 세번째 그룹은 아이들의 장애에 대해 인정하는 어머니들로 구성된다. 이러한 어머니들은 평범한 삶을 지속하고, 가족과 집에서 뿐만 아니라 시민으로서의 사회적인 의무를 지면서 그들의 장애 아동의 특별한 요구에 대해 제공할 능력을 가지고 있다. 장애아들의 기회는 아이들 자체와 그 부족함을 받아들이는 부모님들과 있을 때 가장 극대화된다.

NOTE

Step 1	Survey
Key Words	Mother; handicapped children; attitude
Signal Words	Three; not only… but also; first; second; third
Step 2	**Reading**
Purpose	To describe the three frequent attitudes among mothers of handicapped children
Pattern of Organization	Series
Tone	Neutral
Main Idea	There are three common attitudes among mothers of handicapped children.
Step 3	**Summary**
지문 요약하기 (Paraphrasing)	Three attitudes are common among mothers of handicapped children: rejection, overcompensation, and acceptance. Children who face rejection or are overcompensated for have trouble adjusting to life, while those whose defects are accepted and worked with are able to live a more normal life both in the family and in society.
Step 4	**Recite**
	요약문 말로 설명하기

18 Read the passage and follow the directions.

It is role of the Federal Reserve, known simply as the Fed, to control the supply of money in the U.S. through its system of twelve regional Federal Reserve Banks, each with its own Federal Reserve Bank. Many commercial banks belong to the Federal Reserve System and as members must follow the Fed's reserve requirements, a ruling by the Fed on the percentage of deposits that a member bank must keep either in its own vaults or on deposit at the Fed. If the Fed wants to change the money supply, it can change reserve requirements to member banks; for example, an increase in the percentage of deposits required to be kept on hand would reduce the available money supply. Member banks can also borrow money from the Fed, and an additional way that Fed can control the money supply is to raise or lower the discount rate, the interest rate at which commercial banks borrow from the Fed. An increase in the discount rate would reduce the funds available to commercial banks and thus shrink the money supply. In addition to using _____ and the discount rate to control the money supply, the Fed has another powerful tool, open-market operations.

Fill in the blank with the TWO most appropriate consecutive words from the passage.

NOTE

Step 1	**S**urvey
Key Words	
Signal Words	
Step 2	**R**eading
Purpose	
Pattern of Organization	
Tone	
Main Idea	
Step 3	**S**ummary
지문 요약하기 (Paraphrasing)	
Step 4	**R**ecite
	요약문 말로 설명하기

Answer Key

It is **role of the Federal Reserve**, known simply as the Fed, to control **the supply of money** in the U.S. through its system of twelve regional Federal Reserve Banks, each with its own Federal Reserve Bank. Many commercial banks belong to the Federal Reserve System and as members must follow the Fed's reserve requirements, a ruling by the Fed on the percentage of deposits that a member bank must keep either in its own vaults or on deposit at the Fed. If the Fed wants to change the money supply, it can change **reserve requirements** to member banks; for example, an increase in the percentage of deposits required to be kept on hand would reduce the available money supply. Member banks can also borrow money from the Fed, and an **additional** way that Fed can control the money supply is to raise or lower **the discount rate**, the interest rate at which commercial banks borrow from the Fed. An increase in the discount rate would reduce the funds available to commercial banks and thus shrink the money supply. **In addition to** using **reserve requirements** and the discount rate to control the money supply, the Fed has another powerful tool, **open-market operations**.

▶ key words

①

②

③

모범답안

reserve requirements

구문분석

1. If the Fed wants to change the money supply, it can change reserve requirements to member banks; **for example, an increase in** the percentage of deposits required **to be kept on hand would** reduce the available money supply.
   만일 연준이 통화 공급량을 바꾸고 싶으면 회원 은행의 지급준비금을 바꾸면 된다. 예를 들어 상시 준비시킬 예탁금의 비율을 증가시키면 가용한 통화 공급량은 줄어들 것이다.

2. an additional way that Fed can control the money supply is to raise or lower the discount rate, the interest rate at which commercial banks borrow from the Fed.
   ⇨ 이 문장의 주어는 an additional way이고 동사는 단수동사인 is이며, that은 관계부사 대용으로 사용되었다.
   명사 다음에 comma(,)가 나오고 관사+명사가 나오면 동격일 확률이 매우 높다. 따라서 거기에 맞는 해석을 적용해야 한다. 이때 comma는 '즉'으로 해석하는 것이 좋다. 여기서, the discount rate 다음에 나오는 comma(,)는 동격의 역할을 하여 the interest rate at which commercial banks borrow from the Fed.와 같은 것이 된다. 해석하면, '할인율, 즉, 시중 은행들이 연준으로부터 돈을 빌리는 금리'가 된다.
   ⇨ **at which** commercial banks borrow from the Fed.
   = commercial banks borrow from the Fed at the interest rate.

어휘

a commercial bank 시중 은행; 상업은행
reserve requirements 지급준비 요구
the discount rate 할인율
on hand 가지고 있는; 수중에 있는
ruling 판정, 재정규정
vault (은행의) 금고; 지하 납골당

한글번역

'연준'이라고도 하는 연방 준비 제도의 역할은 각기 자체 연방 준비 지방 은행을 가지고 있는 12개 지역의 연방 준비 은행 제도를 통해 미국의 통화 공급을 통제하는 것이다. 많은 시중 은행들이 연방 준비 제도에 속해 있으며 회원으로서 연준의 준비 요구를 따라야 하는데, 이것은 다름 아닌 회원 은행이 자신의 금고나 연준 예탁고에 확보하고 있어야 하는 예탁금의 비율에 관한 규정이다. 만일 연준이 통화 공급량을 바꾸고 싶으면 회원 은행의 지급준비금을 바꾸면 된다. 예를 들어 상시 준비시킬 예탁금의 비율을 증가시키면 가용한 통화 공급량은 줄어들 것이다. 회원 은행은 연준으로부터 돈을 빌릴 수도 있으며 연준이 통화 공급량을 조절할 수 있는 또 하나의 방법은 할인율을 높이거나 낮추는 것인데, 이는 시중 은행들이 연준으로부터 돈을 빌리는 금리를 말한다. 할인율의 증가는 시중 은행의 가용 자금을 감소하게 만들어 통화 공급을 위축시키게 된다. 지급준비 요구와 할인율을 통해 통화 공급을 조절하는 일 외에도 연준은 공개시장 조작(중앙은행이 금융을 조절하는 것)이라고 하는 또 하나의 강력한 수단을 가지고 있다.

NOTE

Step 1	**S**urvey
Key Words	Role of the Federal Reserve; the money supply; reserve requirements; the discount rate; open-market operations
Signal Words	For example; another
Step 2	**R**eading
Purpose	To explain the functions of the Federal Reserve
Pattern of Organization	Definition; series
Tone	Neutral; objective
Main Idea	The Federal Reserve employs various methods to control the supply of money in the U.S.
Step 3	**S**ummary
지문 요약하기 (Paraphrasing)	The Federal Reserve controls the flow of money in the U.S. through a variety of methods such as reserve requirements, adjusting discount rates, and open-market operations.
Step 4	**R**ecite
	요약문 말로 설명하기

19 Read the passage and follow the directions.

> The democratic doctrine of freedom of speech and of the press, whether we regard it as a natural and inalienable right or not, rests upon certain assumptions. One of these is that men desire to know the truth and will be disposed to be guided by it. Another is that the sole method of arriving at the truth in the long run is by the free competition of opinion in the open market. Another is that, since men will inevitably differ in their opinions, each man must be permitted to urge, freely and even strenuously, his own opinion, provided he accords to others the same right. And the final assumption is that from this mutual toleration and comparison of diverse opinions the one that seems the most rational will emerge and be generally accepted.

MEMO

Describe the main idea of the passage in TEN words or more.

_____

NOTE

Step 1	**S**urvey
Key Words	
Signal Words	
Step 2	**R**eading
Purpose	
Pattern of Organization	
Tone	
Main Idea	
Step 3	**S**ummary
지문 요약하기 (Paraphrasing)	
Step 4	**R**ecite
	요약문 말로 설명하기

Answer Key

The democratic doctrine of freedom of speech and of the press, whether we regard it as a natural and inalienable right or not, rests upon certain assumptions. One of these is that men desire to know the truth and will be disposed to be guided by it. Another is that the sole method of arriving at the truth in the long run is by the free competition of opinion in the open market. Another is that, since men will inevitably differ in their opinions, each man must be permitted to urge, freely and even strenuously, his own opinion, provided he accords to others the same right. And the final assumption is that from this mutual toleration and comparison of diverse opinions the one that seems the most rational will emerge and be generally accepted.

→ key words

모범답안

The freedom of speech and press is based on several important assumptions.

한글번역

언론과 출판의 자유에 관한 민주적인 원리는, 우리가 그것을 타고날 때부터의 양도할 수 없는 권리로 간주하느냐 여부와 무관하게 어떤 가정들 위에 토대를 두고 있다. 이런 가정들의 하나는, 인간은 진실을 알고 싶어 하며 진실에 의해 인도되고 싶어 한다는 것이다. 또 다른 가정은, 진실에 도달하는 유일한 방법은 결국에는 공개 토론장에서 의견을 자유롭게 경쟁시키는 것이라는 것이다. 또 다른 가정은, 사람들이란 어쩔 수 없이 의견이 다르기 마련이므로, 각자가 똑같은 권리를 남에게 주는 한 자신의 의견을 자유롭게 심지어 열렬히 주장하는 것이 허용돼야 한다는 것이다. 그리고 마지막 가정은, 이와 같은 상호 아량과 다양한 의견의 비교로부터 가장 합리적으로 보이는 의견이 나타나서 일반적으로 인정된다는 사실이다.

NOTE

Step 1	Survey
Key Words	Democratic doctrine of freedom of speech and of the press; certain assumptions; truth
Signal Words	One of; Another; Another; the final
Step 2	Reading
Purpose	To explain several assumptions that freedom of speech and of the press is based on
Pattern of Organization	Series
Tone	Analytical; neutral
Main Idea	The freedom of speech and press is based on several important assumptions.
Step 3	Summary
지문 요약하기 (Paraphrasing)	The freedom of speech and press is based on several important assumptions. These are: men should seek the truth; free competition of opinion should drive at the truth; each man is free to urge his opinion; and through competition of these opinions the most rational will be generally accepted.
Step 4	Recite

요약문 말로 설명하기

20 Read the passage and follow the directions.

Since that day, I've had the chance to visit another bomb museum of a different kind: the one that stands in Hiroshima. A serene building set in a garden, it is strangely quiet inside, with hushed viewers and hushed exhibits. Neither ideological nor histrionic, the displays stand entirely without editorial comment. They are simply artifacts, labeled: china saki cups melted together in a stack. A brass Buddha with his hands relaxed into molten pools and a hole where his face used to be. Dozens of melted watches, all stopped at exactly eight-fifteen. A white eyelet petticoat with great, brown-rimmed holes burned in the left side, stained with black rain, worn by a schoolgirl named Oshita-chan. She was half a mile from the hypocenter of the nuclear blast, wearing also a blue short-sleeved blouse, which was incinerated except for its collar, and a blue metal pin with a small white heart, which melted. Oshita-chan lived for approximately twelve hours after the bomb.

MEMO

Why does the writer think the displays in the museum "stand entirely without editorial comment"? Second, explain why the museum visitors are "hushed". Third, what is the significance of all the watches being "stopped at exactly eight-fifteen"?

____
____
____
____
____

NOTE

Step 1	**S**urvey
Key Words	
Signal Words	
Step 2	**R**eading
Purpose	
Pattern of Organization	
Tone	
Main Idea	
Step 3	**S**ummary
지문 요약하기 (Paraphrasing)	
Step 4	**R**ecite
	요약문 말로 설명하기

Answer Key

> Since that day, I've had the chance to visit another **bomb museum of a different kind: the one that stands in Hiroshima**. A serene building set in a garden, it is strangely quiet inside, with hushed viewers and **hushed exhibits**. Neither ideological nor histrionic, **the displays** stand entirely without editorial comment. They are simply artifacts, labeled: china saki cups **melted** together in a stack. A brass Buddha with his hands relaxed into **molten** pools and a hole where his face used to be. Dozens of melted watches, all stopped at exactly eight-fifteen. A white eyelet petticoat with great, brown-rimmed holes burned in the left side, stained with black rain, worn by a schoolgirl named **Oshita-chan**. She was half a mile from the hypocenter of the nuclear blast, wearing also a blue short-sleeved blouse, which was incinerated except for its collar, and a blue metal pin with a small white heart, which **melted**. Oshita-chan lived for approximately twelve hours after the bomb.

→ key word
→ key word
→ key word

모범답안

To maintain a direct connection to the viewer (that resonates on each person's own terms). Second, they are hushed to show respect toward the event and loss, and also because they might be deep in introspection. Third, this was the moment the bomb was detonated(exploded), and broke them.

한글번역

> 그날 이후, 나는 다른 종류의 폭탄 박물관을 방문할 기회가 있었다. 즉, 히로시마에 있는 박물관이다. 정원 속에 세워진 평온한 건물로, 조용한 관람객들과 전시물들과 함께 내부는 이상하게 조용했다. 이념적이지도 과장되지도 않은 전시물들은 전적으로 편집적 논평 없이 서 있다. 그것들은 단순히 라벨이 붙은 물체들이다: 쌓인 채로 함께 녹아버린 도기로 만든 사케 잔들. 손이 녹아 웅덩이로 변하고 얼굴이 있던 곳에 구멍이 난 황동 부처상. 모두 정확히 8시 15분에 멈춘 수십 개의 녹은 시계들. 왼쪽에 큰 갈색 테두리의 구멍이 타들어가고 검은 비에 얼룩진 오시타 찬이라는 여학생이 입었던 흰색 아일릿 페티코트. 그녀는 핵폭발의 중심지로부터 800미터 떨어진 곳에 있었는데, 카라를 제외하고 다 타버린 파란색 반팔 블라우스를 입고 녹아버린 작은 하얀 하트가 있는 파란색 금속 핀을 하고 있었다. 오시타 찬은 폭탄 투하 후 약 12시간 동안 살았다.

NOTE

Step 1	**S**urvey
Key Words	The bomb museum at Hiroshima; the displays; melted
Signal Words	Not clear
Step 2	**R**eading
Purpose	To depict the bomb museum at Hiroshima
Pattern of Organization	Not clear
Tone	Solemn
Main Idea	The bomb museum at Hiroshima shows people the horror of an atomic bomb explosion.
Step 3	**S**ummary
지문 요약하기 (Paraphrasing)	The bomb museum at Hiroshima shows us the horror of an atomic bomb explosion. It presents ruined objects without editorial comment to make an impact. Among the objects is a petticoat that is partially burned and was worn by a schoolgirl who died shortly after the bombing.
Step 4	**R**ecite

요약문 말로 설명하기

21 Read the passage and follow the directions.

I walk into the gym, and there they are, the cardio-bots, half human, half machine, eyes fixed on banks of televisions and ears glued to iPods as they scale imaginary mountains or jog down simulated country roads. How driven they seem, how profoundly self-conscious. Digital monitors strapped around their biceps register their blood pressures and heart rates as their tissues absorb L-glutamine-laced protein drinks that taste like the sort of thing computers would drink if computers got thirsty. And though there must be 30 cardio-bots, lifting their sinewy thighs in unison as their StairMasters and treadmills tick off the number of calories they've burned, each one of them seems to exist in his or her own universe, oblivious to the rest.

What is the writer's opinion of the "Cardio-bots" in the gym? Second, why does the writer describe the cardio-bots as being "half human, half machine"?

_____
_____
_____
_____
_____

NOTE

Step 1	**S**urvey
Key Words	
Signal Words	
Step 2	**R**eading
Purpose	
Pattern of Organization	
Tone	
Main Idea	
Step 3	**S**ummary
지문 요약하기 (Paraphrasing)	
Step 4	**R**ecite
	요약문 말로 설명하기

Answer Key

I walk into the gym, and there they are, **the cardio-bots, half human, half machine,** eyes fixed on banks of televisions and ears glued to iPods as they scale imaginary mountains or jog down simulated country roads. How driven they seem, how profoundly self-conscious. Digital monitors strapped around their biceps register their blood pressures and heart rates as their tissues absorb L-glutamine-laced protein drinks that taste like the sort of thing computers would drink if computers got thirsty. And though there must be 30 cardio-bots, lifting their sinewy thighs in unison as their StairMasters and treadmills tick off the number of calories they've burned, each one of them seems to exist in his or her own universe, oblivious to the rest.

→ key words
 : definition

모범답안

They act exactly as robots, autonomous, unresponsive, which is a metaphorically-suggested judgment of the humans exercising. Second, as the people sitting on the machine do exercise, the two work together as a combined whole.

한글번역

내가 체육관 안으로 걸어 들어가면, 거기에는 그들이 있다. 반쯤은 인간이고, 반쯤은 기계와 같으며, 눈은 방둑처럼 길게 늘어선 텔레비전에 고정돼 있고 귀에는 아이팟이 딱 붙어있는 채 상상의 산을 오르거나 가상의 시골길을 조깅하며 내려가는 심근 강화 운동 로봇들이 말이다. 그들은 얼마나 의욕 넘쳐 보이며, 얼마나 엄청나게 자의식이 강해 보이는가. 컴퓨터가 목마르면 마실 만한 맛이 나는, L-글루타민이 가미된 단백질 음료를 그 로봇들의 세포 조직이 흡수할 때, 그들의 이두박근에 묶여있는 디지털 모니터들은 그들의 혈압과 심장 박동을 기록한다. 그리고 거기엔 자신들이 태워 온 열량의 숫자를 계단 오르기 기계와 트레드밀이 세어 주는 동안 근육질로 된 자기 허벅지를 일제히 들어 올리는 30개의 심근 강화 로봇들이 있음이 분명하지만, 각각의 로봇은 그 혹은 그녀 자신만의 우주 안에서, 나머지 로봇들은 망각한 채 존재하는 것처럼 보인다.

NOTE

Step 1	Survey
Key Words	The cardio-bots: half human, half machine
Signal Words	Not clear
Step 2	**Reading**
Purpose	To describe the cardio-bots in a gym
Pattern of Organization	Definition
Tone	Critical
Main Idea	The practice of exercising at the gym is a very inhuman (in both action and consumption).
Step 3	**Summary**
지문 요약하기 (Paraphrasing)	The practice of exercising is a very inhuman in both action and consumption. The cardio-bots at the gym are fully focused on their exercise with machine-like focus.
Step 4	**Recite**
	요약문 말로 설명하기

22 Read the passage and follow the directions.

> A creative person, first, is not limited in his thinking to "what everyone knows." "Everyone knows" that trees are green. The creative artist is able to see that in certain lights some trees look blue or purple or yellow. The creative person looks at the world with his or her own eyes, not with the eyes of others. The creative individual also knows his or her own feelings better than the average person. Most people don't know the answer to the question, "How are you? How do you feel?" The reason they don't know is that they are so busy feeling what they are supposed to feel, thinking what they are supposed to think, that they never get down to examining their own deepest feelings.

According to the writer, how does the creative person look at the world? Second, why do most people not know the answer to "how are you? How do you feel?" Third, what is the writer's definition of a creative person?

_____
_____
_____
_____
_____

NOTE

Step 1	**S**urvey
Key Words	
Signal Words	
Step 2	**R**eading
Purpose	
Pattern of Organization	
Tone	
Main Idea	
Step 3	**S**ummary
지문 요약하기 (Paraphrasing)	
Step 4	**R**ecite
	요약문 말로 설명하기

Answer Key

A creative person, first, is not limited in his thinking to "what everyone knows." "Everyone knows" that trees are green. The creative artist is able to see that in certain lights some trees look blue or purple or yellow. The creative person looks at the world with his or her own eyes, not with the eyes of others. **The creative individual also knows his or her own feelings better than the average person.** Most people don't know the answer to the question, "How are you? How do you feel?" The reason they don't know is that they are so busy feeling what they are supposed to feel, thinking what they are supposed to think, that they never get down to examining **their own deepest feelings**.

→ key words

→ key word

모범답안

They see the world uniquely, without accepting the conventional perception of things. Second, they usually think about the answer they are expected to give about what they are thinking or feeling. Third, a creative person is one who looks at the world with her/his own thinking and knows her/his own deepest feelings.

한글번역

창의적인 사람은 우선 자신의 사고를 '모두가 아는 것'으로 제한시키지 않는다. "모든 사람은 안다", 나무가 초록색이라는 것을. 창의적인 예술가는 어떤 빛에서는 나무가 파란색으로, 보라색 혹은 노란색으로 보이는 것을 알 수 있다. 창의적인 사람은 남의 눈이 아닌 자신의 눈으로 세상을 바라본다. 창의적인 사람은 또한 보통 사람보다 자신의 감정을 더 잘 안다. 대부분의 사람들은 "어떻게 지내? 기분이 어때?"라는 질문에 대한 대답을 모른다. 모르는 이유는 그들 자신이 느끼기로 돼 있는 것을 느끼고, 그들이 사고해야 하는 것에 대해 사고하기에도 너무 바빠서 그들 자신의 가장 깊은 감정을 진단하는 것에 결코 관심을 기울이지 않기 때문이다.

NOTE

Step 1	Survey
Key Words	A creative person; thinking; feelings
Signal Words	Is; also knows
Step 2	**Reading**
Purpose	To define what a creative person is
Pattern of Organization	Definition
Tone	Subjective
Main Idea	A creative person is one who looks at the world with her thinking and knows her own deepest feelings.
Step 3	**Summary**
지문 요약하기 (Paraphrasing)	A creative person is one who looks at the world with her thinking and knows her own deepest feelings. (or The creative person is able to see with their own eyes, which offers unique and truthful perception of the outside world and their own feelings.)
Step 4	**Recite**

요약문 말로 설명하기

23 Read the passage and follow the directions.

In the 1840s, students protested and acted in violent ways. Students at Yale, for example, objected to their mathematics course and burned their books in the streets. Some captured their tutor and kept him tied up all night, and others shot a cannon through the tutor's bedroom window. In the 1940s and 1950s, students were a fun-loving, game-happy lot. They swallowed live goldfish, took part in dance marathons, and held contests to see how many people could crowd into a phone booth. The more daring males broke into women's rooms in panty raids and then festooned their own rooms with the ill-gotten silks. Then, in the 1960s, students repeated the activities of the 1840s. They objected to their courses, littered the campuses with their books and papers, and locked teachers inside college buildings. They protested against all forms of social injustice, from war to the food in the cafeteria. The more violent threw rocks at the police, and a few planted bombs in college buildings. In the 1970s students repeated the fun and games of the forties and fifties. They held contests to see how many people could squeeze into a phone booth. They had dance marathons. The more daring ran naked across campuses, in a craze called "streaking." The slightly less daring did their streaking with brown paper bags over their heads. History does seem to repeat itself, even in the sometimes violent and sometimes fun-and-games behavior of the students on college campuses.

Describe the main idea of the passage in ONE sentence.

NOTE

Step 1	Ⓢurvey
Key Words	
Signal Words	
Step 2	**Ⓡeading**
Purpose	
Pattern of Organization	
Tone	
Main Idea	
Step 3	**Ⓢummary**
지문 요약하기 (Paraphrasing)	
Step 4	**Ⓡecite**

요약문 말로 설명하기

Answer Key

<u>In the 1840s</u>, **students protested and acted in violent ways**. Students at Yale, <u>for example</u>, **objected** to their mathematics course and **burned** their books in the streets. Some captured their tutor and kept him tied up all night, and others shot a cannon through the tutor's bedroom window. <u>In the 1940s</u> and <u>1950s</u>, **students were a fun-loving, game-happy lot**. They swallowed live goldfish, took part in dance marathons, and held contests to see how many people could crowd into a phone booth. The more daring males broke into women's rooms in panty raids and then festooned their own rooms with the ill-gotten silks. <u>Then, in the 1960s</u>, **students repeated the activities of the 1840s**. They **objected to** their courses, **littered** the campuses with their books and papers, and **locked** teachers inside college buildings. They **protested against** all forms of social injustice, from war to the food in the cafeteria. The more violent threw rocks at the police, and a few planted bombs in college buildings. <u>In the 1970s</u> **students repeated the fun and games of the forties and fifties**. They held contests to see how many people could squeeze into a phone booth. They had dance marathons. The more daring ran naked across campuses, in a craze called "streaking." The slightly less daring did their streaking with brown paper bags over their heads. **History does seem to repeat itself, even in the sometimes violent and sometimes fun-and-games behavior of the students on college campuses.**

→ key word

→ key word

→ key word

main idea

모범답안

Students on college campuses sometimes repeat the same behavior as college students of earlier eras.

한글번역

　1840년대에 학생들은 폭력적인 방식으로 저항하고 행동했다. 예를 들어 예일의 학생들은 그들의 수학 강의에 반기를 들고 거리에서 교과서를 태웠다. 몇몇은 그들의 강사를 잡아 하룻밤 내내 묶어두기도 했고, 다른 이들은 강사의 침실 창문으로 대포를 쏘기도 했다. 1940년대와 1950년대에 학생들은 꽤나 유희를 즐겼고, 게임하는 것을 좋아했다. 그들은 살아 있는 금붕어를 삼키거나 댄스 마라톤(장시간에 걸친 무도회)에 참가하거나, 얼마나 많은 사람이 공중전화 부스 안으로 들어갈 수 있는지 보기 위한 대회를 열기도 했다. 보다 대담한 남자들은 여자들의 방에 침입해 '팬티를 탈취하기 위한 급습'을 감행했고, 그들의 방을 부정하게 얻은 실크로 꾸몄다. 그리고 1960년대에, 학생들은 1840년대의 운동을 반복했다. 그들은 그들의 강의에 반대해 책과 리포트를 캠퍼스 내에 흩뿌렸고, 학교 건물 안에 선생님들을 가뒀다. 그들은 전쟁에서부터 학생 식당의 음식에까지, 모든 종류의 사회적인 부당함에 저항했다. 더 폭력적인 학생들은 경찰에게 돌을 던지고, 몇몇은 학교 건물 내에 폭탄을 설치하기도 했다. 1970년대에 학생들은 40년대와 50년대에 유희와 게임을 즐기던 방식을 반복했다. 그들은 얼마나 많은 사람이 공중전화 부스 안으로 밀려들어갈 수 있는지 보기 위한 대회를 개최했고 댄스 마라톤에 참가했다. 더 대담한 학생들은 '스트리킹'이라 불리는 유행으로서 벌거벗은 채 캠퍼스를 질주했다. 그중에서 다소 덜 대담한 이들은 머리에 누런 종이 봉투를 뒤집어쓰고 뛰었다. 어떤 때는 폭력적이고 어떤 때는 게임을 즐기는 듯한 대학교 학생들의 행동에서조차 역사는 반복되는 것 같다.

NOTE

Step 1	**S**urvey
Key Words	Students; protests; fun; games; violent; repeated
Signal Words	In the 1840s; in the 1940s and 1950s; then, in the 1960s; in the 1970s
Step 2	**R**eading
Purpose	To show that college students of different eras may behave in the same way
Pattern of Organization	Time order
Tone	Informative
Main Idea	Students on college campuses sometimes repeat the same behavior as college students of earlier eras.
Step 3	**S**ummary
지문 요약하기 (Paraphrasing)	When it comes to the behavior of students on college campuses, history sometimes repeats itself. Students in the 1960s carried out protests that were very similar to those made by students in the 1840s, and in the 1970s, students repeated some of the fun and games that students used to do 20 to 30 years before.
Step 4	**R**ecite
	요약문 말로 설명하기

24 Read the passage and follow the directions.

Preparing food for the saute line at the restaurant where I work is a hectic two-hour job. I come to work at 3:00 p.m. knowing that everything must be done by 5:00 p.m. The first thing I do is to check the requisition for the day. Then I have to clean and season five or six prime rib roasts and place them in the slow-cooking oven. After this, I clean and season five trays of white potatoes for baking and put them in the fast oven. Now I have two things cooking, prime ribs and potatoes, at different times and temperatures, and they both have to be watched very closely. In the meantime, I must put three trays of bacon in the oven. The bacon needs very close watching. Next, I make popovers, which are unseasoned rolls. These also go into an oven for baking. Now I have prime ribs, baking potatoes, bacon, and popovers cooking at the same time and all of them needing to be closely watched. With my work area set up, I must make clarified butter and garlic butter. The clarified butter is for cooking liver, veal, and fish. The garlic butter is for stuffing escargots*. I have to make ground meat stuffing also. Half of the ground meat will be mixed with wild rice and will be used to stuff breasts of chicken. The other half of the ground meat mixture will be used to stuff mushrooms. I have to prepare veal, cut and season scampi, and clean and saute mushrooms and onions. In the meantime, I check the prime ribs and potatoes, take the bacon and the popovers out of the oven, and put the veal and chicken into the oven. Now I make au jus, which is served over the prime ribs, make the soup for the day, and cook the vegetables and rice. Then I heat the bordelaise sauce, make the special for the day, and last of all, cook food for the employees. This and sometimes more has to be done by five o'clock. Is it any wonder that I say preparing food for the saute line at the restaurant where I work is a very hectic two-hour job!

*escargots : snails

Describe the main idea of the passage in ONE sentence.

NOTE

Step 1	**S**urvey
Key Words	
Signal Words	
Step 2	**R**eading
Purpose	
Pattern of Organization	
Tone	
Main Idea	
Step 3	**S**ummary
지문 요약하기 (Paraphrasing)	
Step 4	**R**ecite
	요약문 말로 설명하기

Answer Key

> **Preparing food for the saute line at the restaurant** where I work is a **hectic** two-hour job. I come to work at 3:00 p.m. knowing that everything must be done by 5:00 p.m. The first thing I do is to check the requisition for the day. Then, I have to clean and season five or six prime rib roasts and place them in the slow-cooking oven. After this, I clean and season five trays of white potatoes for baking and put them in the fast oven. Now I have two things cooking, prime ribs and potatoes, at different times and temperatures, and they both have to be watched very closely. In the meantime, I must put three trays of bacon in the oven. The bacon needs very close watching. Next, I make popovers, which are unseasoned rolls. These also go into an oven for baking. Now I have prime ribs, baking potatoes, bacon, and popovers cooking at the same time and all of them needing to be closely watched. With my work area set up, I must make clarified butter and garlic butter. The clarified butter is for cooking liver, veal, and fish. The garlic butter is for stuffing escargots. I have to make ground meat stuffing also. Half of the ground meat will be mixed with wild rice and will be used to stuff breasts of chicken. The other half of the ground meat mixture will be used to stuff mushrooms. I have to prepare veal, cut and season scampi, and clean and saute mushrooms and onions. In the meantime, I check the prime ribs and potatoes, take the bacon and the popovers out of the oven, and put the veal and chicken into the oven. Now I make au jus, which is served over the prime ribs, make the soup for the day, and cook the vegetables and rice. Then I heat the bordelaise sauce, make the special for the day, and last of all, cook food for the employees. This and sometimes more has to be done by five o'clock. Is it any wonder that I say **preparing food for the saute line at the restaurant where I work is a very hectic two-hour job!**

→ key words

→ repeltition

모범답안

Preparing food at a restaurant where the speaker works is a very busy job.

한글번역

　내가 일하는 레스토랑에서 볶음 라인 음식을 준비하는 것은 정신없이 바쁜 두 시간짜리 일이다. 난 다섯 시까지 모든 일이 완료돼야 한다는 것을 알고 있기에 3시에 직장에 온다. 내가 가장 먼저 하는 일은 여섯 개의 주문된 최고급 갈비구이를 확인하고 느리게 조리되는 오븐에 넣는 것이다. 그 후 구워야 하는 다섯 쟁반의 하얀 감자들을 씻고 양념을 해, 빨리 조리되는 오븐에 넣는다. 이제 두 가지, 최상품 소갈비와 감자는 다른 시간과 온도에 맞춰져서 요리되고 있고, 두 가지 모두 주의 깊게 지켜봐야 한다. 그동안 오븐에 세 쟁반의 베이컨을 넣어야 한다. 베이컨은 아주 세밀한 관찰이 요구된다. 다음 양념이 안 된 롤빵인 팝오버를 만든다. 이것도 굽기 위해 오븐에 넣는다. 이제 갈비구이, 구운 감자, 베이컨, 팝오버가 동시에 구워지고 있고 모든 요리를 주의 깊게 지켜봐야 한다. 내 근무 구역을 준비하면서 나는 속을 채운 식용 달팽이를 위한 녹인 버터와 마늘 버터를 만들어야 한다. 다진 고기 속도 만들어야 한다. 다진 고기의 절반은 줄풀과 섞어 닭가슴살을 채워 넣기 위해 사용될 것이다. 다진 고기의 또 다른 절반은 버섯 속을 채우기 위해 사용될 것이다. 송아지 고기를 준비하고 자르고 새우튀김을 양념하고 버섯과 양파를 씻고 볶아야 한다. 그러는 동안 소갈비와 감자를 확인하고 베이컨과 팝오버를 오븐에서 꺼내고 송아지 고기와 치킨을 오븐에 넣는다. 이제 소갈비 위에 뿌릴 고기 육즙을 만들고 그날의 수프를 만들고 야채와 쌀을 요리한다. 그리고 보르돌레즈 소스를 데우고 그날의 스페셜 요리를 만들고 마지막으로 직원들을 위한 요리를 한다. 이만큼의, 가끔은 더 많은 양의 일이 다섯 시 정각까지 끝나야 한다. 내가 일하는 레스토랑에서 볶음 라인을 위한 음식을 준비하는 것이 눈코 뜰 새 없이 바쁜 두 시간짜리 일이라고 말하는 것이 이제 놀라운가!

NOTE

Step 1	Survey
Key Words	Preparing food for the saute line at a restaurant; hectic
Signal Words	The first thing; Then; After this; Now; In the meantime; Next; With my work area set up; In the meantime; Now; Then; last of all; by five o'clock
Step 2	**Reading**
Purpose	To describe the hectic job of preparing food for the saute line
Pattern of Organization	Time order(process)
Tone	Informative
Main Idea	Preparing food at a restaurant where the speaker works is a very busy job.
Step 3	**Summary**
지문 요약하기 (Paraphrasing)	Preparing food for the sauté line is a very hectic two-hour job. From 3:00-5:00 p.m., the writer follows a detailed process to prepare the saute line. First, they check requisitions and start cooking prime ribs. Next, they prepare potatoes, bacon, and popovers in sequence. While monitoring these items, they make clarified and garlic butters, followed by meat stuffings for chicken and mushrooms. They then prepare various meats and sauces, while continuing to check and rotate earlier items. Finally, they finish with soups, vegetables, and employee meals, all within the tight two-hour window.
Step 4	**Recite**
	요약문 말로 설명하기

25 Read the passage and follow the directions.

All Americans know that their country began as a British colony, but fewer realize that an American colony went on to become an independent republic. Africa's Liberia began its existence as an American colony established by free African Americans. Then it followed in the footsteps of its parent nation to declare independence and become a separate republic. In 1816, a group of white Americans created the American Colonization Society (ACS). The founders of the ACS wanted to establish an African settlement so that America's 200,000 free blacks, as well as newly emancipated slaves, could return to the continent of their ancestors. The society's motives were humanitarian, social, and religious. Members believed that an American colony like the one they imagined could help end the slave trade, correct the injustices done to enslaved blacks, and aid the spread of Christianity to the African continent. Others, however, advocated the return of free blacks for a different reason. They feared a revolt similar to the one that had occurred in Haiti, where slaves had overthrown their masters and set up a republic. In 1818, with $100,000 of seed money from the U.S. Congress, the ACS sent two representatives to Africa to purchase suitable territory. It wasn't until 1821, however, that a permanent place of settlement was found and bought. According to records, the earliest inhabitants arrived in 1822. In 1824, the colony was officially named Liberia, a name that suggests its purpose as a land of liberty and freedom for black Americans. By 1840, Liberia boasted a population of about 2,500 American expatriates and 28,000 African tribespeople. In 1847, the Liberian government proclaimed its independence from the United States. However, just as Britain had denied America its independence years before, the United States did not immediately recognize Liberia as a separate nation. Many lawmakers were also slaveholders who feared the consequences of acknowledging Liberia's independence. Not until 1862, during the Civil War, did President Abraham Lincoln formally recognize Liberia as a(n) _____.

Fill in the blank with the TWO most appropriate consecutive words from the passage.

_____

NOTE

Step 1	**S**urvey
Key Words	
Signal Words	
Step 2	**R**eading
Purpose	
Pattern of Organization	
Tone	
Main Idea	
Step 3	**S**ummary
지문 요약하기 (Paraphrasing)	
Step 4	**R**ecite
	요약문 말로 설명하기

Answer Key

All Americans know that their country began as a British colony, but fewer realize that an American colony went on to become an independent republic. **Africa's Liberia** began its existence as an American colony established by free African Americans. Then it followed in the footsteps of its parent nation to declare independence and become a separate republic. In 1816, a group of white Americans created **the American Colonization Society (ACS)**. The founders of the ACS wanted to establish an African settlement so that America's 200,000 free blacks, as well as newly emancipated slaves, could return to the continent of their ancestors. The society's motives were **humanitarian, social, and religious**. Members believed that an American colony like the one they imagined could help end the slave trade, correct the injustices done to enslaved blacks, and aid the spread of Christianity to the African continent. Others, however, advocated the return of free blacks for a different reason. They feared a revolt similar to the one that had occurred in Haiti, where slaves had overthrown their masters and set up a republic. // In 1818, with $100,000 of seed money from the U.S. Congress, the ACS sent two representatives to Africa to purchase suitable territory. It wasn't until 1821, however, that a permanent place of settlement was found and bought. According to records, the earliest inhabitants arrived in 1822. In 1824, the colony was officially named Liberia, a name that suggests its purpose as a land of liberty and freedom for black Americans. By 1840, Liberia boasted a population of about 2,500 American expatriates and 28,000 African tribespeople. In 1847, the Liberian government proclaimed its independence from the United States. However, just as Britain had denied America its independence years before, the United States did not immediately recognize Liberia as a separate nation. Many lawmakers were also slaveholders who feared the consequences of acknowledging Liberia's independence. Not until 1862, during the Civil War, did President Abraham Lincoln formally **recognize Liberia as an independent republic**.

key words

time order

모범답안

independent republic

한글번역

　　미국인 중 자신의 모국이 영국 식민지에서 출발했다는 사실을 모르는 사람은 없다. 하지만 미국의 식민지에서 독립 국가로 변모한 나라가 있다는 사실을 아는 미국인은 거의 없다. 아프리카의 라이베리아는 미국 식민지로 시작했으며, 노예제도에서 풀려나 자유의 몸이 된 흑인들에 의해 세워졌다. 그런 후 라이베리아는 모국의 발자취를 쫓아 독립을 선언하고 독자적인 공화국을 형성하게 된다. 1816년, 한 무리의 미국 백인들이 ACS(American Colonization Society: 미국식민협회)를 설립했다. ACS의 설립자들은 아프리카에 정착지 설립을 희망했으며, 이를 통해 미국에 있는 20만 명의 자유의 몸이 된 흑인들뿐만 아니라 새롭게 노예제도에서 해방된 이들까지도 자신들의 선조가 있던 아프리카 대륙으로 되돌아갈 수 있도록 하고자 했다. ACS의 동기는 인도주의적이고, 사회적이며, 종교적이었다. ACS 회원들은 자신들이 구상한 것과 같은 미국 식민지가 노예 교역을 종식시키고, 흑인 노예들에게 가해졌던 불의를 바로잡으며, 아프리카 대륙에 기독교를 전파하는 데 일조할 것으로 믿었다. 하지만 다른 이들은 자유의 몸이 된 흑인들의 귀환을 이와는 다른 이유로 지지했다. 그들은 아이티에서 일어난 것과 같은 반란을 두려워했는데, 아이티의 노예들은 지배층을 뒤엎고, 공화국을 세웠었다. 1818년, 미국 의회로부터 받은 10만 달러의 초기자본과 함께, ACS는 두 명의 대표를 아프리카로 보내 적당한 영토를 구입하도록 했다. 그러나 1821년이 돼서야 영구적으로 정착할 장소를 찾아 구입할 수 있었다. 기록에 의하면, 초기의 거주민들은 1822년에 도착했다고 한다. 그리고 1824년, 그 식민지가 공식적으로 라이베리아라고 명명됐으며, 이 명칭은 미국 흑인들을 위한 자유와 평화의 땅을 목적으로 한다는 사실을 암시하고 있다. 1840년에 이르러서는 라이베리아에 미국에서 2,500명에 달하는 이들이 건너왔고, 아프리카 원주민들은 28,000명에 달하게 됐다. 1847년에는 라이베리아 정부가 미국으로부터 독립을 선언했다. 그러나 이전에 영국이 미국의 독립을 반대했던 것처럼, 미국도 라이베리아를 곧바로 독립국가로 인정하지 않았다. 많은 미국 의원들 또한 노예 소유자들이었기 때문에, 라이베리아를 독립국가로 인정하게 될 경우 일어날 여파에 대해 우려했다. 남북전쟁 중이던 1862년에 이르러서야 에이브러햄 링컨 대통령이 공식적으로 라이베리아를 독립국가로 승인했다.

NOTE

Step 1	**S**urvey
Key Words	American Colonies; Liberia; independent republic
Signal Words	Then it followed; in 1816; in 1818; It wasn't until 1821; in 1822; in 1824; By 1840; in 1847; Not until 1862
Step 2	**R**eading
Purpose	To describe the formation of Liberia and how it gained its independence
Pattern of Organization	Time order
Tone	Informative
Main Idea	Liberia, which began as a U.S. colony, struggled for independence from the United States in much the same way as the United States did from Britain.
Step 3	**S**ummary
지문 요약하기 (Paraphrasing)	Liberia began as an American colony established for free African Americans before declaring independence and becoming a separate republic, mirroring America's own path to independence. In 1816, the American Colonization Society established Liberia as a settlement for free African Americans, motivated by humanitarian concerns and desires to end slave trade and spread Christianity. By 1840, Liberia had 2,500 American expatriates and 28,000 African tribespeople. Liberia declared independence in 1847, but the United States only recognized it in 1862 under Lincoln, during the Civil War.
Step 4	**R**ecite
	요약문 말로 설명하기

26 Read the passage and follow the directions.

Once people wore garlic around their necks to ward off disease. Today, most Americans would scoff at the idea of wearing a necklace of garlic cloves to enhance their well-being. However, you might find a number of Americans willing to ingest capsules of pulverized garlic or other herbal supplements in the name of health. Complementary and alternative medicine, which includes a range of practices outside of conventional medicine such as herbs, homeopathy, massage therapy, yoga, and acupuncture, hold increasing appeal for Americans. In fact, 42% of Americans have used alternative therapies. In all age groups, the use of unconventional healthcare practices has steadily increased in the last 30 years, and the trend is likely to continue, although people born before 1945 are the least likely to turn to these therapies.

Why have so many patients turned to alternative therapies? Many are frustrated by the time constraints of managed care and alienated by conventional medicine's focus on technology. Others feel that a holistic approach to healthcare better reflects their beliefs and values. Others seek therapies that relieve symptoms associated with chronic disease; symptoms that mainstream medicine cannot treat.

<u>Some alternative therapies have even crossed the line into mainstream medicine</u>, as scientific investigation has confirmed their safety and efficacy. For example, physicians may currently prescribe acupuncture for pain management or to control the nausea associated with chemotherapy. Additionally, many U.S. medical schools teach courses in alternative therapies, and many health insurance companies offer some alternative medicine benefits.

Explain what the underlined "Some alternative therapies have even crossed the line into mainstream medicine" means.

___

NOTE

Step 1	**S**urvey
Key Words	
Signal Words	
Step 2	**R**eading
Purpose	
Pattern of Organization	
Tone	
Main Idea	
Step 3	**S**ummary
지문 요약하기 (Paraphrasing)	
Step 4	**R**ecite
	요약문 말로 설명하기

Answer Key

Once people wore garlic around their necks to ward off disease. Today, most Americans would scoff at the idea of wearing a necklace of garlic cloves to enhance their well-being. However, you might find a number of Americans willing to ingest capsules of pulverized garlic or other herbal supplements in the name of health. **Complementary and alternative medicine**, which includes a range of practices outside of conventional medicine such as herbs, homeopathy, massage therapy, yoga, and acupuncture, hold increasing appeal for Americans. In fact, 42% of Americans have used **alternative therapies**. In all age groups, the use of **unconventional healthcare practices** has steadily increased in the last 30 years, and the trend is likely to continue, although people born before 1945 are the least likely to turn to these therapies.

Why have so many patients turned to alternative therapies? Many are frustrated by the time constraints of managed care and alienated by conventional medicine's focus on technology. Others feel that a holistic approach to healthcare better reflects their beliefs and values. Others seek therapies that relieve symptoms associated with chronic disease; symptoms that mainstream medicine cannot treat.

Some alternative therapies have even crossed the line into mainstream medicine, as scientific investigation has confirmed their safety and efficacy. For example, physicians may currently prescribe acupuncture for pain management or to control the nausea associated with chemotherapy. Additionally, many U.S. medical schools teach courses in alternative therapies, and many health insurance companies offer some alternative medicine benefits.

key words

모범답안

It means that certain alternative (or non-traditional) medical treatments have become accepted and integrated into conventional medical practice.

한글번역

예전에는 사람들이 질병을 물리치기 위해 목에 마늘을 걸고 다녔다. 오늘날 대부분의 미국인들은 건강을 증진시키기 위해 마늘 목걸이를 하는 것을 비웃을 것이다. 하지만 건강을 위해 마늘 가루 캡슐이나 다른 허브 보조제를 섭취하려는 미국인들을 쉽게 찾아볼 수 있다. 허브, 동종요법, 마사지 치료, 요가, 침술과 같은 기존 의학 외의 다양한 방법을 포함하는 보완대체의학은 미국인들에게 점점 더 매력적으로 다가가고 있다. 실제로 42%의 미국인들이 대체요법을 사용해 봤다. 모든 연령대에서 비전통적 건강관리 방법의 사용이 지난 30년 동안 꾸준히 증가해 왔으며, 1945년 이전에 태어난 사람들이 이러한 치료법을 가장 적게 찾긴 하지만 이러한 추세는 계속될 것으로 보인다.

왜 이렇게 많은 환자들이 대체요법으로 눈을 돌렸을까? 많은 이들이 관리의료의 시간적 제약에 좌절감을 느끼고 기술에 중점을 둔 전통의학에 거리감을 느끼고 있다. 어떤 이들은 전인적 접근방식의 건강관리가 자신들의 신념과 가치를 더 잘 반영한다고 생각한다. 또 다른 이들은 주류 의학이 치료할 수 없는 만성 질환과 관련된 증상을 완화시키는 치료법을 찾고 있다.

일부 대체요법은 과학적 연구를 통해 안전성과 효능이 입증되면서 주류 의학의 영역으로 들어오기도 했다. 예를 들어, 의사들은 현재 통증 관리나 항암치료와 관련된 메스꺼움을 조절하기 위해 침술을 처방할 수 있다. 또한 많은 미국 의과대학들이 대체요법 과정을 가르치고 있으며, 많은 건강보험 회사들이 일부 대체의학 혜택을 제공하고 있다.

NOTE

Step 1	**S**urvey
Key Words	Alternative therapies; conventional medicine; mainstream medicine; holistic approach; complementary medicine
Signal Words	Because; as a result; due to; therefore; since
Step 2	**R**eading
Purpose	To explain the growing acceptance of alternative medicine in modern healthcare
Pattern of Organization	Problem/solution; cause/effect
Tone	Objective; informative
Main Idea	Alternative medicine is gaining acceptance in mainstream healthcare due to patient demand and scientific validation.
Step 3	**S**ummary
지문 요약하기 (Paraphrasing)	Americans increasingly embrace alternative therapies due to limitations of conventional medicine and desire for holistic treatment approaches. As scientific research validates certain alternative treatments' safety and effectiveness, these therapies are becoming integrated into mainstream medical practice and healthcare systems.
Step 4	**R**ecite
요약문 말로 설명하기	

27 Read the passage and follow the directions.

Modern natural science is a useful starting point because it is the only important social activity that by common consensus is both cumulative and directional, even if its ultimate impact on human happiness is ambiguous. The progressive conquest of nature made possible with the development of the scientific method in the sixteenth and seventeenth centuries has proceeded according to certain definite rules laid down not by man, but by nature and nature's laws. The unfolding of modern natural science has had a homogeneous effect on all societies that have experienced it, for two reasons. In the first place, technology confers decisive military advantages on those countries that possess it, and given the continuing possibility of war in the international system of states, no state that values its independence can ignore the need for defensive modernization. Second, modern natural science establishes a uniform horizon of economic production possibilities. Technology makes possible the limitless accumulation of wealth, and thus the satisfaction of an ever-expanding set of human desires. This process guarantees an increasing homogenisation of all human societies, regardless of their historical origins or cultural inheritances. All countries undergoing economic modernization must increasingly resemble one another : they must unify nationally on the basis of a centralized state, urbanize, replace traditional forms of social organization like tribe, sect, and family with economically rational ones based on function and efficiency, and provide for the universal education of their citizens. Such societies have become increasingly linked with one another through global markets and the spread of a universal consumer culture.

Explain why the development of modern natural science has an uniform effect on all societies.

_____

_____

_____

NOTE

Step 1	**S**urvey
Key Words	
Signal Words	
Step 2	**R**eading
Purpose	
Pattern of Organization	
Tone	
Main Idea	
Step 3	**S**ummary
지문 요약하기 (Paraphrasing)	
Step 4	**R**ecite
	요약문 말로 설명하기

Answer Key

> key words

Modern natural science is a useful starting point because it is the only important social activity that by common consensus is both cumulative and directional, even if its ultimate impact on human happiness is ambiguous. The progressive conquest of nature made possible with the development of the scientific method in the sixteenth and seventeenth centuries has proceeded according to certain definite rules laid down not by man, but by nature and nature's laws. The unfolding of **modern natural science** has had a **homogeneous effect** on all societies that have experienced it, for **two reasons**. In the first place, **technology** confers decisive military advantages on those countries that possess it, and given the continuing possibility of war in the international system of states, no state that values its independence can ignore the need for defensive modernization. Second, **modern natural science** establishes a **uniform** horizon of economic production possibilities. **Technology** makes possible the limitless accumulation of wealth, and thus the satisfaction of an ever-expanding set of human desires. This process guarantees an increasing **homogenisation** of all human societies, regardless of their historical origins or cultural inheritances. All countries undergoing economic modernization must increasingly **resemble** one another: they must unify nationally on the basis of a centralized state, urbanize, replace traditional forms of social organization like tribe, sect, and family with economically rational ones based on function and efficiency, and provide for the **universal** education of their citizens. Such societies have become increasingly linked with one another through global markets and the spread of a **universal** consumer culture.

> key words

모범답안

It is because it forces them to adopt technological advancement for military defense and economic production capabilities, which inevitably leads to similar patterns of social organization and development regardless of their cultural backgrounds.

한글번역

현대 자연과학은 유용한 출발점이다. 그 이유는 이것이 인간의 행복에 대한 궁극적 영향이 모호할지라도, 공통된 합의에 의해 누적적이고 방향성을 가진 유일하게 중요한 사회적 활동이기 때문이다. 16세기와 17세기에 과학적 방법론의 발전으로 가능해진 자연에 대한 점진적 정복은 인간이 아닌 자연과 자연법칙이 정한 특정한 규칙들에 따라 진행돼 왔다. 현대 자연과학의 전개는 두 가지 이유로 이를 경험한 모든 사회에 동질적인 영향을 미쳤다. 첫째로, 기술은 그것을 보유한 국가들에게 결정적인 군사적 이점을 제공하며, 독립성을 중요시한다면 국가 체제에서 전쟁 가능성이 계속되는 한 어떤 국가도 방어적 현대화의 필요성을 무시할 수 없다. 둘째로, 현대 자연과학은 경제적 생산 가능성에 대해 균일한 지평을 확립한다. 기술은 무제한적인 부의 축적을 가능하게 하고, 따라서 끊임없이 확장되는 인간 욕구의 충족을 가능하게 한다. 이 과정은 역사적 기원이나 문화적 유산과 관계없이 모든 인간 사회의 증가하는 동질화를 보장한다. 경제적 현대화를 겪는 모든 국가들은 점점 더 서로 비슷해져야 한다: 그들은 중앙집권화된 국가를 기반으로 국가적 통일을 이뤄야 하고, 도시화돼야 하며, 부족, 종파, 가족과 같은 전통적인 사회 조직 형태를 기능과 효율성에 기반한 경제적으로 합리적인 것으로 대체해야 하고, 시민들을 위한 보편적 교육을 제공해야 한다. 이러한 사회들은 세계 시장과 보편적 소비자 문화의 확산을 통해 서로 점점 더 연결돼 왔다.

NOTE

Step 1	**S**urvey
Key Words	Natural science; modernization; technology; homogenisation; economic production
Signal Words	Because; in the first place; second; thus
Step 2	**R**eading
Purpose	To explain how modern science uniformly affects all societies
Pattern of Organization	Cause/effect
Tone	Analytical
Main Idea	Modern natural science creates uniform effects across all societies for two reasons.
Step 3	**S**ummary
지문 요약하기 (Paraphrasing)	Modern natural science creates uniform effects across all societies for two reasons. First, technology provides decisive military advantages, forcing countries to modernize for defense. Second, it establishes uniform economic production possibilities, leading to similar social and cultural transformations across all societies.
Step 4	**R**ecite
	요약문 말로 설명하기

28 Read the passage and follow the directions.

The question of why we dream has fascinated philosophers and scientists for thousands of years. Despite scientific inquiry into the function of dreams, we still don't have a solid answer for why we do it. While much remains uncertain about dreaming, many experts have developed theories about the purpose of dreams, with new empirical research providing greater clarity.

Sleep allows us to consolidate and process all of the information and memories that we have collected during the previous day. Dreaming is a byproduct, or even an active part, of this experience processing. This model, known as the self-organization theory of dreaming, explains that dreaming is a side effect of brain neural activity as memories are consolidated during sleep. During this process of unconscious information redistribution, it is suggested that memories are either strengthened or weakened. While we dream, helpful memories are made stronger, while less useful ones fade away.

The function of dreams is to help us process and cope with our emotions or trauma in the safe space of slumber. The amygdala, which is involved in processing emotions, and the hippocampus, which plays a vital role in condensing information and moving it from short-term to long-term memory storage, are active during vivid, intense dreaming. This theory suggests that REM sleep plays a vital role in emotional brain regulation. It also helps explain why so many dreams are emotionally vivid and why emotional or traumatic experiences tend to show up on repeat.

While there are many theories for why we dream, more research is needed to fully understand their purpose. Rather than assuming only one hypothesis is correct, dreams likely serve a variety of purposes. Knowing that so much is left uncertain about why we dream, we can feel free to view our own dreams in the light that resonates best with us.

Write a summary following the guidelines below.

| Guidelines |
- Summarize the above passage in ONE paragraph.
- Provide a topic sentence, major supporting details, and a concluding sentence based on the passage.
- Do NOT copy more than FIVE consecutive words from the passage.

NOTE

Step 1	**S**urvey
Key Words	
Signal Words	
Step 2	**R**eading
Purpose	
Pattern of Organization	
Tone	
Main Idea	
Step 3	**S**ummary
지문 요약하기 (Paraphrasing)	
Step 4	**R**ecite
	요약문 말로 설명하기

Answer Key

The question of why we **dream** has fascinated philosophers and scientists for thousands of years. Despite scientific inquiry into the **function of dreams**, we still don't have a solid answer for why we do it. While much remains uncertain about **dreaming**, many experts have developed theories about the **purpose of dreams**, with new empirical research providing greater clarity.

Sleep allows us to **consolidate and process all of the information and memories** that we have collected during the previous day. Dreaming is a byproduct, or even an active part, of this experience processing. This model, known as **the self-organization** theory **of dreaming**, explains that dreaming is **a side effect of brain neural activity** as memories are consolidated during sleep. During this process of unconscious information redistribution, it is suggested that memories are either strengthened or weakened. While we dream, helpful memories are made stronger, while less useful ones fade away.

The function of dreams is to **help us process and cope with our emotions or trauma** in the safe space of slumber. **The amygdala**, which is involved in processing emotions, and the **hippocampus**, which plays a vital role in condensing information and moving it from short-term to long-term memory storage, are active during vivid, intense dreaming. This theory suggests that REM sleep plays a vital role in emotional brain regulation. It also helps explain why so many dreams are emotionally vivid and why emotional or traumatic experiences tend to show up on repeat.

While there are many theories for why we dream, more research is needed to fully understand their purpose. Rather than assuming only one hypothesis is correct, dreams likely serve a variety of purposes. Knowing that so much is left **uncertain** about why we dream, we **can feel free to view our own dreams in the light that resonates best with us**.

key words
theories
①
②
conclusion

모범답안

There are several theories about why people dream. One, the self-organization theory of dreaming, is that dreams aid in memory. Information is processed and memories are managed during dreaming. Another theory is that dreams help process emotions. The amygdala and hippocampus of the brain are both processing emotions and memories together which creates vivid dreams to emotionally regulate the brain. In conclusion, since much is left unclear about the purpose of dreams, we need to use our dreams for our own good.

채점기준

+ 1점: 글의 topic sentence를 다음과 같이 서술하였거나 유사하였다.
"There are several theories about why people dream (or *the role of dreams* or *the goal of dreams*)."

+ 2점: 글의 major supporting details를 다음과 같이 서술하였거나 유사하였다.
"One, the self-organization theory of dreaming, is that information is processed and memories are managed during dreaming. Another theory is that the amygdala and hippocampus of the brain are both processing emotions and memories together which creates vivid dreams to emotionally regulate the brain."
☞ 2개 중 2개 모두를 정확하게 요약한 경우 2점, 1개만 요약한 경우 1점, 요약하지 못한 경우 0점을 준다.

+ 1점: 글의 결론을 "In conclusion, since much is left unclear about the purpose of dreams, we need to use our dreams for our own good."이라 서술하였거나 유사하였다.

● 감점
 • 본문에 나오는 연속되는 6단어 이상을 사용하였다. −1pt
 • 문단을 두 개나 그 이상으로 구성하였다. −1pt
 • grammar나 영어표현이 합쳐 4개 이상 오류가 있다. −1pt

한글번역

우리가 왜 꿈을 꾸는지에 관한 질문은 수천 년 동안 철학자와 과학자들을 매료시켜 왔다. 꿈의 기능에 대한 과학적 탐구에도 불구하고, 우리는 여전히 왜 꿈을 꾸는지에 대한 확실한 답을 가지고 있지 않다. 꿈을 꾸는 것에 대해 여전히 많은 것이 불확실하지만, 많은 전문가들은 더 많은 명확성을 제공하는 새로운 경험적 연구를 통해 꿈의 목적에 대한 이론을 발전시켰다.

수면은 우리가 전날에 수집한 모든 정보와 기억을 통합하고 처리할 수 있게 해준다. 꿈은 이 경험 과정의 부산물 또는 심지어 능동적인 부분이다. 꿈의 자기조직 이론으로 알려진 이 모델은 자는 동안 기억이 굳어지면서 꿈을 꾸는 것이 뇌신경 활동의 부작용이라고 설명한다. 이러한 무의식적인 정보 재분배 과정에서 기억력이 강화되거나 약화된다라는 설이 있다. 우리가 꿈을 꾸는 동안, 도움이 되는 기억은 더 강하게 만들어지는 반면, 도움이 덜 되는 기억은 점점 사라진다.

꿈의 기능은 우리가 잠을 자는 안전한 공간에서 감정이나 트라우마를 처리하고 대처할 수 있도록 돕는 것이다. 꿈을 꾸는 동안 감정을 처리하는 데 관여하는 편도체와 정보를 응축하고 단기 기억 저장에서 장기 기억 저장으로 옮기는 데 필수적인 역할을 하는 해마는 생생하고 강렬하게 활성화된다. 이 이론은 렘 수면이 감정적 뇌 조절에 중요한 역할을 한다는 것을 시사한다. 그것은 또한 왜 그렇게 많은 꿈이 감정적으로 생생한지, 그리고 왜 감정적이거나 충격적인 경험이 반복적으로 나타나는지를 설명하는 데 도움을 준다.

우리가 꿈을 꾸는 이유에 대해 많은 이론이 있지만, 꿈의 목적을 완전히 이해하기 위해서는 더 많은 연구가 필요하다. 오직 하나의 가설만 옳다고 가정하기보다는, 꿈은 다양한 목적을 수행하는 것처럼 보인다. 우리가 왜 꿈을 꾸는지에 대해 너무 많은 것들이 불확실하게 남겨져 있다는 것을 인식할 때, 우리 자신과 가장 잘 공명하는(공감되는) 것을 참조해서 우리는 자유롭게 우리 자신의 꿈을 볼 수 있다.

NOTE

Step 1	Survey
Key Words	Function of dream; theories; the self-organization theory
Signal Words	Why; also; many
Step 2	**Reading**
Purpose	To explain two theories of the purpose of dreams
Pattern of Organization	Cause/effect; series
Tone	Neutral
Main Idea	There are several theories about why people dream.
Step 3	**Summary**
지문 요약하기 (Paraphrasing)	There are several theories about why people dream. One, the self-organization theory of dreaming, is that dreams aid in memory. Information is processed and memories are managed during dreaming. Another theory is that dreams help process emotions. The amygdala and hippocampus of the brain are both processing emotions and memories together which creates vivid dreams to emotionally regulate the brain. In conclusion, since much is left unclear about the purpose of dreams, we need to use our dreams for our own good.
Step 4	**Recite**
	요약문 말로 설명하기

29 Read the passage and follow the directions.

Intellect divides into two major segments, each with a completely different function and mission of its own. The two types of intellect are labeled as the utilitarian intellect and the behavioral intellect or moral virtue.

The utilitarian intellect consists of the various faculties that deal with reasoning, science, technology, contemplation, imagination, creativity, inventions, discoveries, and cognition at large. These are all mental tools at the disposal of humans to achieve all their needs, wants, and desires, large and small, individually and collectively. What is important to recognize, however, is that not all of our pursuits are exclusively good or evil, but often, are a comprise of both. The faculty of utilitarian intellect is the mental element that applies itself unconditionally and indiscriminately to achieve all of them, regardless of if they are noble, evil, or neutral. For instance, the Wright brothers used their utilitarian intellect to invent the airplane, which has immeasurably contributed to human progress. Yet Bin Laden, through his intellect, used this same invention to savagely take 3,800 innocent lives in the most horrifying way, triggering wars that have claimed an even greater more.

On the other hand, the sole function of the behavioral intellect, is the induction of angelic human attributes (justice, honesty, fairness, compassion, virtue, righteousness, and human decency) to all human deeds. Human decency, ethics, compassion, selflessness, and altruistic nature stem from this segment of human intellect, and this of course, is in opposition to the primitive and selfishly blind instincts that exclusively strive for pleasure and satisfaction with total disregard to everything else.

All aspects of intellect are unique to our species and are the essence of being human. Because these two opposing mental elements coexist in the human mind, they inevitably co-function, and cause dualities to emerge. The drastic fluctuation in our conduct is unique to our species and renders humans alone mentally bipolar. When we learn the properties and the missions of these two types of intellect, we clearly see how these forces have created the human condition from inception.

Write a summary following the guidelines below.

| Guidelines |
- Summarize the above passage in ONE paragraph.
- Provide a topic sentence, major supporting details, and a concluding sentence based on the passage.
- Do NOT copy more than FOUR consecutive words from the passage.

NOTE

Step 1	**S**urvey
Key Words	
Signal Words	
Step 2	**R**eading
Purpose	
Pattern of Organization	
Tone	
Main Idea	
Step 3	**S**ummary
지문 요약하기 (Paraphrasing)	
Step 4	**R**ecite
	요약문 말로 설명하기

Answer Key

Intellect divides into **two major segments**, each with a completely different function and mission of its own. **The two types** of intellect are labeled as the utilitarian intellect and the behavioral intellect or moral virtue.

The utilitarian intellect consists of the **various faculties** that deal with reasoning, science, technology, contemplation, imagination, creativity, inventions, discoveries, and cognition at large. These are all mental tools at the disposal of humans to achieve all their needs, wants, and desires, large and small, individually and collectively. What is important to recognize, however, is that not all of our pursuits are exclusively good or evil, but often, are a comprise of both. The faculty of **utilitarian intellect** is the mental element that applies itself unconditionally and indiscriminately to achieve all of them, regardless of if they are noble, evil, or neutral. For instance, the Wright brothers used their utilitarian intellect to invent the airplane, which has immeasurably contributed to human progress. Yet Bin Laden, through his intellect, used this same invention to savagely take 3,800 innocent lives in the most horrifying way, triggering wars that have claimed an even greater more.

On the other hand, the sole function of the **behavioral intellect**, is the induction of **angelic human attributes** (justice, honesty, fairness, compassion, virtue, righteousness, and human decency) to all human deeds. Human decency, ethics, compassion, selflessness, and altruistic nature stem from this segment of human intellect, and this of course, is in opposition to the primitive and selfishly blind instincts that exclusively strive for pleasure and satisfaction with total disregard to everything else.

All aspects of intellect are unique to our species and are the essence of being human. Because **these two opposing mental elements** coexist in the human mind, they inevitably co-function, and cause dualities to emerge. The drastic fluctuation in our conduct is unique to our species and renders humans alone mentally bipolar. When we learn the properties and the missions of **these two types of intellect**, we clearly see how these forces have created the human condition from inception.

key words

모범답안

There are two types of intellect: utilitarian and behavioral. Utilitarian intellect includes invention, creativity, reason and other aspects for achieving human goals with no issue of their being good or evil. On the other hand, behavioral intellect incorporates justice, honesty, fairness and attributes that esteem altruism over the pursuit of pleasure. In conclusion, learning about the importance of both these forces shows how crucial for humans they are and how they should be embraced in a balance.

채점기준

+ 1점: 글의 topic sentence를 다음과 같이 서술하였거나 유사하였다.
"There are two types of intellect: utilitarian and behavioral."
+ 2점: 글의 major supporting details를 다음과 같이 서술하였거나 유사하였다.
"Utilitarian intellect includes invention, creativity, reason and other aspects for achieving human goals with no issue of their being good or evil(=achieving human goals irrespective of their being good or evil). On the other hand, behavioral intellect incorporates justice, honesty, fairness and attributes that esteem altruism over the pursuit of pleasure."
☞ 2개 중 2개 모두를 정확하게 요약한 경우 2점, 1개만 요약한 경우 1점, 요약하지 못한 경우 0점을 준다.
+ 1점: 글의 결론을 "In conclusion, learning about the importance of both these forces shows how crucial for humans they are and how they should be embraced in a balance."라 서술하였거나 유사하였다.

● 감점 · 본문에 나오는 연속되는 5단어 이상을 사용하였다. –1pt
· 문단을 두 개나 그 이상으로 구성하였다. –1pt
· grammar나 영어표현이 합쳐 4개 이상 오류가 있다. –1pt

한글번역

지성은 두 개의 주요 부분으로 나뉘는데, 각각은 완전히 다른 기능과 임무를 가지고 있다. 두 가지 유형의 지성은 공리주의적 지성과 행동적 지성—즉 도덕적 미덕—으로 분류된다.

공리주의적(실용주의적) 지성은 추론, 과학, 기술, 사색, 상상력, 창의성, 발명, 발견, 인지 등을 전반적으로 다루는 다양한 능력으로 구성된다. 이것들은 인간이 모두 크고 작은, 개별적이고 집단적으로, 인간의 모든 필요, 욕구, 욕망을 성취하기 위해 마음대로 사용할 수 있는 정신적 도구들이다. 그러나 인식해야 할 중요한 것은 우리의 모든 추구가 전적으로 선이나 악이 아니라, 종종 두 가지 모두로 구성돼 있다는 점이다. 공리주의적 지성의 능력은 그 어떤 것이라도 성취하기 위해 무조건적이고 무차별적으로 전념하는 심적 요소인데, 이때 성취하고자 하는 것이 고귀하든, 악한 것이든, 아니면 중립적인 것이든 전혀 상관이 없다. 예를 들어, 라이트 형제는 그들의 공리주의적 지성을 이용해 비행기를 발명했는데, 이것은 인간의 진보에 헤아릴 수 없을 정도로 기여했다. 하지만 빈 라덴은 그의 지성을 통해 이 똑같은 발명품(즉 비행기)을 사용해 3,800명의 무고한 생명을 가장 끔찍한 방법으로 잔인하게 앗아갔고, 훨씬 더 많은 생명을 앗아간 전쟁을 촉발시켰다.

반면에 행동적 지성의 유일한 기능은 모든 인간의 행동에 천사 같은 인간의 속성(정의, 정직, 공정, 동정, 미덕, 정의, 인간의 품위)을 유도하는 것이다. 인간의 품위, 윤리, 동정심, 사심, 이타적인 본성은 인간 지성의 이 부분(즉, 행동적 지성)에서 비롯되는데, 당연하게도 이것은 그 밖의 모든 것을 완전히 무시하며 오로지 쾌락과 만족을 위해 노력하는 원시적이고 이기적인 맹목적인 본능에 반대된다.

지성의 이런 측면들(공리주의적지성과 행동적 지성)은 우리 종에게만 고유하며, 인간이 된다라는 것의 본질이다. 이 서로 대립하는 두 가지 정신적 요소가 인간의 마음속에 공존하기 때문에 필연적으로 이 둘은 공존하게 되고, 이중성이 나타나게 된다. 우리 행동의 급격한 변동은 우리 종에게만 있는 독특한 것으로, 이것으로 인해 오직 우리 인간만이 정신적으로 조울증을 겪게 된다. 우리가 이 두 가지 유형의 지성의 특성과 사명을 알게 될 때, 우리는 이러한 힘이 시작부터 어떻게 인간의 조건을 만들어냈는지 분명히 알 수 있다.

Step 1	Ⓢurvey
Key Words	Intellect; utilitarian; behavioral
Signal Words	Two types of…; on the other hand
Step 2	**Ⓡeading**
Purpose	To explain two types of intellect
Pattern of Organization	Series; contrast
Tone	Neutral
Main Idea	There are two types of intellect: utilitarian and behavioral.
Step 3	**Ⓢummary**
지문 요약하기 (Paraphrasing)	There are two types of intellect: utilitarian and behavioral. Utilitarian intellect includes invention, creativity, reason and other aspects for achieving human goals with no issue of their being good or evil. On the other hand, behavioral intellect incorporates justice, honesty, fairness and attributes that esteem altruism over the pursuit of pleasure. In conclusion, learning about the importance of both these forces shows how crucial for humans they are and how they should be embraced in a balance.
Step 4	**Ⓡecite**

요약문 말로 설명하기

30 Read the passage and follow the directions.

From the dawn of civilization, technology has changed—sometimes radically—the way people have lived, how youths have grown up, and how people in society, as a whole, have lived day to day. This includes facets of societal behaviors such as convenience, privacy, communication, and business etc. Technology has typically had both positive and negative effects on society, regardless of how drastic the effects on human behavior have been.

If the modern lifestyle could be characterized in a single word, it would have to be "convenience." From shopping online from one's couch and having goods delivered next-day to the appropriate doorstep, to joining friends for a meetup via a social app without having to leave the house, to booking a flight and hotel across the world for travel the next day, tablet computers, wearable computer systems (i.e. smart watches), and smartphones allow people to perform tasks in a moment, on robust apps via the Internet, that previously would have required going in person. Essentially, technology has helped people to carry out complex tasks in a simpler, quicker manner.

Technology has had a somewhat marred history with regard to the issue of privacy. Most people view cameras, intrusive apps, smart devices like smart homes, and spy-devices as having helped to increasingly compromise the privacy of multitudes. Recently a concept known as "human search" (also referred to as an "Internet mob") has grown in popularity. Unlike the more constructive pursuit known as "crowdsourcing," where people worldwide connect to lend their creativity to some academic, artistic or business endeavor, human search involves people connecting via the Internet to track down information for one another, often to search for someone perceived as having done something wrong.

Technology has had a tremendous, almost unimaginable impact on human life from the dawn of civilization. While it is near impossible to gauge the entire impact on human society, technology clearly has done a lot to make human life easier, more enjoyable, and more convenient. However, when misused or produced irresponsibly, it has had the potential to have devastating consequences, and thus is not without its drawbacks. As humans venture into the future, it is increasingly important for engineers to operate in a more conscientious and responsible manner.

Write a summary following the guidelines below.

| Guidelines |
- Summarize the above passage in ONE paragraph.
- Provide a topic sentence, major supporting details, and a concluding sentence based on the passage.
- Do NOT copy more than FIVE consecutive words from the passage.

NOTE

Step 1	**S**urvey
Key Words	
Signal Words	
Step 2	**R**eading
Purpose	
Pattern of Organization	
Tone	
Main Idea	
Step 3	**S**ummary
지문 요약하기 (Paraphrasing)	
Step 4	**R**ecite
	요약문 말로 설명하기

Answer Key

From the dawn of civilization, **technology** has changed—sometimes radically—the way people have lived, how youths have grown up, and how people in society, as a whole, have lived day to day. This includes facets of societal behaviors such as convenience, privacy, communication, and business etc. **Technology** has typically had **both positive and negative effects on society**, regardless of how drastic the effects on human behavior have been.

If the modern lifestyle could be characterized in a single word, it would have to be "**convenience**." From shopping online from one's couch and having goods delivered next-day to the appropriate doorstep, to joining friends for a meetup via a social app without having to leave the house, to booking a flight and hotel across the world for travel the next day, tablet computers, wearable computer systems (i.e. smart watches), and smartphones allow people to perform tasks in a moment, on robust apps via the Internet, that previously would have required going in person. Essentially, **technology has helped people to carry out complex tasks in a simpler, quicker manner**.

Technology has had a somewhat **marred** history with regard to the **issue of privacy**. Most people view cameras, intrusive apps, smart devices like smart homes, and spy-devices as having helped to increasingly compromise the privacy of multitudes. Recently a concept known as "human search" (also referred to as an "Internet mob") has grown in popularity. Unlike the more constructive pursuit known as "crowdsourcing," where people worldwide connect to lend their creativity to some academic, artistic or business endeavor, human search involves people connecting via the Internet to track down information for one another, often to search for someone perceived as having done something wrong.

Technology has had a tremendous, almost unimaginable impact on human life from the dawn of civilization. While it is near impossible to gauge the entire impact on human society, technology clearly has done a lot to make human life easier, more enjoyable, and more convenient. However, when **misused** or **produced irresponsibly**, it has had the potential to **have devastating consequences**, and thus is not without its drawbacks. As humans venture into the future, **it is increasingly important for engineers to operate in a more conscientious and responsible manner**.

key words

① positive

② negative

conclusion

모범답안

Technology has had positive and negative influences on society. As a benefit, technology has allowed people to live conveniently, simplifying tasks like shopping and travel which saves time and energy by way of such technology as computers and smartphones. On the other hand, privacy has been lost to the new apps, smart homes, spy-devices. Especially, human search engine has negatively been used by tracking down information for other people. In conclusion, technology has helped many but can be misused or dangerous, thus should be given consideration by engineers as it develops.

채점기준

+1점: 글의 topic sentence를 다음과 같이 서술하였거나 유사하였다.
"Technology has had positive and negative influences(or effects/impact) on society."

+2점: 글의 major supporting details를 다음과 같이 서술하였거나 유사하였다.
"As a benefit, technology has allowed people to live conveniently, simplifying tasks like shopping and travel which saves time and energy by way of such technology as computers and smartphones. On the other hand, privacy has been lost to the new apps, smart homes, spy-devices. Especially, human search engine has negatively been used by tracking down information for other people."

☞ 2개 중 2개 모두를 정확하게 요약한 경우 2점, 1개만 요약한 경우 1점, 요약하지 못한 경우 0점을 준다.

+1점: 글의 결론을 "In conclusion, technology has helped many but can be misused or dangerous, thus should be given consideration by engineers (as it develops)."라 서술하였거나 유사하였다.

● 감점
• 본문에 나오는 연속되는 6단어 이상을 사용하였다. −1pt
• 문단을 두 개나 그 이상으로 구성하였다. −1pt
• grammar나 영어표현이 합쳐 4개 이상 오류가 있다. −1pt

한글번역

문명의 시작부터, 기술은 사람들의 삶의 방식, 젊은이들의 성장 방식, 그리고 사회 전체의 일상생활을—때로는 급진적으로—변화시켜 왔다. 여기에는 편의, 사생활, 통신, 그리고 비즈니스 등과 같은 다양한 양상의 사회적 행동이 포함된다. 기술은 보통 인간의 행동에 미치는 영향이 얼마나 극심했는가에 상관없이 사회에 긍정적, 부정적인 영향을 끼쳐왔다.

현대적 생활방식을 한마디로 특징지을 수 있다면, 그것은 '편리함'이어야 할 것 같다. 소파에 앉아서 온라인으로 쇼핑한 것이 다음 날 집 문 앞에까지 배달되는 것에서부터, 집을 나설 필요 없이 소셜 앱을 통해 친구를 만나 모임을 갖는 것, 다음 날 여행을 위해 전 세계 항공편과 호텔을 예약하는 것, 태블릿 컴퓨터, 웨어러블 컴퓨터 시스템(예 스마트 시계) 및 스마트폰은 사람이 이전에는 직접 방문했어야만 했던 일들을, 인터넷에 있는 강력한 앱을 통해, 즉시 작업을 수행할 수 있도록 만들어줬다. 본질적으로, 기술은 복잡한 작업을 더 간단하고 빠르게 수행할 수 있도록 도와줬다.

기술은 사생활 문제와 관련해 다소 손상된 역사를 가지고 있다. 대부분의 사람들은 카메라, 침입형 앱, 스마트 홈과 같은 스마트 장치 및 스파이 장치가 다수의 개인 정보를 점점 더 침해하는 데 도움이 됐다고 본다. 최근 '인간 검색'으로 알려진 개념이 인기를 끌고 있다. '크라우드소싱'—전 세계 사람들이 학문적, 예술적 또는 사업적 노력에 그들의 창의성을 빌려주기 위해 연결하는 것—이라고 알려진 보다 건설적인 추구와는 달리, 인간 검색은—종종 뭔가를 잘못했다고 인식된 사람을 추적해 찾아내는 것과 같은—인터넷을 통해 사람들의 뒤를 캐내는 것을 포함한다.

기술은 문명의 여명기부터 인간의 삶에 엄청난, 거의 상상할 수 없는 영향을 끼쳤다. 인간 사회에 미치는 전체 영향을 가늠하는 것은 거의 불가능하지만, 기술은 분명히 인간의 삶을 더 쉽고, 더 즐겁고, 더 편리하게 만들기 위해 많은 일을 해왔다. 그러나, 잘못 사용되거나 무책임하게 생산될 때, 기술은 파괴적인 결과를 초래할 수 있는 잠재력을 가지고 있으며, 따라서 단점이 없는 것은 아니다. 인간이 (위험을 무릅쓰고) 미래에 발을 들여놓을 때, 엔지니어가 더욱더 양심적이고 책임감 있는 방식으로 운영하는 것이 점점 더 중요해지고 있다.

NOTE

Step 1	Survey
Key Words	Technology; positive; negative; effects; convenience; privacy
Signal Words	Effects
Step 2	Reading
Purpose	To explain technology's positive and negative influences on society
Pattern of Organization	Series
Tone	Subjective
Main Idea	Technology has had positive and negative influences on society.
Step 3	Summary
지문 요약하기 (Paraphrasing)	Technology has had positive and negative influences on society. As a benefit, technology has allowed people to live conveniently, simplifying tasks like shopping and travel which saves time and energy by way of such technology as computers and smartphones. On the other hand, privacy has been lost to the new apps, smart homes, spy-devices. Especially, human search engine has negatively been used by tracking down information for other people. In conclusion, technology has helped many but can be misused or dangerous, thus should be given consideration by engineers as it develops.
Step 4	Recite
	요약문 말로 설명하기

31 Read the passage and follow the directions.

Many of workers fear that a lack of physical office presence will stunt success. And the normalisation of remote work amid the pandemic hasn't necessarily changed this. In 2020, researchers from human-resources software company ADP found that 54% of British workers felt obliged to physically come into the office at some point during the pandemic, especially those in their early-and mid-careers, despite the rise in flexible working. There are two key psychological phenomena that fuel presenteeism.

The first is the 'mere-exposure effect', which holds that the more a person is exposed to someone or something, the more they start to grow affinity. If I've seen one person 10 times for every one time I've seen somebody else, I'm just naturally going to like them more. If a particular worker makes themselves more visible, they may naturally ingratiate themselves to others just by being there—even if the others don't realise it, or can't pinpoint what is it they like about the 'presentee'. Before you know it, the presentee might get a raise or promotion.

This bias exists alongside another psychological concept called the 'halo effect' : associating positive impressions of someone with their actual character. "You start to think of the person who's bringing you coffee or asking about your weekend as maybe 'a sweet guy'—but then I take the mental step of thinking you're a productive worker, too". "You're nice, and then I immediately bloom that out to, 'the guy must be a hard worker as well'—even though you've given me no evidence in this coffee-cup situation to make me think that you're a hard worker." This can lead to promotions or other benefits going to in-person workers.

MEMO

Clinging to a presenteeism culture just favours those who have the time to show up early and leave late. Now, in an era in which work practices have undergone seismic transformations, and have triggered unprecedented scrutiny, there's an urgent need to reduce the emphasis on presenteeism, both physically and digitally.

Write a summary following the guidelines below.

┌─ Guidelines ─┐
- Summarize the above passage in ONE paragraph.
- Provide a topic sentence, major supporting details, and a concluding sentence based on the passage.
- Do NOT copy more than FIVE consecutive words from the passage.

_____

_____

_____

_____

_____

_____

NOTE

Step 1	Survey
Key Words	
Signal Words	
Step 2	**Reading**
Purpose	
Pattern of Organization	
Tone	
Main Idea	
Step 3	**Summary**
지문 요약하기 (Paraphrasing)	
Step 4	**Recite**
	요약문 말로 설명하기

Answer Key

Many of workers fear that a lack of **physical office presence** will stunt success. And the normalisation of remote work amid the pandemic hasn't necessarily changed this. In 2020, researchers from human-resources software company ADP found that 54% of British workers felt obliged to physically come into the office at some point during the pandemic, especially those in their early-and mid-careers, despite the rise in flexible working. **There are two key psychological phenomena that fuel presenteeism.**	key words
	topic sentence
The first is the **'mere-exposure effect'**, which holds that the more a person is exposed to someone or something, the more they start to grow affinity. If I've seen one person 10 times for every one time I've seen somebody else, I'm just naturally going to like them more. If a particular worker makes themselves more visible, they may naturally ingratiate themselves to others just by being there—even if the others don't realise it, or can't pinpoint what is it they like about the 'presentee'. Before you know it, the presentee might get a raise or promotion.	①
This bias exists alongside another psychological concept called the **'halo effect'**: associating positive impressions of someone with their actual character. "You start to think of the person who's bringing you coffee or asking about your weekend as maybe 'a sweet guy'—but then I take the mental step of thinking you're a productive worker, too". "You're nice, and then I immediately bloom that out to, 'the guy must be a hard worker as well'—even though you've given me no evidence in this coffee-cup situation to make me think that you're a hard worker." This can lead to promotions or other benefits going to in-person workers.	②
Clinging to a presenteeism culture just favours those who have the time to show up early and leave late. Now, in an era in which work practices have undergone **seismic transformations**, and have triggered unprecedented scrutiny, **there's an urgent need to reduce the emphasis on presenteeism, both physically and digitally.**	conclusion

모범답안

There are two core psychological reasons that presenteeism, physical office presence, pervades among workers. First, because of "mere-exposure effect" which means that the more exposure given, the more co-workers will prefer the given worker. Second, another advantage is that the "halo effect", which associates good impressions of a person with their real character, leads workers to associate other present workers' good deeds with their whole perception. In conclusion, given the transformations that have happend in workplaces, presenteeism should be counteracted.

> **채점기준**

+ 1점: 글의 topic sentence를 다음과 같이 서술하였거나 유사하였다.
"There are two core psychological reasons that presenteeism, physical office presence, pervades among workers."

+ 2점: 글의 major supporting details를 다음과 같이 서술하였거나 유사하였다.
"First, because of "mere-exposure effect" which means that the more exposure given, the more co-workers will prefer the given worker. Second, another advantage is that the "halo effect", which associates good impressions of a person with their real character, leads workers to associate other present workers' good deeds with their whole perception."

☞ 2개 중 2개 모두를 정확하게 요약한 경우 2점, 1개만 요약한 경우 1점, 요약하지 못한 경우 0점을 준다.

+ 1점: 글의 결론은 "In conclusion, given the transformations that have happend in workplaces, presenteeism should be counteracted."이라 서술하였거나 유사하였다.

● 감점
- 본문에 나오는 연속되는 6단어 이상을 사용하였다. -1pt
- 문단을 두 개나 그 이상으로 구성하였다. -1pt
- grammar나 영어표현이 합쳐 4개 이상 오류가 있다. -1pt

> **한글번역**

많은 노동자들은 사무실에 물리적으로 출근하지 않는 것이 성공을 저해할까봐 두려워한다. 그리고 전염병 기간 동안 이뤄진 원격 근무의 정상화가 이런 상황을 불가피하게 바꾼 것은 아니다. 2020년, 인적 자원 소프트웨어 회사인 ADP의 연구원들은 영국 노동자의 54%가 유연근무의 증가에도 불구하고 전염병 기간 동안 어느 시점에는 사무실에 직접 출근해야 한다고 느꼈다는 사실을 발견했다. 특히 커리어를 시작했거나 중간 수준에 있는 노동자들이 더욱 그렇다. 프리젠티즘(필요 이상으로 직장에서 많은 시간을 보내는 것)을 부추기는 두 가지 핵심적 심리현상이 있다.

첫 번째는 '단순 노출 효과'로, 사람이 누군가나 무언가에 더 많이 노출될수록 친화력이 커지기 시작한다는 것이다. 만약 내가 누군가 다른 사람을 한 번 볼 때마다, 어떤 특정인을 10번씩 봤다면, 나는 10번을 본 사람을 더 좋아하게 될 것이다. 만약 어떤 특정 노동자가 자기 자신을 (남들의) 눈에 더 잘 띄게 만들 수 있다면, 그 노동자는 단지 그곳에 있었다는 것만으로 자연스럽게 다른 사람들에게 환심을 사게 될 수 있다—비록 다른 사람들이 그것을 깨닫지 못하거나, 그 '참석한 사람'에 대해 무엇 때문에 그 사람에 대해 좋아하는지를 정확히 지적하지 못하더라도 말이다. 어느새 그 참석한 사람은 승급이나 승진을 할 수도 있다.

이러한 편견은 '후광(後光) 효과'—누군가에 대한 긍정적 인상을 그들의 실제 성격과 연관시키는—라고 불리는 또 다른 심리적 개념과 나란히 존재한다. "당신은 당신에게 커피를 가져다주거나 당신의 주말에 대해 물어보는 사람을 아마도 '상냥한 남자'로 생각하기 시작하지만, 나는 당신이 생산적인 일꾼이라고 생각하는 정신적인 단계를 밟는다." "당신이 착하면, 나는 즉시 그것을 '그 남자는 성실히 일하는 사람임에 틀림없다'고 꽃피운다. 비록 당신이 이 커피를 주는 상황에서 내가 당신이 성실히 일하는 사람이라고 생각하게 만들 아무런 증거를 제공해주지 않았음에도 말이다." 이것은 현장에 나온 노동자에게 승진이나 다른 혜택으로 이어질 수 있다.

프리젠티즘 문화에 집착하는 것은 일찍 나타나고 늦게 떠날 시간이 있는 사람들에게 유리할 뿐이다. 이제, 업무 관행이 엄청난 변화를 겪고 있고, 전례 없는 정밀 조사를 촉발하고 있는 시대에, 물리적이든 디지털적으로든 프리젠티즘에 대한 강조를 줄일 긴급한 필요가 있다.

NOTE

Step 1	Survey
Key Words	Presenteeism; physical office presence; mere-exposure effect; halo effect
Signal Words	Two; the first; another
Step 2	Reading
Purpose	To explain two core psychological reasons that presenteeism pervades among workers
Pattern of Organization	Cause/effect; series
Tone	Neutral
Main Idea	There are two core psychological reasons that presenteeism pervades among workers.
Step 3	Summary
지문 요약하기 (Paraphrasing)	There are two core psychological reasons that presenteeism, physical office presence, pervades among workers. First, because of "mere-exposure effect" which means that the more exposure given, the more co-workers will prefer the given worker. Second, another advantage is that the "halo effect", which associates good impressions of a person with their real character, leads workers to associate other present workers' good deeds with their whole perception. In conclusion, given the transformations that have happend in workplaces, presenteeism should be counteracted.
Step 4	Recite
	요약문 말로 설명하기

32 Read the passage and follow the directions.

The conventional view of life, based on the "seven ages of man" model first outlined in the 12th century, and later popularized by Shakespeare in his play "As You Like It" in the early 1600s, has the curve going the other way. Adults increase in stature, wealth, experience, and happiness until roughly middle age, after which life becomes a downhill slide to the grave. However, studies first undertaken in the early 1990s began to put this image into doubt. And subsequent studies in various disciplines appear to confirm that in general, life is a U-bend rather than an arch, with people getting happier and enjoying life more as they pass the emotionally low point of middle age.

Several reasons have been postulated for this. One is the effect of emotional experiences at various stages of life. Stress from increasing responsibilities generally begins to rise during the early 20s and continues until middle age, after which it tends to fall sharply. Worry often peaks in middle age and then declines. Middle age, for various reasons, is often accompanied by increased feelings of sadness, which then subside with additional years. Feelings of anger tend to decline with age.

Another reason is the impact of external circumstances. For example, people in their 40s often have teenage children. The low point of middle age could be due to having to share living space with angry or rebellious adolescents. On the other hand, older people may be more content because they tend to be richer and more materially secure than middle-aged folks still burdened with mortgage payments and their children's post-secondary educational expenses.

However, what is really important is internal satisfaction. Older people generally have fewer fights and come up with better solutions to conflict. As they come closer and closer to the end of their life, they get better at living for the present and focusing on things that truly matter.

Write a summary following the guidelines below.

| Guidelines |
- Summarize the above passage in ONE paragraph.
- Provide a topic sentence, major supporting details, and a concluding sentence based on the passage.
- Do NOT copy more than FIVE consecutive words from the passage.

NOTE

Step 1	**S**urvey
Key Words	
Signal Words	
Step 2	**R**eading
Purpose	
Pattern of Organization	
Tone	
Main Idea	
Step 3	**S**ummary
지문 요약하기 (Paraphrasing)	
Step 4	**R**ecite
	요약문 말로 설명하기

Answer Key

The **conventional view of life**, based on the "seven ages of man" model first outlined in the 12th century, and later popularized by Shakespeare in his play "As You Like It" in the early 1600s, has the curve going the other way. Adults increase in stature, wealth, experience, and happiness until roughly middle age, after which life becomes a downhill slide to the grave. However, studies first undertaken in the early 1990s began to put this image into doubt. And subsequent studies in various disciplines appear to confirm that in general, **life is a U-bend rather than an arch**, with **people getting happier and enjoying life more as they pass the emotionally low point of middle age**. ← topic sentence

Several reasons have been postulated for this. One is the effect of **emotional experiences at various stages of life**. Stress from increasing responsibilities generally begins to rise during the early 20s and continues until middle age, after which it tends to fall sharply. Worry often peaks in middle age and then declines. Middle age, for various reasons, is often accompanied by increased feelings of sadness, which then subside with additional years. Feelings of anger tend to decline with age.

Another reason is the impact of **external circumstances**. For example, people in their 40s often have teenage children. The low point of middle age could be due to having to share living space with angry or rebellious adolescents. On the other hand, older people may be more content because they tend to be richer and more materially secure than middle-aged folks still burdened with mortgage payments and their children's post-secondary educational expenses.

However, what is really important is **internal satisfaction**. Older people generally have fewer fights and come up with better solutions to conflict. As they come closer and closer to the end of their life, they get better at **living for the present** and **focusing on things that truly matter**.

모범답안

There are several reasons why people become happier and live better lives as they pass middle age as opposed to the conventional point-of-view. First, after middle age, emotional hardships such as stress and worry tend to reduce. Second, external situations get better because the common presence of teenage children in middle age will no longer be stressful, and more financial security occurs. In conclusion, the internal satisfaction of old age shows better conflict resolution and mastery of life that improves happiness.

채점기준

+ 1점: 글의 topic sentence를 다음과 같이 서술하였거나 유사하였다.
"There are several reasons why people become happier and live better lives as they pass middle age (as opposed to the conventional point-of-view)."

+ 2점: 글의 major supporting details를 다음과 같이 서술하였거나 유사하였다.
"First, after middle age, emotional hardships such as stress and worry tend to reduce. Second, external situations get better because the common presence of teenage children in middle age will no longer be stressful, and more financial security occurs."
☞ 2개 중 2개 모두를 정확하게 요약한 경우 2점, 1개만 요약한 경우 1점, 요약하지 못한 경우 0점을 준다.

+ 1점: 글의 결론을 "In conclusion, the internal satisfaction of old age shows better conflict resolution and mastery of life that improves happiness."이라 서술하였거나 유사하였다.

● 감점
- 본문에 나오는 연속되는 6단어 이상을 사용하였다. −1pt
- 문단을 두 개나 그 이상으로 구성하였다. −1pt
- grammar나 영어표현이 합쳐 4개 이상 오류가 있다. −1pt

한글번역

12세기에 처음 윤곽을 드러내고, 1600년대 초 셰익스피어의 희곡 <뜻대로 하세요>를 통해 대중화된 '인생의 7단계' 모델을 바탕으로 한 기존의 통념적 인생관은 그 곡선이 반대로 가고 있다. 성인은 대략 중년이 될 때까지 신장, 부, 경험, 행복이 증가하며, 그 후 삶은 무덤으로 가는 내리막길이 된다. 그러나 1990년대 초에 처음 수행된 연구들은 이러한 그림을 의심하기 시작했다. 그리고 다양한 분야의 후속 연구들은 삶이 아치형이라기보다는 U자형이라는 것을 확인시켜주고 있는 것처럼 보인다. 즉, 중년의 정서적 저점을 지날수록 사람들은 점점 더 행복해지고 삶을 더 즐기면서 산다는 것이다.

이에 대한 몇 가지 이유가 상정됐다. 하나는 삶의 다양한 단계에서 감정적 경험의 영향이다. 증가하는 책임감으로 인한 스트레스는 일반적으로 20대 초반에 증가하기 시작해 중년까지 지속되며, 그 이후에는 급격히 감소하는 경향이 있다. 걱정은 중년에 절정에 달했다가 쇠퇴하는 경우가 많다. 중년은 다양한 이유로 종종 슬픔이 증가된 감정을 동반하다가 이후엔 점점 나이가 들어가면서 그런 감정은 가라앉게 된다. 분노의 감정은 나이가 들수록 감소하는 경향이 있다.

또 다른 이유는 외부 환경의 영향이다. 예를 들어, 40대의 사람들은 10대 아이들을 자녀로 갖게 되는 경우가 많다. 중년의 저점은 화가 나 있거나 반항적인 청소년들과 생활공간을 공유해야 하기 때문일 수 있다. 반면에 노인들은 주택담보대출 상환과 자녀들의 대학교육비 부담을 지고 있는 중년층보다 더 부유하고 물질적으로 더 안전한 경향이 있기 때문에 더 만족스러울 수 있다.

하지만 정말 중요한 것은 내적 만족이다. 노인들은 일반적으로 싸움을 적게 하고 갈등에 대한 더 나은 해결책을 생각해 낸다. 그들이 삶의 끝에 점점 가까워질수록, 그들은 현재를 위해 사는 것과 진정으로 중요한 것에 집중하는 것에 더 능숙해진다.

NOTE

Step 1	Survey
Key Words	Older people; middle age
Signal Words	Several reasons; One; Another; For example
Step 2	**Reading**
Purpose	To explain why people become happier and live better lives as they pass middle age
Pattern of Organization	Cause/effect; series
Tone	Neutral
Main Idea	There are several reasons why people become happier and live better lives as they pass middle age as opposed to the conventional point-of-view.
Step 3	**Summary**
지문 요약하기 (Paraphrasing)	There are several reasons why people become happier and live better lives as they pass middle age as opposed to the conventional point-of-view. First, after middle age, emotional hardships such as stress and worry tend to reduce. Second, external situations get better because the common presence of teenage children in middle age will no longer be stressful, and more financial security occurs. In conclusion, the internal satisfaction of old age shows better conflict resolution and mastery of life that improves happiness.
Step 4	**Recite**
	요약문 말로 설명하기

33 Read the passage and follow the directions.

Recently published textbooks on art of the post-World War II era include more women, artists of color, out gays and lesbians, and other previously excluded groups than ever before. The call for cultural equity has reached a point where most authors recognize the need to include at least some diversity in their selection of artists. However, inclusion alone does not eradicate the differential treatment of art.

The problem here is not only one of segregation in the guise of integration but also one of point of view : who decides what is an "alternative" and what is considered the normative center? In other cases, gendered or racialized themes provide the pretext for such segregation, such as addressing the theme of domesticity exclusively with works by women. Often this approach wrenches artists and artworks out of their historical contexts in order to have them support a particular theme.

A second problem apparent in recent art history texts about art since 1960 is that they sometimes invoke the Civil Rights and Antiwar Movements as general backdrops to discussions of art of the era, without acknowledging the political challenge these movements posed to the very narratives of art history contained in these texts. Often authors use pictures of key moments in the Civil Rights Movement as background illustrations that reference historical developments in the 1950s and 1960s while excluding artists of color who were actually working at this time. In one text, a prominent author cites the Civil Rights Movement by stating that the "countless displays of extraordinary and anonymous courage on the part of black protestors with their handful of white allies" inspired the development of Happenings in the late 1950s and early 1960s. Yet this same author includes only one artwork by one artist of color among the 116 illustrations in this book.

Many surveys of contemporary art contain a section that clusters artists of color, women, and other groups in a discrete chapter on identity or "alternative" art. This kind of second-rate treatment of works by artists of color should be transformed.

Write a summary following the guidelines below.

--- Guidelines ---
- Summarize the above passage in ONE paragraph.
- Provide a topic sentence, major supporting details, and a concluding sentence based on the passage.
- Do NOT copy more than FIVE consecutive words from the passage.

_____
_____
_____
_____
_____

NOTE

Step 1	**S**urvey
Key Words	
Signal Words	
Step 2	**R**eading
Purpose	
Pattern of Organization	
Tone	
Main Idea	
Step 3	**S**ummary
지문 요약하기 (Paraphrasing)	
Step 4	**R**ecite
	요약문 말로 설명하기

Answer Key

Recently published textbooks on art of the post-World War II era include more women, artists of color, out gays and lesbians, and other previously excluded groups than ever before. The call for cultural equity has reached a point where most authors recognize the need to include at least some diversity in their selection of artists. However, **inclusion alone does not eradicate the differential treatment of art**.

The problem here is not only one of **segregation** in the guise of integration but also one of point of view: who decides what is an "alternative" and what is considered the normative center? In other cases, gendered or racialized themes provide the pretext for **such segregation**, such as addressing the theme of domesticity exclusively with works by women. Often this approach wrenches artists and artworks **out of their historical contexts** in order to have them support a particular theme.

A second problem apparent in **recent art history texts about art** since 1960 is that they sometimes invoke the Civil Rights and Antiwar Movements as **general backdrops** to discussions of art of the era, **without acknowledging the political challenge** these movements posed to the very narratives of art history contained in these texts. Often authors use pictures of key moments in the Civil Rights Movement as background illustrations that reference historical developments in the 1950s and 1960s while excluding artists of color who were actually working at this time. In one text, a prominent author cites the Civil Rights Movement by stating that the "countless displays of extraordinary and anonymous courage on the part of black protestors with their handful of white allies" inspired the development of Happenings in the late 1950s and early 1960s. Yet this same author includes only one artwork by one artist of color among the 116 illustrations in this book.

Many surveys of contemporary art contain a section that clusters artists of color, women, and other groups in a discrete chapter on identity or "alternative" art. **This kind of second-rate treatment of works by artists of color should be transformed**.

key words

tone : critical

모범답안

Though current art history books include previously excluded groups of artists, they have several problems. First, artists from social minorities are being included to address themes in unbalanced ways, which often removes the artists from their historical context. Second, such texts employ the Antiwar and Civil Rights Movement as general settings but fail to acknowledge the political challenges and to feature the artists of color of those times. In conclusion, the poor treatment of artists from social minorities, such as they are contained in an "alternative" chapter, should be improved.

채점기준

+ 1점: 글의 topic sentence를 다음과 같이 서술하였거나 유사하였다.
"Though current art history books include previously excluded groups of artists, they have several problems."

+ 2점: 글의 major supporting details를 다음과 같이 서술하였거나 유사하였다.
"First, artists from social minorities are being included to address themes in unbalanced ways, which often removes the artists from their historical context. Second, such texts employ the Antiwar and Civil Rights Movement as general settings but fail to acknowledge the political challenges and to feature the artists of color of those times."
☞ 2개 중 2개 모두를 정확하게 요약한 경우 2점, 1개만 요약한 경우 1점, 요약하지 못한 경우 0점을 준다.

+ 1점: 글의 결론을 "In conclusion, the poor treatment of artists from social minorities, such as they are contained in an "alternative" chapter, should be improved(= changed)."이라 서술하였거나 유사하였다.

- **감점**
  - 본문에 나오는 연속되는 6단어 이상을 사용하였다. −1pt
  - 문단을 두 개나 그 이상으로 구성하였다. −1pt
  - grammar나 영어표현이 합쳐 4개 이상 오류가 있다. −1pt

한글번역

　　제2차 세계대전 이후 시대의 예술에 대한 최근에 출판된 교과서들은 그 어느 때보다도 더 많은 여성, 유색인종 예술가, 커밍아웃한 게이와 레즈비언, 그리고 이전에는 배제됐던 집단들을 포함시킨다. 문화적 공정에 대한 요구는 대부분의 작가들이 예술가 선정에 적어도 어느 정도의 다양성을 포함할 필요성을 인식하는 지점에 도달했다. 하지만 포용만으로는 예술의 차별적 취급이 근절되지는 않는다.

　　여기서 문제가 되는 점은 통합을 가장한 분리만이 아니라, 관점의 문제이기도 하다 : 어떤 것이 '대안'이고, 어떤 것이 규범적인 중심인지를 (도대체) 누가 결정하는가? (또한) 다른 경우들을 보면, 젠더화되거나 인종화된 주제들이 그러한 분리의 빌미를 제공하기도 하는데, 오직 여성이 만든 작품만을 가지고 가정생활이라는 주제를 다루는 것이 그런 예다. 종종 이런 접근법은 (역사적 맥락에서 따로 떨어져 존재할 수 없는) 예술가와 예술작품을, 어떤 특정 주제를 지지하도록 하기 위해, 역사적 맥락에서 떼어낸다.

　　1960년 이후 예술을 다룬 최근의 예술사 교재들에서 드러나는 두 번째 문제는 다음과 같다. 이 교재들은 민권 운동과 반전 운동을 그 시대의 예술을 논의할 때 그냥 일반적인 배경으로 들먹이곤 하는데, 이러한 운동이 이 교재들에 들어있는 예술사의 바로 그 서사들에 문제제기하는 정치적 도전을 인식하지 못하면서 말이다. 종종 (교재의) 저자들은 1950년대와 1960년대의 역사 발전을 참조하는 배경 삽화로 민권 운동의 핵심적 순간들의 사진들을 사용하지만, 이 시기에 실제로 활동하던 유색인종 예술가들은 배제한다. 어떤 저명한 저자의 한 교재에서는 민권 운동을 인용하면서 "몇 안 되는 백인 협력자들과 함께 흑인 시위자들은 비범하면서도 익명의 용기를 무수히 보여줬고", 1950년대 후반과 1960년대 초반에 일어난 사건들의 전개에 영감을 주었다고 말했다. 하지만, 이 바로 이 저자는 자신의 책에 있는 116개의 삽화 중 한 명의 유색인종 작가의 오직 한 작품만을 (자신의) 책에 실었다.

　　현대 미술에 대한 많은 연구(교재)들은, 정체성 예술이나 '대체' 예술에 대한 별개의 분리된 장에 유색인종 예술가나 여성 예술가, 그리고 다른 (소수) 그룹의 예술가들을 묶는 섹션을 포함하고 있다. 유색인종 예술가를 이런 식의 2류로 취급하는 풍토는 바뀌어야만 한다.

NOTE

Step 1	Survey
Key Words	Cultural equity; inclusion; differential treatment of art
Signal Words	A second problem
Step 2	Reading
Purpose	To criticize current treatment of artists from social minorities
Pattern of Organization	Series
Tone	Subjective
Main Idea	Though current art history books include previously excluded groups of artists, they have several problems.
Step 3	Summary
지문 요약하기 (Paraphrasing)	Though current art history books include previously excluded groups of artists, they have several problems. First, artists from social minorities are being included to address themes in unbalanced ways, which often removes the artists from their historical context. Second, such texts employ the Antiwar and Civil Rights Movement as general settings but fail to acknowledge the political challenges and to feature the artists of color of those times. In conclusion, the poor treatment of artists from social minorities, such as they are contained in an "alternative" chapter, should be improved.
Step 4	Recite
	요약문 말로 설명하기

34 Read the passage and follow the directions.

About eight billion people now live on earth. At the dawn of agriculture, about 8000 B.C., the population of the world was approximately 5 million. Over the 8,000-year period up to 1 A.D. it grew to 200 million with a growth rate of under 0.05% per year. A tremendous change occurred with the industrial revolution. During the 20th century alone, the population in the world has grown from 1.65 billion to 6 billion. Here are several ways eight billion people affect the planet.

By 2025, 1.8 billion people will be living in countries with water scarcity, and fully two-thirds will be living in conditions of water stress. People are using groundwater faster than it can be naturally replenished, putting us in danger of peak water. Also, population growth has forced more than 20 cropland-scarce countries to import grain, making them vulnerable to food-price volatility in the international marketplace. To meet the demands of the future, we must double world food supplies by 2050.

Nearly 90 percent of countries with very young and youthful populations had undemocratic governments. Eighty percent of all new civil conflicts between 1970 and 2007 occurred in countries where at least 60 percent of the population is under age 30. These countries may achieve democracy, but are less likely to sustain it. Neglected "youth bulges" could bolster extremism in fragile states like Somalia and destabilize nascent democracies like Egypt.

Demographic trends significantly impact the planet's resources and peoples' security. Women in developing countries with high fertility rates are more likely to suffer from poor health and low literacy. It is a vicious cycle: More children, inadequate healthcare, and less education make it harder for women to help their families adapt to scarce supplies of food, water, and energy. There are no quick solutions to these problems. But considering them is paramount for the humanity's wellbeing.

Write a summary following the guidelines below.

| Guidelines |
- Summarize the above passage in ONE paragraph.
- Provide a topic sentence, major supporting details, and a concluding sentence based on the passage.
- Do NOT copy more than FIVE consecutive words from the passage.

NOTE

Step 1	Survey
Key Words	
Signal Words	
Step 2	**Reading**
Purpose	
Pattern of Organization	
Tone	
Main Idea	
Step 3	**Summary**
지문 요약하기 (Paraphrasing)	
Step 4	**Recite**
	요약문 말로 설명하기

Answer Key

About eight billion people now live on earth. At the dawn of agriculture, about 8000 B.C., **the population** of the world was approximately 5 million. Over the 8,000-year period up to 1 A.D. it grew to 200 million with a growth rate of under 0.05% per year. A tremendous change occurred with the industrial revolution. During the 20th century alone, **the population** in the world has grown from 1.65 billion to 6 billion. Here are several ways eight billion people affect the planet.

By 2025, 1.8 billion people will be living in countries with water scarcity, and fully two-thirds will be living in conditions of water stress. People are using groundwater faster than it can be naturally replenished, putting us in danger of peak water. Also, **population growth** has forced more than 20 cropland-scarce countries to import grain, making them vulnerable to food-price volatility in the international marketplace. To meet the demands of the future, we must double world food supplies by 2050.

Nearly 90 percent of countries with very young and youthful populations had **undemocratic governments**. Eighty percent of all new **civil conflicts** between 1970 and 2007 occurred in countries where at least 60 percent of the population is under age 30. These countries may achieve **democracy**, but are less likely to sustain it. Neglected "youth bulges" could bolster extremism in fragile states like Somalia and destabilize nascent democracies like Egypt.

Demographic trends significantly impact the planet's resources and peoples' security. Women in developing countries with high fertility rates are more likely to suffer from poor health and low literacy. It is a vicious cycle : More children, inadequate healthcare, and less education make it harder for women to help their families adapt to scarce supplies of food, water, and energy. **There are no quick solutions to these problems. But considering them is paramount for the humanity's wellbeing**.

key words

모범답안

The extreme growth of the human population has created several challenges for the planet. First, population growth has led to water scarcity which has affected many countries, created food shortages that need remedy for future growth. Second, the imbalance of more youths has created political instability creating fragile states which are unlikely to become or remain democratic. In conclusion, some areas of growth are caught in a vicious cycle of having poor care and resources while having more children, therefore, solutions to these problems need to be found.

채점기준

+ 1점: 글의 topic sentence를 다음과 같이 서술하였거나 유사하였다.
"The extreme growth of the human population has created several challenges for the planet."

+ 2점: 글의 major supporting details를 다음과 같이 서술하였거나 유사하였다.
"First, population growth has led to water scarcity which has affected many countries, created food shortages that need remedy for future growth. Second, the imbalance of more youths has created political instability creating fragile states which are unlikely to become or remain democratic."

☞ 2개 중 2개 모두를 정확하게 요약한 경우 2점, 1개만 요약한 경우 1점, 요약하지 못한 경우 0점을 준다.

+ 1점: 글의 결론을 "In conclusion, some areas of growth are caught in a vicious cycle of having poor care and resources while having more children, therefore, solutions to these problems need to be found."이라 서술하였거나 유사하였다.

● 감점
- 본문에 나오는 연속되는 6단어 이상을 사용하였다. -1pt
- 문단을 두 개나 그 이상으로 구성하였다. -1pt
- grammar나 영어표현이 합쳐 4개 이상 오류가 있다. -1pt

한글번역

약 80억 명의 사람들이 현재 지구상에 살고 있다. 기원전 8000년 경, 농업의 여명기에 세계의 인구는 대략 5백만 명이었다. 서기 1년까지 8,000년 동안 매년 0.05% 미만의 성장률로 2억 명으로 성장했다. 산업혁명과 함께 엄청난 변화가 일어났다. 20세기 동안만 해도, 세계의 인구는 16억 5천만 명에서 60억 명으로 증가했다. 여기 80억 명의 사람들이 지구에 영향을 미치는 몇 가지 방법이 있다.

2025년까지, 18억 명의 사람들이 물 부족 국가에 살게 될 것이고, 3분의 2나 되는 많은 사람들이 물 스트레스를 받는 조건에서 살게 될 것이다. 사람들은 자연적으로 보충될 수 있는 것보다 더 빨리 지하수를 사용하고 있어, 우리를 최고치에 도달한 물의 위험에 빠뜨리고 있다. 또한 인구 증가로 인해 20개국 이상이 농경지가 부족해 곡물을 수입해야 했고 국제 시장의 식량 가격 변동성에 취약하게 됐다. 미래의 수요를 충족시키기 위해, 우리는 2050년까지 세계 식량 공급을 두 배로 늘려야 한다.

매우 젊고 젊은 인구를 가진 나라의 거의 90%가 비민주적인 정부를 가지고 있다. 1970년에서 2007년 사이에 발생한 모든 새로운 민족분규의 80%는 인구 중 적어도 60%가 30세 미만인 국가에서 발생했다. 이 국가들은 민주주의를 달성할 수는 있지만, 민주주의를 유지할 가능성은 낮다. 방치된 '청년 팽창'은 소말리아와 같은 취약한 국가에서 극단주의를 강화하고 이집트와 같은 신생 민주주의 국가를 불안정하게 할 수 있다.

인구학적 추세는 지구 자원과 인류의 안전에 중대한 영향을 미친다. 높은 출산율을 보이는 개발도상국의 여성들은 건강 상태가 나쁘고 문해율이 낮을 가능성이 크다. 이는 악순환이다. 아이가 많고, 의료가 부족하며, 교육 기회가 적은 상황은 여성들이 가족이 부족한 식량·물·에너지 자원에 적응하도록 돕는 것을 더욱 어렵게 만든다. 이러한 문제에는 신속한 해결책이 없지만, 그것들을 고려하는 것은 인류의 복지에 있어 무엇보다도 중요하다.

NOTE

Step 1	ⓢurvey
Key Words	Population growth; water scarcity; political instability
Signal Words	Several ways; effect
Step 2	**ⓡeading**
Purpose	To explain challenges of the extreme growth of the human population
Pattern of Organization	Series
Tone	Neutral (but persuasive)
Main Idea	The extreme growth of the human population has created several challenges for the planet.
Step 3	**ⓢummary**
지문 요약하기 (Paraphrasing)	The extreme growth of the human population has created several challenges for the planet. First, population growth has led to water scarcity which has affected many countries, created food shortages that need remedy for future growth. Second, the imbalance of more youths has created political instability creating fragile states which are unlikely to become or remain democratic. In conclusion, some areas of growth are caught in a vicious cycle of having poor care and resources while having more children, therefore, solutions to these problems need to be found.
Step 4	**ⓡecite**
	요약문 말로 설명하기

35 Read the passage and follow the directions.

Current growth patterns stand in the way of sustainable development and its objectives of social, environmental and economic sustainability. Many argue that poor countries should focus on satisfying human needs before attending to nature, especially given their relatively small environmental footprint. This argument is misleading for several reasons.

First, individuals who struggle to feed and house themselves may not see biodiversity protection and climate change mitigation as priorities, but local environmental goods affect their daily lives, with significant impact on income and welfare. The lack of solid waste disposal, for example, is not merely an environmental issue. By clogging drains, it leads to health hazards and flooding, with serious economic and human consequences. In Haiti, poor solid waste disposal is to blame for the resurgence of diseases such as dengue and for vulnerability to storms.

Second, it may be impossible or prohibitively expensive to clean up later. The loss of many environmental assets—most obviously biodiversity—is irreversible. This is also the case with climate. Because greenhouse gases reside in the atmosphere for a long time, each emitted molecule will influence the climate over decades (for methane), centuries (for $CO2$), or longer. Irreversibility may also occur because of economic and technological lock-in. A lot of infrastructure is long lived, and today's choices will be hard to reverse. Urban forms are largely determined when city populations are increasing rapidly and most buildings and transport systems are being built. The consequences of development based on a low-density, individual-vehicle transportation model are largely irreversible, as evidenced by the current struggles of U.S. urban planners to densify and develop public transport systems.

MEMO

Growth drives poverty reduction, though the extent to which it does so depends on the degree of inequality, and greater equality of opportunity. However, for the last 250 years growth has largely come at the expense of the environment. And environmental damage is reaching a scale at which they it is beginning to threaten both growth prospects and the progress achieved in social indicators. Thus, developing countries, especially low income countries, should prioritize policies that are sustainable now, before it's too late.

Write a summary following the guidelines below.

| Guidelines |

- Summarize the above passage in ONE paragraph.
- Provide a topic sentence, major supporting details, and a concluding sentence based on the passage.
- Do NOT copy more than FIVE consecutive words from the passage.

NOTE

Step 1	**S**urvey
Key Words	
Signal Words	
Step 2	**R**eading
Purpose	
Pattern of Organization	
Tone	
Main Idea	
Step 3	**S**ummary
지문 요약하기 (Paraphrasing)	
Step 4	**R**ecite
	요약문 말로 설명하기

Answer Key

Current growth patterns stand in the way of **sustainable development** and its objectives of social, environmental and economic **sustainability**. Many argue that poor countries should focus on satisfying human needs before attending to nature, especially given their relatively small environmental footprint. This argument is misleading for several reasons.

First, individuals who struggle to feed and house themselves may not see biodiversity protection and climate change mitigation as priorities, but local environmental goods affect their daily lives, with significant impact on income and welfare. The lack of solid waste disposal, for example, is not merely an environmental issue. By clogging drains, it leads to health hazards and flooding, with serious economic and human consequences. In Haiti, poor solid waste disposal is to blame for the resurgence of diseases such as dengue and for vulnerability to storms.

Second, it may be **impossible** or **prohibitively expensive** to clean up later. The loss of many environmental assets—most obviously biodiversity—is irreversible. This is also the case with **climate**. Because greenhouse gases reside in the atmosphere for a long time, each emitted molecule will influence the climate over decades (for methane), centuries (for CO_2), or longer. **Irreversibility** may also occur because of economic and technological lock-in. A lot of infrastructure is long lived, and today's choices will be hard to reverse. Urban forms are largely determined when city populations are increasing rapidly and most buildings and transport systems are being built. The consequences of development based on a low-density, individual-vehicle transportation model are largely **irreversible**, as evidenced by the current struggles of U.S. urban planners to densify and develop public transport systems.

Growth drives poverty reduction, though the extent to which it does so depends on the degree of inequality, and greater equality of opportunity. However, for the last 250 years growth has largely come at the expense of the environment. And **environmental damage** is reaching a scale at which they it is beginning to threaten both growth prospects and the progress achieved in social indicators. Thus, **developing countries**, especially low income countries, **should prioritize policies that are sustainable now**, before it's too late.

key words

conclusion

모범답안

There are several reasons developing nations should concentrate on sustainable development. First, placing environmental protection as a secondary goal can result in serious human and economic consequences as shown in the case of poor waste disposal system. Second, an economic-first, environment-later policy is not possible because once the environmental assets are lost, the situation cannot be reversed. Also, as lots of infrastructure tends to be long lasting, our current choices will not be easy to reverse. In conclusion, considering current high degree of environmental damage, poor countries should create sustainable policies right now.

채점기준

+ 1점: 글의 topic sentence를 다음과 같이 서술하였거나 유사하였다.
  "There are several reasons developing nations should concentrate(focus) on sustainable development."

+ 2점: 글의 major supporting details를 다음과 같이 서술하였거나 유사하였다.
  "First, placing environmental protection as a secondary(peripheral/minor) goal can result in serious human and economic consequences as shown in the case of poor waste disposal system(1점). Second, an economic-first, environment-later policy is not possible because once the environmental assets are lost, the situation cannot be reversed(0.5점). Also, as lots of infrastructure tends to be long lasting, our current choices will not be easy to reverse(0.5점)."

+ 1점: 글의 결론을 "In conclusion, considering high degree of environmental damage, poor countries should create sustainable policies right now."라 서술하였거나 유사하였다.

- **감점**
  - 본문에 나오는 연속되는 6단어 이상을 사용하였다. −1pt
  - 문단을 두 개나 그 이상으로 구성하였다. −1pt
  - grammar나 영어표현이 합쳐 4개 이상 오류가 있다. −1pt

한글번역

현재의 성장 양상은 사회적·환경적·경제적 지속가능성을 목표로 하는 지속가능한 발전에 걸림돌이 되고 있다. 많은 사람들은 빈곤 국가들이 상대적으로 환경에 끼치는 영향이 적기 때문에 자연보다 인간의 기본적 필요 충족에 우선 집중해야 한다고 주장한다. 그러나 이러한 주장은 여러 이유에서 잘못됐다.

첫째, 먹고 살 집조차 해결하기 어려운 개인에게는 생물다양성 보호나 기후변화 완화가 우선순위로 보이지 않을 수 있다. 그러나 지역의 환경재는 이들의 일상에 직접적인 영향을 끼치며 소득과 복지에도 중요한 역할을 한다. 예를 들어, 고형폐기물 처리 부재는 단순한 환경 문제가 아니다. 배수로를 막아 보건상의 위험과 홍수를 초래하며 심각한 경제적·인간적 피해로 이어진다. 아이티의 경우, 부실한 폐기물 처리 때문에 뎅기열 같은 질병이 재발하고 폭풍에 취약해졌다.

둘째, 나중에 문제를 해결하는 것이 불가능하거나 막대한 비용을 요구할 수 있다. 환경 자산의 상실, 특히 생물다양성의 상실은 되돌릴 수 없다. 기후 문제도 마찬가지다. 온실가스는 대기 중에 장기간 머물며, 배출된 분자 하나하나가 수십 년(메탄), 수세기(CO_2), 혹은 그 이상 동안 기후에 영향을 준다. 경제적·기술적 고착으로 인한 불가역성 또한 발생할 수 있다. 많은 인프라는 수명이 길기 때문에 오늘날의 선택은 되돌리기 어렵다. 도시의 형태는 주로 인구가 급증하면서 건물과 교통체계가 대거 건설될 때 결정된다. 개인 차량 중심의 저밀도 교통 모델에 기반한 개발은 되돌리기 힘들며, 이는 현재 미국 도시계획가들이 도시 밀도를 높이고 대중교통을 확충하려 애쓰는 모습에서 확인할 수 있다.

성장은 빈곤 감소를 견인하지만, 그 효과는 불평등 정도와 기회의 평등성에 달려 있다. 그러나 지난 250년 동안 성장은 주로 환경을 희생시켜 이뤄졌다. 이제 환경 파괴는 성장 전망뿐 아니라 사회적 지표에서 이룬 성과마저 위협할 수준에 이르렀다. 따라서 개발도상국, 특히 저소득 국가는 늦기 전에 지금 당장 지속가능한 정책을 우선시해야 한다.

NOTE

Step 1	**S**urvey
Key Words	Sustainable development; environmental protection; the loss of environmental assets
Signal Words	Several reasons; First; Second
Step 2	**R**eading
Purpose	To argue why developing nations should concentrate on sustainable development
Pattern of Organization	Series; cause/effect
Tone	Subjective
Main Idea	There are several reasons developing nations should concentrate on sustainable development.
Step 3	**S**ummary
지문 요약하기 (Paraphrasing)	There are several reasons developing nations should concentrate on sustainable development. First, placing environmental protection as a secondary goal can result in serious human and economic consequences as shown in the case of poor waste disposal system. Second, an economic-first, environment-later policy is not possible because once the environmental assets are lost, the situation cannot be reversed. Also, as lots of infrastructure tends to be long lasting, our current choices will not be easy to reverse. In conclusion, considering current high degree of environmental damage, poor countries should create sustainable policies right now.
Step 4	**R**ecite
	요약문 말로 설명하기

36 Read the passage and follow the directions.

Email is a computer-based application for the exchange of messages between users. A worldwide email network allows people to exchange email messages very quickly. There are numerous advantages of email communication, not least that it's fast and reliable. But email has several drawbacks along with its benefits that sometimes make it a challenging way to send information.

The increased use of email has resulted in people receiving hundreds of emails everyday. Yet, thousands of email messages can be archived into folders on your computer or handheld communication device such as a cell phone to be retrieved when you need them. The convenience of email prevents you from having to keep file folders filled with papers. Also, you can send as many messages, files, videos, documents and presentations as you want without having to pay anything. It significantly reduces shipping and postage costs as well as the time.

It would take a manual effort on the part of someone to access all of your important printed documents and destroy them. But all of your emails and important information can be lost with a simple hard-drive crash. If you store your email information on another server, then you could lose your data if that site goes down or out of business. In addition, people tend to treat it like a conversation because email can happen so quickly. They begin to use slang terms and try to carry on conversations via email. However, since email recipients cannot see each other, the emails do not have any voice inflection or emotion that can help with proper interpretation. This can and does cause misinterpretations of the emotion behind the email, leading to hurt feelings, anger, resentment and many more emotions.

Email is an instant form of communication and it's hard to imagine a professional workplace without relying on email for the majority of its internal and external communications. Most people at some point have felt swamped by the large number of emails they have to sift through. But replying to an email is good etiquette, especially if the sender is expecting a response.

Write a summary following the guidelines below.

Guidelines
- Summarize the above passage in ONE paragraph.
- Provide a topic sentence, major supporting details, and a concluding sentence based on the passage.
- Do NOT copy more than FIVE consecutive words from the passage.

_____
_____
_____
_____
_____

NOTE

Step 1	**S**urvey
Key Words	
Signal Words	
Step 2	**R**eading
Purpose	
Pattern of Organization	
Tone	
Main Idea	
Step 3	**S**ummary
지문 요약하기 (Paraphrasing)	
Step 4	**R**ecite
	요약문 말로 설명하기

Answer Key

Email is a computer-based application for the exchange of messages between users. A **worldwide email network** allows people to exchange email messages very quickly. There are numerous **advantages** of email communication, not least that it's fast and reliable. But email has **several drawbacks** along with its benefits that sometimes make it a challenging way to send information.	definition

key words |
The increased use of email has resulted in people receiving hundreds of emails everyday. Yet, thousands of email messages can be archived into folders on your computer or handheld communication device such as a cell phone to be retrieved when you need them. **The convenience** of email prevents you from having to keep file folders filled with papers. Also, you can **send as many messages**, files, videos, documents and presentations as you want without having to pay anything. It significantly reduces shipping and postage costs as well as the time.	① benefits
It would take a manual effort on the part of someone to access all of your important printed documents and destroy them. But all of your emails and important information **can be lost** with a simple hard-drive crash. If you store your email information on another server, then you **could lose** your data if that site goes down or out of business. In addition, people tend to treat it like a conversation because email can happen so quickly. They begin to use slang terms and try to carry on conversations via email. However, since email recipients cannot see each other, the emails do not have any voice inflection or emotion that can help with proper interpretation. This can and does cause **misinterpretations of the emotion** behind the email, leading to hurt feelings, anger, resentment and many more emotions.	② disadvantages
Email is an instant form of communication and it's hard to imagine a professional workplace without relying on email for the majority of its internal and external communications. Most people at some point have felt swamped by the large number of emails they have to sift through. But **replying to an email is good etiquette, especially if the sender is expecting a response**.	conclusion

모범답안

Email, which is a computer-based application, has several benefits and disadvantages. First, regarding advantages, emails make it possible to store and carry a lot of messages very easily and to send lots of things such as documents and files with little or no cost. On the other hand, emails can be lost or destroyed very easily, and also often take on a conversational nature which can lead to misunderstandings due to the lack of voice inflection or emotion. In conclusion, given that email is a key part of the workplace now, though huge number of emails can be overwhelming, it is good etiquette to keep up with email replies.

유희태 일반영어 ❶

> **채점기준**

+ 1점: 글의 topic sentence를 다음과 같이 서술하였거나 유사하였다.
"Email, which is a computer-based application, has several benefits and disadvantages."
+ 2점: 글의 major supporting details를 다음과 같이 서술하였거나 유사하였다.
"First, regarding advantages, emails make it possible to store and carry a lot of messages very easily and to send lots of things such as documents and files with little or no cost. On the other hand, emails can be lost or destroyed very easily, and also often take on a conversational nature which can lead to misunderstandings due to the lack of voice inflection or emotion."
☞ 2개 중 2개 모두를 정확하게 요약한 경우 2점, 1개만 요약한 경우 1점, 요약하지 못한 경우 0점을 준다.
+ 1점: 글의 결론을 "In conclusion, given that email is a key part of the workplace now, though huge number of emails can be overwhelming, it is good etiquette to keep up with email replies."이라 서술하였거나 유사하였다.

● **감점**
 • 본문에 나오는 연속되는 6단어 이상을 사용하였다. −1pt
 • 문단을 두 개나 그 이상으로 구성하였다. −1pt
 • grammar나 영어표현이 합쳐 4개 이상 오류가 있다. −1pt

> **한글번역**

　　이메일은 사용자 간 메시지를 교환하기 위한 컴퓨터 기반 응용 프로그램이다. 전 세계 이메일 네트워크를 통해 사람들은 매우 빠르게 메시지를 주고받을 수 있다. 이메일 통신에는 빠르고 신뢰할 수 있다는 점을 비롯해 수많은 장점이 있다. 그러나 정보 전달 수단으로서의 이메일에는 장점과 함께 몇 가지 단점도 있어 때때로 어려움을 낳는다.

　　이메일 사용이 증가하면서 사람들은 매일 수백 통의 이메일을 받게 됐다. 하지만 수천 개의 메시지를 컴퓨터나 휴대전화 같은 기기에 보관 폴더로 아카이브해 뒀다가 필요할 때 꺼낼 수 있다. 이메일은 종이 문서로 가득 찬 파일철을 유지하지 않아도 되는 편리함을 제공한다. 또한 원하는 만큼의 메시지, 파일, 동영상, 문서, 프레젠테이션을 비용 없이 보낼 수 있다. 이는 운송 및 우편 비용뿐 아니라 시간을 크게 줄여준다.

　　중요한 인쇄 문서를 모두 없애려면 누군가 직접 수작업을 해야 한다. 그러나 이메일은 단순한 하드 드라이브 오류 한 번으로도 모두 잃어버릴 수 있다. 다른 서버에 이메일을 저장한다면, 그 서버가 중단되거나 폐업했을 때 데이터가 손실될 수도 있다. 게다가 이메일은 매우 빠르게 이뤄지기 때문에 사람들은 이메일을 대화처럼 다루는 경향이 있다. 그 결과 속어를 쓰거나 이메일을 대화 수단으로 사용하려 한다. 하지만 이메일에서는 서로를 볼 수 없기 때문에 음성 억양이나 감정이 드러나지 않아 의미를 제대로 해석하기 어렵다. 이 때문에 메시지 뒤에 담긴 감정이 왜곡돼 서운함, 분노, 반감 등 다양한 감정적 갈등을 일으키기도 한다.

　　이메일은 즉각적인 의사소통 수단이며, 오늘날 전문적인 직장에서 내부 · 외부 커뮤니케이션의 대부분을 이메일에 의존하지 않는 상황은 상상하기 힘들다. 많은 사람들이 언젠가는 감당하기 힘든 이메일 양에 압도당한 경험이 있다. 그러나 이메일에 답장을 하는 것은 특히 발신자가 응답을 기대하고 있을 때 예의에 해당한다.

NOTE

Step 1	Survey
Key Words	Email; advantages; drawbacks
Signal Words	Numerous; several; In addition; However
Step 2	Reading
Purpose	To explain email's benefits and disadvantages
Pattern of Organization	Series
Tone	Subjective
Main Idea	Email has several benefits and disadvantages.
Step 3	Summary
지문 요약하기 (Paraphrasing)	Email, which is a computer-based application, has several benefits and disadvantages. First, regarding advantages, emails make it possible to store and carry a lot of messages very easily and to send lots of things such as documents and files with little or no cost. On the other hand, emails can be lost or destroyed very easily, and also often take on a conversational nature which can lead to misunderstandings due to the lack of voice inflection or emotion. In conclusion, given that email is a key part of the workplace now, though huge number of emails can be overwhelming, it is good etiquette to keep up with email replies.
Step 4	Recite
	요약문 말로 설명하기

37 Read the passage and follow the directions.

Career advancements and developments in business can be achieved by expanding professional network. You would be surprised to know how many doors it can open for you. Let's have a sneak peek at a few tips which may help you improve your overall networking skills.

The best way to enhance your networking skills is by simply going outside and meeting new people. Socialization has been further simplified as you can meet new people by merely attending conferences, events, parties, workshops, and different alumni associations. In addition to this, you're always open to surfing on the internet, Amazon, and libraries for resources on business networking specifically. You should seek all sorts of advice but follow only what suits your techniques best and build your strategies. It is not a one size fits all approach.

It will help if you try to stay as visible as possible because people should always be aware of what you're up to. It would be best if you try to keep in touch with people and maintain consistency and regularity. For this, various sources of communication, including emails, blogs, and specific other social networks, are available. In addition to this, you can make your network even more substantial by helping people. Many of such people may prove to be helpful to you in the future, and some might even be more motivated to return the favor. So, you can achieve mutual benefits by sharing thoughts, expertise, accomplishments, and other work.

MEMO

Success is supposed to come to the suave schmoozers and social butterflies. It's true that networking can help you accomplish great things in your business. However, networking is overrated. What is true is that accomplishing great things helps you develop a network. Networking alone leads to empty transactions, not rich relationships. People often believe that if they simply meet more important people, their work will improve. But it's remarkably hard to engage with those people unless you've already put something valuable out into the world.

Write a summary following the guidelines below.

⌐ Guidelines ⌐
- Summarize the above passage in ONE paragraph.
- Provide a topic sentence, major supporting details, and a concluding sentence based on the passage.
- Do NOT copy more than FIVE consecutive words from the passage.

NOTE

Step 1	**S**urvey
Key Words	
Signal Words	
Step 2	**R**eading
Purpose	
Pattern of Organization	
Tone	
Main Idea	
Step 3	**S**ummary
지문 요약하기 (Paraphrasing)	
Step 4	**R**ecite
	요약문 말로 설명하기

Answer Key

Career advancements and developments in business can be achieved by expanding professional network. You would be surprised to know how many doors it can open for you. Let's have a sneak peek at a few tips which may help you improve your overall networking skills.

The best way to **enhance your networking skills** is by simply **going outside and meeting new people. Socialization** has been further simplified as you can meet new people by merely attending conferences, events, parties, workshops, and different alumni associations. In addition to this, you're always open to surfing on the internet, Amazon, and libraries for resources on business networking specifically. You should seek all sorts of advice but follow only what suits your techniques best and build your strategies. It is not a one size fits all approach.

It will help if you try to **stay as visible as possible** because people should always be aware of what you're up to. It would be best if you **try to keep in touch with people** and maintain consistency and regularity. For this, various sources of communication, including emails, blogs, and specific other social networks, are available. In addition to this, **you can make your network even more substantial by helping people**. Many of such people may prove to be helpful to you in the future, and some might even be more motivated to return the favor. So, you can achieve mutual benefits by sharing thoughts, expertise, accomplishments, and other work.

Success is supposed to come to the suave schmoozers and social butterflies. It's true that networking can help you accomplish great things in your business. However, networking is overrated. What is true is that accomplishing great things helps you develop a network. Networking alone leads to empty transactions, not rich relationships. People often believe that if they simply meet more important people, their work will improve. But it's remarkably hard to engage with those people unless **you've already put something valuable out into the world**.

key words

모범답안

There are several ways to network and improve one's career. First, it is effective to go out and meet new people at conferences or consult friends and online resources to find yourself the best techniques. Second, staying as visible as you can and maintaining communication and helping others can benefit your future as well. In conclusion, though networking is important for success, networking is overrated and putting out valuable things will help one engage with other successful people.

채점기준

+ 1점: 글의 topic sentence를 다음과 같이 서술하였거나 유사하였다.
"There are several ways to network and improve one's career."
+ 2점: 글의 major supporting details를 다음과 같이 서술하였거나 유사하였다.
"First, it is effective to go out and meet new people at conferences or consult friends and online resources to find yourself the best techniques. Second, staying as visible as you can and maintaining communication and helping others can benefit your future as well."
☞ 2개 중 2개 모두를 정확하게 요약한 경우 2점, 1개만 요약한 경우 1점, 요약하지 못한 경우 0점을 준다.
+ 1점: 글의 결론을 "In conclusion, though networking is important for success, networking is overrated and putting out valuable things will help one engage with other successful people."이라 서술하였거나 유사하였다.

● 감점
- 본문에 나오는 연속되는 6단어 이상을 사용하였다. -1pt
- 문단을 두 개나 그 이상으로 구성하였다. -1pt
- grammar나 영어표현이 합쳐 4개 이상 오류가 있다. -1pt

한글번역

　　경력 발전과 비즈니스 성장은 전문적 네트워크를 확장함으로써 이뤄질 수 있다. 네트워크 확장이 얼마나 많은 기회를 열어줄 수 있는지 알게 된다면 아마 놀랄 것이다. 여기서는 전반적인 네트워킹 기술을 향상시키는 데 도움이 될 몇 가지 팁을 살펴보자.
　　네트워킹 기술을 향상시키는 가장 좋은 방법은 단순히 밖으로 나가 새로운 사람들을 만나는 것이다. 컨퍼런스, 행사, 파티, 워크숍, 동창회 등에 참석하기만 해도 사회적 교류가 가능하다. 또한 인터넷, 아마존, 도서관에서 비즈니스 네트워킹과 관련된 자료를 찾아볼 수도 있다. 조언은 다양하게 구하되, 자신에게 맞는 방식만 취해 전략을 세워야 한다. 네트워킹에는 일률적인 접근법이 존재하지 않는다.
　　자신의 존재를 최대한 드러내는 것도 중요하다. 사람들이 언제나 당신이 무엇을 하고 있는지 알 수 있어야 한다. 사람들과 지속적이고 규칙적으로 연락을 유지하는 것도 필요하다. 이메일, 블로그, 특정한 소셜 네트워크 등 다양한 소통 수단을 활용할 수 있다. 게다가 다른 사람을 도와줌으로써 네트워크를 더 튼튼하게 만들 수 있다. 이런 사람들 가운데 일부는 훗날 당신에게 도움이 될 수 있으며, 어떤 사람들은 받은 도움을 되갚으려는 동기를 가질 수도 있다. 따라서 생각, 전문성, 성과, 업무 등을 공유함으로써 상호 이익을 얻을 수 있다.
　　일반적으로는 능숙하게 사교하는 사람들에게 성공이 찾아온다고 생각한다. 실제로 네트워킹은 비즈니스에서 큰 성취를 돕는 역할을 할 수 있다. 그러나 네트워킹은 과대평가되는 경향이 있다. 진실은 성취가 네트워크를 만들어낸다는 점이다. 네트워킹만으로는 의미 없는 교환에 그칠 뿐, 풍부한 관계로 이어지지 않는다. 단순히 더 중요한 사람들을 만나면 일이 나아질 것이라고 믿는 경우가 많지만, 세상에 이미 가치 있는 무언가를 내놓지 않았다면 그들과 깊이 교류하기란 매우 어렵다.

NOTE

Step 1	Survey
Key Words	Career; network; improve; going outside and meeting new people; to keep in touch with
Signal Words	A few tips; best way; in addition to
Step 2	**Reading**
Purpose	To suggest several ways to network and improve one's career
Pattern of Organization	Series
Tone	Subjective
Main Idea	There are several ways to network and improve one's career.
Step 3	**Summary**
지문 요약하기 (Paraphrasing)	There are several ways to network and improve one's career. First, it is effective to go out and meet new people at conferences or consult friends and online resources to find yourself the best techniques. Second, staying as visible as you can and maintaining communication and helping others can benefit your future as well. In conclusion, though networking is important for success, networking is overrated and putting out valuable things will help one engage with other successful people.
Step 4	**Recite**
	요약문 말로 설명하기

38 Read the passage and follow the directions.

Sit down, put on a pot, and chalk up another entry in the list of ways that tea drinking may be good for you. Researchers have found new evidence that ordinary tea may prime the immune system to fend off attacks from bacteria and other pathogens. Over the years, credible claims have been made that tea may help protect against various forms of cancer, cardiovascular disease, Alzheimer's, Parkinson's, disease and rheumatoid arthritis.

Researchers looked at the effects of black tea on 11 healthy tea drinkers and compared them with 10 healthy people who began drinking coffee. The researchers found that drinking 20oz. of tea every day for at least two weeks doubled or tripled the immune system's output of an infection-fighting substance called interferon gamma. The coffee drinkers, by contrast, registered no difference in interferon-gamma production. Apparently the body metabolizes the tea into molecules that mimic the surface proteins of bacteria, jump-starting the immune system so that when real bugs show up, they can more easily be dispatched.

While it's been commented on that tea has less caffeine than coffee when given in the same amount of servings, this isn't actually true. Tea has the same amount of caffeine as coffee, and while both are stimulants, coffee has a much bigger depressing effect (not making you sad but reducing your energy levels) than tea, meaning that while both tea and coffee will give you a bigger rush of caffeine, with coffee, the high will also last shorter and drop quicker. If you're wanting something to keep you going through the work day, tea is the best choice.

Tea and coffee have both long been touted for their physical, mental, emotional and social benefits. While both drinks have their advantages, both tea enthusiasts and coffee lovers will defend their drink of choice to the end. However, as always, use a little common sense. Tea is first and foremost one of life's simple pleasures. If you enjoy it, by all means, go ahead and drink it. But don't expect it to make up for bad habits, like smoking, or for bad luck, like whatever genetic shortcomings you were born with.

Write a summary following the guidelines below.

⌐ Guidelines ⌐
- Summarize the above passage in ONE paragraph.
- Provide a topic sentence, major supporting details, and a concluding sentence based on the passage.
- Do NOT copy more than FIVE consecutive words from the passage.

_____
_____
_____
_____
_____

NOTE

Step 1	ⓢurvey
Key Words	
Signal Words	
Step 2	**ⓡeading**
Purpose	
Pattern of Organization	
Tone	
Main Idea	
Step 3	**ⓢummary**
지문 요약하기 (Paraphrasing)	
Step 4	**ⓡecite**
	요약문 말로 설명하기

Answer Key

Sit down, put on a pot, and chalk up another entry in the list of ways that **tea drinking** may be good for you. Researchers have found new evidence that **ordinary tea** may prime the immune system to fend off attacks from bacteria and other pathogens. Over the years, credible claims have been made that **tea** may help protect against various forms of cancer, cardiovascular disease, Alzheimer's, Parkinson's disease and rheumatoid arthritis.

Researchers looked at **the effects of black** tea on 11 healthy tea drinkers and compared them with 10 healthy people who began **drinking coffee**. The researchers found that drinking 20oz. of tea every day for at least two weeks doubled or tripled the immune system's output of an infection-fighting substance called interferon gamma. **The coffee drinkers**, by contrast, registered no difference in interferon-gamma production. Apparently the body metabolizes the tea into molecules that mimic the surface proteins of bacteria, jump-starting the immune system so that when real bugs show up, they can more easily be dispatched.

While it's been commented on that **tea** has less caffeine than **coffee** when given in the same amount of servings, this isn't actually true. Tea has the same amount of caffeine as coffee, and while both are stimulants, coffee has a much bigger **depressing effect** (not making you sad but reducing your energy levels) than tea, meaning that while both tea and coffee will give you a bigger rush of caffeine, with coffee, the high will also last shorter and drop quicker. If you're wanting something to keep you going through the work day, tea is the best choice.

Tea and coffee have both long been touted for their physical, mental, emotional and social benefits. While both drinks have their advantages, both tea enthusiasts and coffee lovers will defend their drink of choice to the end. However, as always, use a little common sense. **Tea is first and foremost one of life's simple pleasures**. If you enjoy it, by all means, go ahead and drink it. But **don't expect it to make up for bad habits**, like smoking, or for bad luck, like whatever genetic shortcomings you were born with.

	key words
	health
	conclusion

모범답안

Tea is linked to more health benefits than coffee. First, unlike coffee, tea can boost the immune system with interferon gamma which can help fight infection. Second, tea has less depressing effect than coffee and its energizing-effects last longer than coffee's shorter-lived rush. In conclusion, tea is a good drink to enjoy, but will not make up for bad habits or bad genetics.

유희태 일반영어 ❶

채점기준

+ 1점: 글의 topic sentence를 다음과 같이 서술하였거나 유사하였다.
"Tea is linked to more health benefits than coffee."
+ 2점: 글의 major supporting details를 다음과 같이 서술하였거나 유사하였다.
"First, unlike coffee, tea can boost the immune system with interferon gamma which can help fight infection. Second, tea has less depressing effect than coffee and its energizing-effects last longer than coffee's shorter-lived rush."
☞ 2개 중 2개 모두를 정확하게 요약한 경우 2점, 1개만 요약한 경우 1점, 요약하지 못한 경우 0점을 준다.
+ 1점: 글의 결론을 "In conclusion, tea is a good drink to enjoy, but will not make up for bad habits or bad genetics."이라 서술하였거나 유사하였다.

● 감점 • 본문에 나오는 연속되는 6단어 이상을 사용하였다. −1pt
　　　 • 문단을 두 개나 그 이상으로 구성하였다. −1pt
　　　 • grammar나 영어표현이 합쳐 4개 이상 오류가 있다. −1pt

한글번역

　　앉아서 주전자에 물을 올리고, 차가 건강에 좋은 또 하나의 이유를 목록에 추가해보자. 연구자들은 일반적인 차가 면역 체계를 활성화시켜 세균이나 기타 병원체의 공격을 막을 수 있다는 새로운 증거를 발견했다. 수년에 걸쳐 차가 여러 형태의 암, 심혈관 질환, 알츠하이머병, 파킨슨병, 류머티즘성 관절염 등을 예방하는 데 도움이 될 수 있다는 신뢰할 만한 주장들이 제기돼 왔다.
　　연구진은 11명의 건강한 차 애호가에게 홍차가 미치는 효과를 살펴보고, 이를 새롭게 커피를 마시기 시작한 10명의 건강한 사람들과 비교했다. 그 결과 하루 20온스(약 0.6리터)의 차를 최소 2주 동안 마신 사람들의 경우, 감염과 싸우는 물질인 인터페론 감마(interferon gamma)의 분비가 두세 배 증가했다. 반면 커피를 마신 사람들에게서는 인터페론 감마 생성의 변화가 관찰되지 않았다. 이는 신체가 차를 대사하면서 세균의 표면 단백질을 모방하는 분자로 전환하기 때문에 면역 체계가 활성화되고, 실제 세균이 침입했을 때 더 쉽게 방어할 수 있는 것으로 보인다.
　　차가 동일한 양으로 제공될 때 커피보다 카페인이 적다는 말이 있지만, 사실이 아니다. 차와 커피에는 같은 양의 카페인이 들어 있으며, 둘 모두 자극제이지만 커피는 차보다 훨씬 큰 "억제 효과"(우울하게 만든다는 뜻이 아니라 에너지 레벨을 낮추는 효과)를 갖는다. 즉, 차와 커피 모두 카페인으로 인한 에너지 상승을 제공하지만, 커피는 상승 효과가 더 짧고 급격하게 떨어진다. 따라서 하루 종일 일을 이어갈 무언가가 필요하다면 차가 더 좋은 선택이다.
　　차와 커피 모두 오랫동안 신체적, 정신적, 정서적, 사회적 효용이 있다고 알려져 왔다. 두 음료에는 각각 장점이 있으며, 차 애호가와 커피 애호가가 모두 끝까지 자신이 선호하는 음료를 옹호할 것이다. 그러나 언제나 상식적으로 접근하는 것이 중요하다. 차는 무엇보다 삶의 단순한 즐거움 중 하나다. 즐긴다면 마음껏 마시면 된다. 하지만 흡연 같은 나쁜 습관이나 타고난 유전적 한계를 보완해 줄 것이라고 기대해서는 안 된다.

NOTE

Step 1	Survey
Key Words	Tea; coffee
Signal Words	By contrast; less... than; much bigger... than
Step 2	**Reading**
Purpose	To argue that tea is better than coffee
Pattern of Organization	Contrast; series
Tone	Subjective
Main Idea	Tea is linked to more health benefits than coffee.
Step 3	**Summary**
지문 요약하기 (Paraphrasing)	Tea is linked to more health benefits than coffee. First, unlike coffee, tea can boost the immune system with interferon gamma which can help fight infection. Second, tea has less depressing effect than coffee and its energizing-effects last longer than coffee's shorter-lived rush. In conclusion, tea is a good drink to enjoy, but will not make up for bad habits or bad genetics.
Step 4	**Recite**
	요약문 말로 설명하기

39 Read the passage and follow the directions.

Multicultural families face challenges similar to other families. Most multicultural families, however, will agree that facing these challenges is more than worth the trouble, considering the benefits of raising children who learn to value differences from an early age.

The issue—where to live—arises from the very beginning. When raising children, connections to extended family are very important, yet many multicultural families do not live close to relatives or have to choose which relatives to live near. Also, they might have to choose job security over travel or moving abroad to help their children learn another language and culture. But in the end, where a family decides to live can be what defines them and makes them unique. Making a conscious decision as a family can lead to greater bonding and a sense of shared purpose.

Multicultural families are much more likely to face prejudice from society, whether because of mixing cultures, languages, or races. Children from multicultural families may feel they have to choose one heritage (and therefore one parent) over another, or may feel they don't fit in anywhere at all. Yet despite the difficulties, in the end multicultural children are at an advantage in today's world because of their intimate familiarity with more than one culture and, perhaps most importantly, their deep understanding of the need to bridges differences. If they are given the proper guidance to weather the prejudice they will inevitably face, they will become savvy yet sensitive citizens of today's increasingly interconnected world.

It is important to remember that multicultural families—like others—were created out of love, and it is that love for each other that can ultimately help them triumph over any challenges they might face. Facing these challenges together can be turned into an advantage that will help cement the family unit.

Write a summary following the guidelines below.

━━━━━━━━━━━━━━━━━━━━━━━ Guidelines ━━━━━━━━━━━━━━━━━━━━━━━
- Summarize the above passage in ONE paragraph.
- Provide a topic sentence, major supporting details, and a concluding sentence based on the passage.
- Do NOT copy more than FOUR consecutive words from the passage.

NOTE

Step 1	**S**urvey
Key Words	
Signal Words	
Step 2	**R**eading
Purpose	
Pattern of Organization	
Tone	
Main Idea	
Step 3	**S**ummary
지문 요약하기 (Paraphrasing)	
Step 4	**R**ecite
	요약문 말로 설명하기

Answer Key

Multicultural families face **challenges** similar to other families. Most multicultural families, however, will agree that facing these challenges is more than worth the trouble, considering the **benefits** of raising children who learn to value differences from an early age.

The issue—where to live—arises from the very beginning. When raising children, connections to extended family are very important, yet many multicultural families **do not live close to relatives or have to choose which relatives to live near.** Also, they might have to choose job security over travel or moving abroad to help their children learn another language and culture. But in the end, **where a family decides to live** can be what defines them and makes them unique. Making a conscious decision as a family can lead to greater bonding and a sense of shared purpose.

Multicultural families are much more likely to face **prejudice** from society, whether because of mixing cultures, languages, or races. **Children from multicultural families** may feel they have to choose one heritage (and therefore one parent) over another, or may feel they don't fit in anywhere at all. Yet despite the difficulties, in the end multicultural children are at an advantage in today's world because of their intimate familiarity with more than one culture and, perhaps most importantly, their deep understanding of the need to **bridges differences**. If they are given the proper guidance to weather the prejudice they will inevitably face, they will become **savvy yet sensitive citizens** of today's increasingly interconnected world.

It is important to remember that multicultural families—like others—were created out of love, and it is that love for each other that can ultimately help them triumph over any challenges they might face. **Facing these challenges together can be turned into an advantage** that will help cement the family unit.

key words

모범답안

Multicultural families face unique challenges and strengths. First, choosing where to live is big challenge for them. They usually do not have relatives nearby and have little chance to give better education to their children. But such difficult situations can create a greater sense of shared purpose. Second, multicultural families confront prejudice but if their children overcome such difficulties, they can become savvy and discerning children because of their capability to bridge differences. In conclusion, it is crucial to remember that these challenges can turn to strengths when a multicultural family shares a tight bond.

유희태 일반영어 ❶

> **채점기준**

+ 1점 : 글의 topic sentence를 다음과 같이 서술하였거나 유사하였다.
"<u>Multicultural families face unique challenges and strengths.</u>"

+ 2점 : 글의 major supporting details를 다음과 같이 서술하였거나 유사하였다.
"First, <u>choosing where to live is big challenge for them. They usually do not have relatives nearby and have little chance to give better education to their children. But such difficult situations can create a greater sense of shared purpose. Second, multicultural families confront prejudice but if their children overcome such difficulties, they can become savvy and discerning children because of their capability to bridge differences.</u>"
☞ 2개 중 2개 모두 정확하게 요약한 경우 2점, 1개만 요약한 경우 1점, 요약하지 못한 경우 0점을 준다.

+ 1점 : 글의 결론을 "<u>In conclusion, it is crucial to remember that these challenges can turn to strengths when a multicultural family shares a tight bond.</u>"라 서술하였거나 유사하였다.

- **감점**
  - 본문에 나오는 연속되는 5단어 이상을 사용하였다. -1pt
  - 문단을 두 개나 그 이상으로 구성하였다. -1pt
  - grammar나 영어표현이 합쳐 4개 이상 오류가 있다. -1pt

> **한글번역**

　　다문화 가정은 다른 가정들과 비슷한 어려움에 직면한다. 그러나 대부분의 다문화 가정은 자녀가 어릴 때부터 차이를 존중하는 법을 배우게 된다는 이점을 고려하면 이러한 어려움이 충분히 감수할 만한 것이라고 동의할 것이다.
　　가장 처음 맞닥뜨리는 문제는 '어디에서 살 것인가'이다. 아이를 키울 때 확대 가족과의 연결은 매우 중요하다. 그러나 많은 다문화 가정은 친척 가까이에 살지 않거나 어느 쪽 친척과 가까이 살지를 선택해야 하는 상황에 놓인다. 또한 자녀가 다른 언어와 문화를 배우도록 해외로 이주하거나 여행하는 대신 직업 안정성을 선택해야 할 수도 있다. 하지만 결국 가족이 어디에서 살기로 결정하느냐가 그들의 정체성을 규정하고 독특하게 만드는 요인이 될 수 있다. 가족이 함께 의식적으로 내린 결정은 더 강한 유대감과 공동의 목적의식을 형성할 수 있다.
　　다문화 가정은 문화, 언어, 인종이 섞였다는 이유로 사회적 편견에 더 많이 직면하는 경우가 많다. 다문화 가정의 아이들은 한쪽 부모의 문화를 선택해야 한다는 압박을 느끼거나, 어느 쪽에도 속하지 못한다는 소외감을 가질 수 있다. 그러나 어려움에도 불구하고 다문화 가정의 아이들은 오늘날 세계에서 분명한 이점을 지닌다. 여러 문화를 친밀하게 접한 경험을 통해 차이를 연결할 필요성을 깊이 이해하기 때문이다. 만약 그들이 불가피하게 맞닥뜨릴 편견을 이겨낼 수 있도록 올바른 지도를 받는다면, 점점 더 상호 연결되는 세계에서 현명하면서도 섬세한 시민으로 성장할 수 있을 것이다.
　　무엇보다 중요한 것은 다문화 가정 역시 다른 가정들과 마찬가지로 '사랑'을 바탕으로 이뤄졌다는 점을 잊지 않는 것이다. 바로 그 상호 간의 사랑이 그들이 직면하는 어떤 어려움도 극복하게 하는 궁극적인 힘이 될 수 있다. 이러한 도전을 함께 맞서 나가는 과정은 가족을 더욱 단단히 결속시키는 이점으로 전환될 수 있다.

NOTE

Step 1	Ⓢurvey
Key Words	Multicultural families; challenges; benefits; where to live; prejudice
Signal Words	More than worth; despite the difficulties
Step 2	**Ⓡeading**
Purpose	To illustrate challenges and strengths multicultural families face
Pattern of Organization	Series
Tone	Subjective
Main Idea	Multicultural families face unique challenges and strengths.
Step 3	**Ⓢummary**
지문 요약하기 (Paraphrasing)	Multicultural families face unique challenges and strengths. First, choosing where to live is big challenge for them. They usually do not have relatives nearby and have little chance to give better education to their children. But such difficult situations can create a greater sense of shared purpose. Second, multicultural families confront prejudice but if their children overcome such difficulties, they can become savvy and discerning children because of their capability to bridge differences. In conclusion, it is crucial to remember that these challenges can turn to strengths when a multicultural family shares a tight bond.
Step 4	**Ⓡecite**
	요약문 말로 설명하기

40 Read the passage and answer the questions.

The economic weakness that underlay the Great Depression had several interrelated causes. The first cause was declining ____ⓐ____. Coal, railroads, textiles, and some other industries were in distress long before 1929, but the major growth industries—automobiles, construction, and mechanized agriculture—had been able to expand as long as consumers bought their products. Frenzied expansion, however, could not continue unabated. When demand leveled off, owners could not accumulate funds to build new plants and hire new workers. Instead, unsold inventories stacked up in warehouses, and laborers were laid off. Underconsumption, which also resulted from maldistribution of income, was important. For example, as the rich grew richer, middle-and lower-income Americans made only modest gains. Though average per capita disposable income rose about 9 percent between 1920 and 1929, the income of the wealthiest 1 percent rose 75 percent, accounting for most of the increase. Much of this increase was put into stock market investments instead of being spent on consumer goods. That American businesses were overloaded with ____ⓑ____ was a cause. In 1929 the top 200 nonfinancial corporations controlled 49 percent of corporate wealth. Many corporations built pyramid-like empires supported by shady, though legal, manipulation of assets and weakly supported liabilities. Finally, the nation's banking system was on precarious footing. For example, when one part of the edifice collapsed, the entire structure crumbled.

Fill in each blank ⓐ and ⓑ with the ONE most appropriate word from the passage respectively.

NOTE

Step 1	**S**urvey
Key Words	
Signal Words	
Step 2	**R**eading
Purpose	
Pattern of Organization	
Tone	
Main Idea	
Step 3	**S**ummary
지문 요약하기 (Paraphrasing)	
Step 4	**R**ecite
	요약문 말로 설명하기

Answer Key

The economic weakness that underlay the Great Depression had several interrelated causes. The first cause was **declining demand**. Coal, railroads, textiles, and some other industries were in distress long before 1929, but the major growth industries—automobiles, construction, and mechanized agriculture—had been able to expand as long as consumers bought their products. Frenzied expansion, however, could not continue unabated. When demand leveled off, owners could not accumulate funds to build new plants and hire new workers. Instead, unsold inventories stacked up in warehouses, and laborers were laid off. **Underconsumption**, which also resulted from **maldistribution of income**, was important. For example, as the rich grew richer, middle-and lower-income Americans made only modest gains. Though average per capita disposable income rose about 9 percent between 1920 and 1929, the income of the wealthiest 1 percent rose 75 percent, accounting for most of the increase. Much of this increase was put into stock market investments instead of being spent on consumer goods. That American businesses were **overloaded with liabilities** was a cause. In 1929 the top 200 nonfinancial corporations controlled 49 percent of corporate wealth. **Many corporations built pyramid-like empires supported by shady**, though legal, manipulation of assets and weakly supported liabilities. Finally, **the nation's banking system was on precarious footing**. For example, when one part of the edifice collapsed, the entire structure crumbled.

모범답안

ⓐ demand ⓑ liabilities

한글번역

　　대공황을 뒷받침한(대공황의 기저를 이루는) 경제적 취약성에는 여러 상호연관된 원인들이 있었다. 첫 번째 원인은 수요 감소였다. 석탄, 철도, 섬유업과 기타 몇몇 산업들은 1929년 훨씬 이전부터 곤경에 처해 있지만, 주요 성장 산업들인 자동차, 건설업, 기계화된 농업은 소비자들이 그들의 제품을 구매하는 한 확장할 수 있었다. 하지만 광란적인 확장은 계속 이어질 수 없었다. 수요가 정체되자 사업주들은 새로운 공장을 건설하고 새로운 노동자를 고용할 자금을 축적할 수 없게 됐다. 대신 팔리지 않은 재고가 창고에 쌓여갔고 노동자들은 해고됐다. 소득의 불균등한 분배에서 비롯된 소비 부족도 중요한 요인이었다. 예를 들어, 부자들은 더욱 부유해졌지만 중간소득층과 저소득층 미국인들은 미미한 수익만 얻었다. 1920년과 1929년 사이에 평균 1인당 가처분소득은 약 9% 증가했지만, 최고 부유층 1%의 소득은 75% 증가해 전체 증가분의 대부분을 차지했다. 이 증가분의 상당 부분은 소비재 구입 대신 주식 투자에 투입됐다. 미국 기업들이 부채에 과부하가 걸린 것도 원인이었다. 1929년에 상위 200개 비금융 기업이 기업 총자산의 49%를 지배했다. 많은 기업들이 교묘하면서도 합법적인 자산 조작과 취약하게 뒷받침된 부채로 지탱되는 피라미드 형태의 제국을 건설했다. 마지막으로 국가의 은행 시스템이 불안정한 기반 위에 있었다. 예를 들어, 이 구조물의 한 부분이 무너졌을 때 전체 구조가 붕괴됐다.

NOTE

Step 1	Surveyy
Key Words	Great Depression; declining demand; underconsumption; maldistribution of income; corporate wealth; pyramid-like empires; banking system; precarious footing
Signal Words	Causes; first cause; also; Finally
Step 2	**Reading**
Purpose	To analyze the underlying economic factors that contributed to the Great Depression
Pattern of Organization	Cause/effect; series
Tone	Neutral
Main Idea	The Great Depression stemmed from multiple interconnected economic weaknesses that had been developing in the American economy throughout the 1920s.
Step 3	**Summary**
지문 요약하기 (Paraphrasing)	The Great Depression stemmed from multiple interconnected economic weaknesses that had been developing in the American economy throughout the 1920s. These included declining demand in major growth industries, underconsumption resulting from income inequality, corporate debt, concentrated business control among top corporations, and a precarious banking system that was vulnerable to collapse.
Step 4	**Recite**
	요약문 말로 설명하기

41 Read the passage and answer the questions.

When it comes to opinions about foreign matter, the cleavage is wide between the general American public and political elites. First of all, the two groups differ in their knowledge of foreign matters, with the public tending to be poorly informed and elites being better informed. For example, the general public has only a vague idea of where Kosovo is, how far it is from Baghdad to Kuwait, or why the Palestinians and the Israelis disagree about the future of Israel. The two groups also differ in their ⓐ_____ of America's international role. To illustrate, while both average citizens and college-educated people initially opposed and then supported our military in Vietnam once it was there, the general public continued to support the troops while the elites dramatically decreased their support and staged antiwar demonstrations. Finally, the public doesn't change their minds as often or as quickly as political elites do. During the Vietnam War, for instance, upper-middle-class people who regularly read several magazines and newspapers underwent a dramatic ⓑ_____ in opinion between 1964 (when they supported the war) and 1968 (when they opposed it), but the views of blue-collar workers scarcely changed at all.

Fill in each blank with the ONE most appropriate word from the passage respectively.

NOTE

Step 1	**S**urvey
Key Words	
Signal Words	
Step 2	**R**eading
Purpose	
Pattern of Organization	
Tone	
Main Idea	
Step 3	**S**ummary
지문 요약하기 (Paraphrasing)	
Step 4	**R**ecite
	요약문 말로 설명하기

Answer Key

When it comes to **opinions about foreign matter**, **the cleavage** is wide between the general American public and political elites. First of all, the two groups differ in their knowledge of **foreign matters**, with the public tending to be poorly informed and elites being better informed. For example, the general public has only a vague idea of where Kosovo is, how far it is from Baghdad to Kuwait, or why the Palestinians and the Israelis disagree about the future of Israel. **The two groups** also differ in their support of **America's international role**. To illustrate, while both average citizens and college-educated people initially opposed and then supported our military in Vietnam once it was there, the general public continued to support the troops while the elites dramatically decreased their support and staged antiwar demonstrations. Finally, **the public** doesn't change their minds as often or as quickly as political **elites** do. During the Vietnam War, for instance, upper-middle-class people who regularly read several magazines and newspapers underwent a dramatic change in opinion between 1964 (when they supported the war) and 1968 (when they opposed it), but the views of blue-collar workers scarcely changed at all.

key words

모범답안

ⓐ support ⓑ change

한글번역

대외 문제에 관한 의견에 있어서 미국의 일반 대중과 정치 엘리트 사이의 격차는 크다. 우선, 두 집단은 대외 문제에 대한 지식에서 차이를 보이는데, 대중은 정보가 부족한 경향이 있고 엘리트들은 더 잘 알고 있다. 예를 들어, 일반 대중은 코소보가 어디에 있는지, 바그다드에서 쿠웨이트까지 얼마나 멀리 떨어져 있는지, 또는 팔레스타인인들과 이스라엘인들이 이스라엘의 미래에 대해 왜 의견이 다른지에 대해 막연한 개념만 가지고 있다. 두 집단은 또한 미국의 국제적 역할에 대한 지지에서도 차이를 보인다. 예를 들어, 일반 시민들과 대학 교육을 받은 사람들 모두 처음에는 베트남 파병을 반대했다가 일단 파병된 후에는 지지했지만, 일반 대중은 계속해서 군대 파병을 지지한 반면 엘리트들은 지지를 극적으로 줄이고 반전 시위를 벌였다. 마지막으로, 대중은 정치 엘리트들만큼 자주 또는 빠르게 마음을 바꾸지 않는다. 예를 들어 베트남 전쟁 동안, 여러 잡지와 신문을 정기적으로 읽는 상류 중산층 사람들은 1964년(전쟁을 지지했을 때)과 1968년(전쟁을 반대했을 때) 사이에 의견의 극적인 변화를 겪었지만, 블루칼라 노동자들의 견해는 거의 변하지 않았다.

NOTE

Step 1	Ⓢurvey
Key Words	Foreign policy; general public; political elites; knowledge gap; Vietnam War; opinion stability; international role; support
Signal Words	Cleavage; First of all; also; Finally
Step 2	Ⓡeading
Purpose	To analyze the contrasting perspectives on foreign policy between ordinary Americans and political elites, explaining the reasons for and implications of these differences
Pattern of Organization	Comparison/contrast; series
Tone	Neutral
Main Idea	The American general public and political elites have fundamentally different approaches to foreign affairs.
Step 3	Ⓢummary
지문 요약하기 (Paraphrasing)	There are significant differences between the American general public and political elites regarding foreign policy opinions. Three key distinctions are highlighted: knowledge levels about international affairs, support for America's global role, and the stability of opinions. The text uses the Vietnam War as a primary example to illustrate these differences, showing how elites were better informed, changed their support more dramatically, and shifted their opinions more quickly than the general public.
Step 4	Ⓡecite
	요약문 말로 설명하기

42 Read the passage and answer the questions.

McDonaldization is the term sociologist George Ritzer derived from the McDonalds' fast food chain to describe the state of our society. He claims our social institutions have become completely dehumanized in the form of a bureaucracy. Health care is an example of one institution that is characterized by the four components : efficiency, predictability, control and quantification. In the past, health care was more simplistic in nature. House calls were no unheard of, and doctors knew all of their patients and their families on a personal level. The doctor who delivered your parents would deliver you as well as your future children. Follow-ups were quite normal; doctors were concerned with your progress for their own peace of mind. Over time the modern health care system emerged into the bureaucratic organization that it is. All the characteristics are easily seen when one examines health care. And ___ⓐ___ is easily seen when you first step into a hospital waiting room and a huge sign tells you a number before you are even able to speak to anyone. After waiting a while your number is called, you must give your health card number to the receptionist before continuing. Efficiency is another characteristic that is prominent in the hospital situation. To make sure things more smoothly you must call ahead and make an appointment with the receptionist. This appointment is to avoid long lines of people waiting to see the doctor. Also, ___ⓑ___ is a big characteristic. Everyone knows what happens when you go see a doctor.

MEMO

Fill in each blank ⓐ and ⓑ with the ONE most appropriate word from the passage respectively. If necessary, change the word form.

NOTE

Step 1	**S**urvey
Key Words	
Signal Words	
Step 2	**R**eading
Purpose	
Pattern of Organization	
Tone	
Main Idea	
Step 3	**S**ummary
지문 요약하기 (Paraphrasing)	
Step 4	**R**ecite
	요약문 말로 설명하기

Answer Key

McDonaldization is the term sociologist George Ritzer derived from the McDonalds' fast food chain to describe the state of our society. He claims our social institutions have become completely **dehumanized** in the form of **a bureaucracy**. **Health care** is an example of one institution that is characterized by the four components : ① **efficiency**, ② **predictability**, ③ **control** and ④ **quantification**. In the past, **health care** was more simplistic in nature. House calls were no unheard of, and doctors knew all of their patients and their families on a personal level. The doctor who delivered your parents would deliver you as well as your future children. Follow-ups were quite normal; doctors were concerned with your progress for their own peace of mind. Over time **the modern health care system** emerged into the **bureaucratic organization** that it is. All the characteristics are easily seen when one examines health care. And **quantification** is easily seen when you first step into a hospital waiting room and a huge sign tells you a number before you are even able to speak to anyone. After waiting a while your number is called, you must give your health card number to the receptionist before continuing. **Efficiency** is another characteristic that is prominent in the hospital situation. To make sure things more smoothly you must call ahead and make an appointment with the receptionist. This appointment is to avoid long lines of people waiting to see the doctor. Also, **predictability** is a big characteristic. Everyone knows what happens when you go see a doctor.

→ key word

→ definition

모범답안

ⓐ quantification ⓑ predictability

한글번역

　　맥도날드화는 사회학자 조지 리처가 맥도날드 패스트푸드 체인점에서 따온 용어로 우리 사회의 상태를 묘사한 것이다. 그는 우리의 사회적 제도들이 관료주의의 형태로 완전히 비인간화됐다고 주장한다. 의료는 효율성, 예측 가능성, 통제, 계량화라는 네 가지 구성요소로 특징되는 제도의 한 예이다. 과거에 의료는 본질적으로 더 단순했다. 왕진은 드물지 않았고, 의사들은 모든 환자와 그들의 가족을 개인적으로 알고 있었다. 당신의 부모를 출산시킨 의사가 당신과 당신의 미래 자녀들도 출산시키곤 했다. 후속 조치는 매우 일반적이었다. 의사들은 자신들의 마음의 평화를 위해 당신의 회복 과정을 걱정했다. (하지만) 시간이 지나면서 현대 의료 시스템은 지금과 같은 관료적 조직으로 전개됐다. 의료를 살펴보면 모든 특징들을 쉽게 볼 수 있다. 그리고 계량화는 병원 대기실에 처음 들어서면 누구와도 말하기도 전에 거대한 표지판이 당신에게 번호를 알려줄 때 쉽게 볼 수 있다. 잠시 기다린 후 당신의 번호가 불리면, 계속 진행하기 전에 접수원에게 건강보험증 번호를 제공해야 한다. 효율성은 병원 상황에서 두드러지는 또 다른 특징이다. 일이 더 순조롭게 진행되기 위해 미리 전화해서 접수원과 예약을 잡아야 한다. 이 예약은 의사를 보기 위해 대기하는 긴 줄을 피하기 위한 것이다. 또한 예측 가능성도 큰 특징이다. 모든 사람들은 의사를 보러 갈 때 무슨 일이 일어나는지 안다.

NOTE

Step 1	Survey
Key Words	McDonaldization; bureaucracy; healthcare; efficiency; predictability; control; quantification
Signal Words	Example; four; another; also
Step 2	**Reading**
Purpose	To explain four components of McDonaldization as they appear in healthcare settings
Pattern of Organization	Series; definition
Tone	Neutral
Main Idea	There are four key elements in McDonaldization of society.
Step 3	**Summary**
지문 요약하기 (Paraphrasing)	McDonaldization is George Ritzer's term describing how social institutions have become dehumanized bureaucracies, exemplified by modern health care. Unlike the past when doctors made house calls and knew patients personally, today's health care system demonstrates the four McDonaldization components: efficiency (appointments to avoid lines), predictability (standardized procedures), control, and quantification (number systems and health card requirements).
Step 4	**Recite**
	요약문 말로 설명하기

43 Read the passage and fill in the blank with the ONE most appropriate word from the passage.

Theresa Amabile has identified several kinds of cognitive and personality characteristics _____ for creativity. The first one is expertise in the field of endeavor, which is directly tied to what a person has learned. A painter or composer must know the paints, techniques, or instruments available. And, a set of creative skills is crucial too. These skills include persistence at problem solving, a capacity for divergent thinking, the ability to break out of old problem-solving habits (mental sets), and a willingness to take risks. The motivation to pursue creative work for internal reasons, rather than for external reasons is necessary. Creative people will produce artistic products for their own satisfaction and not just for rewards such as prize money.

NOTE

Step 1	**S**urvey
Key Words	
Signal Words	
Step 2	**R**eading
Purpose	
Pattern of Organization	
Tone	
Main Idea	
Step 3	**S**ummary
지문 요약하기 (Paraphrasing)	
Step 4	**R**ecite
	요약문 말로 설명하기

Answer Key

Theresa Amabile has identified several kinds of cognitive and **personality characteristics** necessary for **creativity**. The first one is expertise in the field of endeavor, which is directly tied to what a person has learned. A painter or composer must know the paints, techniques, or instruments available. And, a set of **creative skills** is crucial too. These skills include persistence at problem solving, a capacity for divergent thinking, the ability to break out of old problem-solving habits (mental sets), and a willingness to take risks. The motivation to pursue **creative work** for internal reasons, rather than for external reasons is necessary. **Creative people** will produce artistic products for their own satisfaction and not just for rewards such as prize money.

모범답안

necessary

한글번역

　　테레사 아마빌은 창의성에 필요한 여러 종류의 인지적, 성격적 특성들을 규명했다. 첫 번째는 노력 분야에서의 전문 지식으로, 이는 개인이 학습한 것과 직접적으로 연결된다. 화가나 작곡가는 이용 가능한 물감, 기법, 또는 악기들을 알아야 한다. 그리고 창의적 기술들의 집합 역시 중요하다. 이러한 기술들에는 문제 해결에서의 끈기, 확산적 사고 능력, 기존의 문제 해결 습관(사고 틀)에서 벗어날 수 있는 능력, 위험을 감수하려는 의지가 포함된다. 외적 이유보다는 내적 이유로 창의적 작업을 추구하려는 동기가 필요하다. 창의적인 사람들은 상금과 같은 보상을 위해서가 아니라 자신의 만족을 위해 예술적 산물을 창조한다.

NOTE

Step 1	Survey
Key Words	Creativity; expertise; cognitive skills; persistence; divergent thinking; mental sets; risk-taking; intrinsic motivation
Signal Words	Several; first one; too
Step 2	**Reading**
Purpose	To outline the key cognitive and personality characteristics that Theresa Amabile has identified as necessary components for creative production
Pattern of Organization	Series
Tone	Neutral
Main Idea	There are three key elements in creativity.
Step 3	**Summary**
지문 요약하기 (Paraphrasing)	Amabile identifies three essential characteristics for creativity: expertise in one's field, creative skills like persistence and divergent thinking, and intrinsic motivation to create for personal satisfaction rather than external rewards.
Step 4	**Recite**
	요약문 말로 설명하기

44 Read the passage and fill in the blank with the ONE most appropriate word from the passage.

The psychological causes of unhappiness, it is clear, are many and various. But all have something in common. The typical unhappy man is one who, having been deprived in youth of some normal satisfaction, has come to value this one kind of satisfaction more than any other, and has therefore given to his life a one-sided direction, together with a quite undue emphasis upon the achievement as opposed to the activities connected with it. There is, however, a further development which is very common in the present day. A man may feel so completely thwarted that he seeks no form of satisfaction, but only _____. He then becomes a devotee of 'pleasure.' That is to say he seeks to make life bearable by becoming less alive. Drunkenness, for example, is temporary suicide; the happiness that it brings is merely negative, a momentary cessation of unhappiness. The narcissist and the megalomaniac believe that happiness is possible, though they may adopt mistaken means of achieving it; but the man who seeks intoxication, in whatever form, has given up hope except in oblivion. In his case, the first thing to be done is to persuade him that happiness is desirable. Men who are unhappy, like men who sleep badly, are always proud of the fact. Perhaps their pride is like that of the fox who had lost his tail; if so, the way to cure it is to point out to them how they can grow a new tail. Very few men, I believe, will deliberately choose unhappiness if they see a way of being happy. I do not deny that such men exist, but they are not sufficiently numerous to be important.

NOTE

Step 1	**S**urvey
Key Words	
Signal Words	
Step 2	**R**eading
Purpose	
Pattern of Organization	
Tone	
Main Idea	
Step 3	**S**ummary
지문 요약하기 (Paraphrasing)	
Step 4	**R**ecite
	요약문 말로 설명하기

Answer Key

The **psychological causes of unhappiness**, it is clear, are many and various. But all have something in common. The **typical unhappy man** is one who, having been deprived in youth of some normal satisfaction, has come to value this one kind of satisfaction more than any other, and has therefore given to his life a one-sided direction, together with a quite undue emphasis upon the achievement as opposed to the activities connected with it. There is, however, a further development which is very common in the present day. A man may feel so completely thwarted that he seeks no form of satisfaction, but only **oblivion**. He then becomes a devotee of 'pleasure.' That is to say he seeks to make life bearable by becoming less alive. **Drunkenness**, for example, is temporary suicide; the happiness that it brings is merely negative, a momentary cessation of unhappiness. The narcissist and the megalomaniac believe that happiness is possible, though they may adopt mistaken means of achieving it; but the man who seeks **intoxication**, in whatever form, has given up hope except in oblivion. In his case, the first thing to be done is to persuade him that happiness is desirable. Men who are **unhappy**, like men who sleep badly, are always proud of the fact. Perhaps their pride is like that of the fox who had lost his tail; if so, the way to cure it is to point out to them how they can grow a new tail. Very few men, I believe, will deliberately choose **unhappiness** if they see a way of being happy. I do not deny that such men exist, but they are not sufficiently numerous to be important.

모범답안
oblivion

한글번역

불행의 심리적 원인들은 분명히 많고 다양하다. 하지만 모두 공통점이 있다. 전형적인 불행한 남자는 젊은 시절에 어떤 정상적인 만족을 박탈당한 사람으로, 이 한 종류의 만족을 다른 어떤 것보다 더 가치 있게 여기게 됐고, 따라서 자신의 인생에 편향된 방향을 부여했으며, 그것과 연결된 활동들과는 대조적으로 성취에 대해 상당히 부당한 강조를 뒀다. 하지만 현재 여기에는 매우 흔한 추가적인 발전이 있다. 한 남자는 너무나 완전히 좌절감을 느껴서 어떤 형태의 만족도 추구하지 않고, 오직 망각만을 추구할 수 있다. 그러면 그는 '쾌락'의 신봉자가 된다. 즉, 덜 살아있게 됨으로써 인생을 견딜 만하게 만들려고 한다. 예를 들어, 술에 취하는 것은 일시적인 자살이다; 그것이 가져다주는 행복은 단지 부정적인 것으로, 불행의 일시적인 중단일 뿐이다. 자기애주의자와 과대망상증 환자는 행복이 가능하다고 믿는다. 비록 그것을 달성하는 잘못된 수단을 채택할 수도 있지만 말이다; 하지만 어떤 형태든 도취를 추구하는 남자는 망각 외에는 희망을 포기했다. 그의 경우, 해야 할 첫 번째 일은 행복이 바람직하다는 것을 그에게 설득하는 것이다. 불행한 남자들은 잠을 못 자는 남자들처럼, 항상 그 사실을 자랑스러워한다. 아마도 그들의 자부심은 꼬리를 잃은 여우의 그것과 같을 것이다; 만약 그렇다면, 그것을 치료하는 방법은 그들에게 어떻게 새 꼬리를 기를 수 있는지 가르쳐주는 것이다. 매우 적은 수의 남자들이, 내가 믿기로는, 행복해질 방법을 본다면 의도적으로 불행을 선택할 것이다. 그런 남자들이 존재한다는 것을 부정하지는 않지만, 그들은 중요할 만큼 충분히 많지는 않다.

NOTE

Step 1	**S**urvey
Key Words	Unhappiness; deprivation; satisfaction; one-sided direction; achievement; pleasure; intoxication
Signal Words	Causes; further development
Step 2	**R**eading
Purpose	To analyze the psychological causes of unhappiness
Pattern of Organization	Cause/effect →the causes of unhappiness (early deprivation leading to overvaluing certain satisfactions) →the effects (one-sided life direction, emphasis on achievement and seeking escape through pleasure)
Tone	Persuasive
Main Idea	There are different psychological causes and types of unhappiness in men.
Step 3	**S**ummary
지문 요약하기 (Paraphrasing)	There are different psychological causes and types of unhappiness in men. Unhappy men typically were deprived in youth, leading them to overvalue one satisfaction type and focus on achievement over activities. Some seek only escape through "pleasure" like drunkenness—temporary suicide bringing negative happiness. Unlike narcissists who believe happiness possible, these men have given up hope except in oblivion.
Step 4	**R**ecite
	요약문 말로 설명하기

45 Read the passage and fill in the blank with the ONE most appropriate word from the passage.

There were many differing explanations at the time : that he had terminal cancer or money problems, that it was an accident, that he'd quarreled with Mary. None were true. Ernest Hemingway and I were friends for 14 years. I dramatized many of his stories and novels for television specials and film, and we shared adventures in France, Italy, Cuba and Spain, where, as a pretend matador with Ernest as my manager, I participated in a Ciudad Real bullfight. Ernest's zest for life was infectious.

In November, 1960, I went out West for our annual pheasant shoot. When Ernest and our friend Duke MacMullen met my train at Shoshone, Idaho, for the drive to Ketchum, we did not stop at the bar opposite the station as we usually did because Ernest was anxious to get on the road. I asked why the hurry.

"The feds."

"What?"

"They tailed us all the way. Ask Duke."

"Well ... there was a car back of us out of Hailey."

"Why are F.B.I. agents pursuing you?" I asked.

"It's the worst hell. The goddamnedest hell. They've bugged everything. That's why we're using Duke's car. Mine's bugged. Everything's bugged. Can't use the phone. Mail intercepted." We rode for miles in silence.

Decades later, in response to a Freedom of Information petition, the FBI released its Hemingway file. It revealed that beginning in the 1940s J. Edgar Hoover had placed Ernest under surveillance because he was suspicious of Ernest's activities in Cuba. Over the following years, agents filed reports on him and tapped his phones. The surveillance continued all through his confinement at St. Mary's Hospital. It is likely that the phone outside his room was tapped after all. In the years since, I have tried to reconcile Ernest's fear of the F.B.I., which I regretfully misjudged, with the reality of the F.B.I. file. I now believe he truly sensed the _____, and that it substantially contributed to his anguish and his suicide.

NOTE

Step 1	**S**urvey
Key Words	
Signal Words	
Step 2	**R**eading
Purpose	
Pattern of Organization	
Tone	
Main Idea	
Step 3	**S**ummary
지문 요약하기 (Paraphrasing)	
Step 4	**R**ecite
	요약문 말로 설명하기

Answer Key

There were many differing explanations at the time: that he had terminal cancer or money problems, that it was an accident, that he'd quarreled with Mary. None were true. **Ernest Hemingway** and I were friends for 14 years. I dramatized many of his stories and novels for television specials and film, and we shared adventures in France, Italy, Cuba and Spain, where, as a pretend matador with Ernest as my manager, I participated in a Ciudad Real bullfight. Ernest's zest for life was infectious.

In November, 1960, I went out West for our annual pheasant shoot. When Ernest and our friend Duke MacMullen met my train at Shoshone, Idaho, for the drive to Ketchum, we did not stop at the bar opposite the station as we usually did because Ernest was anxious to get on the road. I asked why the hurry.

"**The feds.**"

"What?"

"They tailed us all the way. Ask Duke."

"Well ... there was a car back of us out of Hailey."

"Why are F.B.I. agents pursuing you?" I asked.

"It's the worst hell. The goddamnedest hell. They've bugged everything. That's why we're using Duke's car. Mine's bugged. Everything's bugged. Can't use the phone. Mail intercepted." We rode for miles in silence.

Decades later, in response to a Freedom of Information petition, **the FBI** released its Hemingway file. It revealed that beginning in the 1940s J. Edgar Hoover had placed Ernest under surveillance because he was suspicious of Ernest's activities in Cuba. Over the following years, agents filed reports on him and tapped his phones. **The surveillance** continued all through his confinement at St. Mary's Hospital. It is likely that the phone outside his room was tapped after all. In the years since, I have tried to reconcile Ernest's fear of the F.B.I., which I regretfully misjudged, with the reality of the F.B.I. file. I now believe he truly sensed **the surveillance**, and **that it substantially contributed to his anguish and his suicide.**

모범답안

surveillance

한글번역

당시에는 많은 다른 설명들이 있었다 : 그가 말기 암이나 금전 문제가 있었다는 것, 그것이 사고였다는 것, 그가 메리와 다퉜다는 것. 모두 사실이 아니었다. 어니스트 헤밍웨이와 나는 14년간 친구였다. 나는 그의 많은 이야기와 소설들을 텔레비전 특별 프로그램과 영화로 각색했고, 우리는 프랑스, 이탈리아, 쿠바, 스페인에서 모험을 함께했다. 스페인에서는 어니스트가 내 매니저 역할을 하며 나는 가짜 투우사로서 시우다드 레알 투우에 참가했다. 어니스트의 삶에 대한 열정은 전염성이 있었다.

1960년 11월, 나는 우리의 연례 꿩 사냥을 위해 서부로 갔다. 어니스트와 우리 친구 듀크 맥멀렌이 아이다호주 쇼쇼니에서 내 기차를 마중 나와 케첨으로 드라이브하는 동안, 우리는 평소처럼 역 건너편 술집에 들르지 않았다. 어니스트가 길을 서두르고 있었기 때문이다. 나는 왜 그렇게 급한지 물었다.

"연방 수사관들."

"뭐?"

"그들이 우리를 내내 미행했어. 듀크에게 물어봐."

"음... 헤일리에서 뒤따라오는 차가 있었어."

"왜 FBI 요원들이 자네를 추적하는 거지?" 내가 물었다.

"최악의 지옥이야. 빌어먹을 지옥이야. 그들이 모든 걸 도청했어. 그래서 우리가 듀크 차를 쓰는 거야. 내 차는 도청당했어. 모든 게 도청당했어. 전화를 쓸 수 없어. 우편물도 가로채져." 우리는 수 마일을 침묵 속에서 달렸다.

수십 년 후, 정보자유법 청원에 대한 응답으로 FBI는 헤밍웨이 파일을 공개했다. 그것은 1940년대부터 J. 에드가 후버(FBI 국장)가 어니스트의 쿠바 활동을 의심해 그를 감시했다는 것을 드러냈다. 이후 몇 년간 FBI 요원들은 그에 대한 보고서를 작성하고 그의 전화를 도청했다. 감시는 그가 세인트 메리 병원에 입원해 있는 내내 계속됐다. 결국 그의 병실 밖 전화도 도청당했을 가능성이 높다. 그 이후 몇 년간, 나는 내가 안타깝게도 잘못 판단했던 어니스트의 FBI에 대한 두려움을 FBI 파일의 실제 상황과 맞춰보려고 노력해왔다. 이제 나는 그가 진정으로 감시를 감지했고, 그것이 그의 고뇌와 자살에 실질적으로 기여했다고 믿는다.

NOTE

Step 1	Survey
Key Words	Ernest Hemingway; FBI surveillance; paranoia; J. Edgar Hoover; suicide; government files; mental anguish
Signal Words	Because
Step 2	Reading
Purpose	To reveal how government surveillance affected Ernest Hemingway's mental health and contributed to his suicide, correcting misconceptions about his death
Pattern of Organization	Time order: cause/effect
Tone	Critical; angry
Main Idea	Ernest Hemingway's fears of FBI surveillance played a significant role in his mental deterioration and suicide.
Step 3	Summary
지문 요약하기 (Paraphrasing)	FBI files released decades later confirmed that Hemingway had indeed been under surveillance by J. Edgar Hoover since the 1940s due to his activities in Cuba. The author now believes this surveillance significantly contributed to Hemingway's mental anguish and eventual suicide, contradicting various false explanations circulating at the time.
Step 4	Recite

요약문 말로 설명하기

46 Read the passage and answer the questions.

One of the most dangerous drugs for pregnant women to consume is alcohol. Because alcohol is delivered quickly into the blood and passes quickly into the tissues and membranes, the human fetus is particularly vulnerable to its effects. In fact, the negative effects on a fetus are so pronounced that babies born after exposure to alcohol are said to be suffering from fetal alcohol syndrome. As a pregnant woman drinks alcohol, the alcohol is passed into her bloodstream almost simultaneously. Moreover, because the bloodstream of the fetus is inextricably tied to that of the mother, the alcohol passes directly into the bloodstream of the fetus as well. And what is more, the concentration of alcohol in the fetus is exactly the same as in the mother. For the mother, this concentration is not a problem because her liver can remove one ounce of alcohol from her system per hour. However, the fetus's liver is not completely developed (how developed it is depends on its stage of development). The rate at which it is able to eliminate the alcohol from the blood of the fetus is much slower. Eventually, the alcohol will be returned to the mother's system by passing across the placenta, but this process is slow. By the time this takes place, major neurological damage may have already occurred. Research has shown that as little as one drink of alcohol can produce significant, irreversible damage to the fetus. Babies born after exposure to alcohol generally exhibit facial distortion, inability to concentrate, and difficulty in remembering. Simply speaking, it is imperative that pregnant women avoid alcohol.

According to the passage, why is alcohol particularly dangerous for a developing fetus compared to the pregnant mother?

NOTE

Step 1	Survey
Key Words	
Signal Words	
Step 2	**Reading**
Purpose	
Pattern of Organization	
Tone	
Main Idea	
Step 3	**Summary**
지문 요약하기 (Paraphrasing)	
Step 4	**Recite**
요약문 말로 설명하기	

Answer Key

One of the most dangerous drugs for **pregnant women** to consume is **alcohol**. Because **alcohol** is delivered quickly into the blood and passes quickly into the tissues and membranes, the human fetus is particularly vulnerable to its effects. In fact, the negative effects on a fetus are so pronounced that babies born after exposure to alcohol are said to be suffering from fetal alcohol syndrome. **As a pregnant woman drinks alcohol, the alcohol** is passed into her bloodstream almost simultaneously. Moreover, because the bloodstream of the fetus is inextricably tied to that of the mother, the alcohol passes directly into the bloodstream of the fetus as well. And what is more, the concentration of alcohol in the fetus is exactly the same as in the mother. For **the mother**, this concentration is not a problem because her liver can remove one ounce of alcohol from her system per hour. However, the fetus's liver is not completely developed (how developed it is depends on its stage of development). The rate at which it is able to eliminate the alcohol from the blood of the fetus is much slower. Eventually, the alcohol will be returned to the mother's system by passing across the placenta, but this process is slow. By the time this takes place, major neurological damage may have already occurred. Research has shown that as little as one drink of alcohol can produce significant, irreversible damage to the fetus. Babies born after exposure to alcohol generally exhibit facial distortion, inability to concentrate, and difficulty in remembering. Simply speaking, it is imperative that **pregnant women avoid alcohol**.

모범답안

The fetus's underdeveloped liver cannot process alcohol as quickly as the mother's liver.

한글번역

　　임신한 여성이 섭취하기에 가장 위험한 약물 중 하나는 알코올이다. 알코올은 혈액으로 빠르게 흘러 조직과 막으로 빠르게 전달되기 때문에, 인간 태아는 그 영향에 특히 취약하다. 실제로 태아에 대한 부정적 영향이 너무 뚜렷해서 알코올에 노출된 후 태어난 아기들은 태아 알코올 증후군을 앓고 있다고 한다. 임신한 여성이 알코올을 마시면, 알코올은 거의 동시에 그녀의 혈류로 전달된다. 게다가 태아의 혈류가 어머니의 혈류와 밀접하게 연결돼 있기 때문에, 알코올은 태아의 혈류로도 직접 전달된다. 더욱이 태아의 알코올 농도는 어머니와 정확히 동일하다. 어머니에게는 이 농도가 문제가 되지 않는데, 그녀의 간이 시간당 1온스의 알코올을 시스템에서 제거할 수 있기 때문이다. 하지만 태아의 간은 완전히 발달하지 않았다 (얼마나 발달했는지는 발달 단계에 달려 있다). 태아의 혈액에서 알코올을 제거할 수 있는 속도는 훨씬 느리다. 결국 알코올은 태반을 통과해 어머니 시스템으로 돌아가겠지만, 이 과정은 느리다. 이것이 일어날 때까지 주요한 신경학적 손상이 이미 발생했을 수 있다. 연구에 따르면 단 한 잔의 알코올만으로도 태아에게 심각하고 돌이킬 수 없는 손상을 일으킬 수 있다고 한다. 알코올에 노출된 후 태어난 아기들은 일반적으로 안면 기형, 집중 불능, 기억 장애를 보인다. 간단히 말해서, 임신한 여성들이 알코올을 피하는 것은 불가피하다.

NOTE

Step 1	Survey
Key Words	Alcohol; fetus; fetal alcohol syndrome; neurological damage; pregnancy
Signal Words	Not clear
Step 2	Reading
Purpose	To inform readers about the dangers of alcohol consumption during pregnancy and to emphasize the importance of avoiding it for the health of the fetus
Pattern of Organization	Cause/effect
Tone	Neutral
Main Idea	Alcohol consumption during pregnancy can cause severe and permanent harm to the fetus.
Step 3	Summary
지문 요약하기 (Paraphrasing)	Alcohol consumption during pregnancy poses serious risks to the fetus. Alcohol rapidly enters both the mother's and fetus's bloodstream. Since the fetus's liver is not fully developed, it cannot process alcohol efficiently, leading to potential neurological damage and the development of fetal alcohol syndrome (FAS). Even a single drink can cause irreversible harm, including facial deformities, memory issues, and difficulty concentrating. Pregnant women should avoid alcohol completely to prevent these dangers.
Step 4	Recite
	요약문 말로 설명하기

47 Read the passage and answer the questions.

Common people are often able to take a wider view, and a more "humanistic" view, than is normally being taken by experts. The power of ordinary people, who today tend to feel utterly powerless, does not lie in starting new lines of action, but in placing their sympathy and support with minority groups which have already started. Modern agriculture relies on applying to soil, plants, and animals twenty-eight ever-increasing chemical products, the long-term effect of which on soil fertility and health is subject to very grave doubts. People who raise such doubts are generally confronted with the assertion that the choice lies between "poison or hunger." There are highly _____ in many countries who obtain excellent yields without resort to such chemicals and without raising any doubts about long-term soil fertility and health. Their methods bear the mark of non-violence and humility towards the infinitely subtle system of natural harmony, and this stands in opposition to the life-style of the modern world. The successful farmers have not been able to attract official support or recognition. They have generally been dismissed as "the muck and mystery people," because they are obviously outside the mainstream of modern technological progress.

Fill in the blank with the TWO most appropriate consecutive words from the passage.

NOTE

Step 1	**S**urvey
Key Words	
Signal Words	
Step 2	**R**eading
Purpose	
Pattern of Organization	
Tone	
Main Idea	
Step 3	**S**ummary
지문 요약하기 (Paraphrasing)	
Step 4	**R**ecite
	요약문 말로 설명하기

Answer Key

Common people are often able to take a wider view, and a more "humanistic" view, than is normally being taken by experts. The power of ordinary people, who today tend to feel utterly powerless, does not lie in starting new lines of action, but in placing their sympathy and support with minority groups which have already started. Modern agriculture relies on applying to soil, plants, and animals twenty-eight ever-increasing chemical products, the long-term effect of which on soil fertility and health is subject to very grave doubts. People who raise such doubts are generally confronted with the assertion that the choice lies between "poison or hunger." There are **highly successful farmers** in many countries who obtain excellent yields **without resort to such chemicals** and **without raising any doubts about long-term soil fertility and health**. Their methods bear the mark of non-violence and humility towards the infinitely subtle system of natural harmony, and this stands in opposition to the life-style of the modern world. **The successful farmers** have not been able to attract official support or recognition. They have generally been dismissed as "**the muck and mystery people**," because they are obviously outside the mainstream of modern technological progress.

모범답안
successful farmers

한글번역

일반인들은 전문가들보다 더 넓은 관점과 더 "인본주의적인" 관점을 취할 수 있는 경우가 많다. 오늘날 완전히 무력하다고 느끼는 경향이 있는 보통 사람들의 힘은 새로운 행동 노선을 시작하는 데 있는 것이 아니라, 이미 시작한 소수 집단들에게 그들의 동정과 지지를 보내는 데 있다. 현대 농업은 28가지의 계속 증가하는 화학 제품을 토양, 식물, 동물에 적용하는 데 의존하고 있으며, 이것들이 토양 비옥도와 건강에 미치는 장기적 영향은 매우 심각한 의구심의 대상이다. 그런 의구심을 제기하는 사람들은 일반적으로 선택이 "독 아니면 굶주림" 사이에 있다는 주장에 직면한다. 많은 나라에는 그런 화학 물질에 의존하지 않고 훌륭한 수확량을 얻으며 장기적인 토양 비옥도와 건강에 대해 어떤 의구심도 제기하지 않는 매우 성공적인 농부들이 있다. 그들의 방법은 무한히 미묘한 자연 조화 시스템에 대한 비폭력과 겸손의 특징을 지니고 있으며, 이는 현대 세계의 생활 방식과 대립한다. 성공적인 농부들은 공식적인 지원이나 인정을 받을 수 없었다. 그들은 명백히 현대 기술 발전의 주류에서 벗어나 있기 때문에 일반적으로 "진흙과 신비주의자들"로 치부돼 왔다.

NOTE

Step 1	Ⓢurvey
Key Words	Ordinary people; minority groups; agriculture; chemicals; soil fertility; non-violence; natural harmony; sustainable farming; mainstream
Signal Words	Not clear

Step 2	Ⓡeading
Purpose	To encourage support for alternative farming methods that are more in harmony with nature and challenge the reliance on chemicals in modern agriculture
Pattern of Organization	Contrast/comparison →The passage contrasts modern, chemical-dependent agriculture with more sustainable, chemical-free farming methods.
Tone	Critical
Main Idea	There are two contrasting approaches to modern agriculture.

Step 3	Ⓢummary
지문 요약하기 (Paraphrasing)	There are two contrasting approaches to modern agriculture. Common people can take wider, more humanistic views than experts and should support minority groups already taking action. Modern agriculture relies on 28 increasing chemical products with grave doubts about long-term effects on soil fertility and health. However, highly successful farmers in many countries obtain excellent yields without these chemicals, using methods marked by non-violence and humility toward natural harmony, opposing the modern world's lifestyle.

Step 4	Ⓡecite
	요약문 말로 설명하기

48 Read the passage and answer the questions.

Kindergarten, traditionally a playful port of entry into formal school, is becoming more academic, with children being taught specific skills, taking tests, and occasionally even having homework. Since 1970, the proportion of three- and four-year-olds enrolled in school has risen dramatically, from about one-half million in 1964 to about 5 million in 2003, an increase from about 6 percent to about 60 percent of children ages 3 and 4. These nursery schools have largely joined the push towards academic acceleration in the early grades. Moreover, middle-class nursery schools in recent years have introduced substantial doses of academic material into their daily programs, often using those particular devices originally intended to help culturally deprived preschoolers in compensatory programs such as Headstart to catch up with their middle-class peers. Indeed, some of the increased focus on academic skills in nursery schools and kindergartens is related to the widespread popularity among young children and their parents of *Sesame Street,* a program originally intended to help deprived children attain academic skills, but universally watched by middle-class toddlers as well. Parents of the *Sesame Street* generation often demand a "serious," skill-centered program for their preschoolers in school, afraid that the old-fashioned, play-centered curriculum will bore their alphabet-spouting number-chanting four-and five-year-olds.

Explain the irony regarding the *Sesame Street* shown in the underlined "Parents."

NOTE

Step 1	**S**urvey
Key Words	
Signal Words	
Step 2	**R**eading
Purpose	
Pattern of Organization	
Tone	
Main Idea	
Step 3	**S**ummary
지문 요약하기 (Paraphrasing)	
Step 4	**R**ecite

요약문 말로 설명하기

Answer Key

> **Kindergarten**, traditionally a playful port of entry into formal school, is becoming more academic, with children being taught specific skills, taking tests, and occasionally even having homework. Since 1970, the proportion of three- and four-year-olds enrolled in school has risen dramatically, from about one-half million in 1964 to about 5 million in 2003, an increase from about 6 percent to about 60 percent of children ages 3 and 4. **These nursery schools** have largely joined the push towards academic acceleration in the early grades. Moreover, middle-class nursery schools in recent years have introduced substantial doses of **academic material** into their daily programs, often using those particular devices originally intended to help culturally deprived preschoolers in compensatory programs such as Headstart to catch up with their middle-class peers. Indeed, some of the increased focus on academic skills in nursery schools and kindergartens is related to the widespread popularity among young children and **their parents of *Sesame Street***, a program originally intended to help deprived children attain academic skills, but universally watched by middle-class toddlers as well. **Parents of the *Sesame Street* generation** often demand a **"serious," skill-centered program** for their preschoolers in school, afraid that the old-fashioned, play-centered curriculum will bore their alphabet-spouting number-chanting four-and five-year-olds.

모범답안

The irony is that *Sesame Street*, originally designed to help disadvantaged children catch up academically to middle-class peers, ended up being watched by middle-class kids too, making their parents demand more rigorous academic programs and thus raising educational expectations for everyone.

구문분석

- Original purpose : *Sesame Street* was created to help disadvantaged/poor children learn basic academic skills so they could catch up to middle-class kids when they started school.
- Unintended consequence : Middle-class children also watched *Sesame Street* and learned these same skills. Now their parents expect preschools to be more academically rigorous because their kids already know what *Sesame Street* taught them.

한글번역

전통적으로 정규 학교 교육으로 들어가는 재미있는 입구 역할을 했던 유치원이 점점 더 학문적으로 변하고 있으며, 아이들은 특정 기술을 배우고, 시험을 치르고, 때로는 숙제까지 하고 있다. 1970년 이후 3-4세 아동의 학교 등록 비율이 극적으로 증가했는데, 1964년 약 50만 명에서 2003년 약 500만 명으로 늘어났다. 이는 3-4세 아동의 약 6%에서 약 60%로 증가한 것이다. 이런 보육학교들은 대부분 초등학교 저학년에서의 학문적 가속화 움직임에 동참했다. 게다가 중산층 보육학교들은 최근 몇 년간 일일 프로그램에 상당한 양의 학문적 내용을 도입했는데, 이들은 원래 문화적으로 소외된 미취학 아동들이 헤드스타트 같은 보상 프로그램을 통해 중산층 또래들을 따라잡도록 돕기 위해 고안된 특별한 도구들을 자주 사용한다. 실제로 보육학교와 유치원에서 학문적 기술에 대한 관심이 증가한 것 중 일부는 어린 아이들과 그들의 부모들 사이에서 '세서미 스트리트'가 널리 인기를 끈 것과 관련이 있다. 이 프로그램은 원래 소외된 아이들이 학문적 기술을 습득하도록 돕기 위해 만들어졌지만, 중산층 유아들도 모두 시청했다. '세서미 스트리트' 세대의 부모들은 종종 자녀의 취학 전 교육기관에서 "진지한" 기술 중심 프로그램을 요구한다. 그들은 구식의 놀이 중심 교육과정이 알파벳을 줄줄 외우고 숫자를 노래하는 4-5세 아이들을 지루하게 만들까봐 두려워한다.

NOTE

Step 1	**S**urvey
Key Words	Kindergarten; preschool; academic skills; sesame street; nursery schools; homework; parents; middle-class; educational media
Signal Words	Not clear
Step 2	**R**eading
Purpose	To highlight the shift in preschool and kindergarten education towards more structured, academic-focused curriculums, influenced by cultural trends and media
Pattern of Organization	Not clear
Tone	Objective
Main Idea	Kindergarten and preschool programs are becoming more academic, driven by parental expectations and the influence of educational media.
Step 3	**S**ummary
지문 요약하기 (Paraphrasing)	Kindergarten has shifted from play-based to academic-focused education, with 3-4 year old enrollment rising from 6% to 60% since 1964. This change is driven by *Sesame Street*'s influence and parents demanding skill-centered programs, fearing traditional play curricula will bore children who already know basic academics from educational television.
Step 4	**R**ecite
	요약문 말로 설명하기

49 Read the passage and answer the questions.

Olympians of yesteryear shared the same goal, but they would hardly recognize today's training techniques. To achieve the Olympian ideal of "faster, higher, stronger," coaches now realize, athletes don't have to train more but they do have to train smarter. That's why, these days, cross-country Nordic skiers kneel on skateboards and tug on pulleys to haul themselves up a ramp. Bobsledders practice sprinting in a near-shuffling style that would make world champion sprinter Maurice Greene wince. Pixieish figure skaters hurl 10-pound medicine balls—all because science has parsed nearly every move of every Olympic event and figured out what athletes must do to bring back the gold. That Nordic skier is training to strengthen her upper body, which scientists find is the single greatest determinant of cross-country speed. The bobsled starter's odd sprint stance reflects the realization that he can't impart any forward oomph to the sled if his feet are off the ice, so unlike track sprinters, whose ideal form has them in the air much of the time, the bobsled athlete trains to keep his feet on the ground. The figure skater's medicine ball is strengthening her arms and torso so she can routinely perform triple jumps undreamed of a generation ago.

Write the purpose of the passage.

NOTE

Step 1	**S**urvey
Key Words	
Signal Words	
Step 2	**R**eading
Purpose	
Pattern of Organization	
Tone	
Main Idea	
Step 3	**S**ummary
지문 요약하기 (Paraphrasing)	
Step 4	**R**ecite
	요약문 말로 설명하기

Answer Key

Olympians of yesteryear shared the same goal, but they would hardly recognize **today's training techniques**. To achieve the Olympian ideal of "faster, higher, stronger," coaches now realize, **athletes** don't have to train more but they do have to **train smarter**. That's why, these days, cross-country **Nordic skiers** kneel on skateboards and tug on pulleys to haul themselves up a ramp. **Bobsledders** practice sprinting in a near-shuffling style that would make world champion sprinter Maurice Greene wince. Pixieish figure skaters hurl 10-pound medicine balls—all because science has parsed nearly every move of every Olympic event and figured out what athletes must do to bring back the gold. That Nordic skier is training to strengthen her upper body, which scientists find is the single greatest determinant of cross-country speed. The bobsled starter's odd sprint stance reflects the realization that he can't impart any forward oomph to the sled if his feet are off the ice, so unlike track sprinters, whose ideal form has them in the air much of the time, the bobsled athlete trains to keep his feet on the ground. **The figure skater's** medicine ball is strengthening her arms and torso so she can routinely perform triple jumps undreamed of a generation ago.

모범답안

To illustrate how modern Olympic training has become scientifically-based and sport-specific rather than simply focused on training harder

한글번역

　　과거의 올림픽 선수들도 같은 목표를 공유했지만, 오늘날의 훈련 기법을 보면 거의 알아보지 못할 것이다. "더 빠르게, 더 높게, 더 강하게"라는 올림픽 이상을 달성하기 위해 코치들은 이제 선수들이 더 많이 훈련할 필요는 없지만 더 똑똑하게 훈련해야 한다는 것을 깨달았다. 그래서 요즘 크로스컨트리 노르딕 스키 선수들은 스케이트보드에 무릎을 꿇고 도르래를 당겨서 경사로를 올라간다. 봅슬레이 선수들은 세계 챔피언 단거리 선수인 모리스 그린이 보면 움찔할 만한 거의 발을 끄는 듯한 스타일로 스프린트를 연습한다. 요정 같은 피겨 스케이터들은 10파운드 메디신 볼을 던진다. 이 모든 것은 과학이 모든 올림픽 종목의 거의 모든 동작을 분석해서 선수들이 금메달을 가져오기 위해 무엇을 해야 하는지 알아냈기 때문이다. 노르딕 스키 선수는 상체를 강화하기 위해 훈련하고 있는데, 과학자들은 이것이 크로스컨트리 속도의 가장 중요한 결정 요인이라는 것을 발견했다. 봅슬레이 출발 선수의 이상한 스프린트 자세는 발이 얼음에서 떨어져 있으면 썰매에 앞으로 나아가는 힘을 전달할 수 없다는 깨달음을 반영한다. 따라서 대부분의 시간을 공중에서 보내는 것이 이상적인 폼인 트랙 단거리 선수들과 달리, 봅슬레이 선수는 발을 땅에 붙이고 있도록 훈련한다. 피겨 스케이터의 메디신 볼은 한 세대 전에는 꿈도 꾸지 못했던 트리플 점프를 일상적으로 수행할 수 있도록 팔과 몸통을 강화하고 있다.

NOTE

Step 1	**S**urvey
Key Words	Olympians; train smarter
Signal Words	Not clear
Step 2	**R**eading
Purpose	To illustrate how modern Olympic training has become scientifically-based and sport-specific rather than simply focused on training harder
Pattern of Organization	Series
Tone	Neutral
Main Idea	Modern Olympic training has evolved from simply training more to training smarter, using scientific analysis to develop specialized techniques.
Step 3	**S**ummary
지문 요약하기 (Paraphrasing)	Modern Olympic training has evolved from simply training more to training smarter, using scientifically-designed methods. Cross-country skiers use skateboards and pulleys to strengthen upper bodies, bobsledders practice shuffling sprints to keep feet on ice for maximum force, and figure skaters throw medicine balls to build strength for triple jumps impossible a generation ago.
Step 4	**R**ecite

요약문 말로 설명하기

50. Read the passage and answer the questions.

If you fly over Scottsdale, Arizona, and look down at the vast brown desert, here and there you see little ribbons of green fairways, with country-club communities clustered around them like reeds around ponds, tile-roofed McMansions with mouse-pad lawns and little blue dots where the backyard spas are. Along the nearby roadways you can see massive two-tier malls. In the front tier are strings of chain restaurants that, if they merged, could form Chili's Olive Garden Outback Cantina, serving enough chicken wings to fill a canyon. In the back tier a line of megastores stretches out like a parade of pachyderms: Target and Barnes & Noble etc. Cutting diagonally across the empty parking spaces in between are ninety-eight-pound women in aerobics outfits steering 4,000-pound SUVs. However, suburban life is more arduous than it appears, and provides more character-building experiences than we imagine. Sure, there's less drudgery and backbreaking labor than there was in the past, but there's also far more uncertainty. Almost nobody grows up today assuming that he will work in the same profession, or at the same plant, as his parents. Almost nobody grows up thinking that she will work for one paternalistic organization all her life. Eighty years ago a person who inherited a legacy or grew up in a wealthy WASP family had a reasonably secure status. A person who grew up black or in an ethnic neighborhood encountered certain limits to opportunity. Those limits have been reduced, and although the field is more open, the burden on the individual is much greater. The essence of an information economy is that knowledge is not inheritable: each generation has to earn success over again.

What contrast does the writer create through the image of '98-pound women steering 4,000-pound SUVs'?

___

NOTE

Step 1	ⓢurvey
Key Words	
Signal Words	
Step 2	**ⓡeading**
Purpose	
Pattern of Organization	
Tone	
Main Idea	
Step 3	**ⓢummary**
지문 요약하기 (Paraphrasing)	
Step 4	**ⓡecite**
요약문 말로 설명하기	

Answer Key

If you fly over Scottsdale, Arizona, and look down at the vast brown desert, here and there you see little ribbons of green fairways, with country-club communities clustered around them like reeds around ponds, tile-roofed McMansions with mouse-pad lawns and little blue dots where the backyard spas are. Along the nearby roadways you can see massive two-tier malls. In the front tier are strings of chain restaurants that, if they merged, could form Chili's Olive Garden Outback Cantina, serving enough chicken wings to fill a canyon. In the back tier a line of megastores stretches out like a parade of pachyderms : Target and Barnes & Noble etc. Cutting diagonally across the empty parking spaces in between are ninety-eight-pound women in aerobics outfits steering 4,000-pound SUVs. However, **suburban life** is **more arduous than it appears**, and provides more character-building experiences than we imagine. Sure, there's less drudgery and backbreaking labor than there was in the past, but there's also far more **uncertainty**. Almost nobody grows up today assuming that he will work in the same profession, or at the same plant, as his parents. Almost nobody grows up thinking that she will work for one paternalistic organization all her life. Eighty years ago a person who inherited a legacy or grew up in a wealthy WASP family had a reasonably secure status. A person who grew up black or in an ethnic neighborhood encountered certain limits to opportunity. Those limits have been reduced, and although the field is more open, the burden on the individual is much greater. The essence of an **information economy** is that knowledge is not inheritable : each generation has to earn success over again.

모범답안

The writer creates a striking physical contrast between the tiny, delicate women (98 pounds) and the massive, heavy vehicles (4,000 pounds) (to highlight the absurd excess of suburban consumer culture).

한글번역

애리조나주 스코츠데일 상공을 비행하며 광활한 갈색 사막을 내려다보면, 여기저기서 작은 녹색 페어웨이들을 볼 수 있고, 연못 주변의 갈대처럼 그 주위에 컨트리클럽 공동체들이 모여 있고 마우스패드 같은 잔디밭이 있는 기와지붕의 맥맨션들이 있고 뒷마당 온천욕조가 있는 작은 파란 점들이 있다. 근처 도로를 따라 거대한 2층 쇼핑몰들을 볼 수 있다. 앞쪽 층에는 체인 레스토랑들이 줄지어 있는데, 만약 이들이 합쳐진다면 칠리스 올리브가든 아웃백 칸티나가 될 수 있을 것이고, 협곡을 채울 만큼 충분한 치킨윙을 서빙할 것이다. 뒤쪽 층에는 거대한 상점들이 코끼리 행렬처럼 늘어서 있다 : 타겟과 반스 앤 노블 등. 그 사이의 빈 주차 공간을 대각선으로 가로지르며 98파운드의 여성들이 에어로빅 복장을 하고 4,000파운드짜리 SUV를 운전하고 있다. 하지만 교외 생활은 겉보기보다 더 힘들고, 우리가 상상하는 것보다 더 많은 인격 형성 경험을 제공한다. 물론 과거보다 힘든 일과 등부러지는 노동은 줄었지만, 불확실성은 훨씬 더 많아졌다. 오늘날 거의 아무도 자신이 부모와 같은 직업이나 같은 공장에서 일할 것이라고 가정하며 자라지 않는다. 거의 아무도 평생 하나의 온정주의적 조직에서 일할 것이라고 생각하며 자라지 않는다. 80년 전에는 유산을 물려받거나 부유한 백인 앵글로색슨 개신교도 가정에서 자란 사람은 상당히 안정된 지위를 가졌다. 흑인이거나 소수민족 동네에서 자란 사람은 기회에 대한 특정한 제약을 만났다. 그런 제약들은 줄어들었고, 경쟁의 장이 더 개방됐지만, 개인에게 주어진 부담은 훨씬 더 커졌다. 정보 경제의 본질은 지식이 상속되지 않는다는 것이다 : 각 세대는 성공을 처음부터 다시 얻어야 한다.

NOTE

Step 1	**S**urvey
Key Words	Suburban life; uncertainty; arduous; information economy
Signal Words	Not clear
Step 2	**R**eading
Purpose	To challenge perceptions about suburban life by highlighting how it requires greater adaptability and personal responsibility compared to previous generations despite its comfortable appearance
Pattern of Organization	Not clear
Tone	Observational; somewhat cynical
Main Idea	While suburban life appears comfortable and easy, it actually involves greater uncertainty and individual responsibility than previous generations faced.
Step 3	**S**ummary
지문 요약하기 (Paraphrasing)	Suburban life appears picturesque with green fairways, country-club communities, and sprawling malls. However, beneath this image lies the uncertainty of modern life, where individuals face greater challenges. Success must be earned repeatedly in today's information economy, contrasting with the stability and security of past generations.
Step 4	**R**ecite
	요약문 말로 설명하기

51 Read the passage and fill in the blank with the ONE most appropriate word from the passage.

Ben Yannick stands 6 feet, 7 inches tall. His height makes him especially self-conscious at scientific conferences when he rises to describe his research as a demographer at the London School of Tropical Medicine. "It's always quite embarrassing." he said.

Dr. Yannick, who is Dutch, studies why his fellow citizens are so tall. Today, the Dutch are on average the tallest people on the planet. Just 150 years ago, they were relatively short. In 1860, the average Dutch soldier in the Netherlands was just 5 feet 5 inches. American men were 2.7 inches taller. Since 1860, average heights have increased in many parts of the world, but no people have shot up like the Dutch. The average Dutchman now stands over six feet tall. And while the growth spurt in the United States has stopped in recent years, the Dutch continue to get taller.

For years, scientists have sought to understand why average height has increased, and why the Dutch in particular have grown so quickly. Among other factors, the Dutch have a better diet than in the past, and they also have better medical care. But now Dr. Yannick has found evidence suggesting that evolution is also helping to make them taller.

The new study was made possible thanks to a major medical database recently established in the Netherlands called LifeLines. The database contains a vast amount of information, including genetic profiles and medical records, about tens of thousands of Dutch families. Dr. Yannick analyzed data on 42,612 men and women over age 45, looking at the height of their subjects and how many children they had. Dutch men who were taller than average had more children than those of average or lower than average height. Among those born in the early 1950s, for example, men who were 5 feet 6 inches had on average 2.15 children. Men who were 6 feet 1 inch had 2.39 children. The trend toward taller men having more children persisted for more than 35 years. Under identical conditions, some people will grow taller than others because they carry certain _____ variations.

NOTE

Step 1	**S**urvey
Key Words	
Signal Words	
Step 2	**R**eading
Purpose	
Pattern of Organization	
Tone	
Main Idea	
Step 3	**S**ummary
지문 요약하기 (Paraphrasing)	
Step 4	**R**ecite
	요약문 말로 설명하기

Answer Key

Ben Yannick stands 6 feet, 7 inches tall. His **height** makes him especially self-conscious at scientific conferences when he rises to describe his research as a demographer at the London School of Tropical Medicine. "It's always quite embarrassing." he said.

Dr. Yannick, who is Dutch, studies why **his fellow citizens are so tall**. Today, **the Dutch** are on average the tallest people on the planet. Just 150 years ago, they were relatively short. In 1860, the average Dutch soldier in the Netherlands was just 5 feet 5 inches. American men were 2.7 inches taller. Since 1860, average heights have increased in many parts of the world, but no people have shot up like the Dutch. The average Dutchman now stands over six feet tall. And while the growth spurt in the United States has stopped in recent years, the Dutch continue to get taller.

For years, scientists have sought to understand why **average height has increased**, and why the Dutch in particular have grown so quickly. Among other factors, the Dutch have a better diet than in the past, and they also have better medical care. But now Dr. Yannick has found evidence suggesting that evolution is also helping to make them taller.

The new study was made possible thanks to a **major medical database** recently established in the Netherlands called LifeLines. The database contains a vast amount of information, including genetic profiles and medical records, about tens of thousands of Dutch families. Dr. Yannick analyzed data on 42,612 men and women over age 45, looking at the height of their subjects and how many children they had. Dutch men who were taller than average had more children than those of average or lower than average height. Among those born in the early 1950s, for example, men who were 5 feet 6 inches had on average 2.15 children. Men who were 6 feet 1 inch had 2.39 children. The trend toward taller men having more children persisted for more than 35 years. Under identical conditions, some people will grow taller than others because they carry certain **genetic variations**.

모범답안
genetic

채점기준
- 2점: 모범답안과 같다.
- 0점: 모범답안과 다르다.

한글번역

　벤 야니크는 키가 6피트 7인치(약 2m)이다. 과학 컨퍼런스에 참석해서 런던 열대의학 대학원의 인구통계학자로서 연구를 발표하려고 일어설 때 그의 신장으로 인해 그는 남의 시선을 의식하게 된다. "그건 항상 꽤 당황스러워요."라고 그가 말했다.

　네덜란드 사람인 야니크 박사는 그와 같은 시민들이 그렇게 키가 큰 원인을 연구한다. 오늘날, 네덜란드인들은 평균 신장이 지구에서 제일 크다. 150년 전만 하더라도, 그들은 상대적으로 작았다. 1860년 네덜란드 군인의 평균 신장은 5피트 5인치(약 165cm)였다. 미국 남성들이 2.7인치(약 7cm) 더 컸다. 1860년부터 세계 여러 곳에서 평균 신장이 증가했지만, 네덜란드인만큼 급증한 사람들은 없었다. 현재 네덜란드인의 평균 신장은 6피트(약 182cm) 이상이다. 그리고 미국에서의 성장 급등이 최근 몇 년 멈춰있던 반면에 네덜란드인들은 계속 컸다.

　수년간, 과학자들은 평균 신장이 늘어난 원인과 특히 네덜란드인들이 매우 급속히 성장하는 원인을 이해하려고 했다. 다른 요소 중에, 네덜란드인들은 과거보다 더 좋은 식단을 가지고 있고 또한 더 나은 건강관리를 한다. 하지만 이제 야니크 박사는 진화 또한 그들을 성장시키는 데 도움을 주고 있다는 것을 제안하는 증거를 찾았다.

　LifeLines라 불리는 네덜란드에 최근 설립된 주요 의학 데이터베이스 덕분에 새 연구가 가능해졌다. 이 데이터베이스는 수만 명의 네덜란드인 가족의 유전적 프로파일과 진료기록을 포함한 어마어마한 양의 정보를 담고 있다. 야니크 박사는 실험 대상의 신장과 그들이 얼마나 많은 아이를 가졌는지를 살피면서, 45세 이상 남녀 42,612명에 대한 데이터를 분석했다. 평균보다 큰 네덜란드 사람들이 평균이거나 이하인 사람들보다 더 많은 아이를 가졌다. 예를 들어, 1950년대 초 태어난 사람 중에서 신장이 5피트 6인치(약 167cm)인 사람들은 평균 2.15명의 아이를 가졌다. 6피트 1인치(약 185cm)인 사람들은 평균 2.39명의 아이를 가졌다. 더 큰 사람들이 더 많은 아이를 갖는 추세는 35년 이상 동안 지속됐다. 동일한 조건에서, 어떤 사람들은 특정 유전적 변이를 지니고 있기 때문에 다른 사람들보다 더 성장한다.

NOTE

Step 1	Survey
Key Words	Dutch; average height; evolution; medical database
Signal Words	Why; why; why
Step 2	Reading
Purpose	To explain what might be causing the rising average height of the Dutch
Pattern of Organization	Cause/effect
Tone	Neutral
Main Idea	The cause of greater Dutch height is believed to be evolutionary.
Step 3	Summary
지문 요약하기 (Paraphrasing)	The cause of greater Dutch height is believed to be evolutionary. The Dutch average height is the tallest on the planet and continues to rise. While diet and medical care was theorized to be a cause, a recent revelation assisted by a new major medical database pointed towards evolution as the major cause when it showed that taller men were tending to have more children.
Step 4	Recite
	요약문 말로 설명하기

52 Read the passage and follow the directions.

The sailors who threw Jonah overboard imagined his presence to be the cause of the storm which threatened to wreck their ship. In a similar spirit the Japanese, at the time of the Tokyo earthquake took to massacring Koreans and Liberals. When the Romans won victories in the Punic wars, the Carthaginians became persuaded that their misfortunes were due to a certain laxity which had crept into the worship of Moloch. Moloch liked having children sacrificed to him, and preferred them aristocratic; but the noble families of Carthage had adopted the practice of surreptitiously substituting plebeian children for their own offspring. This, it was thought, had displeased the god, and at the worst moments even the most aristocratic children were duly consumed in the fire. Strange to say, the Romans were victorious in spite of <u>this democratic reform on the part of their enemies</u>. Collective fear stimulates herd instinct, and tends to produce ferocity toward those who are not regarded as members of the herd. So it was in the French Revolution, when dread of foreign armies produced the reign of terror. And it is to be feared that the Nazis, as defeat draws nearer, will increase the intensity of their campaign for exterminating Jews. Neither a man nor a crowd nor a nation can be trusted to act humanely or to think sanely under the influence of the irrational emotion. And for this reason poltroons are more prone to cruelty than brave men, and are also more prone to superstition. When I say this, I am thinking of men who are brave in all respects, not only in facing death. Many a man will have the courage to die gallantly, but will not have the courage to say, or even to think, that the cause for which he is asked to die is an unworthy one.

Explain to what the underlined "this democratic reform on the part of their enemies" refers. Second, what is the main idea of the passage? Write your answer by filling in the blank below with the ONE most appropriate word from the passage.

> Fear and superstition have led societies to commit acts of violence against those they blame for their _____.

NOTE

Step 1	**S**urvey
Key Words	
Signal Words	
Step 2	**R**eading
Purpose	
Pattern of Organization	
Tone	
Main Idea	
Step 3	**S**ummary
지문 요약하기 (Paraphrasing)	
Step 4	**R**ecite
	요약문 말로 설명하기

Answer Key

　　The sailors who threw Jonah overboard imagined his presence to be the cause of the storm which threatened to wreck their ship. In a similar spirit **the Japanese**, at the time of the Tokyo earthquake took to massacring Koreans and Liberals. When the Romans won victories in the Punic wars, **the Carthaginians** became persuaded that their misfortunes were due to a certain laxity which had crept into the worship of Moloch. Moloch liked having children sacrificed to him, and preferred them aristocratic; but the noble families of Carthage had adopted the practice of surreptitiously substituting plebeian children for their own offspring. This, it was thought, had displeased the god, and at the worst moments even the most aristocratic children were duly consumed in the fire. Strange to say, the Romans were victorious in spite of this democratic reform on the part of their enemies. **Collective fear** stimulates **herd instinct**, and tends to produce **ferocity** toward **those who are not regarded as members of the herd**. So it was in the French Revolution, when dread of foreign armies produced the **reign of terror**. And it is **to be feared** that **the Nazis**, as defeat draws nearer, will increase the intensity of their campaign for exterminating Jews. Neither a man nor a crowd nor a nation can be trusted to act humanely or to think sanely under **the influence of the** irrational emotion. And for this reason **poltroons are more prone to** cruelty **than brave men**, and are also **more prone to** superstition. When I say this, I am thinking of men who are brave in all respects, not only in facing death. Many a man will have the courage to die gallantly, but will not have the courage to say, or even to think, that the cause for which he is asked to die is an unworthy one.

ⓐ

ⓑ

ⓒ

key words

ⓓ

ⓔ

모범답안

First, it refers to the practice among the Carthaginians of substituting aristocratic children for plebeian (commoner) children in sacrifices to the god Moloch. Second, the word is "misfortunes".

채점기준

+ 2점: 밑줄 친 부분의 의미를 "the practice among the Carthaginians of substituting aristocratic children for plebeian (commoner) children in sacrifices to the god Moloch."라 서술하였거나 유사하였다.
+ 2점: 빈칸에 들어갈 단어를 "misfortunes"라 정확히 기입하였다.

한글번역

　(구약 성서에서) 요나를 바다에 내던진 선원들은 배를 뒤집을 기세로 불어 닥친 폭풍의 원인이 바로 그라고 상상했다. 이와 비슷한 심정에서 일본인들은 간토 대지진이 일어났을 때 조선인들과 자유주의자들을 학살했다. 포에니 전쟁에서 로마가 승전을 거듭할 무렵, 카르타고인들은 몰렉 신에 대한 자신들의 신앙심의 나태함이 파고들었기 때문에 전투에서 졌다고 믿었다. 몰렉이 좋아하는 제물은 어린아이였는데 특히 귀족 집안의 어린 자제를 선호했다. 그러나 카르타고의 귀족들은 평민 집안의 아이를 남몰래 데려다 자기 아이 대신 제물로 바치는 관행을 일찌감치 마련해 놓았다. 사람들은 이러한 관행 때문에 몰렉 신이 노했다고 여겼고, 이로써 전황이 최악으로 치달을 때는 최고 귀족 가문의 아이들조차도 군말 없이 불 속에 던져져야 했다. 신기하게도, 카르타고인들이 이렇게 민주주의적 개혁을 이뤘는데도 불구하고 정작 전쟁에 이긴 쪽은 로마인들이었다. 집단적 공포는 사람들의 집단 본능을 자극하며, 그 집단의 일원으로 인정받지 못하는 사람에 대한 만행을 촉발하는 경향이 있다. 프랑스 혁명 당시 외국 군대가 쳐들어올지도 모른다는 공포가 만연했을 때도 그러했다. 그리고 나치가, 패배에 가까워졌을 때, 유대인을 몰살시켜야 한다고 주장하는 그들의 캠페인의 강도를 높이려는 것은 곧 그들이 두렵다는 것이다. 거대한 공포의 영향력 아래서는 어떤 개인도 군중도 국가도 자비롭게 행동하거나 올바르게 생각하리라고 기대할 수 없다. 이러한 까닭에 용감한 사람보다는 겁쟁이가 더 쉽게 잔인해지고 더 쉽게 미신에 기대는 것이다. 이렇게 말할 때 내가 염두에 두는 사람은 모든 면에서 용감한 사람이지 죽음에 직면한 경우에만 용감한 사람은 아니다. 의연하게 죽음을 무릅쓸 사람은 많겠지만, 자신에게 목숨을 바치라고 요구하는 명분이 헛된 것이라는 진실에 대해서는 말할 용기는커녕 생각할 용기를 내는 사람도 많지 않을 것이다.

NOTE

Step 1	**S**urvey
Key Words	Collective fear; superstition; irrational emotion; cruelty
Signal Words	The cause of; due to; stimulates; produce; increase; for this reason
Step 2	**R**eading
Purpose	To show the influence of irrational emotions such as fear on stirring cruelty
Pattern of Organization	Cause/effect
Tone	Critical
Main Idea	Fear and superstition have led societies to commit acts of violence against those they blame for their misfortunes.
Step 3	**S**ummary
지문 요약하기 (Paraphrasing)	Throughout history, fear and superstition have led societies to commit acts of violence against those they blame for their misfortunes. This pattern is evident in various incidents, such as sailors blaming Jonah for a storm, the massacre of Koreans and Liberals after the Tokyo earthquake, and Carthaginians altering sacrifices to Moloch after military defeats. These actions, driven by collective fear and irrational beliefs, illustrate a pattern of ferocity towards outsiders and a failure to act humanely or think rationally, revealing a deeper susceptibility to cruelty and superstition under the influence of fear.
Step 4	**R**ecite
	요약문 말로 설명하기

53 Read the passage and follow the directions.

To understand why the National Rifle Association and fellow pro-gun groups have been so successful in stopping gun control legislation, consider the dilemma that faced the former senator Mark Begich, an Alaskan Democrat in April 2013, when the Senate was voting on expanding background checks after the Newtown shooting. Begich was up for re-election in 2014. He knew that many Alaskans were gun owners, and many gun owners are single-issue gun voters. He also knew that while other Alaskans may want tougher gun control, most of these were probably Democrats, who'd support him anyway. And so, along fellow Democrats in gun-dense states like Arkansas, North Dakota and Montana, Begich made the rational political calculus. He voted against gun control, and then lost anyway.

The National Rifle Association poses a credible threat to any lawmaker who crosses it. It uses a clear rating system to evaluate candidates. It helps its 3 million members broadcast their demands. Many will support candidates based on N.R.A. ratings alone. The N.R.A. also spends aggressively in congressional races($28.4 million in outside expenditures in 2014), and can deliver votes, which is even more valuable than money. By contrast, groups that support gun control legislation haven't yet proved they can deliver enough single-issue voters to decide a close election. While these groups are growing in size and membership, they still have a long way to go.

The gun lobby also benefits from geography, particularly in the Senate. Low-population states are more likely to be heavy gun-owning states, and low-population states have disproportionate influence in the Senate. In the House, gun control-supporting Democrats disproportionately concentrate in safe-seat urban districts and swing districts are mostly rural or suburban, and home to higher concentrations of pro-gun voters. For even modest gun control legislation to pass, majorities in both chambers must be convinced that the political cost of opposing ____ⓐ____ is higher than the political cost of crossing the ____ⓑ____.

Fill in each blank with the TWO most appropriate consecutive words from the passage respectively.

_____

NOTE

Step 1	**S**urvey
Key Words	
Signal Words	
Step 2	**R**eading
Purpose	
Pattern of Organization	
Tone	
Main Idea	
Step 3	**S**ummary
지문 요약하기 (Paraphrasing)	
Step 4	**R**ecite
	요약문 말로 설명하기

Answer Key

To understand why the **National Rifle Association** and **fellow pro-gun groups** have been so successful in stopping **gun control legislation**, consider the dilemma that faced the former senator Mark Begich, an Alaskan Democrat in April 2013, when the Senate was voting on expanding background checks after the Newtown shooting. Begich was up for re-election in 2014. He knew that many Alaskans were gun owners, and many gun owners are single-issue gun voters. He also knew that while other Alaskans may want tougher gun control, most of these were probably Democrats, who'd support him anyway. And so, along fellow Democrats in gun-dense states like Arkansas, North Dakota and Montana, Begich made the rational political calculus. He voted against gun control, and then lost anyway.

The National Rifle Association poses a credible threat to any lawmaker who crosses it. It uses **a clear rating system** to evaluate candidates. It helps its 3 million members broadcast their demands. Many will support candidates based on N.R.A. ratings alone. The N.R.A. also **spends aggressively** in congressional races($28.4 million in outside expenditures in 2014), and **can deliver votes**, which is even more valuable than money. By contrast, groups that support **gun control legislation** haven't yet proved they can deliver enough single-issue voters to decide a close election. While these groups are growing in size and membership, they still have a long way to go.

The gun lobby also **benefits** from **geography**, particularly in the Senate. Low-population states are more likely to be heavy gun-owning states, and low-population states have disproportionate influence in the Senate. In the House, gun control-supporting Democrats disproportionately concentrate in safe-seat urban districts and swing districts are mostly rural or suburban, and home to higher concentrations of pro-gun voters. For even modest gun control legislation to pass, majorities in both chambers must be convinced that the political cost of opposing **gun control** is higher than the political cost of crossing **the gun lobby**.

ⓐ
ⓑ
ⓒ
ⓓ

모범답안

ⓐ gun control ⓑ gun lobby

채점기준

- 2점: 모범답안과 같다.
- 1점: 둘 중 하나만 맞았다.
- 0점: 모범답안과 다르다.

한글번역

　　전미총기협회(NRA)와 협회를 따르는 총기 찬성집단이 총기 규제 법안을 저지하는 데 있어서 지금까지 매우 성공적이었음을 이해하기 위해서, 2013년 4월, 상원이 뉴타운 총기 사건 후에 신원 조사를 늘리는 것에 관해 투표할 때 알래스카의 민주당원인 전임 상원의원 마크 베기치가 직면했던 딜레마를 고려해야 한다. 베기치는 2014년 재선에 입후보했다. 그는 알래스카 지역의 많은 주민이 총기 소유자이며, 그들이 총기 문제에만 투표한다는 것을 알았다. 그는 또한 다른 사람들이 더 엄격한 총기 규제를 원할지도 모르지만, 아마 그들의 대부분은 어쨌든 그를 지지할 민주당원임도 알았다. 그래서 아칸소주, 노스다코타주, 몬태나주 같은 총기가 밀집한 지역의 동료 민주당원들을 따라서 베기치는 이성적인 정치적 계산을 했다. 그는 총기 규제에 반대하는 투표를 했는데, 어쨌든 떨어졌다.

　　NRA는 자신을 반대하는 어떤 국회의원에게든 실제적인 위협을 가한다. 협회는 후보자를 평가하기 위해 명확한 순위 제도를 사용한다. 그것은 협회의 3백만 회원들이 자신들의 요구를 널리 알리는 데 도움이 된다. 많은 사람이 NRA 순위만을 근거로 후보자들을 지지할 것이다. NRA는 또한 공격적으로 의회 선거전에 비용을 쓰고(2014년엔 임시비용이 2,840만 달러였다), 돈보다 훨씬 더 가치 있는 표를 모을 수 있다. 반대로, 총기 규제 법안을 지지하는 집단들은 아직 그들이 박빙의 선거전을 끝낼 단일 쟁점에 호소하는(여기서는 총기 규제) 충분한 표를 모을 수 있다는 것을 증명하지 못했다. 이 그룹은 규모와 회원이 성장 중이지만, 여전히 갈 길은 멀다.

　　총기 로비는 또한 지리적으로, 특히 상원에서 혜택을 받는다. 인구가 적은 주들은 총기 소유가 많은 지역일 가능성이 더 높고, 그 지역들은 상원에서 불균형적인 영향력을 갖는다. 하원에서는 총기 규제를 지지하는 민주당원들이 불균형적으로 자리가 보장된 도시지역에 집중하며, 경합주 대부분은 시골이나 교외 지역, 총기 찬성 투표권자들이 더 많이 밀집한 근거지이다. 심지어 가장 완화된 총기 규제 법안이 통과되기 위해선 양원의 대다수가 총기 규제를 반대하는 정치적 비용이 총기 로비를 반대하는 정치적 비용보다 더 높다는 것을 확신해야만 한다.

NOTE

Step 1	Ⓢurvey
Key Words	National Rifle Association; pro-gun groups; gun control; rating system; gun lobby; money; geography
Signal Words	Why; also; also
Step 2	**Ⓡeading**
Purpose	To outline how the NRA's political power functions
Pattern of Organization	Cause/effect; series
Tone	Neutral
Main Idea	The National Rifle Association (NRA) and pro-gun groups have effectively blocked gun control legislation through several means.
Step 3	**Ⓢummary**
지문 요약하기 (Paraphrasing)	The National Rifle Association (NRA) and pro-gun groups have effectively blocked gun control legislation through several means. The NRA's scoring system of candidates can ensure the way its three million members will vote. Likewise, it spends substantially on congressional races. Also, geography benefits the gun lobby from rural areas which have an advantage in the Senate and in the house with states having areas that are heavily gun-owning.
Step 4	**Ⓡecite**

요약문 말로 설명하기

54 Read the passage and follow the directions.

The acid that carries genetic information in every human cell, DNA, contains just four chemicals : adenine, cytosine, guanine, and thymine. But a single gene is "spelled out" by perhaps a million combinations. As the Human Genome Project (which provided a "map" of human genes) was nearing completion in the spring of 2000, there were a number of newspaper headlines about specific discoveries : "Gene Linked to Anxiety." "Gay Gene!" and "Thrill Seeking Due to Genetics." The newspaper articles led people to believe that a single gene is responsible for a certain personality trait, in the same way a single gene can be responsible for a physical characteristic or disease. However, one gene alone cannot cause people to become anxious, homosexual or thrill-seeking. Instead, many _____ work together, and they do direct the combination of chemicals in the body. These chemicals, such as dopamine and serotonin (which affect a person's mood) have a significant influence on personality.

Fill in the blank with the ONE most appropriate word from the passage.

NOTE

Step 1	**S**urvey
Key Words	
Signal Words	
Step 2	**R**eading
Purpose	
Pattern of Organization	
Tone	
Main Idea	
Step 3	**S**ummary
지문 요약하기 (Paraphrasing)	
Step 4	**R**ecite
	요약문 말로 설명하기

Answer Key

The acid that carries genetic information in every human cell, DNA, contains just four chemicals : adenine, cytosine, guanine, and thymine. But **a single gene** is "spelled out" by perhaps a million combinations. As the Human Genome Project (which provided a "map" of human genes) was nearing completion in the spring of 2000, there were a number of newspaper headlines about specific discoveries : "Gene Linked to Anxiety." "Gay Gene!" and "Thrill Seeking Due to Genetics." The newspaper articles led people to believe that a single gene is responsible for a certain **personality trait**, in the same way a single gene can be responsible for a physical characteristic or disease. However, one gene alone cannot cause people to become anxious, homosexual or thrill-seeking. Instead, **many genes** work together, and they do direct the combination of chemicals in the body. These chemicals, such as dopamine and serotonin (which affect a person's mood) have a significant influence on **personality**.

모범답안

genes

채점기준

- 2점: 모범답안과 같다.
- 0점: 모범답안과 다르다.

한글번역

모든 인간 세포 속에 유전적 정보를 지니고 있는 산인, DNA는 단 4개의 화학 물질(즉, 아데닌, 시토신, 구아닌, 그리고 티민)만 가지고 있다. 하지만 단 하나의 유전자만 해도 대략 백만 가지의 조합에 의해 구성된다. (인간 유전자 지도를 제공한) 인간 게놈 프로젝트가 2000년 봄, 완성에 가까워졌을 때, 특정 발견에 대한 수많은 신문들의 1면 머리기사는 다음과 같았다. "불안과 관련 있는 유전자" "게이 유전자!" 그리고 "유전학으로 인한 스릴 추구" 등이 그것들이다. 이런 신문 기사들은 사람들로 하여금 하나의 유전자가 신체적 특성이나 질병에 책임이 있는 것으로 믿게 만들었는데, 이런 방식은 사람들로 하여금 단 하나의 유전자가 어떤 성격적 특성에 책임이 있다고 믿도록 만든 것과 같다. 하지만 (진실은) 하나의 유전자가 단독으로 사람들을 불안하게 하거나, 동성애자가 되게 하거나, 스릴을 추구하게끔 할 수는 없다. 그렇기보단 많은 유전자들은 함께 작동하고, 그래서 이 많은 유전자들이 체내의 화학 물질들의 조합을 지시한다. 바로 이 화학 물질들,—예를 들어 (사람의 기분에 영향을 주는) 도파민과 세로토닌이 성격에 큰 영향을 미친다.

NOTE

Step 1	Survey
Key Words	Genes; personality; characteristic
Signal Words	Influence; led … to; is responsible for; cause
Step 2	**Reading**
Purpose	To clarify how exactly genes play a role in personality
Pattern of Organization	Not clear (약하게 cause/effect)
Tone	Neutral
Main Idea	Personality is influenced by the combination of many genes, not individual genes.
Step 3	**Summary**
지문 요약하기 (Paraphrasing)	Personality is influenced by the combination of many genes, not individual genes. Despite headlines from the Human Genome Project era suggesting single genes determine traits like anxiety, homosexuality, or thrill-seeking, these traits are not controlled by individual genes. Instead, complex interactions among many genes influence chemical balances in the body, like dopamine and serotonin levels, significantly affecting personality.
Step 4	**Recite**

요약문 말로 설명하기

55 Read the passage and follow the directions.

American consumers are addicted to water. The average American uses over 2,000 gallons of water each day—two times the global average. But only a fraction of this water use comes directly from the tap. Most of the water is consumed indirectly, having been funneled into agriculture or commercial production.

This "water footprint" concept—which accounts for the total volume of freshwater used to produce the goods and services we consume—is the most holistic way to look at our water use and is an important tool for identifying wasteful practices.

An incredible 40 percent of the water consumed by Americans goes into meat and dairy production. Livestock must drink water and there is some water use at the farm, but most of this water is used for producing animal feed. Furthermore, a quarter of the water used in the U.S., including water that is polluted in the process, goes toward producing commodities for export.

Is this a wise allocation of the limited supply of freshwater in America? This question is most urgent in the western United States, but it is just as relevant in the rest of the country. The water challenge is also huge worldwide. If we assume an equal share for each global citizen, water use will have to be reduced by 22.5 percent for consumers in China and India, and by 70 percent in the U.S. over the next century.

Improved technologies alone will not be sufficient to achieve the required _____ reduction. The unhealthy U.S. consumption pattern needs to be reconsidered. Taking shorter showers will not suffice. Eating less meat—the biggest water user in the diet—would be much more effective.

Fill in the blank with the TWO most appropriate consecutive words from the passage.

NOTE

Step 1	ⓢurvey
Key Words	
Signal Words	
Step 2	**ⓡeading**
Purpose	
Pattern of Organization	
Tone	
Main Idea	
Step 3	**ⓢummary**
지문 요약하기 (Paraphrasing)	
Step 4	**ⓡecite**
	요약문 말로 설명하기

Answer Key

American consumers are addicted to **water**. The average American uses over 2,000 gallons of **water** each day—two times the global average. But only a fraction of this water use comes directly from the tap. Most of the water is consumed indirectly, having been funneled into **agriculture** or **commercial production**.

This "**water footprint**" concept—which accounts for the total volume of freshwater used to produce the goods and services we consume—is the most holistic way to look at our **water use** and is an important tool for identifying wasteful practices.

An incredible 40 percent of the water consumed by Americans goes into **meat** and **dairy production**. Livestock must drink water and there is some water use at the farm, but most of this water is used for producing animal feed. Furthermore, a quarter of the water used in the U.S., including water that is polluted in the process, goes toward producing **commodities for export**.

Is this a wise allocation of the limited supply of freshwater in America? This question is most urgent in the western United States, but it is just as relevant in the rest of the country. **The water challenge** is also huge worldwide. If we assume an equal share for each global citizen, water use will have to be reduced by 22.5 percent for consumers in China and India, and by 70 percent in the U.S. over the next century.

Improved technologies alone will not be sufficient to achieve the required water **footprint reduction**. The **unhealthy U.S. consumption pattern** needs to be reconsidered. Taking shorter showers will not suffice. Eating less meat—the biggest water user in the diet—would be much more effective.

definition

모범답안
water footprint

채점기준
- 2점: 모범답안과 같다.
- 0점: 모범답안과 다르다.

어휘
dairy production 유제품 생산 fraction 부분, 일부 funnel 이동시키다, 전달하다; 공급하다
holistic 전체적인 per capita 1인당 projected population 추정 인구
suffice 충분하다

한글번역

　미국 소비자들은 물에 중독됐다. 미국인들은 하루 평균—세계 평균의 두 배 이상인—2000갤런(약 3.8리터)의 물을 소비한다. 그러나 이 물 사용의 아주 작은 부분만이 직접적으로 수도꼭지에서 비롯된다. 대다수 물은 간접적으로 소비되는데, 농업이나 상업적 생산을 위해 공급된다.

　이 '물발자국(인간이 사용하는 물의 양을 나타낸 지표)'은—우리가 소비하는 재화나 서비스를 생산하는 데 소비되는 민물의 총량을 설명하는—우리의 물 사용량을 볼 수 있는 가장 전체적인 방식이자 낭비적 물 습관을 확인할 수 있는 가장 중요한 도구이다.

　미국인들에 의해 소비되는 엄청난 40%의 물 사용은 고기나 유제품 생산에 사용된다. 가축들은 물을 마셔야만 하며, 농장에도 약간의 물이 사용된다. 그러나 이 대부분의 물은 동물성 사료를 생산하는 데 사용된다. 더욱이, 이 과정에서 오염되는 물을 포함한 미국에서 사용되는 물의 4분의 1은 수출을 위한 물품을 생산하는 데 소비된다.

　이것이 미국의 한정된 담수 자원을 배분하는 현명한 방식일까? 이 질문은 특히 미국 서부 지역에서 시급하지만, 다른 지역에도 똑같이 적용된다. 물 문제는 전 세계적으로도 막대한 도전이다. 전 세계 모든 시민에게 동일한 몫을 할당한다고 가정할 때, 앞으로 100년 동안 중국과 인도에서는 물 사용을 22.5% 줄여야 하고, 미국에서는 70% 줄여야 한다.

　향상된 기술들만으로는 요구되는 물 사용량 감소를 달성하기에 충분하지 않다. 비정상적인 미국의 물 사용 패턴은 다시 숙고할 필요가 있다. 샤워 시간을 줄이는 것만으로 충분하지 않다. 육류—식단에 있어 가장 큰 물 소비자인—를 적게 소비하는 것이 훨씬 더 효과적이다.

NOTE

Step 1	**S**urvey
Key Words	Water challenge; agriculture; commodities for export; consumption pattern
Signal Words	Furthermore; also
Step 2	**R**eading
Purpose	To diagnose the major components of water consumption and suggest alternatives
Pattern of Organization	Cause/effect; series
Tone	Critical
Main Idea	American water consumption is double the global average, largely due to indirect use in agriculture and exports.
Step 3	**S**ummary
지문 요약하기 (Paraphrasing)	American water consumption is double the global average, largely due to indirect use in agriculture and exports. This vast consumption includes 40% for meat and dairy and a significant portion for exports. Significant reductions are needed : 22.5% in China and India and 70% in the U.S. This challenge cannot be met by technology alone. It requires changing consumption patterns, especially reducing meat intake.
Step 4	**R**ecite

요약문 말로 설명하기

MEMO

56   Read the passage and follow the directions.

There are plenty of emotional arguments both for and against animal testing, but let's start with the most obvious facts. If you examine the history of medicine, you find that experiments on animals have been an important part of almost every major medical advance. Many cornerstones of medical science—the discovery that blood circulates through our veins, understanding the way lungs work, the discovery of vitamins and hormones—were made this way.

Most of the main advances in medicine itself also depended on animal experiments. In the Fifties, between 2000 and 4000 people each year in the UK were paralyzed or killed by polio but, thanks to the polio vaccine, this number has now dropped to just one or two cases a year. Modern surgery would be impossible without today's anaesthetics. The list goes on : organ transplants, heart surgery, hip replacements, drugs for cancer and asthma—animals played an important part in these medical advances.

Animal experimentation wasn't the only type of research necessary to the medical advances that save human lives. Studies on human volunteers were also essential, and test-tube experiments were vital in many cases. But the history of medicine tells us that animal experiments are essential if we want to deal with the diseases.

This is the dilemma we face. We want to prevent suffering. The crucial issue is how we use animals in research. Modern science has developed humane experimental techniques. It is possible to do animal experiments using methods that the animals don't even notice. The worst these animals have to put up with is living in a cage with regular food and water, with animal keepers and vets looking after them.

The golden rule of laboratory animal welfare is to minimize any pain involved using the principle of the three Rs. First, you reduce the number of animals used in each experiment to the minimum that will give a scientific result. Then, whenever possible, you replace animal experiments with alternatives—that don't use animals but will give equally scientific results. Finally, you refine the animal experiments that you do, so they cause the least possible harm to the animals. If an experiment involves surgery on the animal, give it an anaesthetic. When it comes around, give it painkillers and medicine to fight infection.

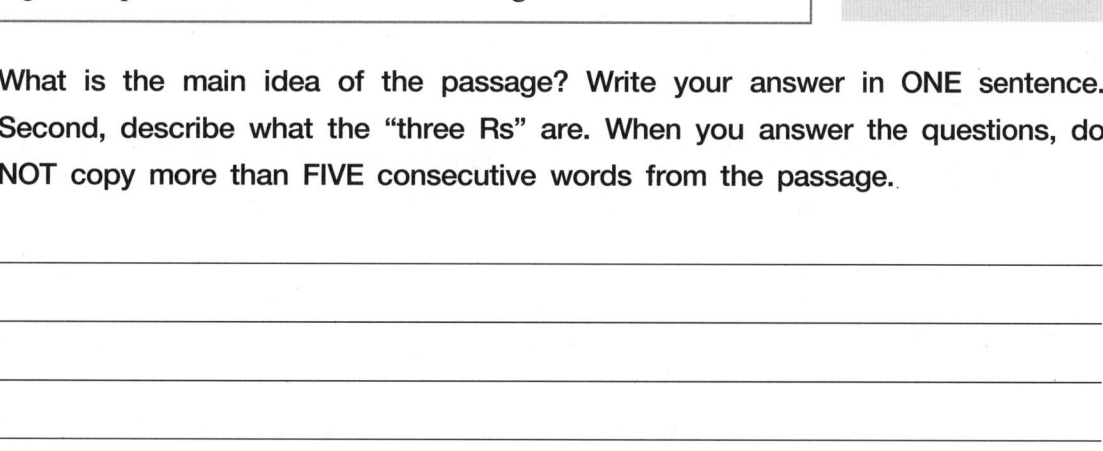

What is the main idea of the passage? Write your answer in ONE sentence. Second, describe what the "three Rs" are. When you answer the questions, do NOT copy more than FIVE consecutive words from the passage.

___
___
___
___
___

NOTE

Step 1	**S**urvey
Key Words	
Signal Words	
Step 2	**R**eading
Purpose	
Pattern of Organization	
Tone	
Main Idea	
Step 3	**S**ummary
지문 요약하기 (Paraphrasing)	
Step 4	**R**ecite
	요약문 말로 설명하기

Answer Key

There are plenty of emotional arguments both for and against **animal testing**, but let's start with the most obvious facts. If you examine the history of medicine, you find that **experiments on animals** have been an important part of almost every major **medical advance**. Many cornerstones of medical science—the discovery that blood circulates through our veins, understanding the way lungs work, the discovery of vitamins and hormones—were made this way.

Most of the main **advances in medicine** itself also depended on **animal experiments**. In the Fifties, between 2000 and 4000 people each year in the UK were paralyzed or killed by polio but, thanks to the polio vaccine, this number has now dropped to just one or two cases a year. Modern surgery would be impossible without today's anaesthetics. The list goes on : organ transplants, heart surgery, hip replacements, drugs for cancer and asthma—animals played an important part in these medical advances.

Animal experimentation wasn't the only type of research necessary to the medical advances that save human lives. Studies on human volunteers were also essential, and test-tube experiments were vital in many cases. But the history of medicine tells us that animal experiments are essential if we want to deal with the diseases.

This is **the dilemma** we face. We want to prevent suffering. The crucial issue is how we use animals in research. Modern science has developed **humane experimental techniques**. It is possible to do animal experiments using methods that the animals don't even notice. The worst these animals have to put up with is living in a cage with regular food and water, with animal keepers and vets looking after them.

The golden rule of **laboratory animal welfare** is to minimize any pain involved using the principle of the **three Rs**. First, you **reduce** the number of animals used in each experiment to the minimum that will give a scientific result. Then, whenever possible, you **replace** animal experiments with alternatives—that don't use animals but will give equally scientific results. Finally, you **refine** the animal experiments that you do, so they cause the least possible harm to the animals. If an experiment involves surgery on the animal, give it an anaesthetic. When it comes around, give it painkillers and medicine to fight infection.

key words

series

모범답안

The main idea is that animal experimentation is an essential practice for medical advances that should be conducted humanely. Second, the three Rs are as follows : reducing the number of animals employed in the experiment to the minimum; replacing animals with alternatives when scientific results are the same; refining animal experiments to minimize the pain inflicted on the animals.

채점기준

+ 2점: 이 글의 요지를 "<u>animal experimentation</u> is an <u>essential step</u> for dealing with <u>human diseases</u>"라고 정확하게 서술하였거나 유사하였다.
  ☞ 또한, 위의 내용이 들어가 있으면서 다른 확장된 내용이 있는 것도 맞는 것으로 한다. 단, 위 밑줄 친 3개가 다 들어가 있어야 한다.
  ☞ "animal experimentation is an essential step"이라고만 했으면 1점을 준다.
+ 2점: three Rs이 무엇인지 "<u>reducing the number of animals employed in the experiment to the minimum</u>; <u>replacing animals with alternatives when scientific results are the same</u>; <u>refining animal experiments to minimize the pain inflicted on the animals</u>"라 정확하게 서술하였다.
  ☞ 셋 중 3개 모두를 서술한 경우 2점, 2개만 서술한 경우 1점, 1개만 서술했거나 서술하지 못한 경우 0점을 준다.

한글번역

　　동물 실험에 대한 찬성과 반대 모두 감정적인 주장들이 많지만, 가장 명백한 사실들로부터 출발하자. 만약 당신이 의학의 역사를 살펴본다면, 당신은 동물에 행하는 실험이 거의 모든 주요 의학적 진보에 중요한 부분이었다는 것을 발견할 것이다. 피가 우리의 혈관을 통해 순환한다는 발견, 폐가 작동하는 방식의 이해, 비타민과 호르몬의 발견과 같은 의학의 많은 초석은 이런 식으로 만들어졌다.

　　의술의 주요 진보 그 자체의 대부분 또한 동물 실험에 의존했다. 15세기에 2000명에서 4000명 사이의 사람들이 영국에서 매년 소아마비에 의해 마비되거나 죽었지만, 소아마비 백신 덕분에 이 숫자는 이제 일 년에 단지 하나 혹은 두 사례로 떨어졌다. 근대 수술은 오늘날의 마취약 없이는 불가능할 것이다. 목록은 계속된다 : 장기 이식, 심장 수술, 골반 교체, 암과 천식을 위한 약—동물은 이 의학적 진보에 중요한 역할을 했다.

　　동물 실험은 인간의 생명을 구하는 의학적 진보에 필요한 유일한 종류의 연구가 아니었다. 인간 자원자에 대한 연구 역시 매우 중요했으며, 시험관 실험은 많은 경우에 필수적이었다. 그러나 의학의 역사는 우리에게 만일 우리가 질병에 대처하고 싶다면 동물 실험은 필수적이라는 것을 말해준다.

　　이것이 우리가 직면한 딜레마이다. 우리는 고통을 방지하고 싶어 한다. 중대한 이슈는 우리가 연구에서 어떻게 동물을 사용하는가이다. 근대 과학은 인간 실험 기술을 발전시켜왔다. 동물이 심지어 알아차리지도 못하는 방법을 사용해 동물 실험을 하는 것이 가능하다. 이 동물들이 견뎌야 하는 가장 최악은 규칙적인 음식과 물이 있는 우리 안에서, 동물 사육사와 그 동물들을 돌봐줄 수의사와 함께 사는 것이다.

　　실험동물 복지의 황금률은 세 R의 원칙을 사용해 개입될 수 있는 어떤 고통도 최소화하는 것이다. 첫째, 당신은 각각의 실험에서 이용되는 동물의 수를 과학적 결과를 줄 수 있는 최소한으로 줄인다. 그다음, 가능한 언제든, 당신은 동물실험에 동물을 사용하지 않지만 동등하게 과학적 결과를 가져다줄 대안으로 교체한다. 마지막으로, 당신은 당신이 하는 동물 실험을 개선해, 그 실험들이 가능성 있는 피해를 가장 적게 야기할 수 있도록 한다. 만약 어떤 실험이 동물에 행하는 수술을 수반한다면, 그 동물에게 마취제를 줘라. 그 동물이 의식을 회복하면, 진통제와 감염에 대항할 약을 줘라.

NOTE

Step 1	Ⓢurvey
Key Words	Animal experimentation; medical advances; technique; dilemma; animal welfare; three Rs
Signal Words	The list goes on...; First; Then; Finally
Step 2	Ⓡeading
Purpose	To outline the importance of animal experimentation and the humane practice
Pattern of Organization	Series
Tone	Persuasive
Main Idea	Animal experimentation is an essential practice for medical advances that should be conducted humanely.
Step 3	Ⓢummary
지문 요약하기 (Paraphrasing)	Animal experimentation is an essential practice for medical advances that should be conducted humanely. It has led to many cures, deeper understanding of anatomy as well as important surgical techniques. However, to minimize suffering that happens in animal testing, humane practices should be used. The principle of minimizing suffering is known as the three Rs: reducing animals used, replacing animals with alternatives and refining experiments to cause the least amount of harm.
Step 4	Ⓡecite
	요약문 말로 설명하기

57 Read the passage and follow the directions.

For the sciences, a new theory is the goal and end result of the creative act. Innovative science produces new propositions in terms of which diverse phenomena can be related to one another in more coherent ways. Such phenomena as a brilliant diamond or a nesting bird are relegated to the role of data, serving as the means for formulating or testing a new theory. The goal of highly creative art is very different: the phenomenon itself becomes the direct product of the creative act. Shakespeare's *Hamlet* is not a tract about the behavior of indecisive princes or the uses of political power, nor is Picasso's painting *Guernica* primarily a propositional statement about the Spanish Civil War or the evils of fascism. What highly creative artistic activity produces is not a new generalization that transcends established limits, but rather an aesthetic particular. Aesthetic particulars produced by the highly creative artist extend, in an innovative way, the limits of an existing form, rather than transcend that form. This is not to deny that a highly creative artist sometimes establishes a new principle of organization in the history of an artistic field: the composer Claudio Monteverdi, who created music of the highest aesthetic value, comes to mind. More generally, however, whether or not a composition establishes a new principle in the history of music has little bearing on its aesthetic worth. Because they embody a new principle of organization, some musical works, such as the operas of the *Florentine Camerata*, are of signal historical importance, but few listeners or musicologists would include these among the great works of music. On the other hand, Mozart's *The Marriage of Figaro* is surely among the masterpieces of music, even though its modest innovations are confined to _____ existing means.

What is the title of the passage? Write your answer in TEN words or less. Second, why does the writer of the passage mention the Florentine Camerata? Write your answer in ONE sentence. Third, fill in the blank with the ONE most appropriate word from the passage. If necessary, change the word form.

NOTE

Step 1	**S**urvey
Key Words	
Signal Words	
Step 2	**R**eading
Purpose	
Pattern of Organization	
Tone	
Main Idea	
Step 3	**S**ummary
지문 요약하기 (Paraphrasing)	
Step 4	**R**ecite
	요약문 말로 설명하기

Answer Key

For the sciences, **a new theory** is the goal and end result of the creative act. Innovative science produces new propositions in terms of which diverse phenomena can be related to one another in more coherent ways. Such **phenomena** as a brilliant diamond or a nesting bird are relegated to the role of data, serving as **the means** for formulating or testing a new theory. **The goal of highly creative art** is very different: **the phenomenon** itself becomes the direct product of the creative act. Shakespeare's *Hamlet* is not a tract about the behavior of indecisive princes or the uses of political power, nor is Picasso's painting *Guernica* primarily a propositional statement about the Spanish Civil War or the evils of fascism. What **highly creative artistic activity** produces is not a new generalization that transcends established limits, but rather an **aesthetic particular**. Aesthetic **particulars** produced by the highly creative artist extend, in an innovative way, **the limits of an existing form**, rather than **transcend that form**. This is not to deny that a highly creative artist sometimes establishes a new principle of organization in the history of an artistic field: the composer Claudio Monteverdi, who created music of the highest aesthetic value, comes to mind. More generally, however, whether or not a composition establishes a new principle in the history of music has little bearing on its **aesthetic worth**. Because they embody a new principle of organization, some musical works, such as the operas of *the Florentine Camerata*, are of signal historical importance, but few listeners or musicologists would include these among the great works of music. On the other hand, Mozart's *The Marriage of Figaro* is surely among the masterpieces of music, even though its **modest innovations** are confined to **extending existing means**.

contrast

모범답안

The title is Differences between Scientific and Artistic Creativity. Second, it is because *the Florentine Camerata* illustrates an example that established a principle of organization but does not demonstrate aesthetic significance. Third, the word to fit the blank is "extending".

채점기준

+ 1점: 글의 제목을 "Differences between Scientific and Artistic Creativity"이라 서술하였거나 유사하였다.
+ 2점: 글의 저자가 *the Florentine Camerata*를 언급한 이유를 "*the Florentine Camerata* illustrates an example that established a principle of organization but does not demonstrate aesthetic significance."이라 서술하였거나 유사하였다.
+ 1점: 빈칸에 들어갈 단어를 "extending"이라 정확히 답하였다.

한글번역

과학에 있어서, 새로운 이론은 목표이며 창조적인 행위의 최종 결과이다. 혁신적인 과학은 어떤 다양한 현상이 다른 현상과 더 일관된 방식으로 관련돼 있을 수 있는지에 관련해 새로운 명제를 낳는다. 눈부신 다이아몬드나 둥지를 트는 새와 같은 현상들은 데이터의 역할로 격하돼, 새로운 이론을 공식화하거나 실험하는 도구로써 역할을 수행한다. 매우 창조적인 예술의 목표는 매우 다르다: 현상 그 자체가 창조적인 행위의 직접적인 산물이 된다. 셰익스피어의 "햄릿"은 우유부단한 군주들의 행동이나 정치적 권력의 사용에 관한 책이 아니며, 피카소의 그림 게르니카가 주로 스페인 내란이나 파시즘의 악함에 대한 명제적 진술인 것도 아니다. 매우 창조적인 예술적 행위가 낳는 것은 확고한 한계들을 초월하는 새로운 일반화가 아니라, 심미적 특수성이다. 매우 창조적인 예술가에 의해 생산되는 심미적인 특색은, 혁신적인 방식으로, 이미 존재하는 형태의 한계를 초월하기보다는 확장하거나 활용한다. 이것은 매우 창조적인 예술가가 때때로 예술적 분야의 역사 속에서 조직의 새로운 원칙을 세운다는 것을 부정하는 것이 아니다: 최상의 심미적 가치를 가진 음악을 창조했던, 클라우디오 몬테베르디가 떠오른다. 그러나 더 일반적으로 한 작곡가가 음악의 역사에서 새로운 원칙을 확립하는가 아닌가는 그 심미적인 가치에 거의 영향이 없다. 조직의 새로운 원칙을 구현하기 때문에 오페라 '피렌체 카메라타'와 같은 몇몇 음악적 작품은 귀중한 역사적 중요성을 가지지만, 음악을 듣는 사람이나 음악학 연구가는 대부분 이런 작품들을 음악의 위대한 작품에 포함하려 하지 않을 것이다. 반면, 모차르트의 '피가로의 결혼'은 비록 그 대단치 않은 수준의 혁신이 기존의 수단을 확장하는 데 국한돼 있다 하더라도 분명히 음악의 걸작 사이에 있다.

NOTE

Step 1	Ⓢurvey
Key Words	Sciences; theory; highly creative art; aesthetic particular; aesthetic worth; extending existing means
Signal Words	On the other hand
Step 2	Ⓡeading
Purpose	To explain the difference between scientific and artistic creativity
Pattern of Organization	Comparison/contrast
Tone	Neutral
Main Idea	In highly creative art, the aesthetic worth comes primarily from innovation extending the limits of an existing form, not from a new organizing principle that is the goal of highly creative acts of science.
Step 3	Ⓢummary
지문 요약하기 (Paraphrasing)	In highly creative art, the aesthetic worth comes primarily from innovation extending the limits of an existing form, not from a new organizing principle. On the other hand, in science, such aesthetic particulars are data intended to be organized under a new theory. In some exceptions, an artist has created a new organizing principle through creation, but this is unrelated to these works' perceived greatness.
Step 4	Ⓡecite
	요약문 말로 설명하기

58 Read the passage and follow the directions.

Evolution has come up with a big innovation. The mammalian hormone oxytocin evolved to play a key role in what makes mammals mammalian. Other newborn animals typically fend for themselves: Crocodiles, for example, are catching insects soon after birth. But mammals develop slowly, and mothers have to feed their newborns. Oxytocin evolved to make this possible, prompting mothers who are nursing to produce more milk as their babies demand it. Evolving the means to nurse the young was only half the battle. You also have to want to take care of them and to invest zillions of calories in generating milk and fending off predators. And you need to be able to recognize your offspring in a crowd, so you don't waste your energy helping others to leave behind copies of their genes. Oxytocin helped to solve <u>both problems</u>. But something truly striking occurred sometime in the past 50,000 years (which is to say, over the last 0.01% of the time during which oxytocin has existed). During that evolutionary blink of an eye, humans embarked on something new, with oxytocin again in a leading role: the domestication of wolves.

How did this occur? Scientists found that modern dogs and their owners secrete oxytocin when they interact with each other. Remarkably, dogs who gaze the most at their humans during interactions had the biggest oxytocin rise— as did their humans. The scientists then spritzed oxytocin (or saline, as a control treatment) up the dogs' noses. The oxytocin caused female dogs to gaze more at their humans whose own oxytocin levels rose as a result. All of this only affected dogs and their owners. Hand-reared wolves and their owners didn't react in the same way to the treatment, and dogs administered oxytocin didn't gaze any longer at humans who weren't familiar to them. In other words, dog and human brains seem to have evolved at lightning speed to co-opt oxytocin for bonding between our species. This sure helps to explain people who use baby talk with their dogs.

What is the main idea of the passage? Write your answer in ONE sentence. Second, identify the underlined "both problems". When you answer this question, do NOT copy more than FIVE consecutive words from the passage.

___
___
___
___
___

NOTE

Step 1	Survey
Key Words	
Signal Words	
Step 2	**Reading**
Purpose	
Pattern of Organization	
Tone	
Main Idea	
Step 3	**Summary**
지문 요약하기 (Paraphrasing)	
Step 4	**Recite**
	요약문 말로 설명하기

Answer Key

Evolution has come up with a big innovation. The mammalian hormone **oxytocin** evolved to **play a key role** in what makes mammals mammalian. Other newborn animals typically fend for themselves : Crocodiles, for example, are catching insects soon after birth. But mammals develop slowly, and mothers have to feed their newborns. **Oxytocin evolved** to make this possible, prompting mothers who are nursing to produce more milk as their babies demand it. **Evolving** the means to nurse the young was only half the battle. You also have to want to take care of them and to invest zillions of calories in generating milk and fending off predators. And you need to be able to **recognize** your offspring in a crowd, so you don't waste your energy helping others to leave behind copies of their genes. **Oxytocin** helped to solve both problems. But something truly striking occurred sometime in the past 50,000 years (which is to say, over the last 0.01% of the time during which oxytocin has existed). During that evolutionary blink of an eye, humans embarked on something new, with oxytocin again in a leading role : **the domestication of wolves**.

How did this occur? Scientists found that modern **dogs** and their owners secrete **oxytocin** when they **interact with** each other. Remarkably, dogs who gaze the most at their humans during interactions had the biggest oxytocin rise—as did their humans. The scientists then spritzed oxytocin (or saline, as a control treatment) up the dogs' noses. The oxytocin caused female dogs to gaze more at their humans whose own oxytocin levels rose as a result. All of this only affected dogs and their owners. Hand-reared wolves and their owners didn't react in the same way to the treatment, and dogs administered oxytocin didn't gaze any longer at humans who weren't familiar to them. In other words, dog and human brains seem to have evolved at lightning speed to co-opt oxytocin for **bonding** between our species. This sure helps to explain people who use baby talk with their dogs.

key words

모범답안

The main idea of the passage is that oxytocin has evolved to play an important role in mankind's preservation of offspring and bonding with dogs. Second, the problems addressed are : parents have to want to take care of their young and they need to be able to recognize their offspring.

채점기준

+ 2점: 이 글의 요지를 "oxytocin has evolved to play an important role in mankind's preservation of offspring and bonding with dogs."라 명확하게 서술하였다.
  ☞ 다음과 같이 서술하였을 경우에도 2점을 준다.
  - "oxytocin played an important role for mankind and ensuring the protection of the young and also bonding humans with dogs."
  - "the hormone oxytocin has evolved into playing an important role in mankind and in bringing humans and dogs together."
  ☞ 다음과 같이 서술하였을 경우엔 1.5점을 준다.
  - "The hormone oxytocin has evolved into playing a major role in bringing humans and dogs together."

+ 2점: 밑줄 친 both problems를 "parents have to want to take care of their young(1점) and they need to be able to recognize their offspring(1점)."이라 명확하게 서술하였다.

한글번역

진화는 큰 혁신을 만들어냈다. 포유류의 호르몬인 옥시토신은 진화해 포유류를 포유류답게 만들어주는 중요한 역할을 하게 됐다. 다른 동물들은 보통 태어나자마자 자기 스스로 살아갈 수 있다. 예를 들어 악어는 태어나자마자 곤충을 잡는다. 하지만 포유동물은 느리게 성장하며 어미들이 새끼들에게 먹이를 먹여야 한다. 옥시토신은 새끼들이 모유를 원할 때 어미들이 모유를 더 만들어낼 수 있도록 촉진함으로써 이것이 가능해지도록 진화했다. 새끼에게 젖을 먹일 수단을 진화시킨 것은 겨우 절반을 해낸 것일 뿐이다. 새끼들을 돌보며 모유를 생산하고 포식자들을 막기 위해 엄청난 칼로리를 투자해야 한다. 여러 개체 속에서 자기 새끼를 알아볼 수도 있어야 한다. 다른 개체들이 그들의 유전자를 남기도록 돕는 데 자신의 에너지를 낭비하지 않기 위해서다. 옥시토신은 두 문제를 모두 해결하는 데 기여한다. 하지만 정말 놀라운 것은 지난 5만 년 사이에 일어났다(옥시토신이 존재했던 기간 중 마지막 0.01%의 기간이다). 진화상으로는 눈 깜박할 사이인 이 기간에 인간은 다시 한번 옥시토신이 주된 역할을 하는 새로운 일을 시작했다. 바로 늑대를 길들인 것이다.

이 일이 어떻게 일어났을까? 학자들은 현대의 개와 그 주인이 상호작용을 할 때 옥시토신이 분비된다는 사실을 밝혀냈다. 놀라운 점은 상호작용 중 인간을 가장 많이 응시한 개들에서 옥시토신이 크게 증가했다는 것이다. 이는 인간도 마찬가지였다. 연구진은 개를 두 그룹으로 나눠 각각 코에 옥시토신과 식염수를 뿌렸다. 옥시토신을 뿌린 개들은 자신의 주인을 더 오래 응시했고 그 결과 옥시토신 수치가 올라갔다. 이 모든 것은 개와 그 개의 주인에게만 영향을 미쳤다. 사람이 기른 늑대들과 그 주인들은 이 실험에 같은 방식으로 반응하지 않았으며, 옥시토신을 뿌린 개들은 낯선 사람은 더 오래 응시하지 않았다. 즉, 개와 인간의 뇌는 두 종 사이의 유대감을 위해 옥시토신을 이용하도록 매우 빠르게 진화한 듯 보인다. 이는 몇몇 사람들이 왜 자신의 개에게 마치 아기를 대할 때처럼 유아어를 사용하는지 설명해준다.

NOTE

Step 1	Survey
Key Words	Evolution; oxytocin; offspring; mammals; dogs; bonding
Signal Words	For example; How did this occur?
Step 2	**Reading**
Purpose	To show how oxytocin came to benefit humankind and bonding with dogs
Pattern of Organization	Series; cause/effect
Tone	Not clear
Main Idea	Oxytocin has evolved to play an important role in mankind's preservation of offspring and bonding with dogs.
Step 3	**Summary**
지문 요약하기 (Paraphrasing)	Oxytocin has evolved to play an important role in mankind's preservation of offspring and bonding with dogs. Through it, parents want strongly to invest time raising and protect their children. Likewise, it came to serve human bonding with dogs as its levels rise in dogs when looking at their owners and vice versa.
Step 4	**Recite**
	요약문 말로 설명하기

59 Read the passage and follow the directions.

After more than forty years of running on parallel tracks, the information and life sciences are beginning to fuse into a single powerful technological and economic force that is laying the foundation for the Biotech Century. The computer is increasingly being used to decipher, manage and organize the vast genetic information that is the raw resource of the new global economy. Already, transnational corporations are creating giant life-science complexes from which to fashion a(n) _____ world.

Food and fiber will likely be grown indoors in giant bacteria baths, partially eliminating the farmer and the soil for the first time in history. Animal and human cloning could be commonplace, with "replication" increasingly replacing "reproduction." Millions of people could obtain a detailed genetic readout of themselves, allowing them to gaze into their own biological future and predict and plan their lives in ways never before possible. Parents may choose to have their children conceived in test-tubes and gestated in artificial wombs outside the human body. Genetic changes could be made in human fetuses to correct deadly diseases and disorders and enhance mood, behavior, intelligence and physical traits.

The Biotech Century promises a cornucopia of genetically engineered plants and animals to feed a hungry world, genetically derived sources of energy and fiber to propel commerce and build a "renewable" society, wonder drugs and genetic therapies to produce healthier babies, eliminate human suffering, and extend the human life span. But, with every step we take into this "Brave New World," the nagging question, "At what cost?" will haunt us. Will the artificial creation of cloned, chimeric, and transgenic animals mean the end of nature and the substitution of a bio-industrial world? Will the mass release of thousands of generically engineered life forms into the environment cause catastrophic genetic pollution and irreversible damage to the biosphere? What are the consequences—for both the global economy and society—of reducing the world's gene pool to patented intellectual property controlled exclusively by a handful of life-science corporations? What will it mean to live in a world where babies are genetically engineered and customized in the womb, and where people are increasingly identified, stereotyped, and discriminated against on the basis of their genotype? What are the risks we take in attempting to design more "perfect" human beings?

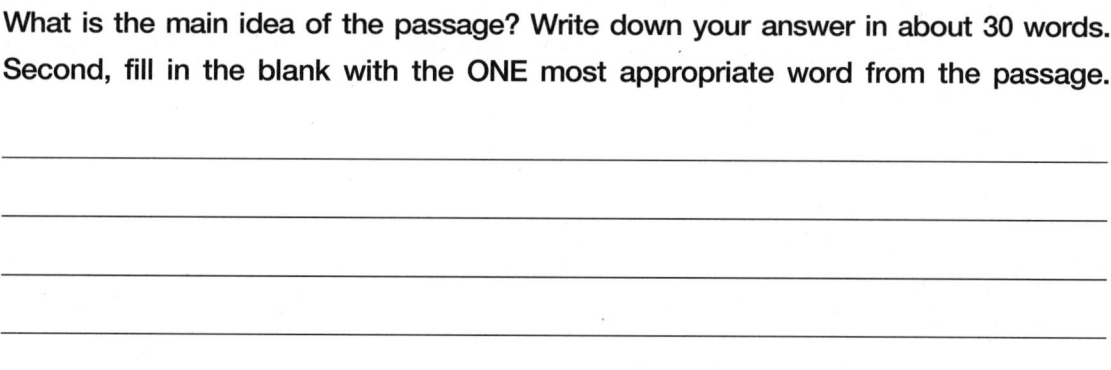

What is the main idea of the passage? Write down your answer in about 30 words. Second, fill in the blank with the ONE most appropriate word from the passage.

NOTE

Step 1	**S**urvey
Key Words	
Signal Words	
Step 2	**R**eading
Purpose	
Pattern of Organization	
Tone	
Main Idea	
Step 3	**S**ummary
지문 요약하기 (Paraphrasing)	
Step 4	**R**ecite
	요약문 말로 설명하기

Answer Key

After more than forty years of running on parallel tracks, the **information** and **life sciences** are beginning to fuse into a single powerful technological and economic force that is laying the foundation for **the Biotech Century**. The computer is increasingly being used to decipher, manage and organize the vast genetic information that is the raw resource of the new global economy. Already, transnational corporations are creating giant **life-science complexes** from which to fashion a **bio-industrial world**.

Food and fiber will likely be grown indoors in giant bacteria baths, partially eliminating the farmer and the soil for the first time in history. Animal and human cloning could be commonplace, with "replication" increasingly replacing "reproduction." Millions of people could obtain a detailed genetic readout of themselves, allowing them to gaze into their own biological future and predict and plan their lives in ways never before possible. Parents may choose to have their children conceived in test-tubes and gestated in artificial wombs outside the human body. Genetic changes could be made in human fetuses to correct deadly diseases and disorders and enhance mood, behavior, intelligence and physical traits.

The Biotech Century promises a cornucopia of **genetically engineered plants and animals** to feed a hungry world, genetically derived sources of energy and fiber to propel commerce and build a "renewable" society, wonder drugs and genetic therapies to produce healthier babies, eliminate human suffering, and extend the human life span. But, with every step we take into this "Brave New World," the nagging question, "**At what cost?**" will haunt us. Will the artificial creation of cloned, chimeric, and transgenic animals mean the end of nature and the substitution of a bio-industrial world? Will the mass release of thousands of generically engineered life forms into the environment cause catastrophic genetic pollution and irreversible damage to the biosphere? What are **the consequences**—for both the global economy and society—of reducing the world's gene pool to patented intellectual property controlled exclusively by a handful of **life-science corporations**? What will it mean to live in a world where babies are genetically engineered and customized in the womb, and where people are increasingly identified, stereotyped, and discriminated against on the basis of their genotype? What are the **risks** we take in attempting to design more "perfect" human beings?

모범답안

The main idea is that though our way of life is likely to be fundamentally transformed in the near future thanks to biotechnology, it raises many ethical questions. Second, the word for the blank is "bio-industrial".

채점기준

+ 2점: 이 글의 요지를 "because of biotechnology (supported by the fusion of the information and life sciences), <u>our way of life is likely to be fundamentally transformed in the near future</u>. However, it raises many ethical questions about its negative side-effects."라 서술하였거나 유사하였다.
  ☞ 내용은 모범답안과 유사하지만 "the biotechnology가 원인"이라는 표현이 빠져있으면 1점만 준다.
  ☞ 내용은 모범답안과 유사하지만 "생명과학이 야기할 윤리적인 문제"에 대한 서술이 없으면 1점만 준다.
+ 2점: 빈칸에 들어갈 한 단어를 "bio-industrial"이라 정확하게 기입하였다.

한글번역

지난 40여 년 동안 평행선을 달리던 정보와 생명과학이 생명공학 시대에 토대가 되는 하나의 강력한 기술적이고 경제적인 힘으로 융합되기 시작했다. 컴퓨터는 새로운 세계화 경제의 원자재인 거대한 유전 정보를 해독하고, 관리하고 조직하는 데 사용되기 시작했다. 이미 초국적 기업들은 거대한 생명과학 복합체를 만들어내고 있는데, 이것들로부터 바이오산업이 나오고 있다.

인류 역사에서 처음으로 음식과 섬유가 실내에 있는 거대한 박테리아 용기 안에서 자랄 것 같은데, 이런 것들은 앞으로 농부와 땅을 없애버릴 가능성이 높다. 동물이나 인간 복제는 '재생산'을 대신하면서 점점 더 증가하는 '복제'로 인해 흔한 일이 될 수 있다. 수백만의 사람들은 그들 자신에 대한 자세한 유전자 해독을 획득할 수 있다. 이 유전자 해독은 전에는 가능하지 않았던 그들의 생물학적인 미래를 바라보고 예측하고 그들의 삶을 여러 방법으로 계획하도록 허락한다. 부모들은 임신하기 위해 테스트 튜브에서 그들의 아이들을 선택할 수도 있고 인간의 몸 밖에 있는 인공적인 자궁 안에 잉태할지도 모른다. 유전적 변화가 인간의 태아 내에서 행해질 수 있는데, 치명적인 병과 장애를 바로잡기 위해서이기도 하고, 또한 기분, 행동, 지능, 그리고 신체적 특징을 향상시키기 위해서이기도 하다.

생명공학 세기는 이 세상의 가난한 사람들을 먹이기 위해 유전적으로 조작된 식물과 동물의 풍요, 상업을 촉진하고 유전적으로 재생 가능 사회를 만들기 위해 에너지와 섬유의 유전적 정보의 풍요, 또한 더 건강한 아이를 생산하고, 인간의 고통을 덜어주고, 인간의 수명을 확장하려는 경이로운 약과 유전적 치료의 풍요를 약속한다. 하지만 우리가 이 '멋진 신세계'로 들어가는 매 발걸음에는 아주 끈질기고 어려운 질문, 즉, "거기에 어떠한 대가가 따르는가?"라는 질문이 우리를 귀신처럼 따라다닐 것이다. 복제된, 공상적인, 그리고 유전자 변형의 동물의 인공적인 생산은 자연의 종말과 생명공학 산업의 세상이 (자연을) 대체하는 것을 의미하는 것인가? 유전적으로 조작된 수많은 생명체들이 환경 속으로 엄청나게 방출되는 것이 재앙적인 유전적 오염과 생물권에 피할 수 없는 피해를 야기할 것인가? 한 줌 밖에 안 되는 생명과학 회사에 의해 독점적으로 통제되는 특허 받은 지적 재산에 세계의 유전자 공급원을 주는 것이 세계 경제와 사회에 어떠한 결과를 미칠까? 아기들이 자궁 안에서 유전적으로 조작되고 주문 제작되는 세상에서, 그리고 사람들이 점점 더 자신의 유전자형에 기초해 신원이 확인되고, 정형화되며, 차별되는 세상에서 산다는 것은 무엇을 의미하게 될까? 우리가 더욱 '완벽한' 인간을 설계하려 시도할 때 닥치게 되는 위험은 무엇일까?

NOTE

Step 1	Survey
Key Words	Biotechnology; bio-industrial world; cost
Signal Words	None
Step 2	Reading
Purpose	To point out the possible effects of biotechnology and raise questions about it
Pattern of Organization	Series
Tone	Concerned; cautious
Main Idea	Though our way of life is likely to be fundamentally transformed in the near future thanks to biotechnology, it raises many ethical questions.
Step 3	Summary
지문 요약하기 (Paraphrasing)	Though our way of life is likely to be fundamentally transformed in the near future thanks to biotechnology, it raises many ethical questions. The growing influence of biotechnology will change food and individuals a great deal and have unforeseeable consequences on the planet. It was only recently that biotechnology came into play with computers and corporate support. This will create new ways of growing food and having children. Likewise, there will be changes across many other fields such as energy and medicine. As all these innovations are unleashed, it is difficult to say what the ultimate effect on the world will be.
Step 4	Recite

요약문 말로 설명하기

60 Read the passage and follow the directions.

We go see a horror movie to reestablish our feelings of essential normality; the horror movie is innately conventional. It urges us to put away our more civilized and adult penchant for analysis and to become children again, seeing things in pure blacks and whites. And we go to have fun. This is where the ground starts to slope away, because this is a very peculiar sort of fun. The fun comes from seeing others menaced—sometimes killed. A critic has suggested that the horror film has become the modern version of the public ①_____. The potential lyncher is in almost all of us, and every now and then, he has to be let loose. Our emotions and our fears form their own body, and we recognize that it demands its own exercise to maintain proper muscle tone. Certain of these emotional muscles are accepted, even exalted, in civilized society. Love, friendship, loyalty, kindness—these are the emotions that we applaud. When we exhibit these emotions, society showers us with positive reinforcement. But anticivilization emotions don't go away, and they demand periodic exercise. The horror movie has a dirty job to do. It deliberately appeals to all that is worst in us. It is morbidity unchained, our most abject instincts set free, our nastiest fantasies realized. The most aggressive of horror films lifts a trapdoor in the civilized forebrain and throws a basket of raw meat to the hungry alligators swimming around in that subterranean river beneath. It keeps them from getting out. It keeps ② them down there and me up here.

MEMO

Fill in the blank ① with the ONE most appropriate word from the passage. If necessary, change the word form. Second, identify what the underlined "② them" refers to.

NOTE

Step 1	**S**urvey
Key Words	
Signal Words	
Step 2	**R**eading
Purpose	
Pattern of Organization	
Tone	
Main Idea	
Step 3	**S**ummary
지문 요약하기 (Paraphrasing)	
Step 4	**R**ecite
	요약문 말로 설명하기

Answer Key

We go see a **horror movie to reestablish** our feelings of essential **normality**; **the horror movie** is innately **conventional**. It urges us to put away our more civilized and adult penchant for analysis and to become children again, seeing things in pure blacks and whites. And we go to have fun. This is where the ground starts to slope away, because this is a very peculiar sort of fun. The fun comes from seeing others menaced—sometimes killed. A critic has suggested that **the horror film** has become the modern version of the public lynching. The potential lyncher is in almost all of us, and every now and then, he has to be let loose. Our emotions and our fears form their own body, and we recognize that it demands its own exercise to maintain proper muscle tone. Certain of these emotional muscles are accepted, even exalted, in civilized society. Love, friendship, loyalty, kindness—these are the emotions that we applaud. When we exhibit these emotions, society showers us with positive reinforcement. But **anticivilization emotions** don't go away, and they demand periodic exercise. **The horror movie** has a dirty job to do. It deliberately appeals to all that is worst in us. It is morbidity unchained, our most abject instincts set free, our nastiest fantasies realized. The most aggressive of **horror films** lifts a trapdoor in the civilized forebrain and throws a basket of raw meat to **the hungry alligators** swimming around in that subterranean river beneath. It keeps them from getting out. It keeps them down there and me up here.

key words

모범답안

The word for the blank is "lynching". Second, the underlined word refers to the hungry alligators.

채점기준

- 4점: 모범답안과 같거나 유사하였다.
- 2점: 둘 중 하나만 맞았다.
- 0점: 모범답안과 다르다.

한글번역

　본질적으로 우리가 정상적인 존재라는 감정을 재확립하기 위해 공포영화를 보러 간다. 공포영화는 태생적으로 과거 지향적이다. 공포영화는 우리가 보다 문명화되고 성숙한 분석으로의 경향을 벗어 던지고 다시 어린이가 되도록, 그리고 사물들을 단지 순수한 흑과 백으로 보도록 요구한다. 우리는 재미 삼아 공포영화를 보러 간다. 공포영화는 땅이 경사지면서 미끄러지는 지점이다. 왜냐하면 공포영화는 아주 특이한 형태의 재미이기 때문이다. 공포영화의 재미는 다른 사람들이 위협을 당하거나 때로는 죽임을 당하는 모습을 볼 때 온다. 한 비평가는 공포영화가 현대화된 공개적인 린치가 됐다고 주장했다. 우리 모두 내면에는 잠재적인 폭력 가해자가 존재한다. 그리고 가끔가다 우리는 이러한 잠재적인 폭력 가해자의 본성을 구속에서 풀어줘야만 한다. 우리의 감정과 두려움은 잠재적인 폭력 가해자의 본체를 형성하게 된다. 우리 안의 잠재적인 폭력 가해자가 적절한 근육 상태를 유지하기 위해 스스로 활동하고자 한다는 것을 우리는 인식한다. 이러한 감정적인 근육의 일부는 문명화된 사회에서 수용된다. 심지어 칭송받기도 한다. 사랑, 우정, 충성, 친절과 같은 것들은 우리가 박수를 보내는 감정들이다. 우리가 이러한 감정을 밖으로 내보일 때, 사회는 긍정적인 강화(= 칭찬)를 퍼붓는다. 하지만 반문화적인 감정은 사라지지 않으며, 이것은 정기적으로 자기 모습을 드러내기를 요구하고 있다. 공포영화는 수행해야 할 더러운 일이 있다. 공포영화는 의도적으로 우리 안에 있는 가장 나쁜 것에 다가온다. 공포영화는 사슬에서 풀린 병적 상태이며, 풀려난 가장 비천한 본능이며, 실현된 가장 고약한 환상이다. 가장 폭력적인 공포영화는 문명화된 전뇌(前腦) 속에 있는 함정문을 들어 올린 후 날고기로 가득 찬 바구니를 지하 깊숙한 강에서 헤엄치고 있는 배고픈 악어들에게 던져준다. 공포영화는 이 배고픈 악어들이 밖으로 나오지 못하도록 억제해준다. 공포영화는 그 악어들을 낮은 그곳에 계속 머물게 하며 나를 여기 위에 있게 해준다.

NOTE

Step 1	**S**urvey
Key Words	Horror film; conventional; anticivilization emotions
Signal Words	Not clear
Step 2	**R**eading
Purpose	To explain how horror films exercise an important outlet in the watchers' psyches
Pattern of Organization	Cause/effect
Tone	Analytical
Main Idea	Horror films are popular because of their use in providing an important release for darker instincts and fantasies, which aren't welcomed in a healthy society.
Step 3	**S**ummary
지문 요약하기 (Paraphrasing)	Horror movies attract audiences by providing a safe outlet for the dark impulses that civilized society typically rejects. While positive emotions like love and kindness are celebrated in daily life, these films allow viewers to temporarily indulge their suppressed antisocial instincts by watching others being threatened or harmed, effectively containing these primitive urges within the realm of entertainment.
Step 4	**R**ecite
	요약문 말로 설명하기

MEMO

2S2R

유희태 일반영어
① 기본

PART 03
2S2R 심화

PART 03 2S2R 심화

01 Read the passage and follow the directions.

There is actually considerable support for this idea that there is a common personality to hard-core smokers. Serious smokers can be separated from nonsmokers along very simple personality lines.

In countless studies the picture of the smoking "type" has been filled out. Heavy smokers have been shown to have a much greater sex drive than nonsmokers. They are more sexually precocious; they have a greater "need" for sex, and greater attraction to the opposite sex. At age nineteen, for example, 15 percent of nonsmoking white women attending college have had sex. The same number for white female college students who do smoke is 55 percent. The statistics for men are about the same. They rank much higher on what psychologists call "anti-social" indexes: they tend to have greater levels of misconduct, and be more rebellious and defiant. They make snap judgments. This characteristic shows itself in the taking of more risks. Interestingly, smokers also seem to be more honest about themselves than nonsmokers. As David Krogh describes it in his treatise *Smoking: The Artificial Passion*, psychologists have what they call "lie" tests in which they insert inarguable statements—"I do not always tell the truth" or "I am sometimes cold to my spouse"—and if test-takers consistently deny these statements, it is taken as evidence that they are not generally truthful. Smokers are much more truthful on these tests. One theory has it that their lack of deference and their surfeit of defiance combine to make them relatively indifferent to what people think of them.

These measures don't apply to all smokers, of course. But as general predictors of smoking behavior they are quite accurate, and the more someone smokes, the higher the likelihood that he or she fits this profile.

Write a summary following the guidelines below.

┤ Guidelines ├
- Summarize the above passage in ONE paragraph.
- Provide a topic sentence, supporting ideas, and a concluding sentence based on the passage.
- Do NOT copy more than FIVE consecutive words from the passage.

NOTE

Step 1	**S**urvey
Key Words	
Signal Words	
Step 2	**R**eading
Purpose	
Pattern of Organization	
Tone	
Main Idea	
Step 3	**S**ummary
지문 요약하기 (Paraphrasing)	
Step 4	**R**ecite
	요약문 말로 설명하기

Answer Key

There is actually considerable support for this idea that there is a common **personality** to **hard-core smokers**. **Serious smokers** can be separated from **nonsmokers** along very simple **personality lines**.

In countless studies the picture of the smoking "type" has been filled out. **Heavy smokers** have been shown to have a much greater sex drive than **nonsmokers**. They are more sexually precocious; they have a greater "need" for sex, and greater attraction to the opposite sex. At age nineteen, for example, 15 percent of **nonsmoking** white women attending college have had sex. The same number for white female college students who **do smoke** is 55 percent. The statistics for men are about the same. They rank much higher on what psychologists call "anti-social" indexes: they tend to have greater levels of misconduct, and be more rebellious and defiant. They make snap judgments. This characteristic shows itself in the taking of more risks. Interestingly, **smokers** also seem to be more honest about themselves than **nonsmokers**. As David Krogh describes it in his treatise *Smoking: The Artificial Passion*, psychologists have what they call "lie" tests in which they insert inarguable statements—"I do not always tell the truth" or "I am sometimes cold to my spouse"—and if test-takers consistently deny these statements, it is taken as evidence that they are not generally truthful. **Smokers** are much more truthful on these tests. One theory has it that their lack of deference and their surfeit of defiance combine to make them relatively indifferent to what people think of them.

These measures don't apply to all smokers, of course. But as general predictors of smoking behavior they are quite accurate, and the more someone smokes, the higher the likelihood that he or she fits this profile.

key words

contrast

모범답안

In hard-core smokers there is a common personality different from non-smokers. Among heavier smokers, studies have found they enjoy an increased level of sex drive, present "anti-social" behavior, make snap judgements and take more risks, and also have a tendency to tell the truth more than those who smoke less. While this does not apply to all smokers, the more one smokes, the more they match this personality.

채점기준

+1점: 글의 topic sentence를 다음과 같이 서술하였거나 유사하였다.
"In hard-core smokers there is a common personality(0.5점) different from non-smokers(0.5점)."
☞ 다음과 같이 서술하였어도 1점을 준다.
- "There are differences in personality traits between heavy smokers and nonsmokers."
- "There are different personality traits between hard-core smokers and non-smokers."
- "Hard-core smokers, as compared with non-smokers, have a different personality."

+2점: 글의 major supporting details를 다음과 같이 서술하였거나 유사하였다.
"they enjoy an increased level of sex drive, present "anti-social" behavior, make snap judgements, and also have a tendency to tell the truth more than those who smoke less."
☞ 4개 중 4개 모두를 정확하게 요약한 경우 2점, 3개만 요약한 경우 1점, 2개만 요약한 경우 0.5점, 1개 또는 요약하지 못한 경우 0점을 준다.

+1점: 글의 결론을 "While(Though) this does not apply to all smokers(0.5점), the more one smokes, the more they match this personality(0.5점)."이라 서술하였거나 유사하였다.

● 감점 • 본문에 나오는 연속되는 6단어 이상을 사용하였다. -0.5pt
 • 문단을 두 개나 그 이상으로 구성하였다. -0.5pt
 • grammar나 영어표현이 합쳐 3개 이상 오류가 있다. -0.5pt

한글번역

중독성 흡연자들에게 공통적인 성격이 있다는 생각을 뒷받침하는 상당한 증거가 실제로 있다. 심각한 흡연자들은 매우 단순한 성격 기준에 따라 비흡연자들과 구분될 수 있다.

수많은 연구에서 흡연 '유형'의 모습이 구체화됐다. 중독성 흡연자들은 비흡연자들보다 훨씬 더 큰 성적 욕구를 가지고 있는 것으로 나타났다. 그들은 성적으로 더 조숙하다. 그들은 성에 대한 더 큰 '욕구'를 가지고 있으며, 이성에 대한 더 큰 매력을 느낀다. 예를 들어, 19세에 대학에 다니는 비흡연 백인 여성의 15%가 성 경험을 가지고 있다. 흡연하는 백인 여대생의 경우 이 수치는 55%이다. 남성의 통계도 거의 같다. 그들은 심리학자들이 '반사회적' 지수라고 부르는 것에서 훨씬 높은 점수를 받는다: 그들은 더 높은 수준의 부정행위를 하는 경향이 있고, 더 반항적이고 도전적이다. 그들은 성급한 판단을 한다. 이 특성은 더 많은 위험을 감수하는 것으로 나타난다. 흥미롭게도, 흡연자들은 또한 비흡연자들보다 자신에 대해 더 정직한 것 같다. 데이비드 크로그가 그의 논문《흡연: 인위적인 열정》에서 설명하듯이, 심리학자들은 그들이 '거짓말' 검사라고 부르는 것을 가지고 있는데, 여기서 그들은 반박할 수 없는 진술들—"나는 항상 진실을 말하지는 않는다" 또는 "나는 때때로 배우자에게 차갑다"—을 삽입하고, 만약 검사 응시자들이 지속적으로 이러한 진술들을 부인한다면, 이것은 그들이 일반적으로 진실하지 않다는 증거로 받아들여진다. 흡연자들은 이러한 검사에서 훨씬 더 진실하다. 한 이론에 따르면 그들의 복종 부족과 그들의 과도한 반항심이 결합돼 사람들이 그들을 어떻게 생각하는지에 대해 상대적으로 무관심하게 만든다는 것이다.

물론 이러한 측정들이 모든 흡연자들에게 적용되는 것은 아니다. 하지만 흡연 행동의 일반적인 예측 요인으로서 그것들은 꽤 정확하며, 누군가가 더 많이 흡연할수록, 그 사람이 이러한 특성에 맞을 가능성이 더 높다.

NOTE

Step 1	Survey
Key Words	Heavy smokers; nonsmokers; personality
Signal Words	Separated from
Step 2	Reading
Purpose	To inform about personality differences between smokers and nonsmokers
Pattern of Organization	Comparison/contrast; series
Tone	Objective; analytical
Main Idea	Heavy smokers have distinct personality traits compared to nonsmokers.
Step 3	Summary
지문 요약하기 (Paraphrasing)	In hard-core smokers there is a common personality different from non-smokers. Among heavier smokers, studies have found they enjoy an increased level of sex drive, present "anti-social" behavior, make snap judgements and take more risks, and also have a tendency to tell the truth more than those who smoke less. While this does not apply to all smokers, the more one smokes, the more they match this personality.
Step 4	Recite

요약문 말로 설명하기

02 Read the passage and follow the directions.

Schools were founded to produce skillful and obedient citizens who would serve the nation loyally. At eighteen, youths needed to be not only patriotic but also literate, so that they could read the brigadier's order of the day and draw up tomorrow's battle plans. They had to know mathematics in order to calculate the shell's trajectory or crack the enemy's secret code. They needed a reasonable command of electronics, mechanics and medicine, in order to operate wireless sets, drive tanks and take care of wounded comrades. When they left the army they were expected to serve the nation as clerks, teachers and engineers, building a modern economy and paying lots of taxes. The same went for the health system. At the end of the nineteenth century countries such as France, Germany and Japan began providing free health care for the masses. They financed vaccinations for infants, balanced diets for children and physical education for teenagers. They drained festering swamps, exterminated mosquitoes and built centralised sewage systems. The aim wasn't to make people happy, but to make the nation stronger. The country needed sturdy soldiers and workers, healthy women who would give birth to more soldiers and workers, and bureaucrats who came to the office punctually at 8 a.m. instead of lying sick at home. Even the welfare system was originally planned in the interest of the nation rather than of needy individuals. When Otto von Bismarck pioneered state pensions and social security in late nineteenth-century Germany, his chief aim was to ensure the loyalty of the citizens rather than to increase their well-being. You fought for your country when you were eighteen, and paid your taxes when you were forty, because you counted on the state to take care of you when you were seventy.

Write a summary following the guidelines below.

--- Guidelines ---
- Summarize the passage in FOUR lines.
- When you summarize, include all examples the writer of the passage employs to prove her/his main point.
- Do NOT copy more than FIVE consecutive words from the passage.

NOTE

Step 1	**S**urvey
Key Words	
Signal Words	
Step 2	**R**eading
Purpose	
Pattern of Organization	
Tone	
Main Idea	
Step 3	**S**ummary
지문 요약하기 (Paraphrasing)	
Step 4	**R**ecite
	요약문 말로 설명하기

Answer Key

> **Schools** were founded to produce skillful and obedient citizens who would serve **the nation loyally**. At eighteen, youths needed to be not only patriotic but also literate, so that they could read the brigadier's order of the day and draw up tomorrow's battle plans. They had to know mathematics in order to calculate the shell's trajectory or crack the enemy's secret code. They needed a reasonable command of electronics, mechanics and medicine, in order to operate wireless sets, drive tanks and take care of wounded comrades. When they left the army they were expected to serve the nation as clerks, teachers and engineers, building a modern economy and paying lots of taxes. The same went for **the health system**. At the end of the nineteenth century countries such as France, Germany and Japan began providing free health care for the masses. They financed vaccinations for infants, balanced diets for children and physical education for teenagers. They drained festering swamps, exterminated mosquitoes and built centralised sewage systems. The aim wasn't to make people happy, but to make the nation stronger. The country needed sturdy soldiers and workers, healthy women who would give birth to more soldiers and workers, and bureaucrats who came to the office punctually at 8 a.m. instead of lying sick at home. Even **the welfare system** was originally planned in the interest of the nation rather than of needy individuals. When Otto von Bismarck pioneered state pensions and social security in late nineteenth-century Germany, **his chief aim** was to ensure **the loyalty of the citizens** rather than to increase **their well-being**. You fought for your country when you were eighteen, and paid your taxes when you were forty, because you counted on the state to take care of you when you were seventy.

[모범답안]

Important national programs of education, health and welfare were aimed to strengthen the nation rather than ensure individual well-being. First, schools were established to provide the nation with obedient and talented soldiers who would later go on to serve in careers and pay taxes. Likewise, the health system was proposed lead strong and numerous citizens to work and fight in wars. Third, the welfare system's chief goal was not to boost the citizens' happiness, but to ensure their loyalty to the nation by ensuring they were taken care of in old age after fighting and paying taxes to the nation through life.

채점기준

+ 2점: 글의 topic sentence를 다음과 같이 서술하였거나 유사하였다.
"National programs(systems) of education, health and welfare were aimed to strengthen the nation rather than ensure individual well-being."

+ 2점: 글의 summary를 다음과 같이 서술하였거나 유사하였다.
"schools were established to provide the nation with obedient and talented soldiers who would later go on to serve in careers and pay taxes. Likewise, the health system was proposed to lead strong and numerous citizens to work and fight in wars. Third, the welfare system's chief goal was not to boost the citizens' happiness, but to ensure their loyalty to the nation."

☞ 3개 중 3개 모두를 정확하게 요약한 경우 2점, 2개만 요약한 경우 1점, 1개 또는 요약하지 못한 경우 0점을 준다.

● **감점**
 • 글의 전체 양이 너무 적은 경우(3줄 이하) −1pt
 • 글의 전체 양이 너무 많은 경우(5줄 이상) −1pt
 • 본문에 나오는 연속되는 6단어 이상을 사용하였다. −0.5pt

한글번역

학교들은 국가에 충성스럽게 봉사할 숙련되고 순종적인 시민들을 양성하기 위해 설립됐다. 18세가 되면, 청년들은 애국적일 뿐만 아니라 문해력도 갖춰야 했다. 그래야 여단장의 일일 명령을 읽고 내일의 전투 계획을 세울 수 있었다. 그들은 포탄의 궤도를 계산하거나 적의 암호를 해독하기 위해 수학을 알아야 했다. 그들은 무선 장비를 조작하고, 탱크를 운전하고, 부상 당한 동료들을 돌보기 위해 전자공학, 기계학, 의학에 대한 합리적인 지식이 필요했다. 군대를 떠날 때 그들은 사무원, 교사, 기술자로서 국가에 봉사하며, 현대 경제를 건설하고 많은 세금을 내는 것이 기대됐다. 보건 시스템도 마찬가지였다. 19세기 말에 프랑스, 독일, 일본 같은 국가들은 대중을 위한 무료 건강관리를 제공하기 시작했다. 그들은 유아 백신접종, 아동을 위한 균형 잡힌 식단, 청소년을 위한 체육교육에 자금을 지원했다. 그들은 고인 늪을 배수하고, 모기를 박멸하고, 중앙집중식 하수 시스템을 건설했다. 목적은 사람들을 행복하게 만드는 것이 아니라 국가를 더 강하게 만드는 것이었다. 국가는 튼튼한 군인과 노동자, 더 많은 군인과 노동자를 낳아줄 건강한 여성들, 그리고 집에서 아파 누워있는 대신 오전 8시에 시간에 맞춰 사무실로 출근하는 관료들이 필요했다. 복지 시스템조차도 원래 도움이 필요한 개인들보다는 국가의 이익을 위해 계획됐다. 비스마르크가 19세기 후반 독일에서 국가 연금과 사회보장을 개척했을 때, 그의 주된 목적은 시민들의 복지를 증진하기보다는 그들의 충성심을 확보하는 것이었다. 당신은 18세에 조국을 위해 싸웠고, 40세에 세금을 냈다. 왜냐하면 70세가 됐을 때 국가가 당신을 돌봐줄 것이라고 기대했기 때문이다.

NOTE

Step 1	**S**urvey
Key Words	Education; health and welfare
Signal Words	Not clear
Step 2	**R**eading
Purpose	To explain how modern national institutions(education, health, welfare) were designed to strengthen the state rather than promote individual happiness
Pattern of Organization	Cause/effect; series
Tone	Objective
Main Idea	Modern nations developed education, health, and welfare systems primarily to strengthen state power rather than individual welfare.
Step 3	**S**ummary
지문 요약하기 (Paraphrasing)	Important national programs of education, health and welfare were aimed to strengthen the nation rather than ensure individual well-being. First, schools were established to provide the nation with obedient and talented soldiers who would later go on to serve in careers and pay taxes. Likewise, the health system was proposed to lead strong and numerous citizens to work and fight in wars. Third, the welfare system's chief goal was not to boost the citizens' happiness, but to ensure their loyalty to the nation.
Step 4	**R**ecite

요약문 말로 설명하기

03   Read the passage and follow the directions.

The only thing worse than being lied to is not knowing you're being lied to. It's true that plastic pollution is a huge problem, of planetary proportions. And it's true we could all do more to reduce our plastic footprint. The lie is that blame for the plastic problem is wasteful consumers and that changing our individual habits will fix it. Recycling plastic is to saving the Earth what hammering a nail is to halting a falling skyscraper. That is to say, punishing individual litterers with hefty fines or jail time, while imposing almost no responsibility on plastic manufacturers for the numerous environmental, economic and health hazards imposed by their products is misdirected.

So what can we do to make responsible use of plastic a reality? Reject the lie. Litterbugs are not responsible for the global ecological disaster of plastic. Humans can only function to the best of their abilities, given time, mental bandwidth and systemic constraints. Our huge problem with plastic is the result of a permissive legal framework that has allowed the uncontrolled rise of plastic pollution, despite clear evidence of the harm it causes to local communities and the world's oceans. Recycling is also too hard in most parts of the U.S. and lacks the proper incentives to make it work well.

Talk about our plastic problem loudly and often. Call your local and federal representatives to support bottle bills, plastic bag taxes and increased producer responsibility for reuse and recycling. Stand up against preemptive bans on local plastic regulation. There are signs that corporations are listening to consumer opinions, too. After numerous petitions from customers and environmental organizations, McDonalds has pledged to use only sustainable packaging materials by 2025 and to phase out styrofoam by the year's end.

A better alternative is the circular economy model, where waste is minimized by planning in advance how materials can be reused and recycled at a product's end of life rather than trying to figure that out after the fact.

Write a summary following the guidelines below.

⌐ Guidelines ⌐

- Summarize the above passage in ONE paragraph.
- Provide a topic sentence, supporting ideas, and a concluding sentence based on the passage.
- Do NOT copy more than FIVE consecutive words from the passage.

NOTE

Step 1	**S**urvey
Key Words	
Signal Words	
Step 2	**R**eading
Purpose	
Pattern of Organization	
Tone	
Main Idea	
Step 3	**S**ummary
지문 요약하기 (Paraphrasing)	
Step 4	**R**ecite

요약문 말로 설명하기

Answer Key

The only thing worse than being lied to is not knowing you're being lied to. It's true that **plastic pollution** is a huge problem, of planetary proportions. And it's true we could all do more to reduce our plastic footprint. The lie is that blame for the plastic problem is wasteful **consumers** and that changing our individual habits will fix it. **Recycling plastic** is to saving the Earth what hammering a nail is to halting a falling skyscraper. That is to say, punishing individual litterers with hefty fines or jail time, while imposing almost no **responsibility** on plastic manufacturers for the numerous environmental, economic and health hazards imposed by their products is misdirected.

So what can we do to make **responsible** use of **plastic** a reality? Reject the lie. Litterbugs are not responsible for the global ecological disaster of plastic. Humans can only function to the best of their abilities, given time, mental bandwidth and systemic constraints. Our huge problem with plastic is the result of a permissive legal framework that has allowed the uncontrolled rise of **plastic pollution**, despite clear evidence of the harm it causes to local communities and the world's oceans. Recycling is also too hard in most parts of the U.S. and lacks the proper incentives to make it work well.

Talk about our **plastic problem** loudly and often. Call your local and federal representatives to support bottle bills, plastic bag taxes and increased producer responsibility for reuse and recycling. Stand up against preemptive bans on local plastic regulation. There are signs that corporations are listening to consumer opinions, too. After numerous petitions from customers and environmental organizations, McDonalds has pledged to use only sustainable packaging materials by 2025 and to phase out styrofoam by the year's end.

A better alternative is the **circular economy model**, where waste is minimized by planning in advance how materials can be reused and recycled at a product's end of life rather than trying to figure that out after the fact.

모범답안

More recycling will not solve plastic pollution, so larger measures need to be taken. As opposed to the conventional thinking that the plastic problem is due to wasteful consumers, a large problem is with the legal framework along with a lack of resources and incentives across the United States. To fix this, we need to talk more about the issues in terms of local regulation and to petition corporations. In conclusion, the better outlook for solving plastic pollution is the circular economy model, which plans in advance for handling waste instead of afterwards.

> **채점기준**

+1점: 글의 topic sentence를 다음과 같이 서술하였거나 유사하였다.
"More recycling will not solve plastic pollution, so larger measures need to be taken."
☞ 다음과 같이 서술하였어도 1점을 준다.
- "Recycling is not enough to save the earth, so larger measures need to be taken."
- "Changing our individual habits such as more recycling cannot fix the environmental problem fix, more active measures need to be taken."
- "Wasteful consumers does not cause the environmental problem and changing our individual habits cannot fix it, more active measures need to be taken."

+2점: 글의 major supporting details를 다음과 같이 서술하였거나 유사하였다.
"As opposed to the conventional thinking that the plastic problem is due to wasteful consumers(0.5점), a large problem is with the legal framework(0.5점) along with a lack of resources and incentives(0.5점) across the United States. To fix this, we need to talk more about the issues in terms of local regulation and to petition corporations(0.5점)."

+1점: 글의 결론을 "the circular economy model, which plans in advance for handling waste instead of afterwards."이라 서술하였거나 유사하였다.

○ 감점
- 본문에 나오는 연속되는 6단어 이상을 사용하였다. −0.5pt
- 문단을 두 개나 그 이상으로 구성하였다. −0.5pt
- grammar나 영어표현이 합쳐 3개 이상 오류가 있다. −0.5pt

> **한글번역**

거짓말을 듣는 것보다 더 나쁜 것은 자신이 거짓말을 듣고 있다는 것을 모르는 것이다. 플라스틱 오염이 지구적 규모의 거대한 문제라는 것은 사실이다. 그리고 우리 모두가 플라스틱 발자국을 줄이기 위해 더 많은 일을 할 수 있다는 것도 사실이다. 거짓말은 플라스틱 문제에 대한 책임이 낭비하는 소비자들에게 있고 우리의 개인적 습관을 바꾸는 것이 이를 해결한다는 것이다. 플라스틱 재활용이 지구를 구하는 것은 망치로 못을 박는 것이 떨어지는 고층 빌딩을 멈추는 것과 같다. 즉, 개별 쓰레기 투기자들에게 무거운 벌금이나 감옥형을 가하면서, 플라스틱 제조업체들이 그들의 제품으로 야기하는 수많은 환경적, 경제적, 건강상의 위험에 대해서는 거의 책임을 지지 않게 하는 것은 잘못된 방향이다.

그렇다면 플라스틱의 책임감 있는 사용을 현실로 만들기 위해 우리는 무엇을 할 수 있을까? 거짓말을 거부하라. 쓰레기 투기자들은 플라스틱의 전 지구적 생태 재앙에 대해 책임이 없다. 인간은 시간, 정신적 여유, 그리고 시스템적 제약이 주어진 상황에서 그들의 능력을 최대한 발휘할 수 있을 뿐이다. 플라스틱에 대한 우리의 거대한 문제는 지역 공동체와 세계 바다에 미치는 해로운 영향에 대한 명확한 증거에도 불구하고 플라스틱 오염의 통제되지 않은 증가를 허용한 관대한 법적 체계의 결과이다. 재활용은 또한 미국 대부분 지역에서 너무 어렵고 제대로 작동하게 만들 적절한 인센티브가 부족하다.

우리의 플라스틱 문제에 대해 크게 그리고 자주 이야기하라. 지역 및 연방 대표들에게 병 법안, 비닐봉지 세금, 그리고 재사용과 재활용에 대한 생산자 책임 증대를 지지하도록 요구하라. 지역 플라스틱 규제에 대한 선제적 금지에 맞서 일어서라. 기업들이 소비자 의견에 귀를 기울이고 있다는 징후들이 있다. 고객들과 환경 단체들의 수많은 청원 후에, 맥도날드는 2025년까지 지속 가능한 포장재만을 사용하고 연말까지 스티로폼을 단계적으로 없애겠다고 약속했다.

더 나은 대안은 순환 경제 모델이다. 여기서 폐기물은 사후에 그것을 알아내려고 하기보다는 제품의 생애 말기에 재료들이 어떻게 재사용되고 재활용될 수 있는지를 미리 계획함으로써 최소화된다.

NOTE

Step 1	Survey
Key Words	Plastic pollution; consumers; recycling; manufacturers; responsibility; environmental hazards; legal framework; circular economy
Signal Words	Not clear
Step 2	**Reading**
Purpose	To expose the false narrative that individual consumers are responsible for plastic pollution and to advocate for systemic solutions
Pattern of Organization	Problem/solution
Tone	Critical; persuasive
Main Idea	More recycling will not solve plastic pollution, so larger measures need to be taken.
Step 3	**Summary**
지문 요약하기 (Paraphrasing)	More recycling will not solve plastic pollution, so larger measures need to be taken. As opposed to the conventional thinking that the plastic problem is due to wasteful consumers, a large problem is with the legal framework along with a lack of resources and incentives across the United States. To fix this, we need to talk more about the issues in terms of local regulation and to petition corporations. In conclusion, the better outlook for solving plastic pollution is the circular economy model, which plans in advance for handling waste instead of afterwards.
Step 4	**Recite**

요약문 말로 설명하기

04 Read the passage and follow the directions.

If you are thinking of becoming a principal, it is crucial that you take all factors of both sides into consideration before making your final decision. Above all, according to *salary.com* the median expected annual salary of a principal is $94,191 while the median expected annual salary of a teacher is $51,243. That is a significant increase in salary and can have a substantial impact on your family's financial status as well as your retirement. There is no denying that a significant increase in salary makes it appealing to a lot of people to make that jump from teacher to principal. However, effective teachers spend a lot of extra time in their classrooms and at home. A principal spends a much greater amount of time doing their jobs than other teachers. Principals are typically the first one to school and the last one to leave. They also have several conferences, professional development and other extra-curricular events in which they are required to attend. In many cases, this can mean attending events five nights a week during the school year. Many principals almost fail to be around their homes and their families during the school year. What is more gloomy about being a principal of a school, you deal with many more negatives than you will positives. The only time you typically deal with students face to face is because of a discipline issue. You also get to handle teachers' complaining about students, parents, and other teachers. When parents request a meeting, they are almost always because they want to complain about a teacher or another student. These constant dealings with all things negative can become overwhelming.

There will be times you will need to shut your office door or go observe a extraordinary teacher's classroom just to escape all the negativity for a few minutes. However, handling all of these negative complaints and issues is a substantial part of your job. You must effectively address each issue or you will not be a principal for long.

Write a summary following the guidelines below.

⌐ Guidelines ⌐
- Summarize the above passage in ONE paragraph.
- Provide a topic sentence and supporting ideas based on the passage.
- Do NOT copy more than FIVE consecutive words from the passage.

NOTE

Step 1	**S**urvey
Key Words	
Signal Words	
Step 2	**R**eading
Purpose	
Pattern of Organization	
Tone	
Main Idea	
Step 3	**S**ummary
지문 요약하기 (Paraphrasing)	
Step 4	**R**ecite
	요약문 말로 설명하기

Answer Key

If you are thinking of becoming **a principal**, it is crucial that you take **all factors of both sides** into consideration before making your final decision. Above all, according to *salary.com* the median expected **annual salary** of a **principal** is $94,191 while the median expected annual salary of a teacher is $51,243. That is a significant increase in salary and can have a substantial impact on your family's financial status as well as your retirement. There is no denying that a significant increase in salary makes it appealing to a lot of people to make that jump from teacher to principal. However, effective teachers spend a lot of extra time in their classrooms and at home. **A principal** spends a much greater amount of time doing their jobs than other teachers. **Principals** are typically the first one to school and the last one to leave. They also have several conferences, professional development and other extra-curricular events in which they are required to attend. In many cases, this can mean attending events five nights a week during the school year. Many **principals** almost fail to be around their homes and their families during the school year. What is more gloomy about being a principal of a school, you deal with many more negatives than you will positives. The only time you typically deal with students face to face is because of a discipline issue. You also get to handle teachers' complaining about students, parents, and other teachers. When parents request a meeting, they are almost always because they want to complain about a teacher or another student. These constant dealings with all things negative can become overwhelming. There will be times you will need to shut your office door or go observe a extraordinary teacher's classroom just to escape all the **negativity** for a few minutes. However, handling all of these **negative** complaints and issues is a substantial part of your job. You must effectively address each issue or you will not be a **principal** for long.

모범답안

You should consider both pros and cons if you want to become a principal of a school. First, becoming a principal means benefits in salary. Your median salary is almost double that of other teachers. There is no doubt that you can financially sustain your family better and will feel less burden after retirement. However, becoming a principal has two disadvantages such as less leisure time and facing a greater share of negative issues. First of all, principals must work far more than teachers, often they are required to attend events and workshops, and hardly ever are able to see their families. Second, principals must focus most of their time on problems coming from student discipline, complaints from parents, students and faculty.

채점기준

+1점: 글의 topic sentence를 다음과 같이 서술하였거나 유사하였다.
"You should consider both pros and cons if you want to become a principal of a school."

+1점: 장점을 다음과 같이 서술하였거나 유사하였다.
"First, becoming a principal means benefits in salary. Your median salary is almost double that of other teachers. There is no doubt that you can financially sustain your family better and will feel less burden after retirement."

+2점: 단점을 다음과 같이 서술하였거나 유사하였다.
"becoming a principal has two disadvantages such as less leisure time and facing a greater share of negative issues. First of all, principals must work far more than teachers, often they are required to attend events and workshops, and hardly ever are able to see their families. Second, principals must focus most of their time on problems coming from student discipline, complaints from parents, students and faculty."

한글번역

교장이 되는 것을 생각하고 있다면, 최종 결정을 내리기 전에 양쪽의 모든 요소들을 고려하는 것이 중요하다. 무엇보다도, salary.com에 따르면 교장의 예상 연간 중간 급여는 94,191달러인 반면 교사의 예상 연간 중간 급여는 51,243달러이다. 이것은 급여의 상당한 증가이고 당신 가족의 재정 상태뿐만 아니라 당신의 은퇴에도 실질적인 영향을 미칠 수 있다. 급여의 상당한 증가가 많은 사람들에게 교사에서 교장으로 도약하는 것을 매력적으로 만든다는 것은 부인할 수 없다. 하지만 효과적인 교사들은 교실과 집에서 많은 추가 시간을 보낸다. 교장은 다른 교사들보다 그들의 일을 하는 데 훨씬 더 많은 시간을 보낸다. 교장들은 일반적으로 학교에 가장 먼저 와서 가장 마지막에 떠나는 사람이다. 그들은 또한 참석해야 하는 여러 회의, 전문성 개발 및 기타 과외 활동들이 있다. 많은 경우, 이것은 학기 중에 주 5일 밤 행사에 참석하는 것을 의미할 수 있다. 많은 교장들은 학기 중에 집과 가족 곁에 있는 것을 거의 못 한다. 학교 교장이 되는 것에 대해 더 우울한 것은, 당신이 긍정적인 것들보다 훨씬 더 많은 부정적인 것들을 다룬다는 것이다. 일반적으로 학생들과 직접 대면하는 유일한 때는 징계 문제 때문이다. 당신은 또한 학생들, 학부모들, 그리고 다른 교사들에 대해 불평하는 교사들을 처리해야 한다. 학부모들이 회의를 요청할 때, 그들은 거의 항상 교사나 다른 학생에 대해 불평하고 싶어서이다. 모든 부정적인 것들과의 이러한 지속적인 상대는 압도적일 수 있다. 당신이 사무실 문을 닫거나 몇 분 동안 모든 부정적인 것들로부터 벗어나기 위해 뛰어난 교사의 교실을 관찰하러 가야 할 때들이 있을 것이다. 하지만 이 모든 부정적인 불평과 문제들을 처리하는 것은 당신 일의 상당한 부분이다. 당신은 각각의 문제를 효과적으로 해결해야 한다. 그렇지 않으면 당신은 오랫동안 교장이 될 수 없을 것이다.

NOTE

Step 1	Survey
Key Words	Principal; salary
Signal Words	Not clear

Step 2	Reading
Purpose	To provide a balanced perspective on the pros and cons of becoming a school principal to help teachers make an informed career decision
Pattern of Organization	Comparison/contrast
Tone	Informative; cautionary
Main Idea	You should consider both pros and cons if you want to become a principal of a school.

Step 3	Summary
지문 요약하기 (Paraphrasing)	You should consider both pros and cons if you want to become a principal of a school. First, becoming a principal means benefits in salary. Your median salary is almost double that of other teachers. There is no doubt that you can financially sustain your family better and will feel less burden after retirement. However, becoming a principal has two disadvantages such as less leisure time and facing a greater share of negative issues. First of all, principals must work far more than teachers, often they are required to attend events and workshops, and hardly ever are able to see their families. Second, principals must focus most of their time on problems coming from student discipline, complaints from parents, students and faculty.

Step 4	Recite
	요약문 말로 설명하기

05 Read the passage and follow the directions.

Both the incidence and impact of epidemics have gone down dramatically in the last few decades. In particular, global child mortality is at and all-time low: less than 5 percent of children die before reaching adulthood. In the developed world the rate is less than 1 percent. This miracle is due to the unprecedented achievements of twentieth-century medicine, which has provided us with vaccinations, antibiotics, improved hygiene and a much better medical infrastructure. For example, a global campaign of smallpox vaccination was so successful that in 1979 the World Health Organization declared that humanity had won, and that smallpox had been completely eradicated. It was the first epidemic humans had ever managed to wipe off the face of the earth. In 1967, smallpox had still infected 15 million people and killed 2 million of them, but in 2014 not a single person was either infected or killed by smallpox.

Every few years we are alarmed by the outbreak of some potential new plague, such as SARS in 2002/3, bird flu in 2005, swine flu in 2009/10 and Ebola in 2014. Yet thanks to efficient counter-measures these incidents have so far resulted in a comparatively small number of victims. SARS, for example, initially raised fears of a new Black Death, but eventually ended with the death of less than 1,000 people worldwide.

Even the tragedy of AIDS, seemingly the greatest medical failure of the last few decades, can be seen as a sign of progress. Since its first major outbreak in the early 1980s, more than 30 million people have died of AIDS, and tens of millions more have suffered debilitating physical and psychological damage. It was hard to understand and treat the new epidemic because AIDS is a uniquely devious disease. Whereas a human infected with the smallpox virus dies within a few days, and HIV-positive patient may seem perfectly healthy for weeks and months, yet go on infecting others unknowingly. In addition, the HIV virus itself does not kill. Rather, it destroys the immune system, there by exposing the patient to numerous other disease. It is these secondary diseases that actually kill AIDS victims. Consequently, when AIDS began to spread, it was especially difficult to understand what was happening.

However, despite these difficulties, after the medical community became aware of the mysterious new plague, it took scientists just two years to identify it, understand how the virus spreads and suggest effective ways to slow down the epidemic. Within another ten years new medicines turned AIDS from a death sentence into a chronic condition.

Write a summary following the guidelines below.

| Guidelines |
- Summarize the above passage in ONE paragraph.
- Provide a topic sentence and supporting ideas.
- Do NOT copy more than FIVE consecutive words from the passage.

NOTE

Step 1	**S**urvey
Key Words	
Signal Words	
Step 2	**R**eading
Purpose	
Pattern of Organization	
Tone	
Main Idea	
Step 3	**S**ummary
지문 요약하기 (Paraphrasing)	
Step 4	**R**ecite
	요약문 말로 설명하기

Answer Key

Both the incidence and impact of **epidemics have gone down** dramatically in the last few decades. In particular, global child mortality is at and all-time low: less than 5 percent of children die before reaching adulthood. In the developed world the rate is less than 1 percent. This miracle is due to the unprecedented achievements of twentieth-century medicine, which has provided us with **vaccinations**, **antibiotics**, improved hygiene and a much better medical infrastructure. For example, a global campaign of **smallpox vaccination** was so successful that in 1979 the World Health Organization declared that humanity had won, and that smallpox had been completely eradicated. It was the first epidemic humans had ever managed to wipe off the face of the earth. In 1967, smallpox had still infected 15 million people and killed 2 million of them, but in 2014 not a single person was either infected or killed by smallpox.

Every few years we are alarmed by the outbreak of some potential **new plague**, such as **SARS** in 2002/3, bird flu in 2005, swine flu in 2009/10 and Ebola in 2014. Yet thanks to efficient counter-measures these incidents have so far resulted in a comparatively small number of victims. SARS, for example, initially raised fears of a new Black Death, but eventually ended with the death of less than 1,000 people worldwide.

Even the tragedy of **AIDS**, seemingly the greatest medical failure of the last few decades, can be seen as a sign of progress. Since its first major outbreak in the early 1980s, more than 30 million people have died of AIDS, and tens of millions more have suffered debilitating physical and psychological damage. It was hard to understand and treat the new epidemic because AIDS is a uniquely devious disease. Whereas a human infected with the smallpox virus dies within a few days, and **HIV-positive** patient may seem perfectly healthy for weeks and months, yet go on infecting others unknowingly. In addition, **the HIV virus** itself does not kill. Rather, it destroys the immune system, there by exposing the patient to numerous other disease. It is these secondary diseases that actually kill AIDS victims. Consequently, when **AIDS** began to spread, it was especially difficult to understand what was happening.

However, despite these difficulties, after **the medical community** became aware of the mysterious new plague, it took scientists just two years to identify it, understand how the virus spreads and suggest effective ways to slow down the epidemic. Within another ten years **new medicines** turned **AIDS** from a death sentence into a chronic condition.

key words

signal words

유희태 일반영어 ❶

모범답안

Worldwide epidemics are now managed thanks to medical expertise and efficiency. Globally, there has been a reduction of child mortality and even the complete eradication of smallpox. Though occasionally new epidemics like SARS break out, they harmed only a very small number of people. Even AIDS, the worst epidemic of the last few decades, has been swiftly identified and treated in order to reduce its harm.

채점기준

+ 1점: 글의 topic sentence를 다음과 같이 서술하였거나 유사하였다.
"<u>Worldwide epidemics are now managed thanks to</u>(due to) <u>medical expertise and efficiency</u> (or <u>medical development</u>)."

+ 3점: 글의 major supporting details를 다음과 같이 서술하였거나 유사하였다.
"there has been <u>a reduction of child mortality</u> and even the complete <u>eradication of smallpox</u>. Though occasionally <u>new epidemics like SARS break out</u>, they harmed only a very small number of people. Even <u>AIDS, the worst epidemic of the last few decades, has been swiftly identified and treated in order to reduce its harm</u>."

☞ 4개 중 4개 모두를 정확하게 요약한 경우 3점, 3개만 요약한 경우 2점, 2개만 요약한 경우 1점, 1개 또는 요약하지 못한 경우 0점을 준다.

● 감점 • 본문에 나오는 연속되는 6단어 이상을 사용하였다. -0.5pt
• 문단을 두 개나 그 이상으로 구성하였다. -0.5pt
• grammar나 영어표현이 합쳐 3개 이상 오류가 있다. -0.5pt

한글번역

전염병의 발생률과 영향력은 지난 몇십 년 동안 극적으로 감소했다. 특히, 전 세계 아동 사망률은 사상 최저 수준이다 : 아이들의 5% 미만이 성인이 되기 전에 죽는다. 선진국에서는 그 비율이 1% 미만이다. 이 기적은 우리에게 백신접종, 항생제, 개선된 위생, 그리고 훨씬 더 나은 의료 인프라를 제공한 20세기 의학의 전례 없는 성취 덕분이다. 예를 들어, 천연두 백신접종의 전 세계적 캠페인은 너무나 성공적이어서 1979년에 세계보건기구는 인류가 승리했고 천연두가 완전히 박멸됐다고 선언했다. 그것은 인간이 지구상에서 완전히 없애는 데 성공한 첫 번째 전염병이었다. 1967년에 천연두는 여전히 1,500만 명을 감염시키고 그중 200만 명을 죽였지만, 2014년에는 단 한 명도 천연두에 감염되거나 죽지 않았다.

우리는 몇 년마다 2002/3년의 사스, 2005년의 조류독감, 2009/10년의 신종플루, 그리고 2014년의 에볼라와 같은 잠재적인 새로운 전염병의 발생에 놀란다. 하지만 효율적인 대응 조치 덕분에 이러한 사건들은 지금까지 비교적 적은 수의 희생자를 낳았다. 예를 들어, 사스는 처음에 새로운 흑사병에 대한 두려움을 불러일으켰지만, 결국 전 세계적으로 1,000명 미만의 죽음으로 끝났다.

지난 몇십 년간 가장 큰 의학적 실패로 보이는 에이즈의 비극조차도 진보의 신호로 볼 수 있다. 1980년대 초 첫 번째 주요 발생 이후, 3,000만 명 이상이 에이즈로 죽었고, 수천만 명이 더 쇠약하게 하는 신체적, 심리적 손상을 겪었다. 에이즈는 독특하게 교활한 질병이기 때문에 새로운 전염병을 이해하고 치료하기가 어려웠다. 천연두 바이러스에 감염된 인간이 며칠 내에 죽는 반면, HIV 양성 환자는 몇 주, 몇 달 동안 완전히 건강해 보일 수 있지만, 자신도 모르게 다른 사람들을 계속 감염시킨다. 게다가, HIV 바이러스 자체는 죽이지 않는다. 오히려, 그것은 면역 체계를 파괴해 환자를 수많은 다른 질병에 노출시킨다. 실제로 에이즈 환자들을 죽이는 것은 이러한 2차 질병들이다. 결과적으로, 에이즈가 퍼지기 시작했을 때, 무슨 일이 일어나고 있는지 이해하기가 특히 어려웠다.

하지만 이러한 어려움에도 불구하고, 의학계가 신비로운 새로운 전염병을 인식한 후, 과학자들이 그것을 식별하고, 바이러스가 어떻게 퍼지는지 이해하고, 전염병을 늦추는 효과적인 방법을 제안하는 데 단지 2년이 걸렸다. 10년 내 새로운 의약품들이 에이즈를 사형 선고에서 만성 질환으로 바꿨다.

NOTE

Step 1	**S**urvey
Key Words	Epidemics; mortality; vaccinations; antibiotics; smallpox; eradicated; SARS; AIDS; HIV; immune system; chronic condition
Signal Words	In particular; for example; such as; SARS for example; even the tragedy of AIDS; due to; thanks to; resulted in
Step 2	**R**eading
Purpose	To demonstrate how modern medicine has dramatically reduced the threat of epidemics and improved global health outcomes
Pattern of Organization	Series; cause/effect
Tone	Informative
Main Idea	Modern medicine has achieved remarkable success in reducing epidemic threats.
Step 3	**S**ummary
지문 요약하기 (Paraphrasing)	Worldwide epidemics are now managed thanks to medical expertise and efficiency. Globally, there has been a reduction of child mortality and even the complete eradication of smallpox. Though occasionally new epidemics like SARS break out, they harmed only a very small number of people. Even AIDS, the worst epidemic of the last few decades, has been swiftly identified and treated in order to reduce its harm.
Step 4	**R**ecite
	요약문 말로 설명하기

06 Read the passage and follow the directions.

Nearly 10 million young Chinese have received their results from the world's largest academic exam, commonly known as the gaokao. The exam is both cherished and despised. It is praised by many as being a relatively corruption-free method of ensuring advancement for those who study hard. The nation rejoiced when the gaokao was restored in 1977 after the death of Mao, who had scrapped it and filled colleges with ill-educated devotees of his cult.

The gaokao is flawed, however. Both the test and the schooling that prepares students for it are unfair and ill-suited to the needs of a country that wants its workers to be more innovative. A common complaint about the gaokao is that it requires so much rote-learning, at least for those parts that do not involve solving mathematical puzzles and the like. That is a problem common to many exams, but the supreme importance of the gaokao means that schools usually focus only on cramming students for it during their three years of senior high school. The government accepts that this must change. But parents complain whenever schools encourage students to do things other than learn gaokao-required facts. That is understandable: they want their children to get into one of China's handful of globally respected colleges. The answer lies in reforming the gaokao and, over time, for the government to focus more on turning China's many bad universities into better ones.

Another worry is that the supposed meritocratic virtues of the gaokao are not what they seem. For sure, those who get into the best universities are chosen for their scores, not their political connections. But those who have the best chance of scoring well are rich city-dwellers. Poorer people in many countries suffer disadvantages in education. Free education ends after junior high school. The crucial part that prepares students for gaokao can involve crippling expenses for poorer families.

Write a summary following the guidelines below.

Guidelines

- Summarize the passage in ONE paragraph.
- When you summarize, include the major supporting details the writer of the passage employs to prove her/his main point.
- Do NOT copy more than FIVE consecutive words from the passage.

NOTE

Step 1	**S**urvey
Key Words	
Signal Words	
Step 2	**R**eading
Purpose	
Pattern of Organization	
Tone	
Main Idea	
Step 3	**S**ummary
지문 요약하기 (Paraphrasing)	
Step 4	**R**ecite
	요약문 말로 설명하기

Answer Key

Nearly 10 million young Chinese have received their results from the world's largest academic exam, commonly known as **the gaokao**. **The exam** is both cherished and despised. It is praised by many as being a relatively corruption-free method of ensuring advancement for those who study hard. The nation rejoiced when the gaokao was restored in 1977 after the death of Mao, who had scrapped it and filled colleges with ill-educated devotees of his cult.

The gaokao is **flawed**, however. Both the test and the schooling that prepares students for it are unfair and ill-suited to the needs of a country that wants its workers to be more innovative. **A common complaint** about **the gaokao** is that it requires so much **rote-learning**, at least for those parts that do not involve solving mathematical puzzles and the like. That is **a problem** common to many exams, but the supreme importance of the gaokao means that schools usually focus only on cramming students for it during their three years of senior high school. The government accepts that this must change. But parents complain whenever schools encourage students to do things other than learn gaokao-required facts. That is understandable: they want their children to get into one of China's handful of globally respected colleges. The answer lies in reforming the gaokao and, over time, for the government to focus more on turning China's many bad universities into better ones.

<u>Another</u> worry is that the supposed **meritocratic** virtues of the gaokao are not what they seem. For sure, those who get into the best universities are chosen for their scores, not their political connections. But those who have the best chance of scoring well are rich city-dwellers. Poorer people in many countries suffer disadvantages in education. Free education ends after junior high school. The crucial part that prepares students for gaokao can involve crippling expenses for poorer families.

key words

series

모범답안

The gaokao exam, which is a central focus of Chinese education, has several problems. First, the gaokao requires too much rote-learning, which does not fit for the current world that emphasizes innovation. Though such a situation is required to change, parents' complaints are not simple. Second, the gaokao does not reflect the meritocratic virtues because it is biased toward city-dwellers who can afford more education, which poorer families cannot keep up with.

유희태 일반영어 ❶

채점기준

+ 2점: 글의 topic sentence를 다음과 같이 서술하였거나 유사하였다.
"The gaokao exam, which is a central focus of Chinese education, has several problems."

+ 2점: 글의 major supporting details를 다음과 같이 서술하였거나 유사하였다.
"First, the gaokao requires too much rote-learning, which does not fit for the current world that emphasizes innovation. (Though such a situation is required to change, parents' complaints are not simple.) Second, the gaokao does not reflect the meritocratic virtues because it is biased toward city-dwellers who can afford more education, which poorer families cannot keep up with."

☞ 2개 중 2개 모두를 정확하게 요약한 경우 2점, 1개만 요약한 경우 1점, 요약하지 못한 경우 0점을 준다.

● 감점 • 본문에 나오는 연속되는 6단어 이상을 사용하였다. -0.5pt
 • 문단을 두 개나 그 이상으로 구성하였다. -1pt

한글번역

거의 1,000만 명의 중국 젊은이들이 흔히 가오카오로 알려진 세계 최대 규모의 학술 시험에서 결과를 받았다. 이 시험은 사랑받기도 하고 증오받기도 한다. 많은 사람들이 열심히 공부하는 사람들의 승진을 보장하는 비교적 부패가 없는 방법이라고 칭찬한다. 가오카오를 폐지하고 대학들을 교육 수준이 낮은 그의 숭배 신봉자들로 가득 채웠던 마오가 사망한 후 1977년에 가오카오가 부활하자 국민은 환호했다.

하지만 가오카오는 결함이 있다. 시험과 학생들을 그것에 대비시키는 학교 교육 모두 불공정하고 노동자들이 더 혁신적이기를 원하는 국가의 필요에 적합하지 않다. 가오카오에 대한 일반적인 불만은 적어도 수학 퍼즐을 푸는 것과 같은 부분이 포함되지 않는 영역들에 대해서는 너무 많은 암기 학습을 요구한다는 것이다. 그것은 많은 시험의 공통된 문제이지만, 가오카오의 최고 중요성은 학교들이 보통 고등학교 3년 동안 학생들을 그것에 대비시키는 주입식 교육에만 집중한다는 것을 의미한다. 정부는 이것이 바뀌어야 한다는 것을 인정한다. 하지만 학교들이 학생들에게 가오카오가 요구하는 사실들을 배우는 것 외의 다른 일들을 하도록 격려할 때마다 부모들이 불평한다. 그것은 이해할 만하다: 그들은 자신의 아이들이 중국 소수의 전 세계적으로 존경받는 대학들 중 하나에 들어가기를 원한다. 해답은 가오카오를 개혁하고, 시간이 지나면서 정부가 중국의 많은 나쁜 대학들을 더 나은 대학들로 만드는 데 더 집중하는 것에 있다.

또 다른 우려는 가오카오의 이른바 능력주의적 미덕들이 보이는 것과 같지 않다는 것이다. 확실히, 최고의 대학에 들어가는 사람들은 정치적 연줄이 아니라 그들의 점수로 선택된다. 하지만 높은 점수를 받을 가장 좋은 기회를 가진 사람들은 부유한 도시 거주자들이다. 많은 국가의 가난한 사람들이 교육에서 불이익을 겪는다. 무료 교육은 중학교 후에 끝난다. 학생들을 가오카오에 대비시키는 중요한 부분은 가난한 가족들에게 치명적인 비용을 수반할 수 있다.

NOTE

Step 1	Survey
Key Words	Gaokao; cherished; despised; flawed; rote-learning; meritocratic
Signal Words	Not clear
Step 2	**Reading**
Purpose	To criticize China's gaokao exam system by highlighting its major flaws and problems
Pattern of Organization	Series; definition
Tone	Critical
Main Idea	The gaokao exam, which is a central focus of Chinese education, has several problems.
Step 3	**Summary**
지문 요약하기 (Paraphrasing)	The gaokao exam, which is a central focus of Chinese education, has several problems. First, the gaokao requires too much rote-learning, which does not fit for the current world that emphasizes innovation. Though such a situation is required to change, parents' complaints are not simple. Second, the gaokao does not reflect the meritocratic virtues because it is biased toward city-dwellers who can afford more education, which poorer families cannot keep up with.
Step 4	**Recite**
	요약문 말로 설명하기

07 Read the passage and follow the directions.

In the 1990's a prime opportunity for study arose when many parents from the US adopted the neglected children in Romanian orphanages. These babies were some of the victims of the governmental instability of the time. They were often left in their cribs to cry, sometimes tied down so they wouldn't escape. With no washing facilities in these orphanages many were covered in their own excrement and were malnourished to boot. Adoptive parents flocked to these orphanages to get them out and scientists flocked to these children for research data. Depending on the age of adoption these children were given a chance at recovery but few made full recoveries. On average they were 40 points below the normal IQ level of other children their age. Many had severe behavioral and emotional disorders and extremely stunted growth.

One case of neglect in the United States I find sort of interesting is that of Jeffrey Dahmer, the cannibalistic serial killer. Unlike most serial killers his childhood was not littered with abuse, but had its fair share of neglect. In his teen years he lived alone in a house because both his parents believed he was with the other one. He seemed to express genuine remorse for his actions and gave a chilling reason for why he'd killed and eaten the people he did. He wanted the perfect complacent companion, the only stable human relationship he could have probably formed. He ate them in an attempt to keep at least a part of them with him forever. He also showed dissociative behaviors, claiming to have no control or memory of the murders, like someone else was doing them.

"Genie" is one of the worst recorded cases of feral* children, children raised with little to no interaction with humans, in the United States. She lived with her blind mother, brother, and domineering father who forbid the rest of the family to talk to her. She spent the first thirteen years of her life strapped to a potty chair in a dark room of the house. She could only speak 20 words. She spent the next four years living with psychologists who studied her and taught her more words and positive behaviors like how to dress herself. However, her improvement didn't last.

feral: wild or neglected

Summarize the passage following the guidelines below.

| Guidelines |
- Summarize the above passage in ONE paragraph.
- Provide a topic sentence and supporting ideas.
- Do NOT copy more than FIVE consecutive words from the passage.

NOTE

Step 1	Ⓢurvey
Key Words	
Signal Words	
Step 2	**Ⓡeading**
Purpose	
Pattern of Organization	
Tone	
Main Idea	
Step 3	**Ⓢummary**
지문 요약하기 (Paraphrasing)	
Step 4	**Ⓡecite**
	요약문 말로 설명하기

Answer Key

In the 1990's a prime opportunity for study arose when many parents from the US adopted **the neglected children** in **Romanian orphanages**. These babies were some of the victims of the governmental instability of the time. They were often left in their cribs to cry, sometimes tied down so they wouldn't escape. With no washing facilities in these orphanages many were covered in their own excrement and were malnourished to boot. Adoptive parents flocked to these orphanages to get them out and scientists flocked to these children for research data. Depending on the age of adoption these children were given a chance at recovery but few made full recoveries. On average they were 40 points below the normal IQ level of other children their age. Many had severe behavioral and emotional disorders and extremely stunted growth. → key words

One case of **neglect** in the United States I find sort of interesting is that of **Jeffrey Dahmer**, the cannibalistic serial killer. Unlike most serial killers his childhood was not littered with abuse, but had its fair share of neglect. In his teen years he lived alone in a house because both his parents believed he was with the other one. He seemed to express genuine remorse for his actions and gave a chilling reason for why he'd killed and eaten the people he did. He wanted the perfect complacent companion, the only stable human relationship he could have probably formed. He ate them in an attempt to keep at least a part of them with him forever. He also showed dissociative behaviors, claiming to have no control or memory of the murders, like someone else was doing them.

"**Genie**" is one of the worst recorded cases of **feral children**, children raised with little to no interaction with humans, in the United States. She lived with her blind mother, brother, and domineering father who forbid the rest of the family to talk to her. She spent the first thirteen years of her life strapped to a potty chair in a dark room of the house. She could only speak 20 words. She spent the next four years living with psychologists who studied her and taught her more words and positive behaviors like how to dress herself. However, her improvement didn't last.

*feral: wild or neglected

모범답안

Childhood neglect has severe and often irreversible consequences on development, behavior, and psychological well-being. First, Romanian orphans, who suffered from neglect, exhibited mental and physical problems and never fully recovered. Second, Jeffrey Dahmer became a serial killer showing dissociative behaviors likely due to his childhood neglect. Finally, "Genie" grew up under extreme conditions of neglect, which severely limited her language ability and behavioral development beyond hope of recovery.

채점기준

+ **1.5점**: 글의 topic sentence를 다음과 같이 서술하였거나 유사하였다.
"Childhood neglect has severe and often irreversible consequences on development, behavior, and psychological well-being." 또는 "Neglect causes serious developmental damage on children."
☞ key word인 "Neglect"가 들어있지 않으면 0점을 준다.

+ **2.5점**: 글의 major supporting details를 다음과 같이 서술하였거나 유사하였다.
"First, Romanian orphans exhibited emotional and psychological problems, stunted growth, and much lower IQs as a result of neglect. Second, Jeffrey Dahmer became a serial killer showing dissociative behaviors likely due to his childhood neglect. Finally, "Genie" was a child who grew up under extreme conditions of neglect, which severely limited her language ability and behavioral development beyond hope of recovery."
☞ 3개 중 3개 모두를 정확하게 요약한 경우 2.5점, 2개만 요약한 경우 2점, 1개만 요약한 경우 1점, 요약하지 못한 경우 0점을 준다.

- **감점**
  - 본문에 나오는 연속되는 6단어 이상을 사용하였다. -0.5pt
  - 문단을 두 개나 그 이상으로 구성하였다. -0.5pt
  - grammar나 영어표현이 합쳐 3개 이상 오류가 있다. -0.5pt

한글번역

1990년대 미국의 많은 부모들이 루마니아 고아원의 방치된 아이들을 입양했을 때 연구를 위한 주요 기회가 생겼다. 이 아기들은 당시 정부 불안정의 희생자들 중 일부였다. 그들은 종종 침대에 방치돼 울었고, 때때로 도망가지 못하도록 묶여 있었다. 이러한 고아원에는 세면 시설이 없어서 많은 아이들이 자신의 배설물로 덮여 있었고 게다가 영양실조였다. 입양 부모들은 그들을 구하기 위해 이 고아원들로 몰려들었고 과학자들은 연구 데이터를 위해 이 아이들에게 몰려들었다. 입양 나이에 따라 이 아이들은 회복의 기회를 얻었지만 완전히 회복한 아이는 거의 없었다. 평균적으로 그들은 같은 나이의 다른 아이들의 정상 IQ 수준보다 40점 낮았다. 많은 아이들이 심각한 행동 및 정서 장애와 극도의 발육 부진을 겪었다.

미국에서 일어난 방치 사례 중 내가 다소 흥미롭다고 생각하는 것은 식인 연쇄 살인마인 제프리 다머의 경우이다. 대부분의 연쇄 살인마들과 달리 그의 어린 시절은 학대로 점철되지 않았지만 상당한 방치가 있었다. 십대 시절에 그는 부모 모두가 그가 다른 쪽과 함께 있다고 믿었기 때문에 집에서 혼자 살았다. 그는 자신의 행동에 대해 진심으로 후회하는 것 같았고 자신이 왜 사람들을 죽이고 먹었는지에 대한 소름끼치는 이유를 제시했다. 그는 완벽하고 순종적인 동반자, 아마도 형성할 수 있었던 유일한 안정적인 인간관계를 원했다. 그는 적어도 그들의 일부를 영원히 자신과 함께 간직하려는 시도로 그들을 먹었다. 그는 또한 해리 행동을 보였는데, 마치 다른 누군가가 살인을 저지르는 것처럼 살인에 대한 통제력이나 기억이 없다고 주장했다.

'Genie'은 미국에서 기록된 야생 아이들, 즉 인간과의 상호작용이 거의 또는 전혀 없이 자란 아이들 중 최악의 사례 중 하나이다. 그녀는 눈먼 어머니, 오빠, 그리고 나머지 가족이 그녀와 대화하는 것을 금지한 지배적인 아버지와 함께 살았다. 그녀는 인생의 첫 13년을 집의 어두운 방에서 변기 의자에 묶인 채로 보냈다. 그녀는 단지 20개의 단어만 말할 수 있었다. 그녀는 다음 4년을 그녀를 연구하고 더 많은 단어와 옷 입는 법과 같은 긍정적인 행동을 가르친 심리학자들과 함께 살았다. 하지만 그녀의 향상은 지속되지 않았다.

NOTE

Step 1	Ⓢurvey
Key Words	Neglect; Romanian orphanages; recovery; Jeffrey Dahmer; Genie; feral children
Signal Words	One case; Unlike most; "Genie" is one of

Step 2	Ⓡeading
Purpose	To demonstrate the severe and lasting effects of childhood neglect through various examples
Pattern of Organization	Series
Tone	Informative; disturbing
Main Idea	Childhood neglect has severe and often irreversible consequences on development, behavior, and psychological well-being.

Step 3	Ⓢummary
지문 요약하기 (Paraphrasing)	Childhood neglect has severe and often irreversible consequences on development, behavior, and psychological well-being. First, Romanian orphans, who suffered from neglect, exhibited mental and physical problems and never fully recovered. Second, Jeffrey Dahmer became a serial killer showing dissociative behaviors likely due to his childhood neglect. Finally, "Genie" grew up under extreme conditions of neglect, which severely limited her language ability and behavioral development beyond hope of recovery.

Step 4	Ⓡecite
	요약문 말로 설명하기

08 Read the passage and follow the directions.

The term "Follow your passion" has increased ninefold in English books since 1990. "Find something you love to do and you'll never have to work a day in your life" is another college-counseling standby of unknown provenance. But passions aren't "found". They're developed.

There are the two mind-sets. One is a "fixed theory of interests"—the idea that core interests are there from birth, just waiting to be discovered—and the other is a "growth theory," the idea that interests are something anyone can cultivate over time.

To examine how these different mind-sets affect our pursuit of different topics, many researchers performed a series of studies on college students—a group that's frequently advised to find their passion in the form of a major or career path.

First, students answered a survey that would categorize them as either "techy"—slang for interested in math and science—or "fuzzy," meaning interested in the arts or humanities. They also filled out a survey determining how much they agreed with the idea that people's core interests don't change over time. They then read an article that mismatched their interests—a piece on the future of algorithms for the fuzzies, and a piece on Derrida for the techies. The more the participants endorsed a "fixed" theory of interests, the less interested they were in the article that mismatched their aforementioned identity as a techy or fuzzy.

This could mean that students who have fixed theories of interest might forgo interesting lectures or opportunities because they don't align with their previously stated passions. Or that they might overlook ways that other disciplines can intersect with their own.

MEMO

Another reason not to buy into the fixed theory is that it can cause people to give up too easily. If something becomes difficult, it's easy to assume that it simply must not have been your passion, after all. The students who thought interests were fixed were also less likely to think that pursuing a passion would be difficult at times. Instead, they thought it would provide "endless motivation."

Summarize the passage following the guidelines below.

⌐ Guidelines ⌐
- Summarize the above passage in ONE paragraph.
- Provide a topic sentence and supporting ideas.
- Do NOT copy more than FIVE consecutive words from the passage.

___
___
___
___
___

NOTE

Step 1	**S**urvey
Key Words	
Signal Words	
Step 2	**R**eading
Purpose	
Pattern of Organization	
Tone	
Main Idea	
Step 3	**S**ummary
지문 요약하기 (Paraphrasing)	
Step 4	**R**ecite

요약문 말로 설명하기

Answer Key

The term "Follow your **passion**" has increased ninefold in English books since 1990. "Find something you love to do and you'll never have to work a day in your life" is another college-counseling standby of unknown provenance. But passions aren't "found". They're developed.

There are the two mind-sets. One is a "**fixed theory of interests**"—the idea that core interests are there from birth, just waiting to be discovered—and the other is a "**growth theory**," the idea that interests are something anyone can cultivate over time.

To examine how these different mind-sets affect our pursuit of different topics, many researchers performed a series of studies on college students—a group that's frequently advised to find their passion in the form of a major or career path.

First, students answered a survey that would categorize them as either "techy"—slang for interested in math and science—or "fuzzy," meaning interested in the arts or humanities. They also filled out a survey determining how much they agreed with the idea that people's core interests don't change over time. They then read an article that mismatched their interests—a piece on the future of algorithms for the fuzzies, and a piece on Derrida for the techies. The more the participants endorsed a "fixed" theory of interests, the less interested they were in the article that mismatched their aforementioned identity as a techy or fuzzy.

This could mean that students who have fixed theories of interest might forgo interesting lectures or opportunities because they don't align with their previously stated **passions**. Or that they might overlook ways that other disciplines can intersect with their own.

Another reason not to buy into **the fixed theory** is that it can cause people to give up too easily. If something becomes difficult, it's easy to assume that it simply must not have been your passion, after all. The students who thought interests were fixed were also less likely to think that pursuing a passion would be difficult at times. Instead, they thought it would provide "endless motivation."

key words

모범답안

The theory that passions are inborn leads people to miss out on the opportunities that the growth theory of passion can provide. For example, students who followed the "fixed" theory had less interest in articles that mismatched with their chosen identity. Thus, they might miss out on the ways in which other knowledge intersects with their field. Additionally, during times of struggle, these fixed theory types might easily give up on their chosen field, assuming it wasn't their true passion.

채점기준

+ 2점: 글의 topic sentence를 다음과 같이 서술하였거나 유사하였다.
"The theory that passions are inborn leads people to miss out on the opportunities that the growth theory of passion can provide."

+ 2점: 글의 major supporting details를 다음과 같이 서술하였거나 유사하였다.
"<u>Students who followed the "fixed" theory had less interest in articles that mismatched with their chosen identity</u>. Thus, <u>they might miss out on the ways in which other knowledge intersects with their field</u>. Additionally, <u>during times of struggle, these fixed theory types might easily give up on their chosen field, assuming it wasn't their true passion.</u>"

☞ 3개 중 3개 모두를 정확하게 요약한 경우 2점, 1~2개만 요약한 경우 1점, 요약하지 못한 경우 0점을 준다.

- **감점**
  - 본문에 나오는 연속되는 6단어 이상을 사용하였다. -0.5pt
  - 문단을 두 개나 그 이상으로 구성하였다. -0.5pt
  - grammar나 영어표현이 합쳐 3개 이상 오류가 있다. -0.5pt

한글번역

"열정을 좇으라"는 말이 책에 등장하는 빈도는 1990년 이후 아홉 배 늘었다. 비슷한 조언으로는 "진정 사랑하는 일을 찾게 되면, 남은 인생 동안 당신은 일을 할 필요가 없어진다." 같은 말도 있다. 하지만 열정은 "찾는" 것이 아니라, 만드는 것이다.

두 가지 마음가짐이 존재한다. 하나는 태어날 때부터 그 사람의 관심사가 고정돼 있어 찾기만을 기다리고 있다는 '관심사 고정설'과 다른 하나는 누구나 자신의 관심사를 키울 수 있다는 '성장설'이 있다.

이런 마음가짐의 차이가 다양한 분야의 일에서 어떤 영향을 미치는지 조사하기 위해, 여러 연구자들은 전공이나 직업에 있어 열정을 느낄 수 있는 일을 찾으라는 조언을 여러 번 들은 바 있는 학부생들을 대상으로 일련의 실험을 수행했다.

우선, 학생들은 수학과 과학에 관심을 가진 '이과(techy)'와 인문학, 예술에 관심을 가진 '문과(fuzzy)'로 나누는 조사에 응했고 한 사람의 관심사는 바뀌지 않는다는 주장에 얼마나 동의하는지에 대해 답했다. 이후 그들은 자신의 관심사와 맞지 않는 내용의 글, 곧 문과에게는 알고리듬의 미래에 대한 글을, 이과에게는 데리다에 대한 글을 읽게 했다. 그 결과, 관심사가 바뀌지 않는다고 생각한 학생들일수록 자신이 읽은 글에 관심을 덜 나타냈다.

이는 관심사가 고정돼 있다고 믿는 학생들은 자신의 관심사와 맞지 않는다는 이유로 흥미로운 수업이나 새로운 기회를 놓치게 될 수 있다는 뜻이다. 곧 새로운 분야에서 자신이 흥미를 발견할 기회를 놓치게 된다는 의미이다.

관심사 고정설의 또 다른 문제는 이를 믿는 사람들은 너무 쉽게 무언가를 포기한다는 것이다. 어떤 문제가 너무 어렵게 느껴질 때, 그 일이 자신에게 맞는 일이 아니라고 생각하기 쉽다. 관심사가 고정돼 있다고 생각하는 학생들은 자신이 열정을 추구하는 것이 때때로 어려운 일이 될 수 있다는 것을 덜 생각했다. 대신에, 그들은 열정이 '무한한 동기'를 부여할 것이라 생각했다.

NOTE

Step 1	Survey
Key Words	passion; fixed theory; growth theory; interests; developed; cultivate
Signal Words	There are the two; first; they also; they then; another reason; instead

Step 2	Reading
Purpose	To argue against the "fixed theory of interests" and advocate for the "growth theory" that interests can be developed
Pattern of Organization	Comparison/contrast; series
Tone	Persuasive; analytical
Main Idea	The theory that passions are inborn leads people to miss out on the opportunities that the growth theory of passion can provide.

Step 3	Summary
지문 요약하기 (Paraphrasing)	The theory that passions are inborn leads people to miss out on the opportunities that the growth theory of passion can provide. For example, students who followed the "fixed" theory had less interest in articles that mismatched with their chosen identity. Thus, they might miss out on the ways in which other knowledge intersects with their field. Additionally, during times of struggle, these fixed theory types might easily give up on their chosen field, assuming it wasn't their true passion.

Step 4	Recite
	요약문 말로 설명하기

09 Read the passage and follow the directions.

Empathy is a powerful motivator of helping. It is elicited when we perceive someone in need, when we value their welfare, and most importantly, when we take their perspective—imagining what it would be like to be in their shoes. This in essence creates an at least temporary sense of shared collective reciprocity. In the right amounts, eliciting empathy can be a very effective way to obtain support. Until you take it too far, that is. Because "I feel your pain" stops working the moment the pain becomes too great. Then the person from whom you are trying to elicit empathy is quite likely to shut down entirely and try to get away from you as soon as possible, probably without helping at all.

Often, those seeking help are so busy trying to establish that they are not personally weak or greedy that they turn the focus away from the helper and onto themselves. They say things like, "I'm not normally the type that asks for help . . ." or "I hate having to ask you for this . . ." The impulse is understandable. Asking for help is uncomfortable. But using disclaimers like these is the wrong way to make it better. I can't get a lot of personal satisfaction from helping you if I know that you hated having to ask me, and that you appear to be miserable about the whole thing.

Because asking for help makes us so uncomfortable, and because we really do expect that people will say no, a common tactic is to portray the help we need as a piddling and negligible little favor. We might emphasize the overall lack of inconvenience helping us will cause, as in, "Could you drop these contracts off at the client's? It's practically on your way home." Or we might highlight how little time it will take the helper to help us: "Would you add these updates to the database? It probably won't take you more than five minutes." The thing is, by minimizing our request, we also minimize the helper's help and thus minimize any warm feelings the act of helping us might have generated.

All these things you can say while asking for help can really backfire.

Summarize the passage following the guidelines below.

Guidelines
• Summarize the above passage in ONE paragraph. • Provide a topic sentence and supporting ideas. • Do NOT copy more than FIVE consecutive words from the passage.

NOTE

Step 1	**S**urvey
Key Words	
Signal Words	
Step 2	**R**eading
Purpose	
Pattern of Organization	
Tone	
Main Idea	
Step 3	**S**ummary
지문 요약하기 (Paraphrasing)	
Step 4	**R**ecite
	요약문 말로 설명하기

Answer Key

Empathy is a powerful motivator of **helping**. It is elicited when we perceive someone in need, when we value their welfare, and most importantly, when we take their perspective—imagining what it would be like to be in their shoes. This in essence creates an at least temporary sense of shared collective reciprocity. In the right amounts, eliciting **empathy** can be a very effective way to obtain support. Until you take it too far, that is. Because "I feel your pain" stops working the moment the pain becomes too great. Then the person from whom you are trying to elicit empathy is quite likely to shut down entirely and try to get away from you as soon as possible, probably without helping at all.

Often, those seeking help are so busy trying to establish that they are not personally weak or greedy that they turn the focus away from the helper and onto themselves. They say things like, "I'm not normally the type that asks for help . . ." or "I hate having to ask you for this . . ." The impulse is understandable. **Asking for help** is uncomfortable. But using **disclaimers** like these is the wrong way to make it better. I can't get a lot of personal satisfaction from helping you if I know that you hated having to ask me, and that you appear to be miserable about the whole thing.

Because **asking for help** makes us so uncomfortable, and because we really do expect that people will say no, a common tactic is to portray the help we need as a piddling and negligible little favor. We might emphasize the overall lack of inconvenience helping us will cause, as in, "Could you drop these contracts off at the client's? It's practically on your way home." Or we might highlight how little time it will take the helper to help us: "Would you add these updates to the database? It probably won't take you more than five minutes." The thing is, by minimizing our request, we also minimize the helper's help and thus minimize any warm feelings the act of helping us might have generated.

All these things you can say while **asking for help** can really backfire.

모범답안

When asking for help, there are several warnings we should consider in order not to backfire. First, it is important not to try to elicit too much empathy, as that can drive people away. Second, using disclaimers about hating to ask for help is similarly unpersuasive. Third, it is important not to minimize the request, as it can have the negative consequence of minimizing the satisfaction the helper might attain.

채점기준

+2점 : 글의 topic sentence를 다음과 같이 서술하였거나 유사하였다.
"When asking for help, there are several warnings we should consider in order not to backfire."

+2점 : 글의 major supporting details를 다음과 같이 서술하였거나 유사하였다.
"First, it is important not to try to elicit too much empathy, as that can drive people away. Second, using disclaimers about hating to ask for help is similarly unpersuasive. Third, it is important not to minimize the request, as it can have the negative consequence of minimizing the satisfaction the helper might attain."

☞ 3개 중 3개 모두를 정확하게 요약한 경우 2점, 1~2개만 요약한 경우 1점, 요약하지 못한 경우 0점을 준다.

● 감점
- 본문에 나오는 연속되는 6단어 이상을 사용하였다. -0.5pt
- 문단을 두 개나 그 이상으로 구성하였다. -0.5pt
- grammar나 영어표현이 합쳐 3개 이상 오류가 있다. -0.5pt

한글번역

　　공감은 도움의 강한 동기부여가 된다. 우리는 누군가 도움이 필요한 상황임을 감지하고, 그 대상이 잘 지내는 데 가치를 두고, 무엇보다 상대의 입장이 될 때 공감을 한다. 본질적으로 이런 공감은 적어도 일시적으로 공유되는 집단상호주의(타인과 무언가를 함께 하고 있기 때문에 타인을 도와야 한다는 생각)의 느낌을 만들어낸다. 적당한 공감을 끌어내는 건 도움을 받기 위해 매우 효과적인 방법이 될 수 있다. 너무 지나치지만 않다면 말이다. 고통이 너무 커지는 순간 "당신의 고통을 알아요"라는 생각은 더 이상 효과가 없기 때문이다. 그런 지경에 이르면, 공감을 끌어내려던 상대는 아예 마음을 닫고, 하나도 도와주지 않으면서 가능한 한 빨리 멀어지려고 할 것이다.

　　종종 도움을 구하는 사람은 자신이 능력이 없어 보이거나 욕심이 많은 것처럼 보이지 않으려고 지나치게 애쓰다가 도움을 줄 사람에서 자신으로 그 초점을 옮겨버린다. 이런 사람은 도움을 구할 때 이런 말을 한다. "저는 평소에 도와달라고 하는 사람이 아닌데요…" 혹은 "도와달라고 하는 게 싫지만…"이라고 말을 한다. 이런 말을 하고 싶은 충동은 이해할 수 있다. 도와달라고 요청하는 건 불편한 일이기 때문이다. 그러나 이렇게 부인하는 말은 상황을 나아지게 하지 않는다. 도움을 구하는 사람이 도움을 요청하는 것을 싫어하고 또 도움을 구하는 상황 자체를 비참해하는 것을 안다면, 도와주는 사람은 도움을 주는 데서 그다지 큰 만족을 느낄 수 없다.

　　사람들은 도움을 요청하는 일을 굉장히 마음 불편한 일로 생각하고 실제로 사람들이 거절하리라고 예상한다. 그래서 어떤 사람들은 필요한 도움을 하찮고 무시해도 될 정도의 작은 도움인 것처럼 표현하는 전략을 흔히 사용한다. 우리는 도와줄 일이 전반적으로 어떤 불편도 끼치지 않을 거라고 강조한다. "이 계약서 좀 고객 사무실에 갖다 줄 수 있을까요? 그 사무실은 당신이 집에 가는 길에 있어요." 이런 식으로 말이다. 아니면 도와줄 사람이 시간을 얼마나 많이 사용하지 않아도 될지 강조하기도 한다. "이 데이터베이스 업데이트해 주실 수 있나요? 5분도 안 걸릴 거예요." 문제는, 이렇게 요청을 최소화하는 것은 도와주는 사람의 도움을 함께 최소화하고, 결과적으로 도움을 준 사람이 갖는 기쁜 마음까지도 최소화해 버린다.

　　이런 모든 말들이 도움을 요청할 때 역효과를 일으키게 하는 것들이다.

NOTE

Step 1	Survey
Key Words	empathy; helping; pain; disclaimers; minimizing; backfire
Signal Words	Not clear
Step 2	**Reading**
Purpose	To explain why common approaches to asking for help are counterproductive and ineffective
Pattern of Organization	Series
Tone	Analytical
Main Idea	When asking for help, there are several warnings we should consider in order not to backfire.
Step 3	**Summary**
지문 요약하기 (Paraphrasing)	When asking for help, there are several warnings we should consider in order not to backfire. First, it is important not to try to elicit too much empathy, as that can drive people away. Second, using disclaimers about hating to ask for help is similarly unpersuasive. Third, it is important not to minimize the request, as it can have the negative consequence of minimizing the satisfaction the helper might attain.
Step 4	**Recite**
	요약문 말로 설명하기

10 Read the passage and follow the directions.

In South Africa, apartheid was not just used to keep blacks in their place, but it was also used to keep gays in theirs. Between 1971-1989, gays were ruthlessly ferreted out of the Apartheid Army. From there they'd be whisked away to medical facilities where shock treatment, psychological aversion therapies, hormone replacement, and drugs were used to change these individuals into heterosexuals. When all else failed, forced sexual reassignment surgery was performed on at least 900 individuals, most, if not all, who were gay, not transsexual. Most of the victims were men between the ages of 16-24.

None of these atrocities conducted on gays were anything new. In the United States most of these procedures had been done in decades past to mental patients. Up until the 1970s being gay was actually considered a mental disorder and in some instances you could be forcibly institutionalized for being afflicted. Aversion therapy became extreme and deranged. For instance, a subject would be shown a nude photo of someone of the same sex while simultaneously being forced to sniff something that smelled really fowl. Other times, they would be injected with vomit inducing drugs, shocked with electricity on all parts of their body, or forced to lie in a bed of their own vomit and wastes. Sometimes these experiments took days and some people actually died. Still, the shame was so great at the time that few of these tragedies have come to light in the present day.

Science is not inherently good or evil, rather it reflects the intentions of those who use it. Today in the United States and in many other countries, it is illegal to experiment on people who don't know they are being experimented on. There are many ethics and guidelines and people whose job it is to make sure that these ideologies are being enforced. We have learned a lot from the past, but we can't undo the bad deeds that have already been done. Instead, we should pay our respects for all those who have suffered in the name of science and vow to never repeat those mistakes again.

Write a summary following the guidelines below.

| Guidelines |
- Summarize the above passage in ONE paragraph.
- Provide a topic sentence and supporting ideas from the passage.
- Do NOT copy more than FIVE consecutive words from the passage.

NOTE

Step 1	Ⓢurvey
Key Words	
Signal Words	
Step 2	**Ⓡeading**
Purpose	
Pattern of Organization	
Tone	
Main Idea	
Step 3	**Ⓢummary**
지문 요약하기 (Paraphrasing)	
Step 4	**Ⓡecite**
	요약문 말로 설명하기

Answer Key

In **South Africa, apartheid** was not just used to keep blacks in their place, but it was also used to keep gays in theirs. Between 1971-1989, gays were ruthlessly ferreted out of **the Apartheid** Army. From there they'd be whisked away to medical facilities where **shock treatment**, psychological aversion therapies, hormone replacement, and drugs were used to change these individuals into heterosexuals. When all else failed, forced sexual reassignment surgery was performed on at least 900 individuals, most, if not all, who were gay, not transsexual. Most of the victims were men between the ages of 16-24.

None of these **atrocities** conducted on **gays** were anything new. In the United States most of these procedures had been done in decades past to mental patients. Up until the 1970s being gay was actually considered a mental disorder and in some instances you could be forcibly institutionalized for being afflicted. **Aversion therapy** became extreme and deranged. For instance, a subject would be shown a nude photo of someone of the same sex while simultaneously being forced to sniff something that smelled really fowl. Other times, they would be injected with vomit inducing drugs, shocked with electricity on all parts of their body, or forced to lie in a bed of their own vomit and wastes. Sometimes these experiments took days and some people actually died. Still, the shame was so great at the time that few of these tragedies have come to light in the present day.

Science is not inherently good or evil, rather it reflects the intentions of those who use it. Today in the United States and in many other countries, it is illegal to experiment on people who don't know they are being experimented on. There are many ethics and guidelines and people whose job it is to make sure that these ideologies are being enforced. We have learned a lot from the past, but we can't undo the bad deeds that have already been done. Instead, we should pay our respects for all those who have suffered in the name of science and vow to never repeat those mistakes again.

key words

모범답안

In the conduct of science there have been many bad deeds committed that should be avoided in the future through ethical mindfulness. For example, in South Africa, during the 1970s and 1980s and the United States until the 1970s, where being gay was considered a mental disease, it was legal to conduct drastic and harmful actions on gays in order to "correct" them, which led to death sometimes. Since, it has become illegal to conduct such experiments and to use people that are unaware in experiments. (Moving forward, we ought to remain vigilante of morality to avoid repeating mistakes like these.)

채점기준

+1점: 글의 topic sentence를 다음과 같이 서술하였거나 유사하였다.
"In the conduct of science there have been many bad deeds committed that should be avoided in the future through ethical mindfulness."

+3점: 글의 major supporting details를 다음과 같이 서술하였거나 유사하였다.
"For example, in South Africa during the 1970s and 1980s and the United States until the 1970s, where being gay was considered a mental disease, it was legal to conduct drastic and harmful actions on gays in order to "correct" them, which led to death sometimes(2점). Since, it has become illegal to conduct such experiments and to use people that are unaware in experiments(1점)."

☞ 3개 중 3개 모두를 정확하게 요약한 경우 3점, 2개만 요약한 경우 2점, 1개만 요약한 경우 1점, 요약하지 못한 경우 0점을 준다.

- **감점**
  - 글의 전체 양이 너무 적은 경우(3줄 이하) -1pt
  - 글의 전체 양이 너무 많은 경우(5줄 이상) -1pt
  - 본문에 나오는 연속되는 6단어 이상을 사용하였다. -0.5pt
  - 문단을 두 개나 그 이상으로 구성하였다. -1pt

한글번역

남아프리카에서 아파르트헤이트는 흑인들을 그들의 위치에 두기 위해서만 사용된 것이 아니라 동성애자들을 그들의 위치에 두기 위해서도 사용됐다. 1971년부터 1989년 사이에 동성애자들은 아파르트헤이트 군대에서 무자비하게 색출됐다. 거기서 그들은 의료 시설로 끌려가 전기충격 치료, 심리적 혐오 요법, 호르몬 대체, 그리고 약물이 이들 개인을 이성애자로 바꾸기 위해 사용됐다. 다른 모든 것이 실패했을 때, 강제 성전환 수술이 최소 900명의 개인에게 시행됐는데, 모두는 아닐지라도 대부분이, 성전환자가 아닌 동성애자였다. 희생자들의 대부분은 16세에서 24세 사이의 남성들이었다.

동성애자들에게 행해진 이러한 잔학 행위들 중 어느 것도 새로운 것이 아니었다. 미국에서는 이러한 절차들의 대부분이 지난 수십 년 동안 정신병 환자들에게 행해졌다. 1970년대까지 동성애자가 되는 것은 실제로 정신장애로 간주됐고 어떤 경우에는 그것에 걸렸다는 이유로 강제로 수용되기도 했다. 혐오 치료는 극단적이고 정신 나간 수준이 됐다. 예를 들어, 실험 대상자는 같은 성의 누군가의 누드 사진을 보면서 동시에 정말 역겨운 냄새를 맡도록 강요당했다. 다른 때는 그들은 구토를 유발하는 약물을 주사당하고, 몸의 모든 부분에 전기 충격을 받고, 또는 자신의 구토물과 배설물의 침대에 누워있도록 강요당했다. 때때로 이러한 실험들은 며칠 동안 지속됐고 어떤 사람들은 실제로 죽었다. 그럼에도 불구하고 당시 수치심이 너무 커서 이러한 비극들 중 거의 대부분이 오늘날까지도 밝혀지지 않았다.

과학은 본질적으로 선하거나 악한 것이 아니라 그것을 사용하는 사람들의 의도를 반영한다. 오늘날 미국과 많은 다른 국가들에서 자신이 실험당하고 있다는 것을 모르는 사람들을 실험하는 것은 불법이다. (오늘날) 많은 윤리와 지침들이 있고, 또한 이러한 이념들(윤리와 지침들)이 (제대로) 시행되고 있는지 확인하는 것이 직업인 사람들이 있다. 우리는 과거로부터 많은 것을 배웠지만, 이미 행해진 나쁜 행위들을 되돌릴 수는 없다. 대신 우리는 과학의 이름으로 고통받은 모든 사람들에게 경의를 표하고 그러한 실수들을 다시는 반복하지 않겠다고 맹세해야 한다.

NOTE

Step 1	Survey
Key Words	Apartheid; gays; shock treatment; aversion therapy; mental disorder; science
Signal Words	Not clear
Step 2	**Reading**
Purpose	To expose the historical medical abuse of gay individuals and emphasize the need for ethical guidelines in scientific research
Pattern of Organization	Series
Tone	Critical
Main Idea	In the conduct of science there have been many bad deeds committed that should be avoided in the future through ethical mindfulness.
Step 3	**Summary**
지문 요약하기 (Paraphrasing)	In the conduct of science there have been many bad deeds committed that should be avoided in the future through ethical mindfulness. For example, in South Africa, during the 1970s and 1980s and the United States until the 1970s, where being gay was considered a mental disease, it was legal to conduct drastic and harmful actions on gays in order to "correct" them, which led to death sometimes. Since, it has become illegal to conduct such experiments and to use people that are unaware in experiments. (Moving forward, we ought to remain vigilante of morality to avoid repeating mistakes like these.)
Step 4	**Recite**
	요약문 말로 설명하기

11 Read the passage and follow the directions.

When we finish using something, we throw it away, but where is away? In our modern cities, away is usually a landfill site, piled high with all those things that we no longer want. A modern American city generates solid waste or garbage at an alarming rate. Every day, New York City produces 17,000 tons of garbage and ships it to Staten Island, where it is added to yesterday's 17,000 tons in a landfill site. We each produce enough garbage every five years to equal the volume of the Statue of Liberty.

In any landfill, gone is not forgotten by nature. By compacting the garbage to reduce its volume, we slow the rate of decomposition, which makes our garbage last longer. In a modern landfill, the process produces a <u>garbage lasagna</u>. There's a layer of compacted garbage covered by a layer of dirt, covered by a layer of compacted garbage and so on. By saving space for more garbage, we cut off the air and water needed to decompose the garbage and, thus, preserve it for future generations. If you could dig far enough, you might still be able to read forty-year-old newspapers. The paper may be preserved, but the news is history.

One of the answers to this problem is recycling. Any object that can be reused in one form or another is an object that shouldn't be found in a landfill. Most of us recycle our paper, which saves energy and resources. Recycled paper can be used again and even turned into other products. Recycling old newspapers is not as valuable as hidden treasure, but when the cost of landfills and the environmental impact of producing more and more newsprint is considered, it can be a bargain. If plastic shopping bags can be recycled into a cloth-like substance which can be used to make reusable shopping bags, maybe American ingenuity can find ways to reduce all that garbage being stored in landfills before the landfills overtake the space for cities.

Write a summary following the guidelines below.

┌─ Guidelines ─┐
- Summarize the above passage in ONE paragraph.
- Provide a topic sentence and supporting ideas including the reason writer mentions "garbage lasagna".
- Do NOT copy more than FIVE consecutive words from the passage.

NOTE

Step 1	**S**urvey
Key Words	
Signal Words	
Step 2	**R**eading
Purpose	
Pattern of Organization	
Tone	
Main Idea	
Step 3	**S**ummary
지문 요약하기 (Paraphrasing)	
Step 4	**R**ecite
	요약문 말로 설명하기

Answer Key

When we finish using something, we throw it away, but where is away? In our modern cities, away is usually a **landfill site**, piled high with all those things that we no longer want. A modern American city generates solid **waste** or **garbage** at an alarming rate. Every day, New York City produces 17,000 tons of garbage and ships it to Staten Island, where it is added to yesterday's 17,000 tons in a **landfill site**. We each produce enough garbage every five years to equal the volume of the Statue of Liberty.

In **any landfill**, gone is not forgotten by nature. By compacting the garbage to reduce its volume, we slow the rate of decomposition, which makes **our garbage** last longer. In a modern **landfill**, the process produces a garbage lasagna. There's a layer of compacted garbage covered by a layer of dirt, covered by a layer of compacted garbage and so on. By saving space for more garbage, we cut off the air and water needed to decompose the garbage and, thus, preserve it for future generations. If you could dig far enough, you might still be able to read forty-year-old newspapers. The paper may be preserved, but the news is history.

One of the answers to this problem is **recycling**. Any object that can be **reused** in one form or another is an object that shouldn't be found in **a landfill**. Most of us **recycle** our paper, which saves energy and resources. **Recycled paper** can be used again and even turned into other products. **Recycling** old newspapers is not as valuable as hidden treasure, but when the cost of **landfills** and the environmental impact of producing more and more newsprint is considered, it can be a bargain. If plastic shopping bags can be **recycled** into a cloth-like substance which can be used to make reusable shopping bags, maybe American ingenuity can find ways to reduce all that garbage being stored in landfills before the **landfills** overtake the space for cities.

key words

모범답안

Recycling is needed to surmount the problem of American cities' growing landfills. These landfills currently grow at an alarming rate, with cities like New York producing thousands of tons daily. The growth is so fast that older waste is rapidly covered over in a type of "garbage lasagna" that prevents the decomposition caused by air and water. Thus, innovative recycling and reduction of waste could help solve this pressing issue before landfills overtake urban space.

채점기준

+ 1점: 글의 topic sentence를 다음과 같이 서술하였거나 유사하였다.
"Recycling is needed to overcome the problem of American cities' growing landfills."

+ 3점: 글의 major supporting details를 다음과 같이 서술하였거나 유사하였다.
"① These landfills currently grow at an alarming rate, with cities like New York producing thousands of tons daily. ② The growth is so fast that older waste is rapidly covered over in a type of "garbage lasagna" that prevents the decomposition caused by air and water. ③ Thus, innovative recycling and reduction of waste could help solve this pressing issue before landfills overtake urban space."

☞ 3개 중 3개 모두를 요약한 경우 3점, ②번 요소를 포함한 2개 요소를 요약한 경우 2점, ②번 요소가 들어가 있지 않고 나머지 2개만 요약한 경우 1점, 요약하지 못한 경우 0점을 준다.

- **감점**
  - 본문에 나오는 연속되는 6단어 이상을 사용하였다. −0.5pt
  - 문단을 두 개나 그 이상으로 구성하였다. −0.5pt
  - grammar나 영어표현이 합쳐 3개 이상 오류가 있다. −0.5pt

한글번역

우리가 무언가를 다 사용하면 그것을 버리지만, 어디로 '버린다'는 것일까? 현대 도시에서 '버린다'는 것은 보통 매립지로, 우리가 더 이상 원하지 않는 모든 것들이 높게 쌓인 곳이다. 현대 미국 도시는 놀라운 속도로 고형 폐기물이나 쓰레기를 발생시킨다. 매일 뉴욕시는 17,000톤의 쓰레기를 생산하고 그것을 스태튼 아일랜드로 운송하는데, 그곳에 어제 버린 17,000톤의 쓰레기 위에 또 쌓인다. 우리 각자는 5년마다 자유의 여신상의 부피와 맞먹는 충분한 쓰레기를 생산한다.

어떤 매립지에서도 사라졌다고 해서 자연이 잊어버리는 것은 아니다(버려진 것들이 자연에서 완전히 사라지는 것은 아니다). 쓰레기의 부피를 줄이기 위해 압축함으로써 우리는 분해 속도를 늦추고, 이것은 쓰레기를 더 오래 지속시킨다. 현대 매립지에서 이 과정은 쓰레기 라자냐를 만든다. 압축된 쓰레기 층이 흙층으로 덮이고, 압축된 쓰레기 층으로 덮이는 식이다. 더 많은 쓰레기를 위한 공간을 절약함으로써 우리는 쓰레기를 분해하는 데 필요한 공기와 물을 차단하고, 따라서 미래 세대를 위해 그것을 보존하게 된다(의도치 않게 쓰레기가 보존돼 미래 세대에게 문제가 된다). 충분히 깊이 팔 수 있다면 여전히 40년 된 신문을 읽을 수 있을지도 모른다. 종이는 보존될 수 있지만 뉴스는 역사다.

이 문제에 대한 해답 중 하나는 재활용이다. 어떤 형태로든 재사용될 수 있는 모든 물체는 매립지에서 발견돼서는 안 되는 물체이다. 우리 대부분은 종이를 재활용하는데, 이것은 에너지와 자원을 절약한다. 재활용된 종이는 다시 사용될 수 있고 심지어 다른 제품으로 바뀔 수도 있다. 오래된 신문을 재활용하는 것은 숨겨진 보물만큼 가치 있지는 않지만, 매립지의 비용과 점점 더 많은 신문 용지를 생산하는 환경적 영향을 고려할 때 그것은 좋은 거래가 될 수 있다. 플라스틱 쇼핑백을 천과 같은 물질로 재활용해 재사용 가능한 쇼핑백을 만들 수 있다면, 아마도 미국의 창의력은 매립지가 도시보다 더 많은 공간을 차지하기 전에(매립지가 계속 확장돼 결국 도시 공간을 잠식하기 전에) 매립지에 저장되는 모든 쓰레기를 줄이는 방법을 찾을 수 있을 것이다.

NOTE

Step 1	Survey
Key Words	Garbage; landfill; decomposition; recycling; reused; environmental
Signal Words	Not clear
Step 2	Reading
Purpose	To explain the garbage problem in modern cities and advocate for recycling as a solution
Pattern of Organization	Not clear
Tone	Informative; concerned; advocating
Main Idea	Recycling is needed to surmount the problem of American cities' growing landfills.
Step 3	Summary
지문 요약하기 (Paraphrasing)	Recycling is needed to surmount the problem of American cities's growing landfills. These landfills currently grow at an alarming rate, with cities like New York producing thousands of tons daily. The growth is so fast that older waste is rapidly covered over in a type of "garbage lasagna" that prevents the decomposition caused by air and water. Thus, innovative recycling and reduction of waste could help solve this pressing issue before landfills overtake urban space.
Step 4	Recite

요약문 말로 설명하기

12 Read the passage and follow the directions.

If you're endlessly distracted by your co-workers in the gaping open office space you all share, you're not alone. Compared to traditional office spaces, face-to-face interaction in open office spaces is not as was expected.

In a recent study, researchers followed two anonymous Fortune 500 companies during their transitions between a traditional office space to an open plan environment and used a sensor called a "sociometric badge" (think company ID on a lanyard) to record detailed information about the kind of interactions employees had in both spaces. The study collected information in two stages; first for several weeks before the renovation and the second for several weeks after.

Many researchers provide three cautionary tales. Open office spaces don't actually promote interaction. Instead, they cause employees to seek privacy wherever they can find it. These open spaces might spell bad news for collective company intelligence or, in other words, an overstimulating office space creates a decrease in organizational productivity. Not all channels of interaction will be effected equally in an open layout change. While the number of emails sent in the study did increase, the richness of this interaction was not equal to that lost in face-to-face interactions.

It seems like it might be time to (first, find a quiet room) and go back to the drawing board with the open office design.

MEMO

Write a summary following the guidelines below.

　　　　　　　　　　　　　　┘ Guidelines ┌
- Summarize the above passage in ONE paragraph.
- Provide a topic sentence and supporting ideas.
- Do NOT copy more than FIVE consecutive words from the passage.

NOTE

Step 1	**S**urvey
Key Words	
Signal Words	
Step 2	**R**eading
Purpose	
Pattern of Organization	
Tone	
Main Idea	
Step 3	**S**ummary
지문 요약하기 (Paraphrasing)	
Step 4	**R**ecite
	요약문 말로 설명하기

Answer Key

If you're endlessly distracted by your co-workers in the gaping **open office space** you all share, you're not alone. Compared to traditional office spaces, face-to-face **interaction** in open office spaces is not as was expected.

In a recent study, researchers followed two anonymous Fortune 500 companies during their transitions between a traditional office space to an open plan environment and used a sensor called a "sociometric badge" (think company ID on a lanyard) to record detailed information about the kind of interactions employees had in both spaces. The study collected information in two stages; first for several weeks before the renovation and the second for several weeks after.

Many researchers provide three cautionary tales. **Open office spaces** don't actually promote **interaction**. Instead, they cause employees to seek privacy wherever they can find it. These open spaces might spell bad news for collective company intelligence or, in other words, an overstimulating office space creates a decrease in organizational productivity. Not all channels of interaction will be effected equally in an **open layout** change. While the number of emails sent in the study did increase, the richness of **this interaction** was not equal to that lost in face-to-face interactions.

It seems like it might be time to (first, find a quiet room) and go back to the drawing board with **the open office** design.

key words

모범답안

Open offices have been proven to be inefficient despite their intended goals. A study followed the changes in work after converting to open office spaces. It learned that employees perform worse in these spaces in terms of three major drawbacks: driving employees to seek privacy, decreasing organizational productivity, and a reduction of the richness of interactivity.

유희태 일반영어 ❶

채점기준

+ **2점**: 글의 topic sentence를 다음과 같이 서술하였거나 유사하였다.
"Open offices have been proven to be inefficient despite their intended goals"
+ **2점**: 글의 major supporting details를 다음과 같이 서술하였거나 유사하였다.
"A study followed the changes in work after converting to open office spaces(0.5점). It learned that employees perform worse in these spaces in terms of three major drawbacks: driving employees to seek privacy, decreasing organizational productivity, and a reduction of the richness of interactivity(1.5점)."
☞ 3개 중 3개 모두를 정확하게 요약한 경우 1.5점, 2개만 요약한 경우 1점, 1개 또는 요약하지 못한 경우 0점을 준다.

- **감점**
  - 본문에 나오는 연속되는 6단어 이상을 사용하였다. -0.5pt
  - 문단을 두 개나 그 이상으로 구성하였다. -0.5pt
  - grammar나 영어표현이 합쳐 3개 이상 오류가 있다. -0.5pt

한글번역

칸막이 없는 사무실에서 다른 사람이 계속 신경 쓰인다면 그건 당신만 그런 것이 아니다. 칸막이 없는 사무실은 기존의 사무실에 비해 직접 얼굴을 보고 이야기하는 비율이 기대만큼 되지도 않았다.

최근 한 연구에서, 연구자들은 전통적인 사무실 구조에서 칸막이 없는 사무실로 구조를 바꾼 포춘 500대 기업에 속하는 두 개의 회사를 조사했다. 그들은 사무실 구조를 바꾸기 몇 주 전, 그리고 구조를 바꾼 몇 주 뒤에 각각 직원들에게 목에 거는 출입증과 비슷하게 생긴 '사회학적 배지'라는 센서를 착용하게 하고 이들과 다른 직원들과의 상호작용을 측정했다.

많은 연구자들은 다음과 같은 세 가지 조심스러운 결론을 내렸다. 칸막이 없는 사무실이 사람들을 더 자주 이야기하게 만들지는 않는다. 오히려 사람들은 가능한 한 자신의 개인 공간을 찾아다니게 된다. (둘째로), 칸막이 없는 사무실은 직원들의 업무 능력에 부정적인 영향을 미친다. 즉, 과도하게 열린 공간은 조직의 생산성을 낮춘다. (셋째로) 사무실의 칸막이를 없앴을 때 사람들 간의 상호작용에는 변화가 온다. 이메일을 통한 상호작용은 증가했지만, 이는 실제 얼굴을 맞대고 하는 대화에 비해 비생산적인 상호작용이다.

(먼저, 조용한 방을 찾고,) 이제 다시 칸막이를 설치할 때가 된 것 같다.

NOTE

Step 1	Survey
Key Words	Open office; interaction; traditional office; privacy; productivity; face-to-face
Signal Words	Not clear

Step 2	Reading
Purpose	To argue against open office designs (by presenting research evidence that contradicts their intended benefits)
Pattern of Organization	Not clear
Tone	Critical
Main Idea	Open offices have been proven to be inefficient despite their intended goals.

Step 3	Summary
지문 요약하기 (Paraphrasing)	Open offices have been proven to be inefficient despite their intended goals. A study followed the changes in work after converting to open office spaces. It learned that employees perform worse in these spaces in terms of three major drawbacks: driving employees to seek privacy, decreasing organizational productivity, and a reduction of the richness of interactivity.

Step 4	Recite
	요약문 말로 설명하기

13 Read the passage and follow the directions.

Modern morals are a mixture of two elements: on the one hand, rational precepts as to how to live together peaceably in a society, and on the other hand traditional taboos derived originally from some ancient superstition, but proximately from sacred books, Christian, Mohammedan, Hindu, or Buddhist. To some extent the two agree; the prohibition of murder and theft, for instance, is supported both by human reason and by Divine command. But the prohibition of pork or beef has only scriptural authority, and that only in certain religions. It is odd that modern men, who are aware of what science has done in the way of bringing new knowledge and altering the conditions of social life, should still be willing to accept the authority of texts embodying the outlook of very ancient and very ignorant pastoral or agricultural tribes. It is discouraging that many of the precepts whose sacred character is thus uncritically acknowledged should be such as to inflict much wholly unnecessary misery. If men's kindly impulses were stronger, they would find some way of explaining that these precepts are not to be taken literally, any more than the command to "sell all that thou hast and give to the poor."

There are logical difficulties in the notion of sin. We are told that sin consists in disobedience to God's commands, but we are also told that God is omnipotent. If He is, nothing contrary to His will can occur; therefore when the sinner disobeys His commands, He must have intended this to happen. St. Augustine boldly accepts this view, and asserts that men are led to sin by a blindness with which God afflicts them. But most theologians, in modern times, have felt that, if God causes men to sin, it is not fair to send them to hell for what they cannot help. We are told that sin consists in acting contrary to God's will. This, however, does not get rid of the difficulty. Those who, like Spinoza, take God's omnipotence seriously, deduce that there can be no such thing as sin. This leads to frightful results. What! said Spinoza's contemporaries, was it not wicked of Nero to murder his mother? Was it not wicked of Adam to eat the apple? Is one action just as good as another? Spinoza wriggles, but does not find any satisfactory answer. If everything happens in accordance with God's will, God must have wanted Nero to murder his mother; therefore, since God is good, the murder must have been a good thing. From this argument there is no escape.

   Those who are in earnest in thinking that sin is _____ to God are compelled to say that God is not omnipotent. As soon as we abandon our own reason, and are content to rely upon authority, there is no end to our troubles.

Describe Spinoza's position about sin and fill in the blank with the ONE most appropriate word from the passage.

NOTE

Step 1	**S**urvey
Key Words	
Signal Words	
Step 2	**R**eading
Purpose	
Pattern of Organization	
Tone	
Main Idea	
Step 3	**S**ummary
지문 요약하기 (Paraphrasing)	
Step 4	**R**ecite
	요약문 말로 설명하기

Answer Key

Modern morals are a mixture of two elements: on the one hand, **rational precepts** as to how to live together peaceably in a society, and on the other hand **traditional taboos** derived originally from some ancient superstition, but proximately from sacred books, Christian, Mohammedan, Hindu, or Buddhist. To some extent the two agree; the prohibition of murder and theft, for instance, is supported both by human reason and by Divine command. But the prohibition of pork or beef has only scriptural authority, and that only in certain religions. **It is odd that modern men, who are aware of what science has done in the way of bringing new knowledge and altering the conditions of social life, should still be willing to accept the authority of texts embodying the outlook of very ancient and very ignorant pastoral or agricultural tribes.** It is discouraging that many of the precepts whose sacred character is thus uncritically acknowledged should be such as to inflict much wholly unnecessary misery. If men's kindly impulses were stronger, they would find some way of explaining that these precepts are not to be taken literally, any more than the command to "sell all that thou hast and give to the poor."

There are logical difficulties in the notion of sin. We are told that **sin consists in disobedience to God's commands, but we are also told that God is omnipotent**. If He is, nothing contrary to His will can occur; therefore when the sinner disobeys His commands, He must have intended this to happen. St. Augustine boldly accepts this view, and asserts that men are led to sin by a blindness with which God afflicts them. But most theologians, in modern times, have felt that, if God causes men to sin, it is not fair to send them to hell for what they cannot help. We are told that sin consists in acting contrary to God's will. This, however, does not get rid of the difficulty. Those who, like Spinoza, take God's omnipotence seriously, deduce that there can be no such thing as sin. This leads to frightful results. What! said Spinoza's contemporaries, was it not wicked of Nero to murder his mother? Was it not wicked of Adam to eat the apple? Is one action just as good as another? Spinoza wriggles, but does not find any satisfactory answer. If everything happens in accordance with God's will, God must have wanted Nero to murder his mother; therefore, since God is good, the murder must have been a good thing. From this argument there is no escape.

Those who are in earnest in thinking that sin is disobedience to God are compelled to say that God is not omnipotent. As soon as we abandon our own reason, and are content to rely upon authority, there is no end to our troubles.

writer's opinion

examples :
① St. Augustine

② Spinoza

모범답안

He thinks there cannot be sin because God is omnipotent. However, if everything happens in accordance with God's will, God must have wanted Nero to kill her mother. Therefore the murder must have been a good thing, since God is good. Second, the word is "disobedience."

한글번역

　현대 도덕은 두 가지 요소의 혼합물이다. 한편에는 한 사회 안에서 평화롭게 공존하는 방법에 관한 이성적 규율이 있고, 다른 한편에는 원래 고대의 미신에서 비롯됐으나 기독교와 이슬람교, 힌두교 또는 불교의 성스러운 경전을 통해 구체적인 틀을 갖춘 전통적 금기들이 있다. 이 두 요소는 어느 선까지는 일치한다. 예컨대 살인과 절도를 금하는 계율에 대해서는 인간의 이성과 신성 모두 찬성한다. 그러나 돼지고기나 소고기를 금하는 계율은 오로지 경전의 권위에 지나지 않고 그마저도 특정 종교에만 국한된다. 현대인들은 새로운 지식을 도입하고 사회생활의 조건을 개선하는 과정에서 과학이 어떤 공헌을 했는지 익히 알고 있다. 그런 그들이 오랜 옛날에 살던 무지한 유목 민족 또는 농경 민족의 세계관이 구현된 문헌의 권위를 지금도 기꺼이 받아들이다니, 기이한 일이 아닐 수 없다. 신성성을 이처럼 맹목적으로 인정하는 계율들 때문에 전혀 불필요한 불행이 일어나는 것을 보면 실로 참담하다. 만약 인간의 선한 충동이 지금보다 더 강하다면, 우리는 이 같은 계율을 "네가 가지고 있는 모든 것을 팔아 가난한 자들에게 주라"고 한 성서 구절과 마찬가지로 문자 그대로 받아들여서는 안 된다고 설명할 방법을 찾아낼 수 있을 것이다.

　죄라는 개념에는 논리적으로 밝히기 곤란한 부분이 있다. 우리는 하느님의 명령에 불복함으로써 죄가 성립한다고 배우지만, 동시에 하느님이 전능하다고도 배운다. 만약 하느님이 전능하다면 그분의 뜻에 어긋나는 일은 그 무엇도 일어날 수 없다. 그러므로 죄인이 하느님의 명령을 거역할 때 하느님께서는 틀림없이 그렇게 되도록 의도하셨을 것이다. 성 아우구스티누스는 이 같은 견해를 담대하게 받아들이고서 인간은 하느님께서 부과하신 무지 때문에 죄에 이른다고 주장했다. 그러나 대다수 현대 신학자들은 만약 하느님께서 인간으로 하여금 죄를 짓도록 하신다면, 인간이 스스로 어찌할 수 없는 일 때문에 지옥에 떨어지는 것은 부당하다고 느꼈다. 우리는 하느님의 뜻을 거슬러 행동함으로써 죄가 성립한다고 배운다. 그러나 이것으로는 그 난점을 해소할 수 없다. 스피노자처럼 하느님의 전능하심을 진지하게 받아들인 이들은 죄 같은 것은 있을 수 없다고 추론했다. 이 추론은 끔찍한 결과로 이어진다. 스피노자의 동시대인들은 이렇게 말했다. "무슨 소리! 어머니를 살해한 네로 황제가 악하지 않단 말인가? 사과를 먹은 아담도 악하지 않았다고? 그 두 가지 행동이 똑같이 선하단 말인가?" 스피노자는 우물쭈물할 뿐 흡족한 답을 내놓지 못했다. 만약 모든 일이 하느님의 뜻에 따라 일어난다면 하느님은 틀림없이 네로가 어머니를 죽이기를 원하셨을 것이며, 하느님은 선하시므로 그 살인 행각 또한 틀림없이 선행이었을 것이다. 이 논의에는 탈출구가 없다.

　죄란 하느님에 대한 불순종이라고 진지하게 믿는 사람들은, 결국 하느님이 전능하지 않다고 말할 수밖에 없다. 우리가 자신의 이성을 버리고 권위에만 의존하기 시작하는 순간, 우리의 곤란은 끝이 없어진다.

NOTE

Step 1	Survey
Key Words	Modern morals; rational precepts; traditional taboos
Signal Words	On the one hand; on the other hand; however; this leads to
Step 2	**Reading**
Purpose	To show comparison between the notion of sin as being a fault of man with the notion that sin was created by God
Pattern of Organization	Compare/contrast
Tone	Concerned; critical
Main Idea	The logical problems of "sin" as a concept are fatally flawed.
Step 3	**Summary**
지문 요약하기 (Paraphrasing)	In religion some rules are rational for keeping the peace, but others are spiritually formed and arbitrary to the betterment of the public. Likewise, the entire concept of sin is logically flawed because God is supposed to be all-powerful, meaning sin would have to be permitted by him. If God does allow all sin then that means that all actions right or wrong are God's will.
Step 4	**Recite**
	요약문 말로 설명하기

14   Read the passage and follow the directions.

The assassination of Julius Caesar on the steps of the Capitol in Rome is one of history's most dramatic events. Many other Roman rulers met similar fates, but Caesar's death has always had a particularly powerful hold on the imagination. This is why Shakespeare wrote *Julius Caesar*. Remember the way he is killed: he is stabbed by some of his closest supporters and friends, notably Brutus. He is betrayed at the entrance to the building which symbolizes his power (the British equivalent today might be the Houses of Parliament). He is killed in public. We respond to these details so strongly because we imagine them to be some of the deepest insecurities of tyrants: a sudden, exposed, humiliating overthrow. Put another way, the event satisfies our own deep doubts about tyrannical power. Myths and legends are ways in which cultures tell stories about themselves in pleasurable forms in order to try to resolve very deep tensions and uncertainties. This 'deep structure' is like the mind's unconscious which contains the hidden, antisocial desires of infancy. Although these desires have been locked away, they are constantly attempting to break through into our conscious life and therefore need regulating. Freud believed dreams served this function, but myths and literature were also ways in which the hidden could 'return' in socially acceptable forms. A story can be endlessly recycled, endlessly experienced, endlessly reproduced. In reading or seeing *Julius Caesar* we can experience unconsciously our desire to rebel against authority, the political equivalent of a parent figure.

In what aspect do myths and literature serve the same function as dreams? Also, why do people respond to the assassination of Julius Caesar so strongly? When you answer each question, do NOT copy more than SIX consecutive words from the passage.

_____
_____
_____
_____
_____

NOTE

Step 1	**S**urvey
Key Words	
Signal Words	
Step 2	**R**eading
Purpose	
Pattern of Organization	
Tone	
Main Idea	
Step 3	**S**ummary
지문 요약하기 (Paraphrasing)	
Step 4	**R**ecite
	요약문 말로 설명하기

Answer Key

The **assassination of Julius Caesar** on the steps of the Capitol in Rome is one of history's most dramatic events. Many other Roman rulers met similar fates, but Caesar's death has always had a particularly powerful hold on the imagination. This is ~~why~~ Shakespeare wrote *Julius Caesar*. Remember the way he is killed: he is stabbed by some of his closest supporters and friends, notably Brutus. He is betrayed at the entrance to the building which symbolizes his power (the British equivalent today might be the Houses of Parliament). He is killed in public. We respond to these details so strongly ~~because~~ we imagine them to be some of the deepest insecurities of tyrants: a sudden, exposed, humiliating overthrow. ~~Put another way~~, the event satisfies our own deep doubts about **tyrannical power**. Myths and legends are ways in which cultures tell stories about themselves in pleasurable forms in order to try to resolve very deep tensions and uncertainties. This '**deep structure**' is like the **mind's unconscious** which contains the hidden, antisocial desires of infancy. Although these desires have been locked away, they are constantly attempting to break through into our conscious life and therefore need regulating. Freud believed dreams served this function, but myths and literature were also ways in which the hidden could 'return' in socially acceptable forms. A story can be endlessly recycled, endlessly experienced, endlessly reproduced. In reading or seeing *Julius Caesar* we can experience **unconsciously** our desire to rebel against authority, the political equivalent of a parent figure.

[모범답안]

Myths and literature serve the same function as dreams in that both of them allow the hidden antisocial desires (of infancy) to return in socially satisfactory forms. Second, the detailed ways Caesar is assassinated satisfy people's deep skepticism (or distrust) about despots.

> 로마 신전 계단에서 줄리어스 시저가 암살된 것은 역사적으로 가장 드라마 같은 사건 중 하나이다. 많은 로마 정치가들도 이와 비슷한 운명에 처했지만 시저의 죽음은 늘 매우 강력하게 상상력을 끌어당긴다. 이것이 셰익스피어가 "줄리어스 시저"를 쓴 이유이다. 그가 어떻게 죽임을 당했는지 생각해보라. 그는 가장 가까웠던 지지자와 친구와 같은 사람들에 의해 공격받았다. 그는 권력을 상징하는 건물(오늘날 영국의 국회의사당) 입구에서 배신을 당했다. 그는 공개적으로 죽임을 당한 것이다. 우리는 이러한 세부내용에 대해 매우 강력하게 반응하는데 그 이유는 우리가 이 내용들이 폭군들의 가장 내면에 있는 불안감이라고 여기기 때문이다. 갑작스럽고 노출돼있으며 불명예스러운 파멸 말이다. 달리 말하면, 이 사건은 무도한 권력에 대한 우리의 깊은 의구심을 만족시켜 준다. 신화나 전설은 긴장이나 불확실성을 해결하기 위해 문화가 재미있는 형식으로 이야기 해주는 방식들이다. 이 심층구조는 유아기의 숨겨진 반사회적 욕망을 포함하는 무의식과 같다. 이런 욕망들이 갇혀있더라도 욕망은 우리의 의식적 생활 속으로 나오려고 지속적으로 시도하고 있기 때문에 규범이 필요하다. 프로이트는 꿈이 이런 기능을 한다고 믿었지만 신화나 문학 또한 숨겨진 것이 사회적으로 수용될 수 있는 형태로 돌아올 수 있는 길이었다. 이야기는 끊임없이 재활용되고 끊임없이 경험되며 끊임없이 재생산된다. 줄리어스 시저의 작품을 보거나 읽으면서 우리는 무의식적으로 권위에 반항하고 싶은 욕구를 경험할 수 있는데, 권위는 정치적으로 부모와 같은 존재이다.

NOTE

Step 1	ⓢurvey
Key Words	The assassination of Julius Caesar; deep structure; tyrants
Signal Words	Why; put another way; because
Step 2	**ⓡeading**
Purpose	To explain why the assassination of Julius Caesar remains a popular story
Pattern of Organization	Cause/effect
Tone	Objective
Main Idea	The assassination of Julius Caesar remains a popular story due to the resonant structure surrounding the event's details.
Step 3	**ⓢummary**
지문 요약하기 (Paraphrasing)	The assassination of Julius Caesar remains a popular story due to the resonant structure surrounding the event's details. As Caesar's death fits with what we want to see for tyrants, being overthrown suddenly by those close to them, it appeals to our desires and unconscious urges towards rebellion against authority.
Step 4	**ⓡecite**

요약문 말로 설명하기

15 Read the passage and follow the directions.

In what has been said of the evolution of the vicarious leisure class and its differentiation from the general body of the working classes, reference has been made to a further division of labour,—that between the different servant classes. One portion of the servant class, chiefly those persons whose occupation is vicarious leisure, come to undertake a new, subsidiary range of duties—the vicarious consumption of goods. The most obvious form in which this consumption occurs is seen in the wearing of liveries and the occupation of spacious servants' quarters. Another, scarcely less obtrusive or less effective form of vicarious consumption, and a much more widely prevalent one, is the consumption of food, clothing, dwelling, and furniture by the lady and the rest of the domestic establishment. But already at a point in economic evolution far antedating the emergence of the lady, specialized consumption of goods as an evidence of pecuniary strength had begun to work out in a more or less elaborate system. The beginning of a differentiation in consumption even antedates the appearance of anything that can fairly be called pecuniary strength. It is traceable back to the initial phase of predatory culture, and there is even a suggestion that an incipient differentiation in this respect lies back of the beginnings of the predatory life. This most primitive differentiation in the consumption of goods is like the later differentiation with which we are all so intimately familiar, in that it is largely of a ceremonial character, but unlike the latter it does not rest on a difference in accumulated wealth. The utility of consumption as an evidence of wealth is to be classed as a derivative growth. It is an adaption to a new end, by a selective process, of a distinction previously existing and well established in men's habits of thought.

Complete the idea that the writer is conveying by filling in the blank with the TWO most appropriate consecutive words from the passage.

> The most significant difference between primitive society and later society in terms of consumption of goods is that unlike the former, the latter depends on _____.

NOTE

Step 1	**S**urvey
Key Words	
Signal Words	
Step 2	**R**eading
Purpose	
Pattern of Organization	
Tone	
Main Idea	
Step 3	**S**ummary
지문 요약하기 (Paraphrasing)	
Step 4	**R**ecite
	요약문 말로 설명하기

Answer Key

In what has been said of the evolution of **the vicarious leisure class** and its differentiation from the general body of the working classes, reference has been made to a further **division of labour**,—that between the different servant classes. One portion of the servant class, chiefly those persons whose occupation is vicarious leisure, come to undertake a new, subsidiary range of duties—**the vicarious consumption of goods**. The most obvious form in which this consumption occurs is seen in the wearing of liveries and the occupation of spacious servants' quarters. (Another) scarcely less obtrusive or less effective form of vicarious consumption, and a much more widely prevalent one, is the consumption of food, clothing, dwelling, and furniture by the lady and the rest of the domestic establishment. // But already at a point in economic evolution far antedating the emergence of the lady, **specialized consumption of goods** as an evidence of pecuniary strength had begun to work out in a more or less elaborate system. The **beginning of a differentiation** in consumption even antedates the appearance of anything that can fairly be called pecuniary strength. It is traceable back to the initial phase of predatory culture, and there is even a suggestion that an incipient differentiation in this respect lies back of the beginnings of the predatory life. **This most primitive differentiation in the consumption of goods** is like the later differentiation with which we are all so intimately familiar, in that it is largely of a ceremonial character, but unlike the latter it does not rest on a **difference in accumulated wealth**. The utility of consumption as an evidence of wealth is to be classed as a derivative growth. It is an adaption to a new end, by a selective process, of a distinction previously existing and well established in men's habits of thought.

→ key words (the vicarious leisure class)
→ key words (division of labour)
ⓐ
ⓑ
→ key words (specialized consumption of goods)
→ key words (beginning of a differentiation)
→ key words (This most primitive differentiation in the consumption of goods)
→ key words (difference in accumulated wealth)

모범답안

accumulated wealth

어휘

adaptation to~ ~에 적응
domestic establishment 지배계급 여성들
incipient 시작의, 처음의, 초기의
obtrusive 눈에 띄는
prevalent 일반적인, 널리 퍼져있는
spacious 널찍한
traceable back to ~까지 거슬러 올라가는

back of~ ~의 배후에 있는
elaborate 정교한, 복잡한
leisure class 유한계급
pecuniary 금전상의
scarcely less 거의 유사하게
subsidiary 부수적인
vicarious 대리의, 대신하는, 대신하여 받는

derivative 파생적인
habits of thought 사고방식
livery 제복
predatory 약탈하는
servant's quarters 행랑채; 응접실

한글번역

　　대리적 유한계급의 진화와 전체 노동자 계급으로부터 그 계급을 구별하는 것에 대해 말할 때 언급돼야 할 것은 다름 아닌 더 심화된 (노동) 분업—즉, 서로 다른 하인 계급들 사이에서 발생한 분업이다. 주로 직업이 대리적 여가인 한 그룹의 하인 계급은 새로운 부수적인 의무를 떠맡게 되는데, 그것은 바로 대리적 상품 소비이다. 이러한 소비를 발생시키는 가장 명백한 형태는 제복의 착용과 널찍한 행랑채의 공간으로 보여진다. 거의 유사하게 눈에 띄거나 효과적인 형태의 간접적인 소비이지만 훨씬 더 널리 만연한 대리적 소비는 식품, 옷, 주거와 가구인데, 이는 귀부인들과 그 외 지배계급 여성들에 의해 행해진 것들이다. 하지만 이미 귀부인의 출현을 훨씬 앞서는 경제 발전의 어떤 시점에서는, 금전적 강점(돈이 많다는 것)의 증거로서의 상품에 대한 특화된 소비는 정도의 차이는 있지만 정교한 시스템에서 작동되기 시작했다. 소비에서 차별화의 시작은 꽤 금전상의 강점으로 불릴 수 있는 것의 출현을 앞서는 것이다. 초창기 약탈 문화로 거슬러 올라가면, 상품 소비에서 원시적 차별화는 주로 제의적 성격을 지니고 있다는 점에서 우리가 너무나 잘 알고 있는 후대(현대)의 차별화와 다르지 않다. 하지만, 현대의 차별과는 다르게 원시적 차별화는 축적된 부의 차이에 기반하고 있지 않다. 부의 증거로서 소비를 이용하는 것은 파생적 성장으로서 분류될 수 있다. 그것은, 선택 과정을 통해 새로운 목적에 맞게 적응된 것인데, 그 목적이라는 것은 이미 존재해 인간들의 사고방식에 확고히 뿌리내린 (남과 자신을) 구별(하는 것)이라는 것이다.

NOTE

Step 1	Survey
Key Words	Vicarious leisure class; vicarious consumption; differentiation in the consumption
Signal Words	Differentiation; like; unlike; less
Step 2	Reading
Purpose	To outline the ways in which a new kind of consumption grew and created changes
Pattern of Organization	Comparison/contrast; cause/effect
Tone	Objective
Main Idea	The vicarious leisure class developed its unique consumption in divergence to other working classes through changes in thought and thusly consumption of goods.
Step 3	Summary
지문 요약하기 (Paraphrasing)	The vicarious leisure class developed its unique consumption in differentiation to other working classes through changes in thought and thusly consumption of goods. The first form of this differentiation was the development of predatory culture and ceremonial character, then derived into consumption of goods.
Step 4	Recite

요약문 말로 설명하기

16 Read the passage and follow the directions.

According to criminologists working in the conflict tradition, crime is the result of conflict within societies that is brought about through the inevitable processes of capitalism. Dispute exists between those who espouse a 'pluralist' view of society and those who do not. Pluralists, following from writers like Mills, are of the belief that power is exercised in societies by groups of interested individuals (businesses, faith groups, government organizations for example) vying for influence and power to further their own interests. These criminologists have been called 'conservative conflict theorists.' They hold that crime may emerge from economic differences, differences of culture, or from struggles concerning status, ideology, morality, religion, race or ethnicity. These writers are of the belief that such groups, by claiming allegiance to mainstream culture, gain control of key resources permitting them to criminalize those who do not conform to their moral codes and cultural values. These theorists, therefore, see crime as having roots in symbolic or instrumental conflict occurring at multiple sites within a fragmented society.

Others are of the belief that such 'interests,' particularly symbolic dimensions such as status are epiphenomenological by-products of more fundamental economic conflict. For these theorists, societal conflict from which crime emerges is founded on the fundamental economic inequalities that are inherent in the processes of capitalism.

Drawing on the work of Marx, Engels, and Bonger among others, such critical theorists suggest that the conditions in which crime emerges are caused by the appropriation of others' labor through the generation of what is known as surplus value, concentrating in the hands of the few owners of the means of production, disproportionate wealth and power.

In the passage, there are TWO different points of view about the causes of crime. First, for conservative conflict theorists, who are criminals? Second, for critical theorists, what causes crime in a society? When you answer each question, do NOT copy more than SIX consecutive words from the passage.

_____
_____
_____
_____

NOTE

Step 1	**S**urvey
Key Words	
Signal Words	
Step 2	**R**eading
Purpose	
Pattern of Organization	
Tone	
Main Idea	
Step 3	**S**ummary
지문 요약하기 (Paraphrasing)	
Step 4	**R**ecite
	요약문 말로 설명하기

Answer Key

According to criminologists working in the **conflict tradition**, **crime** is the result of **conflict** within societies that is brought about through the inevitable processes of capitalism. Dispute exists between those who espouse a '**pluralist**' view of society and those who do not. **Pluralists**, following from writers like Mills, are of the belief that power is exercised in societies by groups of interested individuals (businesses, faith groups, government organizations for example) vying for influence and power to further their own interests. **These criminologists** have been called '**conservative conflict theorists**.' They hold that crime may emerge from economic differences, differences of culture, or from struggles concerning status, ideology, morality, religion, race or ethnicity. These writers are of the belief that such groups, by claiming allegiance to mainstream culture, gain control of key resources permitting them to criminalize those who do not conform to their moral codes and cultural values. These theorists, therefore, see crime as having roots in symbolic or instrumental conflict occurring at multiple sites within a fragmented society.

Others are of the belief that such 'interests,' particularly **symbolic** dimensions such as status are epiphenomenological by-products of more **fundamental economic conflict**. For these theorists, **societal conflict** from which crime emerges is founded on the fundamental economic inequalities that are inherent in the processes of capitalism.

Drawing on the work of Marx, Engels, and Bonger among others, such **critical theorists** suggest that the conditions in which **crime** emerges are caused by the appropriation of others' labor through the generation of what is known as surplus value, concentrating in the hands of the few owners of the means of production, disproportionate wealth and power.

key words

모범답안

First, according to conservative conflict theorists, criminals are those who do not conform to mainstream moral and cultural values (or codes). Second, critical theorists argue that crime is caused by social conflict, which is based on the fundamental economic inequalities, that is, the exploitation of other people's labor through the generation of surplus value.

한글번역

갈등 전통에 관련해서 종사하는 범죄학자들에 따르면, 범죄는 자본주의의 불가피한 과정을 통해 야기되는 사회 내부 갈등의 결과이다. 사회에 대한 '다원주의자'의 관점을 옹호하는 사람들과 그렇지 않은 사람들 사이의 논쟁이 존재한다. 밀스와 같은 작가들로부터 나온 다원주의자들은 자신들의 이익을 늘릴 영향력과 힘을 겨루는 이해관계에 있는 개인들의 집단들(예를 들어 사업체, 종교 단체, 정부 기관)에 의해 권력이 사회에서 행사된다는 믿음을 가진다. 이 범죄학자들은 '보수적 갈등 이론가들'이라고 불려왔다. 그들은 범죄가 경제적 차이, 문화의 차이, 혹은 지위, 이데올로기, 도덕성, 종교, 인종, 민족성과 관련된 투쟁으로부터 출현할지도 모른다고 생각한다. 이러한 작가들은 그러한 집단들이 주류의 문화에 충성을 요구함으로써 그들의 도덕적인 관례와 문화적 가치에 순응하지 않는 사람들을 불법화하는 것을 허용하는 주요 자원의 통제권을 획득한다고 믿는다. 그래서 이러한 이론가들은 범죄를 파편화된 사회 내 다양한 곳에서 발생하는 상징적이거나 도구적인 갈등에 뿌리를 두고 있다고 본다.

다른 사람들은 이러한 '이익', 특히 지위와 같은 상징적 차원이 보다 근본적인 경제 갈등의 현상학적 부산물이라고 믿는다. 이러한 이론가들에게 범죄가 발생하는 사회의 갈등은 자본주의 과정에 내재된 근본적인 경제 불평등에 기반한다.

마르크스, 엥겔, 봉거 등의 업적에 기반해, 이러한 비판적 이론가들은 범죄가 출현하는 조건들이 잉여가치라 알려진 것을 만들어내는 과정에서 다른 사람들의 노동이 소수의 생산수단 소유자에게 전유(專有)됨으로써, 부와 권력이 소수에게 불균형적으로 집중되는 데서 비롯된다고 주장한다.

NOTE

Step 1	Survey
Key Words	Conflict; crime; pluralists; interest; conservative conflict theorists; symbolic conflict; fundamental economic conflict; critical theorists; surplus value
Signal Words	Others

Step 2	Reading
Purpose	To explain the difference between conservative conflict theorists and critical theorists in terms of the cause of crime
Pattern of Organization	Comparison/contrast
Tone	Objective
Main Idea	Conservative conflict theorists believe crime to spring from a defined set of values those in power put into place to protect their own values. Alternatively, critical theorists believe crime to stem from economic inequalities caused by those appropriating others' labor and giving just a small group power and wealth.

Step 3	Summary
지문 요약하기 (Paraphrasing)	Conservative conflict theorists believe crime to spring from a defined set of values those in power put into place to protect their own values. Alternatively, critical theorists believe crime to stem from economic inequalities caused by those appropriating others' labor and giving just a small group power and wealth.

Step 4	Recite
	요약문 말로 설명하기

17 Read the passage and follow the directions.

Elected by the greatest personal triumph of any Governor ever chosen by a State, John P. Altgeld fearlessly and knowingly bared his devoted head to the fiercest, most vindictive criticism ever heaped upon a public man by the media, because he loved justice and dared to do the right. John Peter Altgeld, the son of a illiterate farm labourer, was born in Selters, Germany on 30th December, 1847. The following year the family moved to the United States and settled in Mansfield, Ohio. After a brief schooling he started work on the family farm when he was twelve years old. Altgeld became an itinerant worker in Arkansas, where he joined a railroad-building crew. Eventually Altgeld became a school teacher in Missouri. He continued to study until he qualified as a lawyer. A member of the Democratic Party, he developed a reputation for protecting the rights of the poor and in 1874 was elected district attorney of Andrew County. Altgeld moved to Chicago, Illinois, in 1875, where he wrote his book, *Our Penal Machinery and Its Victims*. The book, that argued that the United States criminal system favoured the rich over the poor, influenced a generation of social reformers, including the lawyer, Clarence Darrow and Jane Addams, the founder of the Hull House Settlement. In 1877 Altgeld returned to Ohio and married Emma Ford, a teacher. Over the next few years Altgeld became a successful businessman. Altgeld specialized in the buying and selling of real estate. One of his most successful ventures was the purchase of the sixteen-story Unity Block in Chicago. Despite his wealth, Altgeld developed a strong sympathy for the plight of the poor. He became involved in politics and with the support of the Democrats and various socialist groups, Altgeld was elected Governor of Illinois in 1892. Once in power Altgeld's embarked on an ambitious program of social reform, which included attempts to prohibit child labour and the inspection of factories. He also introduced a law prohibiting discrimination against trade union members. Altgeld controversially pardoned three men, Oscar Neebe, Samuel Fielden and Michael Schwab, convicted after the Haymarket Bombing. In 1894 President Grover Cleveland and Attorney General Richard Olney sent in federal troops to deal with the Pullman Strike. Altgeld protested against this violation of state's rights, but the action was popular with industrialists in Illinois. During the 1896 election Altgeld was attacked by the _____ for his liberal record and his love for justice.

Fill in the blank with the ONE most appropriate word from the passage.

NOTE

Step 1	**S**urvey
Key Words	
Signal Words	
Step 2	**R**eading
Purpose	
Pattern of Organization	
Tone	
Main Idea	
Step 3	**S**ummary
지문 요약하기 (Paraphrasing)	
Step 4	**R**ecite
	요약문 말로 설명하기

Answer Key

Elected by the **greatest personal triumph** of any Governor ever chosen by a State, **John P. Altgeld** fearlessly and knowingly bared his devoted head to the fiercest, most vindictive criticism ever heaped upon a public man by the media, because **he loved justice** and **dared to do the right**. John Peter Altgeld, the son of a illiterate farm labourer, was born in Selters, Germany on 30th December, 1847. The following year the family moved to the United States and settled in Mansfield, Ohio. After a brief schooling he started work on the family farm when he was twelve years old. **Altgeld** became an itinerant worker in Arkansas, where he joined a railroad-building crew. Eventually Altgeld became a school teacher in Missouri. He continued to study until he qualified as a lawyer. A member of the Democratic Party, he developed a reputation for protecting the rights of the poor and in 1874 was elected district attorney of Andrew County. **Altgeld** moved to Chicago, Illinois, in 1875, where he wrote his book, *Our Penal Machinery and Its Victims*. The book, that argued that the United States criminal system favoured the rich over the poor, influenced a generation of social reformers, including the lawyer, Clarence Darrow and Jane Addams, the founder of the Hull House Settlement. In 1877 Altgeld returned to Ohio and married Emma Ford, a teacher. Over the next few years Altgeld became a successful businessman. Altgeld specialized in the buying and selling of real estate. One of his most successful ventures was the purchase of the sixteen-story Unity Block in Chicago. Despite his wealth, Altgeld developed a strong sympathy for the plight of the poor. He became involved in politics and with the support of the Democrats and various socialist groups, Altgeld was elected Governor of Illinois in 1892. Once in power Altgeld's embarked on an ambitious program of social reform, which included attempts to prohibit child labour and the inspection of factories. He also introduced a law prohibiting discrimination against trade union members. **Altgeld** controversially pardoned three men, Oscar Neebe, Samuel Fielden and Michael Schwab, convicted after the Haymarket Bombing. In 1894 President Grover Cleveland and Attorney General Richard Olney sent in federal troops to deal with the Pullman Strike. **Altgeld** protested against this violation of state's rights, but the action was popular with industrialists in Illinois. During the 1896 election Altgeld was attacked by **the media** for **his liberal record** and his love for justice.

key words

모범답안

media

한글번역

　미국의 주에서 지금까지 선출됐던 주지사 가운데 가장 위대한 개인적 승리에 의해 선출된 존 알트겔드는 지금까지 공인에게 가해졌던 가장 격렬하고 보복적인 비난에도 두려움 없이 당당히 온몸으로 맞섰다. 왜냐하면 그는 정의를 사랑했고 대담하게도 올바른 것을 하기로 결심했기 때문이다. 한 문맹인 농장 노동자의 아들인 존 알트겔드는 1847년 12월 30일 독일의 젤터스에서 태어났다. 다음 해 그의 가족은 미국으로 이동해 맨스필드 오하이오주에 정착했다. 간단한 교육 후에 그는 12살 때 가족 농장에서 일을 시작했다. 알트겔드는 철도를 짓는 크루에 참여하게 됐던 알칸사스주에서 순회 노동자가 됐다. 끝내 알트겔드는 미주리주의 학교 선생님이 됐다. 그는 변호사 자격을 얻을 때까지 공부를 계속해 나갔다. 민주당의 한 일원이었던 그는 가난한 이들의 권리를 보호한다는 평판을 얻었고 1874년 그는 앤드류 카운티의 지방 검사로 선출됐다. 1875년이 되던 해 알트겔드는 그의 책 「Our Penal Machinery and Its Victims」를 저술했던 시카고 일리노이주로 떠났다. 서민보다는 상류층 위주로 특혜를 받던 미국 범죄체계에 대해 논했던 그 책은 변호사인 클래런스 대로와 헐 하우스 인보관 설립자였던 제인 애덤스를 포함한 사회 개혁자들의 세대에게 영향을 미쳤다. 1877년 알트겔드는 오하이오로 돌아와 교사였던 엠마 포드와 결혼했다. 향후 몇 년이 지난 후 알트겔드는 성공한 사업가가 됐다. 알트겔드는 부동산 매매를 전문으로 했다. 그의 가장 성공적이었던 벤처 사업들 중 하나는 시카고의 16층짜리 Unity Block을 매입한 것이었다. 그의 부유함에도 불구하고, 알트겔드는 가난한 이들의 역경에 대한 강한 연민을 가졌다. 그는 정치에 개입하기 시작했고 민주 당원, 그리고 각종 사회주의 단체들과 함께 했으며, 알트겔드는 1892년에 일리노이의 주지사로 선출됐다. 권력을 잡은 알트겔드는 아동 노동을 금지하고 공장을 검사하려는 시도를 포함한 야심찬 사회 개혁 프로그램을 추진했다. 그는 또한 노동조합원에 대한 차별을 금지하는 법을 도입했다. 알트겔드는 헤이마켓 폭격 후 유죄를 선고받았던 세 사람인 오스카 니브, 사무엘 필든 그리고 마이클 슈왑을 논란을 일으키며 사면했다. 1894년 그로버 클리블란드 대통령과 법무장관 리처드 올니는 풀먼 파업 사태를 처리하기 위해 연방 병력을 파견했다. 알트겔드는 이러한 주권의 위반에 대해서 항의했지만 그 행동은 일리노이의 상공업자들에게 인기있었다. 1896년 선거 운동 기간 중 알트겔드는 그의 진보적 업적과 정의에 대한 사랑에 대해 언론들로부터 공격받았다.

NOTE

Step 1	Survey
Key Words	John Altgeld; liberal record
Signal Words	30th December; 1847; The following year; Eventually; in 1874; in 1875; In 1877; Over the next few years; in 1892; In 1894; During the 1896
Step 2	**Reading**
Purpose	To illustrate John Altgeld's great life
Pattern of Organization	Time order
Tone	Admiring
Main Idea	John P. Altgeld spent his whole career protecting and sympathizing with the poor even though his conservative opponents had attacked his progressive policy.
Step 3	**Summary**
지문 요약하기 (Paraphrasing)	John P. Altgeld spent his whole career protecting and sympathizing with the poor though his conservative opponents had attacked his progressive policy. Born to an illiterate farm laborer, Altgeld rose from a farm worker to a respected lawyer and social reform advocate. His book influenced key reformers, and despite personal wealth, he championed the poor's rights, implementing significant social reforms and challenging federal intervention in the Pullman Strike, which marred his re-election prospects due to media backlash against his liberal policies.
Step 4	**Recite**
	요약문 말로 설명하기

18 Read the passage and follow the directions.

> In Plato's early works, the so-called Socratic dialogues, there are no indications that the search for virtue and the human good goes beyond the human realm. This changes with the growing interest in an all-encompassing metaphysical grounding of knowledge in Plato's middle dialogues that leads to the recognition of the 'Forms'—the true nature of all things, culminating in the Form of the Good as the transcendent principle of all goodness. Moral values must be based on an appropriate political order that can be maintained only by leaders with a rigorous philosophic training. Though the theory of the Forms is not confined to human values but embraces the nature of all there is, Plato at this point seems to presuppose no more than an analogy between human affairs and _____ harmony. The late dialogues, by contrast, display a growing tendency to see a unity between the microcosm of human life and the order of the entire universe. Such holistic tendencies would seem to put the attainment of the requisite knowledge beyond human boundaries. Though Plato's late works do not display any readiness to lower the standards of knowledge as such, in his discussion of cosmic order he leaves room for conjecture and speculation, a fact that is reflected in <u>a more pragmatic treatment</u> of ethical standards and political institutions.

Choose the ONE most appropriate word from the passage that best completes the blank. Then, describe what the underlined "a more pragmatic treatment" means.

NOTE

Step 1	**S**urvey
Key Words	
Signal Words	
Step 2	**R**eading
Purpose	
Pattern of Organization	
Tone	
Main Idea	
Step 3	**S**ummary
지문 요약하기 (Paraphrasing)	
Step 4	**R**ecite
	요약문 말로 설명하기

Answer Key

In **Plato's early works**, the so-called Socratic dialogues, there are no indications that the search for **virtue** and **the human good** goes beyond the human realm. This changes with the growing interest in an all-encompassing **metaphysical grounding** of knowledge in Plato's **middle dialogues** that leads to the recognition of the 'Forms'—the true nature of all things, culminating in the Form of the Good as the transcendent principle of all goodness. **Moral values** must be based on an appropriate **political order** that can be maintained only by leaders with a rigorous philosophic training. Though the theory of the Forms is not confined to **human values** but embraces the nature of all there is, **Plato** at this point seems to presuppose no more than an analogy between human affairs and cosmic harmony. The late dialogues, by contrast, display a growing tendency to see a unity between the microcosm of human life and the order of the entire universe. Such holistic tendencies would seem to put the attainment of the requisite knowledge **beyond human boundaries**. Though **Plato's late works** do not display any readiness to lower the standards of knowledge as such, in his discussion of **cosmic order** he leaves room for conjecture and speculation, a fact that is reflected in a more **pragmatic treatment** of **ethical standards** and **political institutions**.

time order

모범답안

The word is "cosmic". Next, the "more pragmatic treatment" means that Plato became more realistic and flexible in his approach to ethics and politics, moving away from rigid philosophical ideals to focus on what worked practically in the real world.

한글번역

플라톤의 초기 저작들, 이른바 소크라테스의 대화편이라고 하는 작품들에서는 미덕과 인간의 선에 대한 탐구가 인간적 영역을 초월하고 있음을 전혀 보여주고 있지 않다. 이러한 상황은 플라톤의 중기 대화편에서 모든 것을 아우르는 지식의 형이상학적 토대에 대한 관심이 커지면서 변화하게 된다. 이로 인해 '형상'을 인식하게 되는데, 이것은 모든 선의 초월적 원리로서의 '선의 형상'의 절정에 도달하게 되는 모든 존재의 참된 본질이다. 도덕적 가치관은 철저한 과학적 훈련을 받은 지도자들에 의해서만 유지될 수 있는 적절한 정치적 질서의 기반 위에 정립돼야 한다. 형상 이론이 인간적 가치관에만 한정된 것이 아니라, 존재하는 모든 것들의 본질을 포함하긴 하지만, 플라톤은 이 시점에서는 인간사와 우주적 조화 간의 유사성만을 전제로 하는 것으로 보인다. 이와는 대조적으로, 후기 대화편에서는 인간의 삶이라는 소우주와 전체 우주의 질서 사이에 존재하는 통일성을 바라보는 경향이 점점 커지는 것을 볼 수 있다. 그러한 전체론적 경향은 필수적인 지식의 성취를 인간의 영역 너머에 두는 것처럼 보인다. 플라톤의 후기 저작들에서 지식의 기준을 낮추려는 의지는 전혀 보이지 않지만, 그가 우주적 질서를 논할 때는 추측과 짐작의 여지를 남겨 놓고 있어서 윤리적 기준과 정치제도에 대해 좀 더 실용적인 접근을 하고 있음을 반영하고 있다.

NOTE

Step 1	Survey
Key Words	Plato; virtue; human good; ethical; metaphysical; transcendent
Signal Words	In early works; middle; the late dialogues
Step 2	**Reading**
Purpose	To show how Plato's philosophy developed over time
Pattern of Organization	Time order
Tone	Neutral
Main Idea	Plato's philosophical views evolved through three distinct phases.
Step 3	**Summary**
지문 요약하기 (Paraphrasing)	Plato's philosophical views evolved through three distinct phases. His early works, the Socratic dialogues, focused solely on human virtue. In his middle period, he introduced the theory of Forms and the Form of the Good as the foundation of knowledge, suggesting an analogy between human and cosmic harmony. His later dialogues emphasized the unity between human life and universal order, but acknowledged the limitations of human knowledge, leading to a more practical approach to ethics and politics rather than strict philosophical ideals.
Step 4	**Recite**
	요약문 말로 설명하기

19 Read the passage and follow the directions.

No artist has reinvented the visible world in a more radical way than Picasso. In his stringent early Cubist paintings, composed with fragmentary geometric planes, the differences between figure and ground are hardly distinguishable, testing the limits of representation. After the First World War, he developed a very different kind of painting, paradoxically both flat and suggestive of intangible depth, hard-edged and often brightly coloured. Recently, T. J. Clark focuses on those paintings of the 1920s and 30s in his book, *Picasso and Truth*. Picasso's works from this period have now become so familiar that their complexity and radical strangeness are often taken for granted, even overlooked. Clark's book sets out to explore just how radical and how strange these paintings are.

Ugliness and monstrosity cannot always be co-opted into another form of beauty; they are sometimes meant to shake the very foundations of the viewer's beliefs and reveal new kinds of truth. Clark sees Picasso as a kind of wizard, who had the uncanny gift of being able to see the world around him in a clearer, more truthful way than his contemporaries. Clark's book attempts to show how Picasso extends and even redefines conventional notions of truth through complex relationships between spaces and objects and subject matter, most especially through a courageous engagement with monstrosity.

Because Picasso's works of these years departed so radically from accepted norms, they were often greeted with hostility or puzzlement. In 1932, the psychologist Carl G. Jung famously compared Picasso's paintings to the pictures made by schizophrenics, and called him an "underworld" personality who followed "the demonic attraction of ugliness and evil." Although Clark does not mention Jung in this context, he casts his own similar position in a positive light, celebrating rather than damning the eerie power of Picasso's paintings. Clark acknowledges that Picasso's art contains pathological elements, but he sees them as reflections of the pathology of an age rather than of an individual. For him, Picasso's art is a judgement on a century that was rife with disaster.

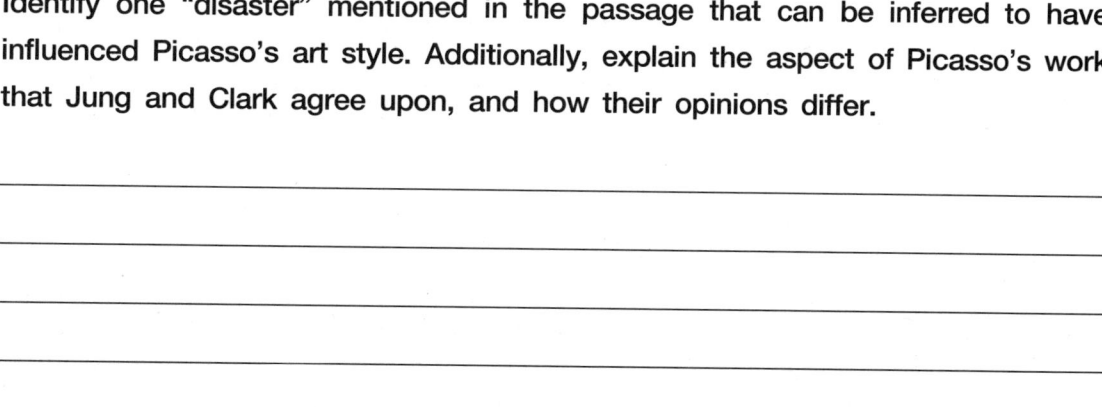

Identify one "disaster" mentioned in the passage that can be inferred to have influenced Picasso's art style. Additionally, explain the aspect of Picasso's work that Jung and Clark agree upon, and how their opinions differ.

_____
_____
_____
_____

NOTE

Step 1	**S**urvey
Key Words	
Signal Words	
Step 2	**R**eading
Purpose	
Pattern of Organization	
Tone	
Main Idea	
Step 3	**S**ummary
지문 요약하기 (Paraphrasing)	
Step 4	**R**ecite
	요약문 말로 설명하기

Answer Key

No artist has reinvented the visible world in a more radical way than **Picasso**. In his stringent early Cubist paintings, composed with fragmentary geometric planes, the differences between figure and ground are hardly distinguishable, testing the limits of representation. After the First World War, he developed a very different kind of painting, paradoxically both flat and suggestive of intangible depth, hard-edged and often brightly coloured. Recently, **T. J. Clark** focuses on those paintings of the 1920s and 30s in his book, Picasso and Truth. **Picasso's works** from this period have now become so familiar that their complexity and radical strangeness are often taken for granted, even overlooked. Clark's book sets out to explore just how radical and how strange these paintings are.

Ugliness and monstrosity cannot always be co-opted into another form of beauty; they are sometimes meant to shake the very foundations of the viewer's beliefs and reveal new kinds of truth. Clark sees Picasso as a kind of wizard, who had the uncanny gift of being able to see the world around him in a clearer, more truthful way than his contemporaries. Clark's book attempts **to show how Picasso extends and even redefines conventional notions of truth through complex relationships between spaces and objects and subject matter, most especially through a courageous engagement with monstrosity**.

Because Picasso's works of these years departed so radically from accepted norms, they were often greeted with hostility or puzzlement. In 1932, the psychologist Carl G. Jung famously compared Picasso's paintings to the pictures made by schizophrenics, and called him an "underworld" personality who followed "the demonic attraction of ugliness and evil." Although Clark does not mention Jung in this context, he casts his own similar position in a positive light, **celebrating** rather than damning **the eerie power of Picasso's paintings**. Clark acknowledges that Picasso's art contains pathological elements, but he sees them as **reflections of the pathology of an age** rather than of an individual. For him, **Picasso's art is a judgement on a century that was rife with disaster**.

→ key words

모범답안

One "disaster" to influence Picasso that is referred to in the passage is World War I. Both Jung and Clark agree on the eeriness and pathological quality of Picasso's work, but Jung viewed the work as ugly and akin to schizophrenics' art whilst Clark saw them as reflecting the problem of the era's mindset, not the artist's.

어휘

co-opt 선임하다, 끌어들이다
schizophrenic 정신 분열병 환자
hard-edged 냉철한, 철저히 현실에 입각한
stringent 엄중한, 엄격한, 긴박한

한글번역

피카소보다 더 급진적인 방식으로 가시적인 세상을 보여준 예술가는 없었다. 파편화된 기하학적인 평면들로 구성된 그의 엄격한 초기 입체파 그림들에서는 인물과 배경 사이의 차이점이 거의 구분이 되지 않으며 구상적 재현의 한계를 시험하고 있다. 제1차 세계대전이 끝난 뒤, 그는 역설적으로 평평하면서도 뭐라 꼬집어 말할 수 없는 깊이를 암시하고, 현실을 예리하게 묘사하면서도 종종 밝게 채색된 매우 다른 종류의 그림을 그렸다. 최근에 T. J. 클락은 그의 저서인 <피카소와 진실>에서 1920년대와 30년대의 피카소 그림들에 초점을 맞추고 있다. 이 시기의 피카소 그림들은 지금은 아주 익숙해져서 그림들의 복잡함과 극단적인 생소함이 종종 당연한 것으로 여겨지고 있고 심지어 간과되기도 한다. 클락의 책은 이 그림들이 얼마나 급진적이고 생소한지를 탐구하고 있다.

추악함과 기괴함이 항상 또 다른 형태의 아름다움이라고 내세워질 수는 없다; 왜냐하면 그러한 것들은 때때로 그림을 보는 사람들의 믿음의 토대를 흔들어 새로운 종류의 진실을 드러내도록 의도했기 때문이다. 클락은 피카소를 동시대인들보다 더 분명하고 더 진실된 방식으로 자신의 주변 세상을 볼 수 있는 초자연적인 재능을 가진 일종의 마법사로 여기고 있다. 클락의 책은 피카소가 어떻게 공간과 물체 그리고 주제 사이의 복잡한 관계를 통해, 특히 기괴함을 대담하게 수용함으로써 틀에 박힌 진실의 개념을 확대하고 심지어 재정의하는지를 보여주고 있다.

이 몇 년간 피카소의 작품들은 보편적인 규범들로부터 아주 급진적으로 이탈돼 있었기 때문에 종종 적대감이나 혼란스러움으로 받아들여졌다. 1932년에 심리학자인 칼 융은 피카소의 그림을 정신분열증 환자가 그린 그림과 비교해 그를 '추악함과 사악함의 악마적 매력'을 추구하는 '저승에서 온 인간'이라 불렀다. 비록 클락은 이러한 맥락에서 융을 언급하지는 않지만 긍정적인 관점에서 그와 비슷한 자신의 의견을 드러내고 피카소 그림들의 섬뜩한 힘을 혹평하기보다는 오히려 높이 평가하고 있다. 클락은 피카소의 작품에 병적인 요소가 포함됐음을 인정하고 있지만 그는 피카소의 작품들이 한 개인의 병적 상태라기보다는 한 시대의 병적 상태를 반영하고 있다고 보고 있다. 그에게 피카소의 그림은 재난으로 가득했던 한 세기에 대한 판단이다.

NOTE

Step 1	Survey
Key Words	Picasso's art; T. J. Clark; truth; monstrosity
Signal Words	Not clear
Step 2	**Reading**
Purpose	To explain author T. J. Clark's view of Picasso's art
Pattern of Organization	Not clear
Tone	Neutral
Main Idea	Although Picasso's work contains ugly, monstrous elements, T. J. Clark argues it is a radical and truthful reflection of the age and therefore valuable.
Step 3	**Summary**
지문 요약하기 (Paraphrasing)	Although Picasso's work contains ugly, monstrous elements, T. J. Clark, the author of *Picasso and Truth*, argues it is a radical and truthful reflection of the age and therefore valuable. Picasso's art was a departure from the norms of art in his time, which some viewed with hostility and puzzlement. However, Clark asserts that Picasso was able to see the world in a more truthful way than his contemporaries and that the pathological elements in Picasso's art reflect the character of an age rather than of the artist himself.
Step 4	**Recite**
	요약문 말로 설명하기

20 Read the passage and follow the directions.

At precisely 4 P.M., Monday through Friday, Oprah appears on innumerable television sets in her shows. First, before the live action starts, a theme song is heard. Oprah sings her own song, in which the main lyrics are, I will rise: Various photographic stills of Oprah are flashed on the screen. Some of these snapshots include Oprah hugging a distraught fan, Oprah laughing with that signature smile, Oprah dancing with her hands clapped together, Oprah bent down on one knee like a preacher holding a young girl's hand. All of these images are there to relax the television viewing audience and to assure them that Oprah is a kind, caring, fun-loving individual who really is real.

When Oprah first appears, she sets the stage and the mood for what is to come. The show begins after a brief commercial break with an excited-looking Oprah running onto the set to the cheers of a very enthusiastic audience. Oprah gives audience members high fives; on her face is a huge grin as she prances onto the stage. The applause goes on for a moment or two as Oprah bows, and then the cheering dies out. Speaking loudly into her handheld microphone, Oprah greets the audience in a very friendly manner and points out some things about the audience that she finds funny. Often she relates to the audience something that occurred to her backstage. After cheerfully bantering with the audience, Oprah explains what she has in store for them today. Sometimes she has a celebrity guest, other times she has a regular person whose story has inspired her. Her celebrity guests have included stars like Julia Roberts and Will Smith; her regular guests have shared their triumphs and problems. On other _____ she picks a topic like how to handle your money and invites financial experts on the show. They may cover such skills as how to save money at the grocery store or how to balance your checkbook.

Fill in the blank with the ONE most appropriate word from the passage.

NOTE

Step 1	Ⓢurvey
Key Words	
Signal Words	
Step 2	**Ⓡeading**
Purpose	
Pattern of Organization	
Tone	
Main Idea	
Step 3	**Ⓢummary**
지문 요약하기 (Paraphrasing)	
Step 4	**Ⓡecite**
요약문 말로 설명하기	

Answer Key

At precisely 4 P.M., Monday through Friday, **Oprah** appears on innumerable television sets in her shows. First, before the live action starts, [a theme song is heard.] Oprah sings her own song, in which the main lyrics are, "I will rise." [Various photographic stills of Oprah] are flashed on the screen. Some of these snapshots include Oprah ⓐ hugging a distraught fan, Oprah ⓑ laughing with that signature smile, Oprah ⓒ dancing with her hands clapped together, Oprah bent down on one knee like a preacher ⓓ holding a young girl's hand. All of these images are there to relax the television viewing audience and to assure them that Oprah is a kind, caring, fun-loving individual who really is "real."

When Oprah first appears, she sets the stage and the mood for what is to come. [The show begins after a brief commercial break with an excited-looking Oprah running onto the set] to the ⓐ cheers of a very enthusiastic audience. Oprah gives audience members ⓑ high fives; on her face is a huge grin as she prances onto the stage. The ⓒ applause goes on for a moment or two as Oprah bows, and then the cheering dies out. Speaking loudly into her handheld microphone, Oprah ⓓ greets the audience in a very friendly manner and points out some things about the audience that she finds funny. Often she relates to the audience something that occurred to her backstage. After cheerfully bantering with the audience, [Oprah explains what she has in store for them today.] Sometimes she has ⓐ a celebrity guest, other times she has a "regular" person whose story has inspired her. Her celebrity guests have included stars like Julia Roberts and Will Smith; her "regular" guests have shared their triumphs and problems. On other shows she picks ⓑ a topic like how to handle your money and invites financial experts on the show. They may cover such skills as how to save money at the grocery store or how to balance your checkbook.

▶ key word
— major supporting details: the theme songs
— minor supporting details: Oprah song

▶ *appearance* (반복됨)
— major supporting details: the photographic still of Oprah
— minor supporting details:
ⓐ hugging a fan
ⓑ laughing
ⓒ dancing
ⓓ holding a girl's hand

main idea
— major supporting details: Oprah running onto the set and starts the shows
— minor supporting details:
ⓐ cheering
ⓑ high fives
ⓒ applauding
ⓓ sharing something funny that occurred backstage

— major supporting details: explains the day's program
— minor supporting details:
ⓐ guests
ⓑ special topic

모범답안
shows

어휘

banter 잡담을 나누다(=chat)
distraught (흥분해서) 제정신이 아닌

prance 걸어 다니다, 휘젓고 다니다

한글번역

　월요일부터 금요일까지 정확히 오후 4시에 오프라는 수많은 티비에 등장한다. 먼저 생방송이 시작되기 전에 주제곡이 흘러나온다. 오프라는 주 가사가 "나는 일어날 거야"라는 자신의 노래를 부른다. 화면에는 수많은 오프라의 스틸 사진이 비친다. 오프라가 (흥분해서) 제정신이 아닌 팬을 끌어안는 장면, 오프라의 그 특유의 미소로 웃는 모습, 오프라가 박수를 치며 춤추는 장면, 오프라가 목사님처럼 한쪽 다리를 구부리고 어린 소녀의 손을 잡고 있는 장면 등이 이들 스냅샷이다. 이 모든 이미지들은 텔레비전을 보는 시청자들을 이완하게 해주고, 오프라가 친절하고, 따뜻하며, 재미있고, 사랑이 많은 '진짜' 인물임을 확신시켜 주기 위함이다.

　오프라가 일단 들어오면, 그녀는 무대와 분위기를 앞으로 진행될 일에 맞춰 놓는다. 쇼는 짤막한 광고 이후에 열광적인 관중들의 환호를 받으며 흥분한 표정의 오프라가 세트로 뛰어 들어오면서 시작된다. 오프라는 관중들과 하이파이브를 하고 무대를 걸어 다니는 동안 얼굴에는 환한 미소를 띠고 있다. 오프라가 인사를 하는 동안 박수는 한동안 계속되고 환호는 가라앉는다. 손에 쥔 마이크에 크게 말을 하면서 오프라는 관중들을 대단히 친근한 매너로 맞이하고 자신이 관중들 사이에서 재미있다고 생각한 것들을 말한다. 가끔 그녀는 무대 뒤편에서 일어난 일들에 대해 관중들에게 말한다. 관중들과 활기차게 몇 마디를 나눈 후 오프라는 오늘의 주제가 무엇인지를 설명한다. 어떤 때는 유명인사가 손님일 때도 있고, 또 어떤 경우는 그녀에게 인상을 준 '보통 사람'을 데려올 때도 있다. 그녀의 유명인 손님은 줄리아 로버츠나 윌 스미스 같은 스타들을 포함한다. 일반인 손님은 자신들의 성취나 문제점들을 공유한다. 또 어떤 쇼에서는 어떻게 돈을 관리할지와 같은 주제를 선정하고 쇼에 경제 전문가를 초대하기도 한다. 이들 쇼에서는 식품점에서 돈을 아끼는 기술이라든지 어떻게 체크북 잔액을 관리하는지 등을 알려준다.

NOTE

Step 1	**S**urvey
Key Words	Oprah; appearance; television show
Signal Words	At precisely 4 P.M.; First; When; after
Step 2	**R**eading
Purpose	To depict the Oprah Winfrey show
Pattern of Organization	Time order; series
Tone	Cheerful; informative
Main Idea	Oprah's show presents herself as real and friendly as she gives her thoughts and talks with both celebrity and inspiring guests.
Step 3	**S**ummary
지문 요약하기 (Paraphrasing)	Oprah's show opens with images establishing her as real and friendly. After this she gives some thoughts and observations before talking with both celebrity and inspiring guests about various topics.
Step 4	**R**ecite
	요약문 말로 설명하기

MEMO

21 Read the passage and follow the directions.

In the Medieval Age, when personal attention was focused more on securing a place in the next world, virtue was what every good Christian aspired to. To lead a virtuous life and to be of good virtue assured eternal salvation. In the Modern Age, virtue began drifting to the margins as society became increasingly production oriented. The bourgeoisie began to substitute character for virtue. By the nineteenth century, character had become one of the most important descriptive words in the English vocabulary. To be of good character was the highest compliment one could extend to a bourgeois man or woman. Character, more than anything else, conjured up the notion of self-control and self-mastery. The term character became associated with citizenship, hard work, industriousness, determination, frugality, integrity, and, above all else, adulthood. It represented both a secularization of the values of the Protestant work ethic and a reaffirmation of the kind of producer values deemed so important to advancing the capitalist agenda and propertied regime.

By the early 1920s, however, _____ was beginning to wane in importance and a new concept of self was beginning to emerge, first in the pages of self-improvement manuals and books and later in the popular culture. Commentators of the day urged Americans to develop their personalities. Orison Swett Marden, who just a generation earlier had written on the qualities of good character, published a new book, *The Masterful Personality*, in 1921, in which he urged his readers to learn to exhibit personal charm. Marden reminded his followers that "so much of our success in life depends upon what others think of us."

He counseled that manners, proper clothes, good conversation ("to know what to say and how to say it"), energy, life efficiency, and poise all are qualities that everyone can use to "sway great masses." The words used to describe personality were quite different from those used to describe character. Someone is said to have personality if he or she is attractive, creative, fascinating, forceful, magnetic, engaging, vivacious, demonstrative, and warm. To have personality is to stand out in a crowd, to be noticed, to command attention, to influence others. To "be yourself," to "express your individuality." To "have self-confidence" became the rallying cry of a generation. Those very qualities, in turn, became the psychological raw material for mass marketing techniques and national advertising campaigns designed to turn a nation of savers and producers into a nation of spenders and consumers.

Fill in the blank with the ONE most appropriate word from the passage. Also, write a summary following the guidelines below.

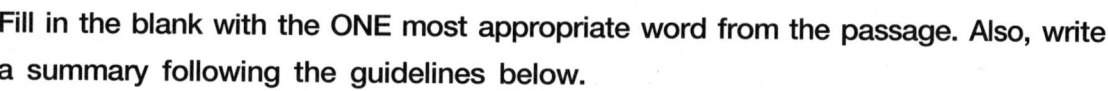 Guidelines

- Summarize the above passage in ONE paragraph.
- Provide a topic sentence and supporting details from the passage.
- Do NOT copy more than FIVE consecutive words from the passage.

NOTE

Step 1	**S**urvey
Key Words	
Signal Words	
Step 2	**R**eading
Purpose	
Pattern of Organization	
Tone	
Main Idea	
Step 3	**S**ummary
지문 요약하기 (Paraphrasing)	
Step 4	**R**ecite
	요약문 말로 설명하기

Answer Key

In the Medieval Age, when personal attention was focused more on securing a place in the next world, **virtue** was what every good Christian aspired to. To lead a virtuous life and to be of good virtue assured eternal salvation. In the Modern Age, virtue began drifting to the margins as society became increasingly production oriented. The bourgeoisie began to substitute character for virtue. By the nineteenth century, **character** had become one of the most important descriptive words in the English vocabulary. To be of good character was the highest compliment one could extend to a bourgeois man or woman. **Character**, more than anything else, conjured up the notion of self-control and self-mastery. The term character became associated with citizenship, hard work, industriousness, determination, frugality, integrity, and, above all else, adulthood. It represented both a secularization of the values of the Protestant work ethic and a reaffirmation of the kind of producer values deemed so important to advancing the capitalist agenda and propertied regime.

By the early 1920s, however, **character** was beginning to wane in importance and a new concept of self was beginning to emerge, first in the pages of self-improvement manuals and books and later in the popular culture. Commentators of the day urged Americans to develop their **personalities**. Orison Swett Marden, who just a generation earlier had written on the qualities of good **character**, published a new book, *The Masterful Personality*, in 1921, in which he urged his readers to learn to exhibit personal charm. Marden reminded his followers that "so much of our success in life depends upon what others think of us." He counseled that manners, proper clothes, good conversation ("to know what to say and how to say it"), energy, life efficiency, and poise all are qualities that everyone can use to "sway great masses." The words used to describe **personality** were quite different from those used to describe **character**. Someone is said to have personality if he or she is attractive, creative, fascinating, forceful, magnetic, engaging, vivacious, demonstrative, and warm. To have **personality** is to stand out in a crowd, to be noticed, to command attention, to influence others. To "be yourself," to "express your individuality." To "have self-confidence" became the rallying cry of a generation. Those very qualities, in turn, became the psychological raw material for mass marketing techniques and national advertising campaigns designed to turn a nation of savers and producers into a nation of spenders and consumers.

모범답안

The word in the blank should be "character". Second, the value by which people were primarily celebrated and weighed has changed over time. From the Medieval age to the nineteenth century, "virtue" was the primary factor to considering a person's merit. Subsequently, and until the 1920s, "character" became the leading quality. Following this, there was a clear shift towards "personality". Those who stood out and had strengths and unique properties as individuals were given praise(were praised).

채점기준

+ 1점: 빈칸에 들어갈 한 단어를 "character"라 기입하였다. 이외에는 답이 될 수 없다.
+ 1점: 글의 topic sentence를 다음과 같이 서술하였거나 유사하였다.
"The value by which people were primarily celebrated and weighed has changed over time."
+ 2점: 글의 major supporting details를 다음과 같이 서술하였거나 유사하였다.
"① From the Medieval age to the nineteenth century, "virtue" was the primary factor to considering a person's merit. ② Subsequently, and until the 1920s, "character" became the leading quality. ③ Following this, there was a clear shift towards "personality". Those who stood out and had strengths and unique properties as individuals were given praise."
☞ 3개 중 3개 모두를 정확하게 서술한 경우 2점, 2개만 서술한 경우 1점, 1개 또는 서술하지 못한 경우 0점을 준다. 이때 시간을 나타내는 signal words가 없으면 각각 0.5점씩 감점한다.

한글번역

중세인의 가장 큰 관심사는 내세에서 안전한 자리를 차지하는 것이었다. 그래서 선량한 기독교도라면 누구나 덕을 쌓고 싶어 했다. 덕을 쌓은 사람은 영원한 구원을 받을 수 있다고 그들은 믿었다. 그러나 근대로 들어와 사회가 점점 생산 지향적으로 움직이면서 덕은 변방으로 밀려나기 시작했다. 부르주아는 덕보다는 양식을 강조하기 시작했다. 19세기로 오면 양식이라는 단어는 영어 어휘 중에서 가장 중요한 묘사어의 하나로 굳건히 자리 잡는다. 양식이 있다는 말은 남녀를 불문하고 부르주아가 가장 듣고 싶어하는 말이었다. 양식은 무엇보다도 자기 절제와 자기 통제라는 관념을 연상시켰다. 양식은 시민의식, 근면, 성실, 의지, 검약, 청렴, 그리고 성숙함과 자연스럽게 연결됐다. 그것은 프로테스탄트의 노동 윤리에 담긴 정신을 세속화시키면서 동시에 자본주의와 사유 재산 체제를 앞으로 밀고 나가는 데 중요한 역할을 할 생산자 정신의 가치를 재확인하는 말이었다.

그러나 1920년대부터는 상황이 달라졌다. 양식의 중요성이 점점 약해지고, 새로운 자아의 개념이 처음에는 자아를 향상시키려는 요령을 가르치는 책에서 나타나더니 나중에는 대중문화로까지 침투했다. 당시 이 방면의 전문가들은 매력을 갈고 닦아야 한다고 강조했다. 불과 한 세대 전까지만 하더라도 바람직한 양식의 특성에 대해서 글을 썼던 오리즌 스웨트 마든이 1921년에는 "매력 있는 인간"이라는 책을 써서 독자들에게 개인적 매력을 발산하는 비결을 배우라고 촉구했다. 마든은 그의 추종자들에게 "남들이 우리를 어떻게 생각하느냐에 따라 우리는 성공할 수도 있고 실패할 수도 있다"고 강조했다. 그는 예의범절, 경우에 맞는 옷차림, 원만한 화술(언제 무슨 말을 해야 할지 아는 것), 활력, 절도 있는 생활, 바른 몸가짐만 익히면 누구나 "만인을 자기편으로 만들 수 있다"고 조언했다. 매력 있는 인간을 묘사하는 데 동원되는 단어는 양식 있는 인간을 묘사하는 데 쓰이던 단어와는 판이하게 달랐다. 호감을 주고 창조적이고 흡인력 있고 끄는 힘이 있고 애교 있고 쾌활하고 속을 드러내는 포근한 사람을 두고 우리는 매력 있는 인간이라고 말한다. 그런 사람은 수많은 군중 속에 있어도 단번에 좌중의 시선을 끌어들이는 힘이 있고 남에게 영향을 미칠 수 있는 능력이 있다. "나 자신이 되자", "나의 개성을 표현하자", "자기 확신을 가지자" 같은 구호가 시대를 풍미했다. 이런 구호는 저축과 생산 중심의 사회를 지출과 소비 중심의 사회로 탈바꿈시키기 위해 고안된 마케팅 기법과 국가 차원의 선전을 위한 심리적 재료가 됐다.

NOTE

Step 1	Ⓢurvey
Key Words	Virtue; character; personalities
Signal Words	In the Medieval Age; By the nineteenth century; By the early 1920s
Step 2	**Ⓡeading**
Purpose	To explain how the value by which people were primarily celebrated and weighed has changed over time
Pattern of Organization	Time order
Tone	Neutral
Main Idea	The value by which people were primarily celebrated and weighed has changed over time.
Step 3	**Ⓢummary**
지문 요약하기 (Paraphrasing)	The value by which people were primarily celebrated and weighed has changed over time. From the Medieval age to the nineteenth century, "virtue" was the primary factor to considering a person's merit. Subsequently, and until the 1920s, "character" became the leading quality. Following this, there was a clear shift towards "personality". Those who stood out and had strengths and unique properties as individuals were given praise(were praised).
Step 4	**Ⓡecite**
	요약문 말로 설명하기

22   Read the passage and follow the directions.

According to a recent Gallup survey, only 15 percent of Americans think that Homo sapiens evolved through natural selection alone, free of all divine intervention; 32 percent maintain that humans may have evolved from earlier life forms in a process lasting millions of years, but God orchestrated this entire show; 46 percent believe that God created humans in their current form sometime during the last 10,000 years, just as the Bible says. Spending three years in college has absolutely no impact on these views. Though schools evidently do a very poor job teaching evolution, religious zealots still insist that it should not be taught at all. Alternatively, they demand that children must also be taught the theory of intelligent design, according to which all organisms were created by the design of some higher intelligence. "Teach them both theories," say the zealots, "and let the kids decide for themselves."

Why does the theory of evolution provoke such objections, whereas nobody seems to care about the theory of relativity or quantum mechanics? How come politicians don't ask that kids be exposed to alternative theories about matter, energy, space and time? After all, Darwin's ideas seem at first sight far less threatening than the monstrosities of Einstein and Werner Heisenberg. The theory of evolution rests on the principle of the survival of the fittest, which is a clear and simple—not to say humdrum—idea. In contrast, the theory of relativity and quantum mechanics argue that you can twist time and space, that something can appear out of nothing, and that a cat can be both alive and dead at the same time. This makes a mockery of our common sense, yet nobody seeks to protect innocent schoolchildren from these scandalous ideas. The theory of relativity makes nobody angry, because it doesn't contradict any of our cherished beliefs. Most people don't care an iota whether space and time are absolute or relative. If you think it is possible to bend space and time, well, be my guest. Go ahead and bend them. What do I care? In contrast, Darwin has deprived us of our souls. If you really understand the theory of evolution, you understand that there is no soul.

Summarize the passage following the guidelines below.

| Guidelines |

- Summarize the above passage in ONE paragraph.
- Provide a topic sentence and supporting ideas from the passage.
- Be sure to include the main reason the theory of evolution provokes much antagonism in your summary.
- Do NOT copy more than FIVE consecutive words from the passage.

_____
_____
_____
_____
_____

NOTE

Step 1	**S**urvey
Key Words	
Signal Words	
Step 2	**R**eading
Purpose	
Pattern of Organization	
Tone	
Main Idea	
Step 3	**S**ummary
지문 요약하기 (Paraphrasing)	
Step 4	**R**ecite
	요약문 말로 설명하기

Answer Key

According to a recent Gallup survey, only 15 percent of Americans think that Homo sapiens evolved through **natural selection** alone, free of all divine intervention; 32 percent maintain that humans may have evolved from earlier life forms in a process lasting millions of years, but God orchestrated this entire show; 46 percent believe that God created humans in their current form sometime during the last 10,000 years, just as the Bible says. Spending three years in college has absolutely no impact on these views. Though schools evidently do a very poor job teaching evolution, **religious zealots** still insist that it should not be taught at all. Alternatively, they demand that children must also be taught the theory of intelligent design, according to which all organisms were created by the design of some higher intelligence. "Teach them both theories," say the zealots, "and let the kids decide for themselves."

Why does the theory of evolution provoke such objections, whereas nobody seems to care about the theory of relativity or quantum mechanics? How come politicians don't ask that kids be exposed to alternative theories about matter, energy, space and time? After all, Darwin's ideas seem at first sight far less threatening than the monstrosities of Einstein and Werner Heisenberg. The theory of evolution rests on the principle of the survival of the fittest, which is a clear and simple—not to say humdrum—idea. In contrast, **the theory of relativity and quantum mechanics** argue that you can twist time and space, that something can appear out of nothing, and that a cat can be both alive and dead at the same time. This makes a mockery of our common sense, yet nobody seeks to protect innocent schoolchildren from these scandalous ideas. **The theory of relativity makes nobody angry, because it doesn't contradict any of our cherished beliefs.** Most people don't care an iota whether space and time are absolute or relative. If you think it is possible to bend space and time, well, be my guest. Go ahead and bend them. What do I care? In contrast, **Darwin has deprived us of our souls**. If you really understand **the theory of evolution**, you understand that there is no soul.

→ key words

key question

answers
①

②

모범답안

The theory of evolution in the United States elicits strong opposition from people who believe God created the world. Not more than 15 percent of American people believe evolutionary theory while more than 75 percent of Americans reject it. Though other scientific theories, such as quantum theory and the theory of relativity, have much deeper implications about the nature of reality, they face no such challenge. It is because evolutionary theory challenges "cherished beliefs" and proves "that there is no soul".

> **채점기준**

+1점: 글의 topic sentence를 다음과 같이 서술하였거나 유사하였다.
"The theory of evolution in the United States elicits strong opposition from people who believe God created the world." 또는 "The theory of evolution, unlike other scientific theories, elicits strong opposition from religious people who believe God created the world."

+1점: 글의 첫 번째 문단을 다음과 같이 요약하였다.
"Not more than 15 percent of American people believe evolutionary theory while more than 75 percent of Americans reject it."

☞ 답안에 구체적인 숫자 대신에 "소수"와 "대다수"라는 표현을 썼어도 맞는 것으로 한다.
☞ 위와 유사한 내용을 서술하였고, 학교 교육의 현실에 대한 설명이 추가로 있어도 맞는 것으로 한다.

+2점: 문제에서 요구한 내용을 다른 과학이론과의 관계 속에서 다음과 같이 설득력 있게 요약하였다.
"<u>Though other scientific theories, such as quantum theory and the theory of relativity, have much deeper implications about the nature of reality, they face no such challenge</u>(1점). It is because <u>evolutionary theory challenges "cherished beliefs" and proves "that there is no soul"</u>(1점)."

☞ 답안에 "other scientific theories"만 언급하고 "quantum theory and the theory of relativity"를 서술하지 않았으면 0.5점 감점을 한다.

● **감점**
• 본문에 나오는 연속되는 6단어 이상을 사용하였다. -0.5pt
• 문단을 두 개나 그 이상으로 구성하였다. -0.5pt

> **한글번역**

최근 갤럽조사에 따르면 미국인의 오직 15%만이 호모사피엔스가 신의 개입 없이 자연선택만을 통해 진화했다고 생각한다; 32%는 인간이 초기 생명 형태부터 수백만 년에 걸쳐 진화했을 가능성이 있지만 신이 이 쇼 전체를 지휘했다고 주장한다; 46%의 미국인은 성경에 적힌 그대로 신이 지난 1만 년 동안의 어느 시점에 지금의 형태로 인간을 창조했다고 믿는다. 3년간 대학을 다녀도 이러한 견해는 절대 바뀌지 않는다. 학교가 진화에 대해 제대로 가르치지 못한 것이 분명하지만, 열성적인 신자들은 그것도 모자라 진화를 아예 가르치지 말아야 한다고 주장한다. 혹은 지적설계론도 함께 학생들에게 가르치라고 요구한다. 지적설계론에 따르면 모든 생명체는 어떤 지적 존재(신)의 설계로 창조됐다. 신자들은 "아이들에게 두 이론을 모두 가르치고 아이들 스스로 결정하게 하라"고 주장한다.

그런데 왜 진화론에는 이렇듯 격렬한 반대를 일으키면서도 상대성이론이나 양자역학에는 아무도 신경 쓰지 않을까? 왜 정치인들은 물질, 에너지, 공간, 시간에 대한 대안이론들을 아이들에게 가르치라고 요구하지 않을까? 따지고 보면 다윈의 이론들은 처음에는 아인슈타인과 베르너 하이젠베르크의 기괴한 이론들보다 훨씬 덜 위협적으로 보인다. 진화이론의 토대인 최적자 생존원리는 단조롭다고 말할 수는 없어도 간단명료한 개념이다. 반면 상대성 이론과 양자역학은 시간과 공간을 구부릴 수 있고 무에서 어떤 것이 출현할 수 있으며 고양이가 살아 있는 동시에 죽은 상태일 수 있다고 주장한다. 이런 주장은 우리의 상식을 조롱하지만, 아무도 이 해괴망측한 이론들로부터 죄 없는 학생들을 보호하려고 하지 않는다. 상대성이론은 아무도 화나게 하지 않는다. 왜냐하면 우리의 소중한 믿음 가운데 어떤 것과도 모순되지 않기 때문이다. 대부분의 사람들은 공간과 시간이 절대적인지 상대적인지 눈곱만큼도 관심이 없다. 만일 당신이 공간과 시간을 구부리는 것이 가능하다고 생각한다면 마음대로 하라는 식이다. 가서 그것을 구부려라. 내가 무슨 상관인가? 반면 다윈은 우리에게서 영혼을 박탈했다. 당신이 진화론을 제대로 이해한다면 그것이 영혼은 없다는 이야기임을 알아차릴 것이다.

NOTE

Step 1	Survey
Key Words	Natural selection; the theory of evolution; religious zealots; the theory of relativity and quantum mechanics
Signal Words	Why; because; in contrast
Step 2	**Reading**
Purpose	To explain why the theory of evolution provokes such objections
Pattern of Organization	Cause/effect
Tone	Critical
Main Idea	The theory of evolution in the United States elicits strong opposition from people who believe God created the world. It is because evolutionary theory challenges "cherished beliefs" and proves "that there is no soul".
Step 3	**Summary**
지문 요약하기 (Paraphrasing)	The theory of evolution in the United States elicits strong opposition from people who believe God created the world. Not more than 15 percent of American people believe evolutionary theory while more than 75 percent of Americans reject it. Though other scientific theories, such as quantum theory and the theory of relativity, have much deeper implications about the nature of reality, they face no such challenge. It is because evolutionary theory challenges "cherished beliefs" and proves "that there is no soul".
Step 4	**Recite**
	요약문 말로 설명하기

23 Read the passage and follow the directions.

One of the most striking tendencies of our time is the expansion of markets and market-oriented reasoning into spheres of life traditionally governed by non-market norms. We consider the moral questions that arise, for example, when countries hire out military service and the interrogation of prisoners to mercenaries or private contractors; or when parents outsource pregnancy and child-bearing to paid laborers in the developing world; or when people buy and sell kidneys on the open market. Other instances abound: Should students in under performing schools be offered cash payments for scoring well on standardized tests? Should teachers be given bonuses for improving the test results of their students? Should states hire for-profit prison companies to house their inmates? Should the United States simplify its immigration policy by adopting the proposal of a University of Chicago economist to sell U.S. citizenship for a $100,000 fee? These questions are not only about utility and consent. They are also about the right ways of valuing key social practices— military service, child-bearing, teaching and learning, criminal punishment, the admission of new citizens, and so on. Since marketizing social practices may corrupt or degrade the norms that define them, we need to ask what non-market norms we want to protect from market intrusion. This is a question that requires public debate about <u>competing conceptions</u> of the right way of valuing goods. Markets are useful instruments for organizing productive activity. But unless we want to let the market rewrite the norms that govern social institutions, we need a public debate about the moral limits of markets.

MEMO

Summarize the passage following the guidelines below.

| Guidelines |

- Summarize the above passage in ONE paragraph.
- Provide a topic sentence, supporting ideas from the passage, and a concluding sentence.
- Be sure to identify the "competing conceptions" of the underlined section in your summary.
- Do NOT copy more than FIVE consecutive words from the passage.

NOTE

Step 1	Survey
Key Words	
Signal Words	
Step 2	**Reading**
Purpose	
Pattern of Organization	
Tone	
Main Idea	
Step 3	**Summary**
지문 요약하기 (Paraphrasing)	
Step 4	**Recite**
	요약문 말로 설명하기

Answer Key

One of the most striking tendencies of our time is **the expansion of markets and market-oriented reasoning into spheres of life traditionally governed by non-market norms**. We consider the moral questions that arise, for example, when countries hire out military service and the interrogation of prisoners to mercenaries or private contractors; or when parents outsource pregnancy and child-bearing to paid laborers in the developing world; or when people buy and sell kidneys on the open market. Other instances abound: Should students in under performing schools be offered cash payments for scoring well on standardized tests? Should teachers be given bonuses for improving the test results of their students? Should states hire for-profit prison companies to house their inmates? Should the United States simplify its immigration policy by adopting the proposal of a University of Chicago economist to sell U.S. citizenship for a $100,000 fee? // **These questions** are not only about **utility** and **consent**. They are also about the right ways of valuing key social practices—military service, child-bearing, teaching and learning, criminal punishment, the admission of new citizens, and so on. **Since marketizing social practices may corrupt or degrade the norms that define them, we need to ask what non-market norms we want to protect from market intrusion**. This is a question that requires public debate about competing conceptions of the **right way of valuing goods**. Markets are useful instruments for organizing productive activity. But unless we want to let the market rewrite the norms that govern social institutions, we need a **public debate** about **the moral limits of markets**.

- key words
- series
- key words
- key idea
- key words

모범답안

The marketization of spheres of life traditionally free of this influence is a new and controversial shift. The following social practices and institutes have been influenced by markets in ways that raise ethical questions: military service, the treatment of child-bearing, education, criminal punishment, and immigration. Currently, there are "competing conceptions" that are comprised of those who would see these sectors organized in the morally-questionable terms of markets, and those who would keep them unaffected. Therefore, our society needs to start a serious debate where we apply marketization in the realms of morality and public services.

> **채점기준**

+ 1점 : 글의 topic sentence를 다음과 같이 서술하였거나 유사하였다.
"The marketization of spheres of life traditionally free of this influence is a new and controversial shift."

+ 1점 : 글의 핵심 내용인 social practices or institutions에 대한 요약이 다음과 같이 들어가 있다.
"social practices and institutes have been effected by markets in ways that raise ethical questions: <u>military service</u>, <u>the treatment of child-bearing</u>, <u>education</u>, <u>criminal punishment</u>, and <u>immigration</u>."
  ☞ social practices 다섯 가지 중 4개 이상을 서술한 경우 1점, 2개 또는 3개 이상을 서술한 경우 0.5점, 1개 또는 서술하지 못한 경우 0점을 준다.

+ 1점 : 문제에서 요구한 "competing conceptions"이 무엇인지 다음과 같이 명확하게 서술하였고 이것이 전체 글의 요약에 녹아 들어가 있다.
"The "competing conceptions" are comprised of <u>those who would see these sectors organized in the morally-questionable terms of markets</u>, and <u>those who would keep them unaffected</u>."
  ☞ 두 개 중 하나만 맞았으면 0.5점을 준다.

+ 1점 : 글의 결론을 "Therefore, our society needs to start a serious debate where we apply marketization in the realms of morality and public services."이라 서술하였거나 유사하였다.

● 감점 • 본문에 나오는 연속되는 6단어 이상을 사용하였다. -0.5pt
        • 문단을 두 개나 그 이상으로 구성하였다. -0.5pt

> **한글번역**

우리시대에 가장 두드러진 성향 하나는 시장과 시장 친화적 사고가 시장과는 거리가 먼 기준의 지배를 받던 전통적 삶의 영역까지 파고든다는 점이다. 이를테면 국가가 병역이나 죄수 심문을 민간 도급업체나 별도 인력을 고용해 맡길 때, 부모가 개발도상국가 사람들에게 돈을 주고 임신과 출산을 의뢰할 때, 콩팥을 공개시장에서 사고팔 때 어떤 도덕 문제들이 생기는지 앞에서 살펴본 바 있다. 이런 예는 많다. 학업 성취도가 부진한 학교에 다니는 학생들이 표준화된 시험에서 좋은 성적을 낼 경우 상금으로 포상해야 하는가? 학생들의 시험성적이 올라갔다면 교사가 보너스를 받아야 하는가? 국가는 이익을 추구하는 기업에 재소자 수용을 맡겨야 하는가? 미국은 시카고대학 경제학자의 제안을 받아들여 미국 시민권을 10만 달러에 파는 방법으로 외국인 이민 정책을 단순화해야 하는가? 이는 공리와 합의만을 묻는 게 아니다. 그것은 군 복무, 출산, 가르침과 배움, 범죄자 처벌, 새시민을 받아들이는 일 같은 중요한 사회적 행위의 가치를 측정하는 올바른 방법에 관한 물음이기도 하다. 사회적 행위를 시장에 맡기면 그 행위를 규정하는 규범이 타락하거나 질이 떨어질 수 있기에, 시장이 침입하지 못하도록 보호하고 싶은 비시장 규범이 무엇인지 물을 필요가 있다. 이를 위해서는 선의 가치를 측정하는 올바른 방법을 놓고 공개 토론을 벌여야 한다. 시장은 생산 활동을 조직하는 데 유용한 도구다. 그러나 우리가 사회제도를 지배하는 규범을 시장이 고쳐 쓰기를 원치 않는다면, 시장의 도덕적 한계를 공론에 부칠 필요가 있다.

NOTE

Step 1	ⓢurvey
Key Words	The expansion of markets; market-oriented reasoning; spheres of life traditionally governed by non-market norms; utility; consent; public debate; the moral limits of markets
Signal Words	For example; when···; when···; when···; Other instances; Should···; Should···
Step 2	**ⓡeading**
Purpose	To call for a public debate about the moral limits of markets
Pattern of Organization	Series
Tone	Critical
Main Idea	The marketization of spheres of life traditionally free of this influence is a new and controversial shift.
Step 3	**ⓢummary**
지문 요약하기 (Paraphrasing)	The marketization of spheres of life traditionally free of this influence is a new and controversial shift. The following social practices and institutes have been influenced by markets in ways that raise ethical questions: military service, the treatment of child-bearing, education, criminal punishment, and immigration. Currently, there are competing conceptions that are comprised of those who would see these sectors organized in terms of markets, and those who would keep them unaffected. Therefore, our society needs to start a serious debate where we apply marketization in the realms of morality and public services.
Step 4	**ⓡecite**
	요약문 말로 설명하기

24 Read the passage and follow the directions.

In 1966, *Time* magazine famously examined whether the United States was on a path to secularization when it published its now-iconic "Is God Dead?" cover. However, the question proved premature.

In fact, Americans pray more often, are more likely to attend weekly religious services and ascribe higher importance to faith in their lives than adults in other wealthy, Western democracies, such as Canada, Australia and most European states. For instance, more than half of American adults (55%) say they pray daily, compared with 25% in Canada, 18% in Australia and 6% in Great Britain. (The average European country stands at 22%.) Actually, when it comes to their prayer habits, Americans are more like people in many poorer, developing nations—including South Africa (52%), Bangladesh (57%) and Bolivia (56%)—than people in richer countries.

As it turns out, the U.S. is the only country out of 102 examined that has higher-than-average levels of both prayer and wealth. In every other country surveyed with a gross domestic product of more than $30,000 per person, fewer than 40% of adults say they pray every day. The U.S. tendency to run counter to international trends on religiosity has long fascinated social scientists. One idea popular among modern sociologists for a number of decades held that America's unregulated and open religious "market"—where different faiths compete freely for new members without government interference—has fostered fertile ground for religious growth. More recently, some sociologists have argued that there is a link between relatively high levels of income inequality in the U.S. and continued high levels of religiosity. These researchers posit that less-well-off people in the U.S. and other countries with high levels of income inequality may be more likely to seek comfort in religious faith because they also are more likely to experience financial and other insecurities.

But even though the U.S. is more religious than other wealthy countries, it hasn't been completely immune from the secularization that has swept across many parts of the Western world. Indeed, previous Pew Research Center studies have shown slight but steady declines in recent years in the overall number of Americans who say they believe in God. This lines up with the finding that American adults under the age of 40 are less likely to pray than their elders, less likely to attend church services and less likely to identify with any religion—all of which may portend future declines in levels of religious commitment.

Write a summary following the guidelines below.

| Guidelines |
- Summarize the above passage in ONE paragraph.
- Provide a topic sentence, supporting ideas, and a concluding sentence based on the passage.
- Do NOT copy more than FIVE consecutive words from the passage.

NOTE

Step 1	Survey
Key Words	
Signal Words	
Step 2	**Reading**
Purpose	
Pattern of Organization	
Tone	
Main Idea	
Step 3	**Summary**
지문 요약하기 (Paraphrasing)	
Step 4	**Recite**
	요약문 말로 설명하기

Answer Key

In 1966, *Time* magazine famously examined whether the United States was on a path to **secularization** when it published its now-iconic "Is God Dead?" cover. However, the question proved premature. → key word

In fact, Americans pray more often, are more likely to attend weekly **religious services** and ascribe higher importance to faith in their lives than adults in other wealthy, Western democracies, such as Canada, Australia and most European states. For instance, more than half of American adults (55%) say they pray daily, compared with 25% in Canada, 18% in Australia and 6% in Great Britain. (The average European country stands at 22%.) Actually, when it comes to their prayer habits, Americans are more like people in many poorer, developing nations—including South Africa (52%), Bangladesh (57%) and Bolivia (56%)—than people in richer countries.

As it turns out, the U.S. is the only country out of 102 examined that has higher-than-average levels of both prayer and wealth. In every other country surveyed with a gross domestic product of more than $30,000 per person, fewer than 40% of adults say **they pray every day**. The U.S. tendency to run counter to international trends on **religiosity** has long fascinated social scientists. One idea popular among modern sociologists for a number of decades held that America's **unregulated and open religious "market"**—where different faiths compete freely for new members without government interference—has fostered fertile ground for **religious growth**. More recently, some sociologists have argued that there is a link between relatively high levels of **income inequality** in the U.S. and continued high levels of **religiosity**. These researchers posit that less-well-off people in the U.S. and other countries with high levels of **income inequality** may be more likely to seek comfort in religious faith because they also are more likely to experience financial and other insecurities. → key word

→ key word

But even though the U.S. is **more religious** than other wealthy countries, it hasn't been completely immune from the **secularization** that has swept across many parts of the Western world. Indeed, previous Pew Research Center studies have shown slight but steady declines in recent years in the overall number of Americans who say they believe in God. This lines up with the finding that American adults under the age of 40 are less likely to **pray** than their elders, less likely to **attend church services** and less likely to **identify with any religion**—all of which may portend future declines in levels of **religious commitment**.

모범답안

The U.S. remains a robustly religious country and the most devout of all the rich Western democracies. Americans' prayer habits exceed other wealthy democracies and are more like people of poorer, developing nations. The unique combination of high prayer and wealth levels has been attributed to the U.S.'s open religious situation encouraging growth, and, on the other hand, to the nation's income inequality creating a need for people to use faith for comfort. However, secularization is slightly growing in the U.S. as more young people show less likelihood to believe in God or practice prayer.

채점기준

+ 1점: 글의 topic sentence를 다음과 같이 서술하였거나 유사하였다.
"The U.S. remains a robustly religious country and the most devout of all the rich Western democracies."
+ 1점: 글의 핵심 내용인 "Americans' prayer habits exceed other wealthy democracies and are more like people of poorer, developing nations."가 잘 요약되었다.
+ 1점: 글의 핵심 내용인 "The unique combination of high prayer and wealth levels has been attributed to the U.S.'s open religious market encouraging growth(0.5점), and, on the other hand, to the nation's income inequality creating a need for people to use faith for comfort(0.5점)."이 두 번째 요인이라는 점이 잘 요약되었다.
+ 1점: 글의 결론을 "secularization is slightly growing in the U.S. as more young people show less likelihood to believe in God or practice prayer."이라 서술하였거나 유사하였다.

● 감점 • 본문에 나오는 연속되는 6단어 이상을 사용하였다. -0.5pt
• 문단을 두 개나 그 이상으로 구성하였다. -0.5pt
• grammar나 영어표현이 합쳐 3개 이상 오류가 있다. -0.5pt

한글번역

지난 1966년, "타임"은 이제는 매우 유명한 "신은 죽었는가?"라는 표지를 펴내며 미국이 세속화로 향하는 길에 있는가에 대해 공공연하게 질문을 던졌다. 그러나, 그 질문은 너무 이른 것이었던 것으로 나타났다.

실제로, 미국인은 캐나다, 호주, 그리고 다른 대부분 유럽 국가와 같은 부유한 서구 민주주의의 성인들보다 더 자주 기도하고, 매주 교회를 비롯한 종교 시설에 가는 사람도 많았으며, 자신의 삶에서 신앙이 중요하다고 생각하는 사람도 더 많다. 예를 들어 미국인 성인의 과반수(55%)가 매일 기도한다고 답했으며, 이는 캐나다 25%, 호주 18%, 영국 6%와 비교된다. (유럽 국가들의 평균은 22%이다.) 사실, 그들의 기도 습관에 대해 말하자면, 미국인들은 선진국에 있는 사람들보다는 남아프리카공화국(52%), 방글라데시(57%), 볼리비아(56%)와 같은 경제적으로 더 궁핍한 개발도상국의 사람들과 더 비슷하다.

드러난 바와 같이, 미국은 조사 대상 102개국 가운데 기도하는 사람의 비율과 부유한 정도 모두 평균을 웃도는 유일한 나라이다. 나머지 1인당 국내총생산이 3만 달러를 넘는 모든 나라는 매일 기도한다고 응답하는 국민의 비율이 40%가 되지 않는다. 종교적 독실함에 대한 국제적인 추세에 역행하는 미국의 경향은 여러 사회과학자의 마음을 오랫동안 사로잡아왔다. 현대 사회학자들 사이에서 지난 수십 년간 널리 받아들여진 한 가설은 미국의 규제 없고 개방된 종교 '시장', 즉 서로 다른 신앙이 정부의 개입 없이 자유롭게 새 신도를 위해 경쟁하는 장이 종교의 성장을 위한 비옥한 토지를 조성해왔다는 것이다. 최근에는 일부 사회학자들이 미국 내에서 상대적으로 높은 수준의 수입 불평등과 계속해서 높은 수준으로 유지되는 신앙적 독실함 간에 연관성이 있음을 주장해왔다. 이 연구자들은 미국이나 소득 불평등이 심한 다른 나라에 사는 저소득층 사람들이 재정적인 불안함과 그 외 다른 종류의 불안함을 겪을 가능성이 더 높기 때문에 종교적 신앙 안에서 위안을 구하려고 할 가능성도 더 높다고 주장한다.

하지만 비록 미국이 다른 선진국보다는 더 종교적이기는 해도, 서구 국가들 대부분을 휩쓴 세속화의 물결로부터 완전히 영향을 받지 않았던 것은 아니다. 실제로, 퓨 리서치 센터가 앞서 진행한 조사 결과들은 신을 믿는다고 말하는 미국인의 전반적인 숫자가 미세하지만, 꾸준히 감소함을 보여줬다. 이는 40세 미만 성인 미국인들은 더 나이 든 미국인들보다 기도도 덜 하고, 교회 등 종교 행사에도 덜 나갔으며, 자신을 어떤 종교와도 동일시하는 경향이 더 적다는 연구 결과와 일맥상통한다. 이 모두는 종교적 헌신의 수준이 미래에 감소할 것이라는 전조가 될 수 있다.

NOTE

Step 1	**S**urvey
Key Words	Secularization; religiosity; pray; unregulated and open religious market; income inequality
Signal Words	For instance; one idea; because
Step 2	**R**eading
Purpose	To explain why the U.S. remains a robustly religious country
Pattern of Organization	Series; cause/effect
Tone	Objective
Main Idea	The U.S. remains a robustly religious country and the most devout of all the rich Western democracies.
Step 3	**S**ummary
지문 요약하기 (Paraphrasing)	The U.S. remains a robustly religious country and the most devout of all the rich Western democracies. Americans' prayer habits exceed other wealthy democracies and are more like people of poorer, developing nations. The unique combination of high prayer and wealth levels has been attributed to the U.S.'s open religious situation encouraging growth, and, on the other hand, to the nation's income inequality creating a need for people to use faith for comfort. However, secularization is slightly growing in the U.S. as more young people show less likelihood to believe in God or practice prayer.
Step 4	**R**ecite
	요약문 말로 설명하기

MEMO

25. Read the passage and follow the directions.

Many scientists believe that the aging process is caused by the gradual buildup of a huge number of individually tiny faults—some damage to a DNA strand here, a deranged protein molecule there, and so on. This degenerative buildup means that the length of our lives is regulated by the balance between how fast new damage strikes our cells and how efficiently this damage is corrected. The body's mechanisms to maintain and repair our cells are wonderfully effective—which is why we live as long as we do—but these mechanisms are not perfect. Some of the damage passes unrepaired and accumulates as the days, months and years pass by. We age because our bodies keep making mistakes.

We might well ask why our bodies do not repair themselves better. Actually we probably could fix damage better than we do already. In theory at least, we might even do it well enough to live forever. The reason we do not is because it would have cost more energy than it was worth when our aging process evolved long ago, when our hunter-gatherer ancestors faced a constant struggle against hunger. Under the pressure of natural selection to make the best use of scarce energy supplies, our species gave higher priority to growing and reproducing than to living forever. Our genes treated the body as a short-term vehicle, to be maintained well enough to grow and reproduce, but not worth a greater investment in durability when the chance of dying an accidental death was so great. In other words, genes are immortal, but the body—what the Greeks called soma—is disposable.

Since the late 1970s, the evidence to support this <u>disposable soma theory</u> has grown significantly. In my laboratory some years ago we showed that longer-lived animals have better maintenance and repair systems than short-lived animals do. If you can avoid the hazards of the environment for a bit longer by flying away from danger or being cleverer or bigger, then the body is correspondingly a bit less disposable, and it pays to spend more energy on repair.

The writer proposes a "disposable soma theory" to provide an answer to why human bodies do not repair themselves better. What is the "disposable soma theory"? Do NOT copy more than SIX consecutive words from the passage.

NOTE

Step 1	**S**urvey
Key Words	
Signal Words	
Step 2	**R**eading
Purpose	
Pattern of Organization	
Tone	
Main Idea	
Step 3	**S**ummary
지문 요약하기 (Paraphrasing)	
Step 4	**R**ecite
	요약문 말로 설명하기

Answer Key

　　Many scientists believe that **the aging process** is caused by the gradual buildup of a huge number of individually tiny faults—some damage to a DNA strand here, a deranged protein molecule there, and so on. This degenerative buildup means that the length of our lives is regulated by the balance between how fast new damage strikes our cells and how efficiently this damage is corrected. The body's mechanisms to maintain and repair our cells are wonderfully effective—which is why we live as long as we do—but these mechanisms are not perfect. Some of the damage passes unrepaired and accumulates as the days, months and years pass by. We age because our bodies keep making mistakes. ▶ key word

　　We might well ask **why** our bodies do not repair themselves better. Actually we probably could **fix damage** better than we do already. In theory at least, we might even do it well enough to live forever. The reason we do not is because **it would have cost more energy than it was worth when our aging process evolved long ago, when our hunter-gatherer ancestors faced a constant struggle against hunger**. Under the pressure of natural selection to make the best use of **scarce energy supplies**, our species gave higher priority **to growing and reproducing** than to **living forever**. **Our genes** treated the body as a short-term vehicle, to be maintained well enough to grow and reproduce, but not worth a greater investment in **durability** when the chance of dying an accidental death was so great. In other words, **genes are immortal**, but **the body**—what the Greeks called **soma**—is **disposable**. ▶ key question ▶ key words

　　Since the late 1970s, the evidence to support **this disposable soma theory** has grown significantly. In my laboratory some years ago we showed that longer-lived animals have better maintenance and repair systems than short-lived animals do. If you can avoid the hazards of the environment for a bit longer by flying away from danger or being cleverer or bigger, then the body is correspondingly a bit less **disposable**, and it pays to spend more **energy** on **repair**. ▶ key words

모범답안

It is a theory that explains why human beings' bodies do not repair themselves better than now. According to the theory, human beings only have a limited amount of energy that has to be divided between reproductive activities and the repair of the non-reproductive aspects of the body(soma). In that situation, human beings tend to give high priority to reproductive activities at the expense of maintaining of the non-reproductive activities.

한글번역

　많은 과학자들은 노화 과정이 개별적으로는 미미하지만 수많은 결함들의 점진적 축적에 의해 일어난다고 믿는다—여기서는 DNA 가닥 손상, 저기서는 변성된 단백질 분자 등. 이러한 퇴행성 축적은 우리 삶의 길이가 새로운 손상이 세포를 공격하는 속도와 이 손상이 얼마나 효율적으로 교정되는지 사이의 균형에 의해 조절되는 것을 의미한다. 우리 세포를 유지하고 복구하는 신체 기전은 놀랍도록 효과적이다—그래서 우리가 지금만큼 오래 사는 것이다—하지만 이러한 기전들은 완벽하지 않다. 일부 손상은 복구되지 않은 채 남아서 매일, 매달, 매년이 지나면서 축적된다. 우리가 노화하는 이유는 우리 몸이 계속해서 실수를 저지르기 때문이다.

　우리 몸이 왜 더 스스로 잘 복구하지 않는지 의문을 가질 수 있다. 사실 우리는 현재보다 더 손상을 잘 고칠 수 있을 것이다. 적어도 이론적으로는 영원히 살 수 있을 정도로 충분히 잘 할 수도 있다. 우리가 그렇게 하지 않는 이유는 오래전 우리의 노화 과정이 진화했을 때, 우리의 수렵채집 조상들이 기아와의 끊임없는 투쟁에 직면했던 시기에 그것이 가치에 비해 더 많은 에너지를 소모했을 것이기 때문이다. 부족한 에너지 공급을 최대한 활용하라는 자연선택의 압력 하에서, 우리 종은 영원히 사는 것보다 성장하고 번식하는 것에 더 높은 우선순위를 뒀다. 우리의 유전자는 몸을 단기 수단으로 취급했는데, 성장하고 번식할 수 있을 정도로만 잘 유지하되, 사고로 죽을 가능성이 그토록 클 때 내구성에 더 큰 투자를 할 가치는 없다고 본 것이다. 다시 말해, 유전자는 불멸이지만 몸—그리스인들이 소마라고 부른 것—은 일회성이다.

　1970년대 후반 이후로, 이 일회성 소마 이론을 뒷받침하는 증거가 상당히 늘어났다. 몇 년 전 내 연구실에서 우리는 수명이 긴 동물들이 수명이 짧은 동물들보다 더 나은 유지 및 복구 시스템을 가지고 있다는 것을 보여줬다. 위험으로부터 날아서 도망가거나 더 영리하거나 더 큰 몸집으로 환경의 위험을 조금 더 오래 피할 수 있다면, 몸은 그에 상응해 조금 덜 일회성이 되고, 복구에 더 많은 에너지를 쓰는 것이 이득이 된다.

NOTE

Step 1	Survey
Key Words	The aging process; repair; to live forever; reproducing; soma; disposable; energy
Signal Words	Why; the reason; in other words
Step 2	**Reading**
Purpose	To explain why our bodies do not repair themselves better
Pattern of Organization	Cause/effect
Tone	Neutral
Main Idea	The disposable soma theory proposes that bodies are treated as disposable by genes and given the ability to repair based on their reproduction rather than on living forever.
Step 3	**Summary**
지문 요약하기 (Paraphrasing)	The disposable soma theory proposes that bodies are treated as disposable by genes and given the ability to repair based on their reproduction rather than on living forever. Aging is understood by scientists to be the accumulation of damage that our bodies aren't able to repair over time. The reason for this is that it would cost more energy to perfectly repair than natural selection could allow, so instead the species made growing and reproducing higher priorities.
Step 4	**Recite**
	요약문 말로 설명하기

26 Read the passage and follow the directions.

Popular among laymen but not fully confirmed by empirical research, greater fool theory portrays bubbles as driven by the behavior of a perennially optimistic market participants (the fools) who buy overvalued assets in anticipation of selling it to other speculators (the greater fools) at a much higher price. According to this explanation, the bubbles continue as long as the fools can find greater fools to pay up for the overvalued asset. The bubbles will end only when the greater fool becomes the greatest fool who pays the top price for the overvalued asset and can no longer find another buyer to pay for it at a higher price. Some argue that the cause of bubbles is excessive monetary liquidity in the financial system, inducing lax or inappropriate lending standards by the banks, which then causes asset markets to be vulnerable to volatile hyperinflation caused by short-term, leveraged speculation. According to the explanation, excessive monetary liquidity (easy credit, large disposable incomes) potentially occurs while fractional reserve banks are implementing expansionary monetary policy (i.e. lowering of interest rates and flushing the financial system with money supply). When interest rates are going down, investors tend to avoid putting their capital into savings accounts. Instead, investors tend to leverage their capital by borrowing from banks and invest the leveraged capital in financial assets such as equities and real estate. Simply put, economic bubbles often occur when too much money is chasing too few assets, causing both good assets and bad assets to appreciate excessively beyond their fundamentals to an unsustainable level. Once the bubble bursts the central bank will be forced to reverse its monetary accommodation policy and soak up the liquidity in the financial system or risk a collapse of its currency. The removal of monetary accommodation policy is commonly known as a contractionary monetary policy. When the central bank raises interest rates, investors tend to become risk averse and thus avoid leveraged capital because the cost of _____ may because too expensive.

Complete the last sentence by filling in the blank with the ONE most appropriate word from the passage.

NOTE

Step 1	Survey
Key Words	
Signal Words	
Step 2	**Reading**
Purpose	
Pattern of Organization	
Tone	
Main Idea	
Step 3	**Summary**
지문 요약하기 (Paraphrasing)	
Step 4	**Recite**
	요약문 말로 설명하기

Answer Key

Popular among laymen but not fully confirmed by empirical research, **greater fool theory** portrays **bubbles** as driven by the behavior of a perennially optimistic market participants (the fools) who buy overvalued assets in anticipation of selling it to other speculators (the greater fools) at a much higher price. According to this explanation, the **bubbles** continue as long as the fools can find greater fools to pay up for the overvalued asset. The bubbles will end only when the greater fool becomes the greatest fool who pays the top price for the overvalued asset and can no longer find another buyer to pay for it at a higher price. Some argue that **the cause of bubbles** is **excessive monetary liquidity** in the financial system, inducing lax or inappropriate lending standards by the banks, which then **causes** asset markets to be vulnerable to volatile hyperinflation **caused** by short-term, leveraged speculation. According to the explanation, **excessive monetary liquidity** (easy credit, large disposable incomes) potentially occurs while fractional reserve banks are implementing expansionary monetary policy (i.e. lowering of interest rates and flushing the financial system with money supply). When interest rates are going down, investors tend to avoid putting their capital into savings accounts. Instead, investors tend to leverage their capital by borrowing from banks and invest the leveraged capital in financial assets such as equities and real estate. Simply put, **economic bubbles** often occur when too much money is chasing too few assets, **causing** both good assets and bad assets to appreciate excessively beyond their fundamentals to an unsustainable level. Once **the bubble** bursts the central bank will be forced to reverse its monetary accommodation policy and soak up the liquidity in the financial system or risk a collapse of its currency. The removal of monetary accommodation policy is commonly known as a contractionary monetary policy. When the central bank raises interest rates, investors tend to become risk averse and thus avoid leveraged capital because the cost of borrowing may become too expensive.

> key word 1
> one explanation of the bubbles by the theory definition (the great fool theory)

> key word 2
> another explanation of the bubbles definition (excessive monetary liquidity)

> key word 3
> summary of the explanation 2

모범답안
borrowing

구문분석

이 글을 두 문단으로 나눈다면, "Some argue~"에서 시작된다. 이 글의 제목은 'What is the cause of bubbles?'이고, 이 질문에 대한 답이 글 전체의 내용이 된다. 거품의 원인에 대한 첫 번째 설명은 "greater fool theory"이며; 두 번째는 "금융시스템에서의 과잉 유동성(excessive monetary liquidity in the financial system)"이다. 따라서 나머지 내용들은 이 두 이론의 구체적 내용을 설명하는 supporting details에 해당한다.

어휘

be driven by ~에 의해 추동되다(움직이다)
disposable 처분 가능한, 가처분
flush 홍수가 나게 하다, 범람시키다
induce ~을 장려하다, 유발하다
liquidity 유동성
reverse 뒤바꾸다
soak up 빨아들이다
burst 터지다
equities 주식
in anticipation of ~을 기대하며
leverage (자금을) 조달하다
perennially 영원히, 항상, 지속적으로
risk averse 위험 회피
speculation 투기

한글번역

보통 사람들 사이에서 인기가 있지만, 실증적 연구에 의해서는 아직 확증되지 않은, '더 큰 바보 이론'은 거품이 시장을 항상 낙관적으로 바라보는 시장 참여자(바보)의 행위에 의해 추동되는 것으로 설명한다. 이들은 과잉 평가된 자산을 그것보다 더 높은 가격에 다른 투기자(더 큰 바보)에게 팔려는 기대를 가지고 산다. 이 이론에 따르면, 거품은 과잉 평가된 자산을 산 바보들이 그 과잉 평가된 자산을 사줄 수 있는 더 큰 바보들을 발견할 수 있을 때까지 지속된다. 버블은 오직 '더 큰 바보'가 '가장 큰 바보'가 될 때 꺼지게 된다. 이때 '가장 큰 바보'는 과잉 평가된 자산을 가장 높은 가격에 지불해 더 이상 그 높게 올라간 가격으로 사줄 사람을 찾을 수 없게 된다. 어떤 사람들은 버블의 원인을 느슨하거나 부적절한 은행의 대출 관행을 포함한, 금융시스템에서의 과잉 유동성에서 찾고 있다. 그런데 이것은 자산시장이 단기로 차입된 투기자본에 의해 야기되는 폭발적인 하이퍼인플레이션에 취약해지도록 만든다. 이 설명에 따르면, 각 준비은행의 지점들에서 통화 팽창 정책(예를 들어, 이자율을 낮춘다든가, 돈을 공급해 금융시스템이 굴러가도록 하는 것 등)을 시행하고 있을 때, 금융시스템에서의 과잉 유동성(손쉬운 신용, 풍부한 가처분소득 등)은 잠재적으로 발생한다. 이자율이 낮아지면, 투자자들은 자신들의 자본을 저축통장에 넣는 것을 피하는 경향이 있다. 오히려, 투자자들은 은행으로부터 자본을 빌려 그 차입된 자본을 주식이나, 부동산 등 금융자산에 투자한다. 간단히 말하면, 경제 거품은 너무 많은 돈이 너무 적은 자산을 추구할 때 종종 발생하는데, 이것에 의해서 건전한 자산이든 불량자산이든 모두 자신들의 기초 체력을 넘어서 지속 불가능한 수준까지 과하게 평가받게 된다. 일단 거품이 터지면, 중앙은행은 통화 대부 정책을 되돌려, 금융시스템에서 유동성을 회수할 수밖에 없는데 그렇지 않으면, 통화 붕괴라는 위험을 감수해야만 하기 때문이다. 통화 대부 정책을 되돌리는 것은 보통 통화 수축 정책이라 불린다. 중앙은행이 이자율을 올리면, 투자자는 위험을 회피하는 경향이 있으며, 따라서 (은행으로부터) 돈을 빌리는 비용이 너무 높기 때문에 자본을 차입하는 것을 피하게 된다.

NOTE

Step 1	Survey
Key Words	Greater fool theory; (economic) bubbles; excessive monetary liquidity
Signal Words	According to this explanation; Some; causes; According to the explanation; Simply put
Step 2	**Reading**
Purpose	To give the two explanations of the cause of the bubbles
Pattern of Organization	Definition; cause/effect; series
Tone	Neutral (objective)
Main Idea	There are a few of explanations of the causes of economic bubbles.
Step 3	**Summary**
지문 요약하기 (Paraphrasing)	There are several explanations of the causes of economic bubbles. According to the great fool theory bubbles are fed by optimism towards assets which become heavily over-valued to a breaking point, at which point they burst and the value descends rapidly, causing the market to once again adjust to the reversal. Next, according to the second explanation, excessive monetary liquidity cause bubbles in the financial system.
Step 4	**Recite**

요약문 말로 설명하기

27 Read the passage and follow the directions.

The Civil War preserved the unity of the American nation while ousting from power a planter class that had controlled the national government since its inception. It made the Republican Party the dominant political force for the next six decades. It created a new banking and tariff system that set the stage for the rapid expansion of industrial capitalism. It destroyed the largest slave system the modern world has known and established equality before the law, regardless of race, as an essential element of American citizenship. All these results produced winners and losers. Among the winners were African-Americans, Union veterans, the Republican party, industrialists and Wall Street bankers. The _____ⓐ_____ included anyone who had tied his or her fortunes to the struggle for southern independence, believers in white supremacy and many farmers and laborers whose protests against the new fiscal-industrial system help to shape the volatile politics of the Gilded Age. From the vantage point of 1900, after the experiment in interracial democracy during postwar Reconstruction failed, it seemed that the white South, in some ways, had won the war. Racism pervaded the nation, and sharecropping, disenfranchisement, lynching and other elements of the Jim Crow system severely proscribed blacks' freedom. But despite the disappointments that followed, it is important to remember that the Union's triumph foreclosed an even more oppressive outcome. Had the Confederacy emerged victorious, not only would _____ⓑ_____ there have lasted into the 20th century, but an independent South would have moved to create a slave empire encompassing much of the Caribbean and Central America. Union victory helped to propel Cuba and Brazil, the last great slave systems, down the road to abolition. Southern victory would have reinvigorated slavery throughout the hemisphere.

MEMO

Fill in each blank with the ONE most appropriate word from the passage.

NOTE

Step 1	**S**urvey
Key Words	
Signal Words	
Step 2	**R**eading
Purpose	
Pattern of Organization	
Tone	
Main Idea	
Step 3	**S**ummary
지문 요약하기 (Paraphrasing)	
Step 4	**R**ecite
	요약문 말로 설명하기

Answer Key

The Civil War ① <u>preserved</u> the unity of the American nation while ousting from power **a planter class** that had controlled the national government since its inception. It ② <u>made</u> the Republican Party the dominant political force for the next six decades. It ③ <u>created</u> a new banking and tariff system that set the stage for the rapid expansion of industrial capitalism. It ④ <u>destroyed</u> the largest slave system the modern world has known and ⑤ <u>established</u> equality before the law, regardless of race, as an essential element of American citizenship. // **All these results** produced **winners and losers**. Among **the winners** were African-Americans, Union veterans, the Republican party, industrialists and Wall Street bankers. **The losers** included anyone who had tied his or her fortunes to the struggle for southern independence, believers in white supremacy and many farmers and laborers whose protests against the new fiscal-industrial system help to shape the volatile politics of the Gilded Age. // From the vantage point of 1900, after the experiment in interracial democracy during postwar Reconstruction failed, it seemed that the white South, in some ways, had won the war. Racism pervaded the nation, and sharecropping, disenfranchisement, lynching and other elements of the Jim Crow system severely proscribed blacks' freedom. ̲B̲u̲t̲ despite the disappointments that followed, **it is important to remember that the Union's triumph foreclosed an even more oppressive outcome**. Had the Confederacy emerged victorious, not only would **slavery** there have lasted into the 20th century, but an independent South would have moved to create a slave empire encompassing much of the Caribbean and Central America. Union victory helped to propel Cuba and Brazil, the last great slave systems, down the road to abolition. Southern victory would have reinvigorated slavery throughout the hemisphere.

key words

results:
①
②
③
④
⑤

main idea

evidence

모범답안
ⓐ losers ⓑ slavery

어휘

abolition 폐지	down the road 장래에	foreclose ~을 막다; (가능성)을 배제하다
hemisphere 반구	oppressive 억압적인	oust 몰아내다
pervade 만연하다	proscribe 금지하다	reinvigorate 활기를 불어넣다

vantage point (무엇을 지켜보기에) 좋은 위치; (특히 과거를 생각해 보는) 시점[상황]

한글번역

　남북전쟁은 그것의 시초부터 중앙 정부를 통제했던 농장주 계급을 권력에서 몰아내는 동안에도 미국의 통일을 지켰다. 그것은 그 후 60년간 공화당을 주도적인 정치 세력으로 만들었다. 그것은 산업 자본주의의 급격한 팽창을 준비시킬 수 있었던 새로운 금융과 관세 제도를 만들어냈다. 그것은 현대 세계가 알고 있는 가장 큰 노예 제도를 부숴버렸고, 미국 시민권의 중요한 요소로서 인종에 상관없이 법 앞에 평등을 확립시켰다. 이러한 모든 것의 결과들은 승자와 패자를 양산시켰다. 승자들은 미국 흑인, 참전 용사, 공화당, 기업가와 월 스트리트 자본가들이었다. 패자는 남부 독립을 위한 투쟁에 그들의 미래를 건 사람들, 백인 우월주의를 믿는 사람들, 그리고 새롭게 등장하던 금융 산업제도에 대항해 싸웠던 많은 농부와 노동자들이었다. 그런데 이 농부와 노동자들의 투쟁이 도금시대(미국 남북전쟁 후의 대호황 시대)의 불안한 정치를 형성하는 데 일조했다. 1900년이라는 역사적으로 유리한 시점에서 보면, 전후의 재건운동(1865-1877년에 있었던 남북전쟁 후 미국을 새롭게 건설하는 것) 동안 서로 다른 인종 간의 민주주의 실험이 실패했기 때문에, 어떤 면에서 보면 남부 백인들이 전쟁에서 이겼다고 보일 수도 있다. 인종차별주의가 미국 전반에 만연했고 소작, 시민권 박탈, 억압과 짐 크로우 법(재건시대부터 1965년까지 남부에서 흑인을 비롯한 유색인종을 차별하던 법)의 여러 다른 요소들이 흑인의 자유를 엄격히 금했다. 하지만 그 이후에 이뤄진 실망스러운 결과에도 불구하고, 우리가 중요하게 기억해야 할 것이 있다. 즉, 미합중국(북군)의 승리는 훨씬 더 억압적인 결과가 일어나지 못하게 했다는 사실 말이다. 만일 남부 연합(남군)이 승리했었더라면, 노예제도가 20세기까지 이어졌을 뿐만 아니라 독립적인 남부가 캐리비안과 중앙아메리카를 둘러싼 노예 제국을 건설하기 위해 움직였을 것이다. 미합중국의 승리는 쿠바와 브라질이라는 마지막으로 남은 최대 규모의 노예제를 장차 폐지하도록 몰고 갔다. 남부 연합이 승리했다면 반구 전역(중남미)의 노예제에 활기를 불어넣었을 것이다.

NOTE

Step 1	Survey
Key Words	The Civil War; equality; postwar; slavery
Signal Words	Made; created; results
Step 2	**Reading**
Purpose	To assess the Civil War's mixed historical impact by weighing its immediate transformative achievements against its unfulfilled promises of racial equality
Pattern of Organization	Cause/effect; series
Tone	Analytical
Main Idea	The Union's victory in The Civil War has several crucial contributions to the history of USA. Though there were limitations, the Union's victory excluded a much more oppressive result.
Step 3	**Summary**
지문 요약하기 (Paraphrasing)	The Union's victory in The Civil War has several crucial contributions to the history of USA. The Union's victory expelled southern rullers, created a new financial system, and above all destroyed slavery. Though there were limitations such as severe racism in the southern states of United States, the Union's victory excluded a much more oppressive result. Also, it helped other slave nations to abolish slavery.
Step 4	**Recite**
	요약문 말로 설명하기

MEMO

28   Read the passage and follow the directions.

A man awakens with chest pain and writes it off as indigestion. His wife urges him to go to the emergency room, where he is diagnosed as having a heart attack. A woman awakens with chest pain and thinks she might be having a heart attack. She goes immediately to the emergency room, where all tests of her heart function are normal. <u>Doctors throw up their hands</u> and send her on her way.

Possible explanations for these differences are complex, ranging from the physiological to the cultural. It's not clear whether women actually feel pain more intensely, as some —but not all—laboratory experiments have found, or whether they simply tend to describe their pain more expansively. Women do have thinner skin and a higher density of nerve fibers than men. And estrogen, the so-called female hormone, influences women's pain response in many ways. Fluctuations in hormone levels might contribute to variations in the severity of women's pain symptoms across the menstrual cycle, during pregnancy and immediately after delivery, and during and after menopause*. Menstrual cramps and childbirth themselves might help explain differences in how women and men perceive pain. When women feel pain, their brains don't respond the same as men's do. Because women are brought up to be more nurturing than men, they're more likely to regard pain as a call to action. In other words, women tend to think, "OK, it hurts. Now, let's go do something about it." Men, on the other hand, are taught from boyhood that crying and other expressions of distress are for sissies. Partly because women tend to seek _____ more often than men, their pain complaints are often less likely to be taken seriously. Some doctors might discount a woman's pain because they think it's all in her head. Even if doctors do acknowledge the validity of a woman's pain, they may think she has a higher pain tolerance because she's built to give birth. Either way, they say the outcome is the same: less aggressive medical help women's pain.

*menopause: the permanent cessation of ovarian function occurring some time before the end of the natural lifespan

Fill in the blank with the TWO most appropriate consecutive words from the passage. Second, explain what the underlined "Doctors throw up their hands" means.

___
___
___
___
___

유희태 일반영어 ❶

NOTE

Step 1	**S**urvey
Key Words	
Signal Words	
Step 2	**R**eading
Purpose	
Pattern of Organization	
Tone	
Main Idea	
Step 3	**S**ummary
지문 요약하기 (Paraphrasing)	
Step 4	**R**ecite
	요약문 말로 설명하기

Answer Key

A **man** awakens with chest **pain** and writes it off as indigestion. His wife urges him to go to the emergency room, where he is diagnosed as having a heart attack. **A woman** awakens with chest **pain** and thinks she might be having a heart attack. She goes immediately to the emergency room, where all tests of her heart function are normal. Doctors throw up their hands and send her on her way.

Possible explanations for these differences are complex, ranging from **the physiological** to **the cultural**. It's not clear whether women actually feel pain more intensely, as some—but not all—laboratory experiments have found, or whether they simply tend to describe their pain more expansively. **Women** do have thinner skin and a higher density of nerve fibers than men. And estrogen, the so-called female hormone, influences **women's pain** response in many ways. Fluctuations in hormone levels might contribute to variations in the severity of women's pain symptoms across the menstrual cycle, during pregnancy and immediately after delivery, and during and after menopause. Menstrual cramps and childbirth themselves might help explain differences in how **women and men perceive pain**. When **women** feel **pain**, their brains don't respond the same as men's do. Because **women** are brought up to be more nurturing than **men**, they're more likely to regard pain as a call to action. In other words, **women** tend to think, "OK, it hurts. Now, let's go do something about it." **Men**, on the other hand, are taught from boyhood that crying and other expressions of distress are for sissies. Partly because women tend to seek medical help more often than men, their pain complaints are often less likely to be taken seriously. Some doctors might discount a **woman's pain** because they think it's all in her head. Even if doctors do acknowledge the validity of a woman's pain, they may think she has a higher pain tolerance because she's built to give birth. Either way, they say the outcome is the same: less aggressive medical help **women's pain**.

→ key word
① behavioral

② physiological

signal words

③ cultural

모범답안

The words are "medical help." Second, it means that the doctors gesture in a way that shows frustration, helplessness, or surrender. In this context, it suggests that the doctors are giving up or admitting defeat because they can't find the cause of the woman's chest pain through standard heart tests. (The phrase implies they're dismissing her problem rather than investigating further, highlighting the different medical treatment between men and women described in the passage.)

한글번역

　한 남자가 흉부 통증이 있는 채로 잠에서 깨어나고 그 통증을 소화불량 정도로 치부한다. 그의 아내는 그에게 응급실에 가라고 강력히 권고했고, 거기서 그는 심근경색이 있다고 진단받는다. 한 여성이 흉부 통증이 있는 채로 잠에서 깨어나고 자신이 심근경색이 있을지도 모른다고 생각한다. 그녀는 곧장 응급실로 가며, 거기서 그녀의 심장 기능에 대한 모든 검사는 정상으로 나온다. 의사들은 손을 들고 그녀를 보낸다.

　이러한 여러 차이점에 대해 가능한 설명들은 복합적인데, 생리적인 설명에서부터 문화적인 설명까지 이른다. 일부—그러나 전부는 아닌—실험실 실험이 발견해왔듯, 여성이 실제로 고통을 더 강렬하게 느끼는지, 혹은 여성들이 그저 자신의 고통을 더 크게 묘사하는 것인지는 분명하지 않다. 여성은 남성에 비해 더 얇은 피부와 더 높은 신경 섬유 밀도를 가지고 있다. 그리고 소위 여성 호르몬이라 불리는 에스트로겐은 여성이 고통에 반응하는 것에 많은 방식으로 영향을 미친다. 호르몬 레벨의 변동은 월경 주기, 임신 기간 동안과 출산 직후, 그리고 폐경기 동안과 이후에 걸쳐서 여성의 통증의 강도 변화에 일조할 수도 있다. 월경통과 출산 그 자체가 여성과 남성이 고통을 어떻게 받아들이는지의 차이들을 설명하는 것을 도울 수도 있다. 여성이 고통을 느낄 때, 그들의 뇌는 남성의 뇌가 하는 것처럼 반응하지 않는다. 여성이 남성보다 더 보살핌을 받도록 키워지기 때문에, 여성들은 고통을 조치가 필요한 신호로 간주할 가능성이 더 높다. 다시 말해, 여성은 "아, 아프네. 이제, 이 고통에 뭘 좀 해보러 가야겠네."라고 생각하는 경향이 있다. 반면에, 남성은 소년기부터 울음이나 그 외에 고통에 대한 다른 표현들은 계집애들이나 하는 것이라고 배운다. 부분적으로는 여성이 남성보다 더 자주 의학적 도움을 구하는 경향이 있기 때문에, 여성들의 고통 불평은 종종 진지하게 받아들여질 가능성이 더 적다. 일부 의사는 여성의 고통이 모두 그녀의 상상에서 나온 것이라고 생각하기 때문에 그 고통을 무시할지도 모른다. 비록 의사들이 어떤 여성의 고통이 유효함을 깨닫는다 할지라도, 그들은 그 여성이 아이를 낳도록 만들어졌기 때문에 더 높은 고통 저항력을 가진다고 생각할 수도 있다. 어느 쪽이든, 그 의사들은 결과는 같다고 말한다: 결과는 여성의 고통에 덜 적극적인 치료이다.

NOTE

Step 1	Survey
Key Words	A man; a woman; pain
Signal Words	These differences; differences; on the other hand
Step 2	**Reading**
Purpose	To show how men and women are different concerning pain
Pattern of Organization	Contrast
Tone	Analytical; critical
Main Idea	In the realm of pain, men and women differ in their behavioral responses, the way their bodies sense and the way their pain is perceived by others.
Step 3	**Summary**
지문 요약하기 (Paraphrasing)	In the realm of pain, men and women differ in their behavioral responses, the way their bodies sense and the way their pain is perceived by others. First, concerning behavior, a man would be less likely to respond to pain with urgency, while a woman might misread a slight pain as being something more serious. Additionally, women have more thorough ways to describe pains, as well as hormonal and nervous systems that may in fact explain the differences in how women perceive pain. Finally, in terms of how they are perceived by others, men are expected to be strong and showing pain defines them as "sissies," while women see pain as a "call to action," and even can be ignored by some doctors for being so sensitive.
Step 4	**Recite**
	요약문 말로 설명하기

29 Read the passage and follow the directions.

More than forty years since the beginning of affirmative action programs and the social change that led to them, Jews, women, African Americans, Latinos, and Asian Americans sit on the boards of the country's largest corporations; presidential cabinets have become increasingly diverse; and the highest ranks of the military are no longer filled solely by white men. The rules, however remain the same as in 1956 when C. Wright Mills' *The Power Elite* described the exclusively white, male, and Christian makeup of the leading members of America's political, military, and business institutions. The broad social movements of the 1960s and '70s sought to diversify this elite—and, in the process, shift its values to reflect greater social equity—but failed to change the three most important factors in attaining membership. Indeed, the diversity "forced" upon the power elite has given it buffers, <u>ambassadors, and tokens, through the women and minorities who share its prevailing values</u>. For the most part, it takes at least three generations to rise from the bottom to the top. Fully one-third of women in the elite are from the upper class. Most of the Cuban Americans and Chinese Americans come from ruling-class families displaced by political upheaval. The Jews and Japanese Americans are the products of two-and three- generational climbs up the social ladder. And the first African Americans to serve in cabinets and on the boards of large corporations tended to come from the small black middle class that predated the civil rights movement. Also, the women and minorities who make it into the corporate elite are typically better educated than the white males who are already a part of it, but time and again they emerge from the same institutions Harvard, Yale, Princeton, and MIT on the East Coast; the University of Chicago in the Midwest; Stanford and the University of California at Berkeley on the West Coast. Finally, African Americans and Latinos who do make it into the power elite are lighter-skinned than other prominent members of their racial group. As Colin Powell told Henry Louis Gates Jr. in the *New Yorker*, explaining his popularity among whites: "Thing is, I ain't that black."

Explain what the underlined "ambassadors, and tokens, through the women and minorities who share its prevailing values" means. Second, explain what Colin Powell is implying in the underlined "Thing is, I ain't that black."

NOTE

Step 1	Survey
Key Words	
Signal Words	
Step 2	**Reading**
Purpose	
Pattern of Organization	
Tone	
Main Idea	
Step 3	**Summary**
지문 요약하기 (Paraphrasing)	
Step 4	**Recite**
	요약문 말로 설명하기

Answer Key

More than forty years since the beginning of affirmative action programs and the social change that led to them, Jews, women, African Americans, Latinos, and Asian Americans sit on the boards of the country's largest corporations; presidential cabinets have become increasingly diverse; and the highest ranks of the military are no longer filled solely by white men. The rules, however remain the same as in 1956 when C. Wright Mills' *The Power Elite* described the exclusively white, male, and Christian makeup of the leading members of America's political, military, and business institutions. The broad social movements of the 1960s and '70s sought to diversify **this elite**—and, in the process, shift its values to reflect greater social equity—but failed to change the **three most important factors** in attaining membership. Indeed, the diversity "forced" upon the power elite has given it buffers, ambassadors, and tokens, through the women and minorities who share its prevailing values. For the most part, it takes at least three generations to rise from the bottom to the top. Fully one-third of **women** in **the elite** are from **the upper class**. Most of the Cuban Americans and Chinese Americans come from ruling-class families displaced by political upheaval. The Jews and Japanese Americans are the products of two-and three-generational climbs up the social ladder. And the first African Americans to serve in cabinets and on the boards of large corporations tended to come from the small **black middle class** that predated the civil rights movement. // Also, the women and minorities who make it into the corporate elite are typically **better educated** than the white males who are already a part of it, but time and again they emerge from the same institutions Harvard, Yale, Princeton, and MIT on the East Coast; the University of Chicago in the Midwest; Stanford and the University of California at Berkeley on the West Coast. // Finally, African Americans and Latinos who do make it into **the power elite** are **lighter-skinned** than other prominent members of their racial group. As Colin Powell told Henry Louis Gates Jr. in the *New Yorker*, explaining his popularity among whites: "Thing is, I ain't that black."

① class

② education

③ skin color

모범답안

It means that diverse individuals who enter the power elite while conforming to its established values serve as strategic intermediaries and symbolic representatives who legitimize the system without challenging its fundamental structure. (*ambassadors: these diverse members function as **representatives who can effectively communicate between the power elite and their identity groups**. They give the elite access and credibility when dealing with minority communities while still prioritizing elite interests. *tokens: this term refers to **symbolic representation without substantive change**. These individuals are included primarily to create the appearance of diversity while the fundamental power structure and its values remain intact. Their presence can be pointed to as evidence of inclusion, even when they represent minimal actual redistribution of power.) Second, Colin Powell is implying that his acceptability to white Americans stems partly from being perceived as less physically "black" than other African Americans. (His lighter skin tone makes him less threatening to white Americans. / His success depends partly on being viewed as an "exception" rather than representative of African Americans broadly.)

한글번역

(소수자들에게 혜택을 주는) 평등실현제도 프로그램들과 그 프로그램들을 가능하게 했던 사회 변화가 시작된 지 40년이 넘었고, 유대인, 여성, 아프리카계 미국인, 라틴계, 아시아계 미국인들이 미국의 가장 큰 기업들의 이사회에 앉아 있다. 대통령의 내각은 점점 더 다양해졌고, 군대의 최고 계급은 더 이상 백인 남성들만으로 채워지지 않는다. 하지만 규칙들은, 라이트 밀즈가 (자신의 책인) <파워 엘리트>에서 미국의 정치, 군사, 비즈니스 기관의 지도적 구성원들이 오직 백인, 남성, 기독교인으로만 이뤄져 있다고 설명한 1956년과 같다. 1960년대와 70년대의 광범위한 사회 운동은 이 엘리트 계층을 다양화하고—그렇게 하는 과정에서 이 엘리트 계층의 가치관을 더 큰 사회적 형평성을 반영하기 위해 바꾸려 했지만—멤버십 획득(엘리트 계층에 들어가는 것)을 위한 가장 중요한 세 가지 요소를 바꾸는 데 실패했다. 사실, 파워 엘리트에게 '강요된' 다양성은 (비록 소수자임에도.) 지배적 가치관을 공유하는 여성과 소수자들로 하여금 자신들(파워 엘리트)을 위한 완충 장치, 대사, 상징적 인물(실질적인 권한이나 영향력 없이 다양성을 보여주기 위해 있는 듯한 존재)이 되도록 했다. 대부분 바닥에서 정상까지 오르는 데는 적어도 3세대가 걸린다. 엘리트 여성 중 정확히 3분의 1은 상류층 출신이다. 대부분의 쿠바계 미국인과 중국계 미국인은 정치적 격변으로 인해 쫓겨난 지배계급 가족 출신이다. 유대인과 일본계 미국인은 사회적 사다리를 2~3세대에 걸쳐 올라온 결과물이다. 그리고 내각과 대기업 이사회에서 일한 첫 아프리카계 미국인들은 시민권 운동 이전에 존재했던 많지 않았던 흑인 중산층 출신인 경향이 있다. 또한, 기업 엘리트에 진입하는 여성과 소수자들은 전체적으로 이미 그 기업 엘리트의 구성원인 백인 남성들보다 교육 수준이 더 높다. 하지만 이 여성과 소수자들은 동일한 기관—동부 해안의 하버드, 예일, 프린스턴, MIT 또는 중서부의 시카고 대학, 서부 해안의 스탠퍼드와 버클리 대학(U.C. Berkeley)—에서 계속해서 나온다. 마지막으로, 파워 엘리트에 들어가는 아프리카계 미국인과 라틴계는 자신들의 인종 집단에 속해 있는 다른 저명한 구성원들보다 피부색이 더 밝다. 콜린 파월(부시 행정부 국무장관)이 <뉴요커>에서 헨리 루이스 게이츠 주니어(미국의 저명한 흑인 학자이자 지도자)에게 말한 것처럼, 백인들 사이에서 자신의 인기를 설명하며: "핵심은 내가 그렇게 흑인스럽지 않다는 거지요."

NOTE

Step 1	Survey
Key Words	The power elite; women from the upper class; more educated; lighter-skinned
Signal Words	Also; Finally
Step 2	**Reading**
Purpose	To point out lingering problems despite major changes in society to better minorities' place in the workforce
Pattern of Organization	Series
Tone	Critical; analytical
Main Idea	Despite increased diversity in America's power elite since the 1960s, the fundamental requirements for entry remain unchanged.
Step 3	**Summary**
지문 요약하기 (Paraphrasing)	Despite increased diversity in America's power elite due to social movements and the affirmative action policies since the 1960s, some of the most important factors have not changed in the slightest, specifically, such issues as class, education, and skin-color. It still takes several generations to enter the highest rung of society. So the high-standing among minorities are those which, exceptionally, have had wealthy and successful parents. With regard to education, minorities who achieve high positions often greatly outmatch their White counterparts in the elite, while emerging from the very same schools. Finally, the Africans and Latino-Americans who do manage to enter into the upper crust of society are "lighter-skinned," or more like Whites in their appearance.
Step 4	**Recite**
	요약문 말로 설명하기

30 Read the passage and follow the directions.

Sigmund Freud, the Austrian founder of psychoanalysis, called dreams the "royal road to the unconscious." He therefore paid close attention to their content. Through his study of dreams, Freud identified several specific ways in which they disguise their underlying meaning. According to Freud, dreams make use of condensation. In other words, one dream figure or object might well represent several different real-life people or things. Thus, a person in a dream could look like your instructor yet speak and gesture like your father, which Freud, at least, would say was a condensed figure representing authority. Displacement was another one of Freud's dream disguises. When displacement is at work in a dream, violent or angry actions, unacceptable in real life, are directed toward safe objects. For example, a teenager who goes to sleep furious at parents who are planning to divorce might dream of smashing a set of dishes rather than dreaming about being angry at the parents she loves. In what Freud called "dream work," symbolization is often at play, and he believed that dream imagery should be interpreted in symbolic rather than real terms. A student who dreams of walking into class naked, for example, might well be motivated not by exhibitionist tendencies but by the fear of being weak and vulnerable. Secondary elaboration involves not the dream itself but the memory of it. It was Freud's position that when remembering dreams, we elaborate on them, adding logical connections not originally present in the dream itself.

Write a summary following the guidelines below.

┌─────────────── Guidelines ───────────────┐
- Summarize the above passage in ONE paragraph.
- Provide a topic sentence and supporting details from the passage.
- Do NOT copy more than FIVE consecutive words from the passage.
└──┘

_____
_____
_____
_____
_____

NOTE

Step 1	**S**urvey
Key Words	
Signal Words	
Step 2	**R**eading
Purpose	
Pattern of Organization	
Tone	
Main Idea	
Step 3	**S**ummary
지문 요약하기 (Paraphrasing)	
Step 4	**R**ecite
	요약문 말로 설명하기

Answer Key

Sigmund Freud, the Austrian founder of psychoanalysis, called **dreams** the "royal road to **the unconscious**." He therefore paid close attention to their content. <u>Through his study of dreams, Freud identified several specific ways in which they disguise their underlying meaning</u>. According to Freud, **dreams** make use of **condensation**. In other words, one dream figure or object might well represent several different real-life people or things. Thus, a person in a dream could look like your instructor yet speak and gesture like your father, which Freud, at least, would say was a condensed figure representing authority. // **Displacement** was another one of Freud's dream disguises. When displacement is at work in a dream, violent or angry actions, unacceptable in real life, are directed toward safe objects. For example, a teenager who goes to sleep furious at parents who are planning to divorce might dream of smashing a set of dishes rather than dreaming about being angry at the parents she loves. // In what Freud called "dream work," **symbolization** is often at play, and he believed that dream imagery should be interpreted in symbolic rather than real terms. A student who dreams of walking into class naked, for example, might well be motivated not by exhibitionist tendencies but by the fear of being weak and vulnerable. // **Secondary elaboration** involves not the dream itself but the memory of it. It was Freud's position that when remembering dreams, we elaborate on them, adding logical connections not originally present in the dream itself.

→ key words

① condensation

② displacement

③ symbolization

④ secondary elaboration

[모범답안]

Sigmund Freud identified four different ways that dreams disguise their hidden meanings. Through the process of "condensation", one person in a dream may actually represents several different people. Second, "displacement" allows antisocial actions (or emotions) unacceptable in reality to be redirected toward a safe target. Third, "symbolization" means that symbols should be interpreted symbolically, not literally. Finally, "secondary elaboration" takes place when the dream is over and the dreamer adds logical details to what (s)he remembers about the dream.

채점기준

+ 1점: 글의 topic sentence를 다음과 같이 서술하였거나 유사하였다.
"Sigmund Freud identified <u>four</u> different ways that <u>dreams disguise their hidden meanings</u>."
☞ "four"가 없으면 0.5점 감점한다.

+ 3점: 글의 major supporting details를 다음과 같이 서술하였거나 유사하였다.
"Through the process of "<u>condensation</u>", one person in a dream may actually represents several different people. Second, "<u>displacement</u>" allows antisocial actions (or emotions) unacceptable in reality to be redirected toward a safe target. Third, "<u>symbolization</u>" means that symbols should be interpreted symbolically, not literally. Finally, "<u>secondary elaboration</u>" takes place when the dream is over and the dreamer adds logical details to what (s)he remembers about the dream."
☞ 4개 중 4개 모두를 정확하게 서술한 경우 3점, 3개만 서술한 경우 2점, 2개만 서술한 경우 1점, 1개 또는 서술하지 못한 경우 0점을 준다.

한글번역

정신분석학의 오스트리아인 창립자인 지그문트 프로이트는 꿈을 '무의식을 향하는 왕도'라고 불렀다. 따라서 그는 꿈의 내용에 깊은 주의를 기울였다. 자신의 꿈 연구를 통해, 프로이트는 꿈이 그 기저에 깔린 의미를 숨기는 여러 구체적인 방법을 찾아냈다. 프로이트에 따르면, 꿈은 압축을 사용한다. 다시 말해, 꿈의 어떤 인물이나 대상은 아마 여러 다른 실제 삶의 사람들이나 사물들을 나타낼 수도 있다. 따라서, 꿈속에 있는 어떤 사람은 당신의 교사처럼 보이면서도 당신의 아버지처럼 말하고 몸짓할 수 있는데, 적어도 프로이트는, 이를 권위를 나타내는 응축된 인물이라고 말했을 것이다. 치환은 프로이트의 꿈 위장술 중 또 다른 하나이다. 치환이 꿈에서 작동할 때, 실제 생활에서 받아들여질 수 없는 난폭하거나 화난 행동들이 안전한 대상을 향한다. 예를 들어, 이혼을 계획하는 부모에 성이 난 채로 잠자리에 드는 10대는 자신이 사랑하는 부모에 화를 내는 것에 대한 꿈을 꾸기보다는 식기 한 세트를 부수는 것을 꿈꿀지도 모른다. 프로이트가 '꿈 작업'이라고 불렀던 것 중, 상징화가 종종 영향을 미치며, 그는 꿈의 형상이 실제보다는 상징적인 용어로 해석돼야 한다고 믿었다. 예를 들어, 나체로 수업에 걸어 들어가는 꿈을 꾸는 학생은, 아마도 노출증적인 경향보다는 나약해지고 취약해지는 것에 대한 공포에 의해 동기부여를 받았을지도 모른다. 이차적 정교화는 꿈 자체가 아니라 그 꿈에 대한 기억과 연관돼 있다. 꿈을 기억할 때, 우리는 그 꿈 자체에 원래 존재하지 않았던 논리적인 연관성을 더함으로써, 꿈을 정교화한다는 것이 프로이트의 입장이었다.

NOTE

Step 1	Ⓢurvey
Key Words	Sigmund Freud; dreams; the unconscious; condensation; displacement; symbolization; secondary elaboration
Signal Words	Specific ways; another
Step 2	**Ⓡeading**
Purpose	To explain Sigmund Freud's theory about dreams
Pattern of Organization	Series
Tone	Neutral
Main Idea	Sigmund Freud identified four different ways that dreams disguise their hidden meanings.
Step 3	**Ⓢummary**
지문 요약하기 (Paraphrasing)	Sigmund Freud identified four different ways that dreams disguise their hidden meanings. Through the process of "condensation", one person in a dream may actually represents several different people. Second, "displacement" allows antisocial actions (or emotions) unacceptable in reality to be redirected toward a safe target. Third, "symbolization" means that symbols should be interpreted symbolically, not literally. Finally, "secondary elaboration" takes place when the dream is over and the dreamer adds logical details to what (s)he remembers about the dream.
Step 4	**Ⓡecite**
	요약문 말로 설명하기

2S2R
유희태 일반영어 ① 기본

초판 1쇄	2009년 12월 1일	
2쇄	2010년 1월 5일	
3쇄	2010년 5월 10일	
2판 1쇄	2010년 12월 15일	
2쇄	2011년 1월 30일	
3쇄	2012년 2월 23일	
4쇄	2012년 12월 30일	
5쇄	2013년 7월 25일	
3판 1쇄	2014년 11월 30일	
2쇄	2015년 1월 25일	
4판 1쇄	2016년 4월 29일	
5판 1쇄	2017년 1월 3일	
2쇄	2017년 12월 20일	
6판 1쇄	2019년 1월 3일	
2쇄	2019년 3월 20일	
7판 1쇄	2022년 1월 10일	
2쇄	2022년 4월 15일	
3쇄	2023년 8월 25일	
4쇄	2025년 1월 20일	
8판 1쇄	2026년 1월 15일	

저자와의
협의하에
인지생략

저자 유희태 **발행인** 박 용 **발행처** (주)박문각출판
표지디자인 박문각 디자인팀
등록 2015. 4. 29. 제2019-000137호
주소 06654 서울시 서초구 효령로 283 서경 B/D
팩스 (02) 584-2927
전화 교재 문의 (02) 6466-7202 동영상 문의 (02) 6466-7201

이 책의 무단 전재 또는 복제 행위는 저작권법 제136조에 의거, 5년 이하의 징역 또는 5,000만원 이하의 벌금에 처하거나 이를 병과할 수 있습니다.

정 가 39,000원
ISBN 979-11-7519-460-1